PHILOSOPHERS WITHOUT GODS

LOUISE M. ANTONY

EDITOR

Philosophers without Gods

Meditations

on Atheism

and the

Secular Life

OXFORD
UNIVERSITY PRESS
2007

OXFORD
UNIVERSITY PRESS

Oxford University Press, Inc., publishes works that further
Oxford University's objective of excellence
in research, scholarship, and education.

Oxford New York
Auckland Cape Town Dar es Salaam Hong Kong Karachi
Kuala Lumpur Madrid Melbourne Mexico City Nairobi
New Delhi Shanghai Taipei Toronto

With offices in
Argentina Austria Brazil Chile Czech Republic France Greece
Guatemala Hungary Italy Japan Poland Portugal Singapore
South Korea Switzerland Thailand Turkey Ukraine Vietnam

Published by Oxford University Press, Inc.
198 Madison Avenue, New York, New York 10016

www.oup.com

Philosophers without gods: meditations on Atheism and the secular life /
[edited by]
Louise M. Antony.
p. cm.
Includes bibliographical references and index.
ISBN 978-0-19-517307-9
1. Atheism. I. Antony, Louise M.
BL2710.P45 2007
211'8—dc22
2007060082

9 8 7 6 5 4 3 2 1
Printed in the United States of America
on acid-free paper

CONTENTS

INTRODUCTION

Louise M. Antony

Atheism is a minority position in today's world. At least in the parts of the globe accessible to pollsters, most people believe in God. The rate of theism has little to do with the level of scientific or technological development of the society in question. Consider, for example, the United States, where, despite the country's constitutional commitment to the "separation of church and state," most institutions of daily life are infused with theism.[1] U.S. coins carry the proclamation "In God We Trust," sessions of the U.S. Congress open with a prayer offered by the official congressional chaplain, and national and civic leaders routinely invoke the name of God in campaign and policy speeches.

Within this climate, skeptics and atheists are viewed with suspicion. We are presumed to be arrogant, devoid of moral sentiments, and insensitive to a wide variety of human goods. Indeed, according to the authors of a recent survey from the University of Minnesota, "Atheists are at the top of the list of groups that Americans find problematic in both public and private life."[2] Forty-seven percent of those surveyed said that they would "disapprove" if their child "wanted to marry a member of this group."[3] The survey's authors hasten to point out that these opinions seemed not to reflect their respondents' actual encounters with real, live atheists—most people in the survey claimed not to know any—but rather reflected a stereotypical construction, one that linked disbelief with egotism, consumerism, and ethical relativism.

This volume is meant to contribute to a more just understanding of those who have rejected religious belief. It collects original essays by twenty leading philosophers from Great Britain and the United States, all of whom abjure traditional religious faith. Contributors to the first section, "Journeys," write in a personal vein, describing and reflecting upon the development of their own positions on issues like the existence of God and the basis of moral value. Authors in the second section, "Reflections," discuss in a more general way philosophical questions that arise in connection with religion and theology: Is religious faith really a form of belief? Can an atheist affirm the meaningfulness of human existence? Without God, is anything sacred?

None of us are casual atheists. Some of us were once religious; others never believed. But all of us have had long and serious engagements with religious questions and religious people, both through our professional work and in the course of our daily lives. As professional philosophers, all of us have studied and taught the main philosophical arguments for and against the existence of God, and several of us have published scholarly work on the philosophy of religion. We have discussed religion with colleagues at professional conferences, and with friends over dinner.[4] We have made common cause with religious people in social and political movements. We have seen friends find courage, inspiration, hope, and solace in their religious beliefs, and support and fellowship from their religious communities. We know what we are rejecting. But more importantly, we know *why* we are rejecting it.

I hope the reader will be struck, as I was, by the marvelous diversity of perspectives expressed in these pages, some of which the reader may find quite surprising. Many of the authors, for example, express great affection for particular religious traditions, even as they explain why they cannot, in good conscience, embrace them. Stewart Shapiro ("Faith and Reason, the Perpetual War: Ruminations of a Fool") and Joseph Levine ("From Yeshiva Bochur to Secular Humanist)," both raised in Orthodox Jewish homes, make vivid both the lofty intellectual pleasures of Torah study and the mundane gratifications of a Torah-governed life. Daniel Garber is Jewish by descent but was raised in a secular home. In his essay ("Religio Philosophi"), he expresses a poignant longing for the Christian religiosity that inspired the philosophers he studies, particularly Pascal. Walter Sinnott-Armstrong ("Overcoming Christianity") explains how his loneliness as a displaced Southerner was eased by the fellowship he found in the Amherst College Christian community. Marvin Belzer ("Mere Stranger") recounts with unalloyed pleasure the joyous experiences of his childhood in an evangelical Protestant home.

Still, every one of these writers found reason to give up religious belief. Although Shapiro maintains a kosher home and participates with his wife and children in the life of their local synagogue, his faith has dissolved. He explains his paradoxical relationship to Judaism in his essay. Levine explains, in his, how he came to reject both the doctrines and the practice of orthodoxy, despite the heavy personal costs his rejection entailed. Belzer recounts the gradual process whereby the defining doctrines of his family's Christianity came to seem, one by one, irrelevant to the core of his religiosity. Sinnott-Armstrong explains how, forced to choose between an ethos of faith and one of rational inquiry, he abandoned religion and took up his life work as a philosopher. I describe a similar dynamic in my own essay ("For the Love of Reason").

Only a few of us in these pages engage in what might be called "evangelical atheism." Like Sinnott-Armstrong, Edwin Curley ("On Becoming a Heretic") urges atheists to abandon their quietism when religion is invoked in defense of immoral and regressive social policies. Simon Blackburn ("Religion and Respect") descries the way the mere designation of a belief as "religious" is held by many to immunize it from all criticism. In my essay ("For the Love of Reason"), I indict dogmatic religion, like the Catholicism in which I was raised, for lionizing the irrational acceptance of preposterous claims.

Several authors acknowledge the losses that can be suffered when faith dissolves. Daniel Farrell ("Life without God: Some Personal Costs") was a Jesuit seminarian when his crisis developed. He explains that in losing his vocation he lost forever the kind of clarity of purpose that had hitherto defined his life. David Owens ("Disenchantment") considers, by means of a brilliantly creepy thought-experiment, the way a thoroughgoing naturalism about human behavior threatens to undermine our most fundamental self-conceptions. Levine laments the loss of what he used to experience as personal connection with a transcendent being.

Other contributors, however, argue that secular life can provide rewards as great and as rich as those claimed by the religious. Anthony Simon Laden ("Atheism and Invisibility") contends that transcendent experiences are possible without transcendent beings, through a loving and open refocusing of attention toward other people. Daniel Dennett, writing in the aftermath of a life-threatening heart attack, shares his appreciation of the thoroughly human skills and kindnesses that contributed to his survival and that now sustain his recovery. It's not necessary to thank God, he insists, when we can, instead, literally "Thank Goodness." Kenneth Taylor ("Without the Net of Providence: Atheism and the Human Adventure") explains why he thinks human beings have the capacity to generate moral value from within, and how our mutual recognition of these capacities in each other can form the basis of moral communities. He also points out that the notion of "divine providence" can offer no psychological bulwark against the horrors that threaten us in everyday human life. At least according to traditional texts, God's plan may well include untold suffering for any particular human being. In my essay, I add that religion can actually increase one's psychic distress by populating the world with supernatural beings and powers. Simon Blackburn articulates a secular conception of the "sacred" as that which is held separate and apart, beyond comparison with things of merely mundane value. Marcia Homiak ("An Aristotelian Life") finds in Aristotle's theory of *eudaimonia* ("human flourishing") a compelling model of attainable virtue and fulfillment. Laden, Taylor, Homiak, and I all argue that a naturalistic understanding of the human condition reveals a set of heroic challenges—to pursue our goals without illusions, to act morally without hope of reward—challenges that, if taken up, can impart a durable value to finite and fragile human lives.

Atheists are frequently accused by religious people of caricaturing religious doctrine, of attacking straw positions to which few enlightened believers subscribe. Religious people, we are told, need not be fundamentalists; they need not acquiesce to the Bible's apparent endorsement of slavery, genocide, and collective punishment. With more nuanced readings of Scripture, they say, and more sophisticated theology, belief in God can be reconciled with moral rationalism. Several authors consider and reject this reformist expedient. Levine and Sinnott-Armstrong point out that such recommendations invalidate the religious faith of a great many people. Levine insists that anyone who dismisses fundamentalism as unsophisticated effectively disparages the entire tradition of Torah Judaism. Shapiro and Tappenden ("An Atheist's Fundamentalism") argue that attempts to read religious texts and doctrines in a "non-realist" way, to treat them as not in the realm of literal truth or falsehood, must, in the case of Judaism and Christianity, founder on the fact that certain claims of fact are essential to these religions as we know them. Tappenden argues that a properly respectful atheism must take religious narratives at face value, so as to acknowledge the power these stories have held for human beings through the centuries.

But what does "respect" come to in this context? Two authors explicitly consider the question what it means to "respect" views that one believes to be deeply mistaken. Simon Blackburn ("Religion and Respect") argues that it's one thing to demand that we atheists show respect for the projects and needs that people so often address by means of religion: the search for meaning, the struggle to overcome weakness, the need to mark life's passages. This demand is wholly legitimate. But it's quite another thing, and not at all legitimate, to demand that we applaud or endorse people's embrace of doctrines that seem to us unjustified and unjustifiable. Richard Feldman ("Reasonable Religious Disagreement") writes more generally about the puzzle of religious "tolerance:" if I genuinely believe that my religion is true, and if my religion makes claims that yours rejects, how can I think it "reasonable" for you to hold to yours? How can we solve this puzzle without either stiffening into a repressive intolerance, or lapsing into a lazy relativism?

Another charge routinely leveled at atheists is that we have no moral values. The essays in this volume should serve to roundly refute this. Every writer in this volume adamantly affirms the objectivity of right and wrong. I rehearse the main argument—an ancient one, from Plato—for thinking that the existence of God is neither necessary nor sufficient for morality. Taylor develops a positive secular account of the basis of moral value, inspired by the work of Immanuel Kant. Homiak and Laden both explain what they find compelling in Aristotle's secular conception of the connection between virtue and human flourishing.

Several authors take the moral argument further. They argue that traditional religion not only fails to ground morality, but is, in fact, incompatible with it. These authors point to what they see as irreconcilable tensions between the moral messages in Scripture, and the dictates of common-sense morality. Elizabeth Anderson ("If God Is Dead, Is Everything Permitted?") contends that, if one relied on scriptural evidence, one would have to conclude that God is monstrously evil. David Lewis ("Divine Evil") concurs. In his view, the strongest challenge to rational theism is not the traditional argument from evil, which concerns "evils God fails to prevent" but rather the argument from "divine evil," concerning "the evils God himself perpetrates." Curley and Shapiro express their horror at the moral standardly drawn from the story of Abraham and Isaac—that it is right to obey God even when He commands murder. Sinnott-Armstrong, Levine, and I explain how moral scruples about doctrines in our respective traditions contributed to our loss of faith.

While Anderson and Lewis look at the dark side of religious *doctrine,* Georges Rey and Jonathan Adler examine what they contend are pathological features of religious *belief.* Rey ("Meta-Atheism: Religious Avowal as Self-Deception") observes that there are many psychological peculiarities about religious "belief." For example, many doctrinal beliefs professed by the faithful are not emotionally or behaviorally manifest in their daily lives in the way typical of beliefs about more mundane matters. Religious doctrines, Rey concludes, are not so much believed as merely avowed. Jonathan Adler takes up the question of why fanaticism is so frequently grounded in religious belief. His answer is that the notion of religious faith is at odds with ordinary norms of knowledge, norms that serve to block extremist inferences in ordinary circumstances.

Humility is a premier religious virtue. I think that all the contributors to this volume are humble, perhaps more humble than most religious people. Like theists, we affirm the limitations and fallibility of the human mind; like them, we acknowledge, with awe, the vastness and complexity of the natural world. Unlike theists, however, we have no master story to tell about the origins or the ultimate future of the world. Human science has learned a great deal, we think, but it's not a patch on what there is left to know. We have no sacred texts, no authorities with definitive answers to our questions about the nature of morality or the purpose of life, no list of commandments that cover every contingency and dilemma. We can have no confidence, the evidence of history being as it is, that the truth will win out, or that goodness will triumph in the end. We have no fear of eternal punishment, but no hope, either, of eternal reward. We have only our ideals and our goals to motivate us, only our sympathy and our intelligence to make us good, and only our fellow human beings to help us in time of need. When we speak, we speak only for ourselves—we cannot claim inspiration or sanction from the Creator and Lord of the universe.

What we offer here, then, are not manifestos or creeds. We want simply to explain what we believe, and why we believe. That, in the end, is the best we can do.

ACKNOWLEDGMENTS

I'd like to express my most sincere gratitude to my authors. I know that these essays were not easy to write, and I'm delighted that you all persevered. Thanks, too, to Peter Ohlin, our editor at Oxford University Press, for encouraging me to start this project and for supporting me throughout its completion. To my husband, Joe Levine, and my daughter, Rachel Antony-Levine, who had to share living space with me while I worked on this book—thanks for your patience and for all your help. Finally, a special thank-you to Rachel and to my son, Paul Antony-Levine, for proving that wonderful people can emerge from godless homes.

PART ONE

Journeys

ONE 

Faith and Reason, the Perpetual War: Ruminations of a Fool

Stewart Shapiro

> The fool hath said in his heart, "There is no God."
>
> —Ps. 14:1

> And the angel of the Lord called unto Abraham a second time out of heaven, and said: "By Myself have I sworn, saith the Lord, because thou hast done this thing, and hast not withheld thy son, thine only son, that in blessing I will bless thee, and in multiplying I will multiply thy seed as the stars of the heaven, and as the sand which is upon the seashore; and thy seed shall possess the gate of his enemies; and in thy seed shall all the nations of the earth be blessed; because thou hast hearkened to My voice."
>
> —Gen. 22:15–18

In the spirit of this volume, let me begin with a short, autobiographical note. We'll get to some philosophy or, better, meta-philosophy, after that.

I still remember the moment when the last remnants of my religious faith died. One day in February of 1984, I was driving and listening to a radio news story about David Vetter, otherwise known as the "bubble-boy." The announcer said that he had been born, twelve years before, with a condition, known as severe combined immune deficiency (SCID), that robbed him of the usual defenses against infectious diseases. Since any infection would prove fatal, David lived in a sterile environment, a plastic bubble. He had no physical contact with any living organism. Eventually, the defense was breached, and his doctors had to enter the bubble. David then hugged his mother for the first time, and died a short time later, thus prompting the news story that day.

When I heard that story, something in me snapped, and I have not had a sustained religious thought since. Once or twice, particularly when in the stunningly beautiful highlands of Scotland, or the northern regions of Israel, old feelings stirred, but it never lasted very long. All I had to do was to start to think about it.

Of course, the story of the bubble-boy was only the straw that broke the back of my religious faith. It was a major tragedy, to be sure, but certainly not the worst one I had heard of. My more or less typical Jewish education included a grounding in the Holocaust, covering that period in history from innumerable angles and perspectives. And of course stories of war, pestilence, famine, earthquakes, and so on, abound in both history and the daily news. In retrospect, it is easy to see that my faith had been waning, and the news story that day was the one that put it away for good, or at least for these last twenty years.

I am fortunate that I have not experienced a personal tragedy at anywhere near the level of David Vetter or his family. In my religious days, I would have added "Baruch Hashem" to that statement. But it now seems outright silly to praise or bless God for sparing *me* from such tragedies. I don't deserve it. And there is no way that the bubble-boy deserved what happened to him. He was *born* with the condition that robbed him of the simple pleasures of human contact. President Carter once reminded us that life is not fair. We all know that. So why should we believe that this universe was created by a being driven by principles of fairness? And if the universe was created by a sentient being of some sort or other, why does this being deserve our worship, let alone our praise? Free thinkers have been asking these questions for centuries, and I have yet to hear a hint of an acceptable answer.

My immediate family remains religious, as modern Orthodox Jews, and I go along with much of the ritual for the sake of family unity. Since I lean toward being a vegetarian, keeping at least some level of a kosher diet is not a major issue, either in or outside the home. There is a lot of wisdom in the Torah, and high among it is the Sabbath. Every Friday night, all work and school shuts down in our home, and we spend the evening and next day together, having nice, relaxed meals, catching up with each other, reading for pleasure, or studying religious texts. This is not negotiable, nor is it susceptible to deadlines on any project from any arena (other than life or death matters, of course). I admit to enjoying this, both for the sheer pleasure and for the psychological harmony it brings to our family. I also admit that if left on my own, I would not maintain the rigor of the Sabbath very long. It is too easy to let outside influences—editors' deadlines for example—push aside what is really important. At least for me, the Sabbath has to be observed religiously to maintain the benefits of it. I seem to have stumbled on a way to keep it religiously without being religious. In this respect, among many others, I am fortunate to be in a religious family.

A few years ago, our community lost a vibrant woman to breast cancer. She was in her early forties and left behind four children, the youngest not yet bat mitzvah (aged eleven). For a few weeks, I went into a rebellious state, refusing to go to synagogue or participate in any rituals (i.e., any positive commandments between man and God). Friends pointed out to me that I had no business to stay away, since those directly affected by the tragedy were maintaining their faith, dutifully and meticulously fulfilling the commandments for mourners. The boys showed clear intent and depth of faith as they recited the Kaddish. For those who do not know, the Kaddish is a prayer recited by Jewish people who have lost a close relative (parent, child, etc.). It must be said several times each day, in the presence of ten adult Jewish males. Although it is usually recited in a solemn tone, the mourners' Kaddish contains no references to the departed and no words of comfort. It consists entirely of praises of God. This is how Judaism requires one to behave after getting kicked in the teeth by Mother Nature. The bereaved one must publicly declare praise for God.

I am in awe and admiration of the faith of those who pursue this mitzvah, especially after a tragedy like this one. I have nothing but respect for them. But I cannot follow them. Some say that this is pompous and ungrateful, but if so, so be it.

That is enough about me, or almost so. I hope the gentle reader does not mind my *qvelling* a bit (to use a Yiddish expression). What follows is an essay that my eldest daughter, Rachel, wrote when she was a senior in high school, as part of her applications to some colleges:

> I am the product of a Jewish day school. For thirteen years, I have attended the same school with the same people. Half of my day consists of English, physics, speech, and the other classes that most high school students drudge through. The other half, however, is comprised of religious learning, where I study Hebrew language, biblical texts, and Jewish History.
>
> But when I say that I am the product of a Jewish day school, I mean more than that I attend one. My family and I live in a small heavily Jewish area, and practically everyone in my school lives near me or attends the same synagogue. Even my extracurricular activities, which include playing sports at my school and leading a junior congregation, all directly relate to my religion. For better or worse, Judaism is my identity. It is my morality, my strength, my meaning. Growing up in an intimate community, where religion is more than a burden to endure, but something transcendent and inspiring, has been more fulfilling than I can articulate. I always assumed that I would raise my family the same way. I never questioned that. Until recently.
>
> My father is a philosophy professor and is consistently pragmatic. What he cannot calculate he does not accept. He sometimes lacks emotion and faith. He understands only cold, hard logic. Yet despite his suspicions about G-D and religion, he has always acted like any other Orthodox Jewish man. For the sake of our family, he regularly attended synagogue with us and participated in all Jewish customs. I sometimes forgot that he even doubted. And then, earlier this year, a young and special woman in

> our community passed away from cancer, leaving four young children, one exactly my age, and forcing all those who knew her to question their faith. My father's, which already hinged on such a precarious thread, was now permanently and finally lost. He stopped attending synagogue and severed most of his religious ties. When I asked him how he could surrender on his religion so quickly, he replied that no G-D would allow such tragedies to exist, and that people can live meaningful, important, rewarding lives without a higher authority. Although my father never challenges my beliefs and even respects my commitment, he is the first important person in my life to ever throw my world into upheaval, to make me re-examine how and why I believe.
>
> At eighteen, it is hard to surmise philosophical and ideological reasons for my beliefs. I was raised to hold my religion and my morality on equal ground, and to barely separate one from the other. My father's sudden vocal skepticism of G-D has forced me to re-evaluate many of my strongly held, innate values. My commitment to Judaism is as strong now as ever. Jewish life is an inherent part of where I decide to attend college. Yet despite my deeply rooted faith, I cannot help but wonder if there is credence to my father's ideas. In college, I look forward to expanding my horizons and learning from new and unique people. I am thankful for my warm and affable upbringing. But it is now time to see how my beliefs will serve me in a bigger, more complicated world. I used to be frightened at the prospect of such a transition. Now, because of my father, I have a newly acquired curiosity and a burning desire to broaden my views. After leading a protected, sheltered life, college will still be scary. But suddenly I can't wait.

I admit that I sometimes fail to show emotion, but I do not see this as connected, in any way, to my lack of faith. I would have preferred that Rachel say "sweet reason" instead of "cold, hard logic," but I could not be more proud of her. Most of all, I am grateful and humbled to be a member of the philosophical tradition that breeds the skepticism that led to this confrontation in her mind.

It is not news that religion (or at least organized religion) has had a troubled relationship with philosophy and science, at least in recent centuries. For the most part, the best that can be said is that the two enterprises occasionally manage an uncomfortable and grudging mutual toleration, and even that relationship is not particularly stable. When I teach Jewish philosophy, we study two sorts of figures: philosophers like Philo Judaeus, who attempt to reconcile rabbinic Judaism with traditional philosophical sources, and great rabbis, like Saadya Gaon or Yehuda Halevi, whose works contain philosophical interpretations and speculations. It is perhaps not a great exaggeration to think of this latter work as dabbling in philosophy. There are precious few figures comfortable in both philosophy and the rabbinic world.

On the other hand, the few exceptions to this generalization are among the most powerful minds ever—enough so to give my growing skepticism some pause. One is Maimonides and another is the late Rabbi Joseph Soloveithchik, affectionately referred to as "the Rav" ("the rabbi"). Christianity and Islam have figures like this in their traditions, and in their midst today. And on a more mundane level, some of the most respected and influential scientists and philosophers today are religious, some deeply so.

Nevertheless, I think it is fair to say that among contemporary philosophers, the seriously religious are a small minority. It would not take much effort from the editor of this volume to include ten or twenty times as many authors. One day last year, I was visiting the Israel Museum in Jerusalem. My sister-in-law picked up a book on religious artifacts and suggested that my Christian colleagues might enjoy it. I replied that I did not know if I have any Christian colleagues. She reacted with surprise: "What? Are they all Jewish?!" Putting aside the possibility that some members of my department might be Muslims, Buddhists, and so on, I told her that, for all I knew, my colleagues are atheists. She laughed, and noted, "Ah, yes, philosophers."

It is worth asking why most philosophers are skeptical of religion and why most rabbis shun philosophy. What is it about philosophy and religion, or at least philosophy and traditional Judaism, that leads to a clash in all but a few minds? Why does it seem to take a mind like that of Maimonides or the Rav to thrive in both worlds? A first hypothesis is that the level of faith demanded by typical Western religions is in conflict with the questioning, probing, and doubting that underlie scientific and philosophical methodology. This is the place where the spade turns.

To speak (very) roughly, there are three stances one can take on the interaction between religion and science or philosophy—between faith and reason. The first is that they are at war. The idea here is that religious faith is inherently irrational. Religion and philosophy each stand in the way of the other, in eyeball-to-eyeball confrontation. Neither can accomplish its goal without vanquishing the other.

Bertrand Russell occupies an extreme, and perhaps overly simplistic, version of this perspective. His "Has Religion Made Useful Contributions to Civilization?" (1930) begins, "My . . . view on religion is that of Lucretius. I regard it as a disease born of fear and as a source of untold misery to the human race." And the essay ends thus:

> The knowledge exists by which universal happiness can be secured; the chief obstacle to its utilization for that purpose is the teaching of religion. Religion prevents our children from having a rational education; religion prevents us from removing the fundamental causes of war; religion prevents us from teaching the ethic of scientific co-operation in place of the old fierce doctrines of sin and punishment. It is possible that mankind is

> on the threshold of a golden age; but, if so, it will be necessary first to slay the dragon that guards the door, and this dragon is religion.

The view that religion and rationality are at war finds some articulation within the religious camp as well. These combatants maintain that to engage in philosophy at all, or to think of a religion as a (part of a) *Weltanschauung* subject to the usual criteria on the rational acceptability of such things (whatever those are), is the ultimate in hubris. To reason about religious faith is to adopt what Karl Barth (1956) calls a standpoint of "unbelief." As Alvin Plantinga (1983, 70–71) put it, on Barth's behalf: "[To] be in the standpoint of unbelief is to hold that belief in God is rationally acceptable *only if it is more likely than not with respect to the deliverances of reason.* [For one] who holds this belief, says Barth, his ultimate commitment is to the deliverances of reason rather than God. Such a person 'makes reason a judge over Christ' . . . a posture that is for a Christian totally inappropriate, a manifestation of sinful human pride." From this perspective, the very attempt to reason one's way through to religion runs directly against the command to subject one's personal will to the divine will. The directive is to obey, not to think first and then obey if it seems reasonable to do so. According to Exodus (24:7), when God gave the Torah at Sinai, the children of Israel said, as one, "We will do, and we will understand." The rabbis take the order of these pronouncements to be crucial. The Israelites agreed to obey the commandments before they understood them, expressing faith that they would eventually come to understand them. For this act of faith, they are praised. The merit for this is invoked by contemporary Jews, as they plea for forgiveness each Yom Kippur.

Fundamentalists in our day have to reconcile the accounts in Genesis with the findings of modern science. It certainly *looks like* the universe is much older than scripture says it is. So from the fundamentalist perspective, when God made the world, he planted evidence in it that misleads the rational mind. It is undeniable that if the creation story is literally true, then the world contains evidence that did mislead many rational minds. Why is this? One speculative answer, which I have heard from some Jews and Christians, is that God planted the evidence for evolution, or for the existence of stars more light years from us than the number of years since creation (etc.), in order to test our faith and to increase the merit of those who come to believe anyway. I take it that this attitude is a natural (logical?) extension of the thesis that religious faith is irrational and that one should have faith nevertheless.

If there is war between religion and philosophy/science or, indeed, rationality itself, then we have left the bounds of rational persuasion, so there is not much more to say in an essay of this type. If my opponent concedes that her position is irrational, then what can a philosopher do to convince her to change? How can one appeal to a neutral observer? How can you convince someone that it is better to be rational? Will a rational argument do the trick?

The thesis of war is, of course, not universally held by either believers or skeptics. Thank goodness. I hope that, at least today, the war hypothesis is a marginal, minority view among the world's religions. As noted above, many of the paradigms of rationality in the Western world—doctors, scientists, philosophers—are personally religious. Most of the organized religions of the world support universities, some of them among the best worldwide.

There are two other orientations that one can take on the relationship between religion and philosophy or science. The *rationalist* tradition has attracted some of the best minds in history. The underlying thesis is that religion, properly understood, and rationality, properly applied, pull in the same direction. The rational mind that comes standard with the human body is a gift that God has bestowed on us, and we are supposed to use this gift to negotiate the world and to understand God's ways. As Descartes argued, God would not—could not—give us tools that lead us badly astray when they are used properly. This perspective permeates Maimonides' *Guide for the perplexed.* For Maimonides, it is axiomatic that God would not ask anyone to believe something unreasonable. Passages in scripture that do not make sense, such as the various anthropomorphisms of God, are not to be understood literally. Make no mistake. Maimonides held that the five books of the Torah were written by God himself and that every statement in them is true. But not every statement is to be understood literally. The tradition, and our rational minds, help us tell which are the literal truths and which are metaphorical.

I conceded above that there is a lot of wisdom in the Torah. It has enormous insights on how human beings should treat each other, centuries ahead of its time. The laws concerning gossip and idle speech (*lashon hara*) are jewels, well ahead of the mores of our own time. The Jewish and non-Jewish world would be an immensely better place if these commandments were followed.

My religious friends want to explain to me how the wisdom got into the document. Unlike Maimonides and perhaps Rabbi Soloveithchik, however, I remain perplexed and cannot see the worldview of traditional Judaism as rational. Quite the contrary. The problem, as I see it, is that the Torah is not perfect (despite the fact that the Psalms 17:7 say it is). Human life is valued, to be sure, but individual autonomy is not. Democracy, freedom of speech, and religious tolerance are not among the values of the Torah. Within Torah Judaism, all serious decisions, even personal decisions, are vested in a male-dominated hierarchy. The Torah tolerates and, indeed, encourages and in some cases requires slavery, and the laws concerning divorce, illegitimacy, and other issues related to women are nothing less than pernicious. Modern Orthodox rabbis have developed a way to use the *secular* legal system to attenuate a deep ethical problem concerning divorce in the Torah. One of the most problematic aspects of the Torah's worldview is the thesis of a chosen people. Most of the ethical insights noted above become true, lasting insights only when they are extended from how Jews should treat each other to how people should treat each other. I cannot accept the chauvinism that underlies the literal reading of many of the laws, even the wise ones.

In short, I cannot buy *all* of the Torah, and so I cannot believe it has a divine source. Within the tradition, and according to Jewish law, Judaism is a package deal. One is not allowed to pick and choose among the various commandments and doctrines. You either accept the package as a whole, or reject it. Maimonides, the quintessential rationalist, insists on belief in every one of his thirteen principles of faith and obedience to every one of the 613 commandments. Of course, humans are not perfect, and everyone inevitably falls short in practice, but the Torah itself must be accepted in toto. I submit that the level of faith demanded by traditional Judaism is inconsistent with the philosophical doubt or questioning we engage in daily, the same doubt and Socratic questioning that philosophers instill in students and anyone else who will listen, the same doubt that gave birth to and sustains the scientific enterprise.

The clash between faith and reason is exemplified in the biblical story of the sacrifice of Isaac. Even if we put the matter of morality aside, the commandment to sacrifice Isaac makes no sense. God had given Abraham and Sarah a son in their old age: at Isaac's birth, Abraham was a hundred years old and Sarah was ninety. A miracle. And Abraham was explicitly promised that Isaac would have children: "for through Isaac shall seed be raised unto you" (Gen. 21:12). A few verses after this prophecy, Abraham is commanded to give up his son as a sacrificial offering. And Abraham obeys, or tries to. God sends an angel to stop Abraham, just before he kills Isaac.

The praise that God's angel heaps on Abraham serves as an epigraph to this essay. Abraham had passed this final test, with flying colors. Apparently, the test was to see if Abraham would obey this command, despite its irrationality and despite its immorality. Following Søren Kierkegaard, I cannot help seeing this episode as a refutation of rationalism. The Torah is saying that sometimes it is outright irrational to have faith, and yet one should have this faith nevertheless—just as the enemies of rationality have been urging. God's commandment not only trumps morality, it trumps rationality. Maybe it takes an Abraham to get to that level of faith, and the rest of us should stick to what is moral and rational. But the story is in scripture for a reason. It is to teach us something. For me at least, the message of the story is clear, and I reject it with all of my being.

It need hardly be mentioned that this biblical story is not an obscure item added to the corpus. One cannot take it or leave it. The story lies at the heart of the worldview. A religious Jew recites it every morning shortly after rising.

There are a number of other interpretations of this biblical story, some more consistent with the tradition than others. None come close to satisfying me or getting to the heart of the problem. One reading is that Abraham actually *failed* the test. He was supposed to stand up to God, and reject the command to sacrifice his son. Abraham had established a precedent of arguing with God, before the destruction of Sodom. On the reading in question, he should have argued here and refused to obey. Instead, we are told that Abraham got up early, anxious to obey this most unusual command. A *Midrash* ("legend") has it that Abraham rose early so that Sarah would not find out what was going to happen. The thought behind this *Midrash* is that Sarah would have prevented Abraham from (trying to) sacrifice their son. If so, then I submit that she is the hero of this story, the one to serve as a role model for future generations of parents and believers. In her apparent willingness to stand up to God, did she somehow have less faith than her husband, or did she have the good sense to think before acting, and to wonder how authentic the (supposed) command is? We have learned from David Hume that a seed of doubt and skepticism is healthy. It would not have taken much here. Could Abraham have gone through with the sacrifice if he entertained the thought that he misunderstood the command, or that it was not authentic?

In any case, the proposition that Abraham failed this test is inconsistent with the text itself. Abraham is praised to the nth degree after he is prevented from murdering Isaac. And it is explicit that he is praised for his willingness to sacrifice his son. The angel stops the sacrifice with the words, "Do not lay your hand on the boy, and do nothing to him; for I know now that you revere God, seeing that you have not refused me your son, your only son." It just does not make sense to praise someone for failing a test.

It is sometimes pointed out (or claimed) that in the historical context, the commandment to sacrifice Isaac did not seem as immoral as it would today. Since human sacrifice was (supposedly) common among the world's religions at that time, God was not asking Abraham to do anything very much out of the ordinary. Of course, God had indicated earlier that Abraham would have many descendants through Isaac, but Abraham had already witnessed miracles. He might have found it probable—or certain—that another miracle would occur, and that Isaac would be resurrected after the sacrifice. How else could the earlier prophecy, which Abraham presumably did not doubt, come to pass? On this reading, the sacrifice of Isaac does not fare all that poorly on grounds of the mores of the time or on grounds of consistency with previous pronouncements.

This interpretation, if correct, diminishes the praise due to Abraham. If he was confident that Isaac would somehow be resurrected, or not be killed in the act due to some miracle or other, then Abraham was not really sacrificing anything (in his own mind). On this reading, he did not believe that he was giving anything up in favor of his faith or obedience to God. And if child sacrifice was indeed common, then Abraham was not doing anything very much out of the ordinary. Lots of people did what Abraham was prepared to do—sacrifice a close relative in obedience to a higher power. We are told, more than once, that Abraham loved Isaac. I presume that at least some of the pagans loved their children too. It is only natural to love one's offspring. The only difference between the pagan who sacrificed a child, and Abraham who tried and was stopped, is that the latter was (supposedly) following the true religion. But does one get special credit, and praise, just for being right? If it is indeed praiseworthy to (be prepared to) kill one's child in obedience to a deity, then Abraham and his pagan counterparts are on a par. If the pagan's child sacrifice was too immoral to deserve praise, then so was Abraham's.

Nowadays, we read almost daily of people who kill innocent human beings, claiming that they are doing what God wants. We call them terrorists, or would-be terrorists if (like Abraham) they are stopped at the last minute. Whatever else we may think of such people, I presume that we do not doubt the sincerity of their beliefs. They must be sincere, since many of them deliberately kill themselves in the process. It is the beliefs themselves that are sick, demented, irrational. No God would want this, we tell ourselves. The philosopher in me still asks the question: What's the difference between the near sacrifice of Isaac and contemporary religious terrorism?

I do not claim to have said the last word on the sacrifice of Isaac in this context. I do submit, however, that this biblical story represents a deep challenge to rationalism, perhaps the deepest in the (so-called) Old Testament. Contemporary rationalists have attempted to come to grips with the story. Here is Louis Pojman (1998): "Many Old Testament scholars dismiss the literalness of the story and interpret it within the context of Middle Eastern child sacrifice. The story, according to these scholars, provides pictorial grounds for breaking with this custom." As noted above, this account is not consistent with the praise heaped on Abraham for passing the test, or at least it diminishes the praise. Pojman continues: "But even leaving aside this plausible explanation, we might contend that Abraham's action can be seen as rational given his noetic framework."[1] One can imagine his replying to a friendly skeptic years after the incident in the following manner:

> I heard a voice. It was the same voice (or so I believed) that commanded me years before to leave my country, my kindred, and my father's house to venture forth into the unknown. It was the same voice that promised me that I would prosper. I hearkened, and though the evidence seemed weak, the promise was fulfilled. It was the same voice that promised me a son in my old age and Sarah's old age, when childbearing was thought to be impossible. Yet it happened. My trust was vindicated. My whole existence has been predicated on the reality of that voice. . . . This last call was in a tone similar to the other calls. The voice was unmistakable. To deny its authenticity would be to deny the authenticity of the others. . . . I prefer to take the risk of obeying what I take to be the voice of God and disobey certain norms than to obey the norms and miss the possibility of any absolute relation to the Absolute. And what's more, I'm ready to recommend that all people who feel so called by a higher power do exactly as I have done.

I find this last statement chilling, but our topic here is rationality, not chillingness. I know that other thinkers whose rationality is beyond question come to conclusions similar to Pojman's concerning this story, and perhaps I have not picked the strongest rationalistic interpretation of it. But I cannot follow this line. It seems to me that Abraham's action was outrightly irrational, and that *this* was the message of the story. He was praised for acting in an irrational manner, following his faith. To use Pojman's apt phrase, the social "norms" in question here are not those concerning the polite way to address someone or concerning petty theft. The focus is on the norm against the deliberate murder of an innocent human being—a child. How on Earth can it be rational to violate that, especially after receiving prophecy that said child will himself have children? When we are dealing with matters that are this fundamental, perhaps there is no neutral standpoint from which one can evaluate the dispute. But for me at least, the issue here is whether the level of faith demanded of an Abraham, or anyone else for that matter, is compatible with entertaining doubts about the authenticity of the source of the faith. The Torah's message is that it is not. One of the sins that Jews confess each Yom Kippur is the sin of doubt. I submit that at least some doubt is no sin at all. This, I believe, is the most important lesson of philosophy. Even the slightest inkling of doubt would have been sufficient to stay Abraham's hand. Since there was no doubt, an angel had to come to stay his hand.

Let me insert one more personal anecdote. There was only one occasion during my career when I lost my temper at a professional philosophy event. It was a departmental colloquium, and the speaker was a well-known philosopher defending the rationality of a belief that God has spoken directly to (or otherwise communicated with) an agent. The colloquium speaker argued that a subject can be rationally justified in the belief that the communication is genuine—that it comes from the Divine source. Of course, it is not enough just to think, or even to be subjectively certain, that God is talking to you. According to the speaker, the hypothesis that God is talking to you is defeasible, and as such, it can be "overridden" by other epistemic factors.

During the question period, I got the floor and suggested that at least some of the Inquisitors thought that they were being commanded directly by God to torture the unbelievers into submission. He agreed. I asked him what went wrong (presuming that something had gone wrong). His response was that the Inquisitors' belief that they were in communication with God was overriden by other factors and that they should have seen this. "What were the overriding factors?" I asked. "Basic morality," he said.

At this point, I asked the speaker if he held that basic morality *always* overrides (i.e., defeats) the hypothesis that God has spoken. He said "no," that the situation is more complex than that. This was the point where I lost it. I said that my people, and others, have suffered enough from Christians' thinking that they were talking with God. After the colloquium, two religious philosophy students told me that they appreciated my reaction, and it gave them pause in their own thinking. So perhaps some good came of the session.

In retrospect, I suspect that the speaker balked at the suggestion that basic morality always trumps a hypothesis of prophecy because he wanted—or needed—to maintain that Abraham's actions concerning the sacrifice of Isaac fit into the religious epistemology developed in the talk. That is, the speaker needed to maintain that, according to the presented epistemology, Abraham was rationally *justified* in murdering Isaac. I am enough of a Quinean to reject foundationalism.[2] Just about every belief is fallible, and subject to revision, if the going gets rough enough. But I would think that it is patently obvious that the immorality of slitting the throat of an innocent child would override any belief that a morally divine deity has commanded someone to do just that. I concede that there is no knock-down argument here. Holism is hard to negotiate, especially when things this fundamental are called into question. So let us leave our discussion of rationalism.

One further orientation on the relationship between religious faith and rational belief is that the two are incommensurable—they do not engage each other at all. Science and perhaps even philosophy are at cross-purposes with religion. A defense of this, perhaps desperate, orientation begins with Hume's is–ought dichotomy. Science, and rational speculation generally, concern facts. The goal is to figure out what is true about the universe: whether or not it had a beginning and, if it did, how it began; how the universe operates; how planet Earth developed into what it is; and so on. In contrast, religion is normative. It concerns how we should live our lives. On this view, the Torah is a handbook for what Plato calls the art of living, and it is not a scientific, historical, or cosmological treatise. A famous, contemporary Orthodox rabbi was once asked if he believed that humans descended from other primates, as evolution contends. His response: "Why are you asking me? This is a scientific question. Ask a scientist." This is of-a-piece with the incommensurability orientation.

The world might be better off if believers and skeptics alike adopted a view like this. We would not have to fight over scientific textbooks, and perhaps the ugly disputes between various religions would be attenuated. For example, if one gives up the factual belief that a chunk of land belongs to his group, by divine decree, then he might find some reason to come to grips with others who make claims to the land.

As pleasant as this orientation may be, I do not know how tenable it is. Incommensurability does not fit with religion as we know it. Can the world's religions withdraw from *all* factual claims (other than the existence of God, perhaps)? Many years ago, in an Introduction to the Philosophy of Religion class, a Christian student rejected the incommensurability thesis, remarking that "if they find the body, the game is up." Can Christians maintain their faith without defending the historical reality of Christ walking on Earth? Closer to home, I gather that most modern Orthodox Jews have come to accept the truth of evolution. After all, the evidence for it is damn good. So they hold that the creation story is not to be taken literally. Its truths are metaphorical. Maybe one can take the same orientation toward the story of the great flood, and perhaps even the actual historical existence of the Patriarchs: Abraham, Isaac, Jacob, and their wives and children. But the concession to science ends there, or at least close to there. As emphasized in Joseph Levine's contribution to this volume, Orthodox Judaism is predicated on a special relationship between God and the children of Israel, a relationship that was consummated historically at Mount Sinai. If there was no Sinai, then Orthodox Judaism loses its hold on the children of Israel. The Bible says that God's presence descended on the mountain. A friend pointed out that we do not know what that means and that we have some room to interpret this sentence in a non-literal manner. But, he added, if there were no Jews at Sinai, we are in trouble. I do not know what an Orthodox Judaism stripped of all of its factual claims would look like, but it would be nothing like the religion we have now.

In short, I do not know how well religion can stay on the "ought" side of the is–ought dichotomy (assuming that it is a dichotomy). A deeper problem for the incommensurability thesis comes from the other side of the divide. Rationality, and certainly philosophy, are not—and should not be—content to stay on the "is" side. The incommensurability thesis is that religion tells us how to live. It instructs us on how to treat each other, how to treat the planet, and so on. And, as noted above, there are indeed deep insights along those lines in the holy texts. However, it seems to me that moral matters are susceptible to rational appraisal. That is, rationality has something to say about the best way to live and does not abandon that arena to the world's religions.

This is not to insist on moral realism, the thesis that moral discourse is objective. Moral non-cognitivists from Hume to Simon Blackburn insist that moral assertions, such as the wrongness of killing innocent children, do not express matters of fact, or have truth conditions. But it does not follow from such views that moral discourse lies outside the norms of rational appraisal altogether. Hume admits as much, when he discusses the senses in which we hold that a given feeling or action is rational or irrational. Moreover, Blackburn's quasi-realism is a sustained attempt to show that there is a logic of morality. To say that moral pronouncements are not cognitive, and, with Hume's *Treatise of Human Nature,* that morality is not *primarily* a rational matter ("reason is, and ought only to be, the slave of the passions," 2.3.3.4) is not to deny reason an important (albeit secondary) role in moral deliberation. Abraham was not stopped by his faith in his attempt to murder Isaac. Something should have stopped him.

I am not an expert in meta-ethics, and I may have mis-described the territory. But it seems clear to me, at least, that it is simply not true that religion and science/philosophy are incommensurable. I do think that religion has nothing to say to science, on the "is" side of the dichotomy, but philosophy and rational reflection generally do have something to say about the "ought." It is dangerous and unethical to leave that realm to the world's religions. Frankly, they do not have a good track record.

So I am forced to the conclusion that the two peace proposals, rationalism and incommensurability, are untenable with at least the mainstream Judeo-Christian traditions, or, to be specific, traditional Torah Judaism. If this is correct, then religious faith is at war with rationality, and all there is to do is choose sides. The best the camps can hope for is a grudging, mutual respect—agreeing to disagree, keeping the dispute from getting violent. Rationality dictates this much, perhaps. Hopefully, the believer's faith will go along, although the history of religious tolerance is not promising.

There is indeed mystery in life, a lot of unanswered questions of vital importance. I would not be a philosopher if I did not believe that, with all my being. Religion and philosophy alike grapple with the deepest questions of all: What is it all about? How should we live? Philosophy is sometimes chided for failing to provide compelling answers to its questions. Perhaps one of the most important lessons of philosophy is to teach us how to live with the questions unanswered, rather than settle for unsatisfactory but popular answers. This is our legacy from Socrates onward and is the source of at least some of the conflict with religion. In exchange for the security, comfort, and certainty of the world's religions, we offer only doubt and uncertainty, a cold, hard logical look at the universe. But I'll take it.

Many thanks to Louise Antony for encouraging me to contribute to this volume. Thanks also to Louise, Dan Farrell, and Joseph Levine for commenting on an earlier draft.

TWO 

From Yeshiva Bochur to Secular Humanist

Joseph Levine

Introduction—Brief Autobiography

I was born in Brooklyn, New York, of Eastern European Jewish descent. My parents were born in the States, but their parents came from Europe, and both my parents spoke Yiddish as their first language. When I was just three, my family moved to Los Angeles, California. Both of my parents were raised in Torah Jewish homes, and that's how they raised my two brothers and myself.[1]

The Torah, in the broad sense in which I intend it here, is the entire body of law, legend, and inspirational literature that encompasses the Old Testament of the Bible, the Talmud, Midrash, and numerous other religious writings down through the centuries, including today. To be a Torah Jew is to live in conformity with the Torah, and to believe its precepts. "Strictly Orthodox," *shomer shabbas* (translated literally as "guardian of the Sabbath"), and, I would claim, "fundamentalist," are other terms one could use to describe this way of life. While the first two are common, you don't hear "fundamentalist" used very often in connection with Judaism, though it is with Christianity and Islam. But Torah Jews really are fundamentalists; I was taught that the world was literally created in six days almost six thousand years ago, and that the theory of evolution was mistaken.

In our milieu, to qualify as a Torah Jew, one had to keep kosher both at home and when eating out, and also refrain from any of the prohibited activities from sundown Friday to Saturday evening. This means you couldn't turn on or off lights, tear anything, carry anything outside your home, light or adjust a fire on the stove, drive or ride in a car, or perform any of a host of other activities. When it comes to eating, no meat and milk together—you had to wait six hours after eating meat before you could eat any dairy—no unkosher meat, two sets of dishes (four actually, if you count Passover dishes).

While this may sound like an awfully restrictive form of life—well OK, it is actually—there are important compensating advantages. For instance, on the Sabbath, one spends time in synagogue with one's friends and neighbors, one has leisurely feasts with singing and a lot of fellow feeling, there are no outside distractions, and it's typical to have a nice nap or walk to round out the day. If you're used to eating only kosher food, it's not that hard to refrain from eating non-kosher food, especially if you live in a community where everyone is doing the same.

Another significant feature of Torah Judaism has to do with schooling. If at all possible, a Torah Jewish family does not send a child—especially a male child—to a public school. I was sent to a religious Jewish school—a "yeshiva"—in Los Angeles.[2] At the age of six or seven, I began to study Talmud (I was a bit precocious), along with other religious subjects. The school day was long, as half the day was devoted to Torah study and the other half to our secular subjects. We were expected to master the standard academic curriculum, and indeed yeshiva students tended to do well when applying to college.

One significant element of my upbringing that certainly distinguished it from most others in the Torah tradition was that it took place in Los Angeles in the 1960s. From very early on, I was subjected to the conflicting messages of traditional (Eastern European) Jewish life and modern American culture, in particular the cutting edge represented by 1960s counterculture. As a small child this didn't affect me much, but by the age of twelve or thirteen, the clash of influences started to have an effect. In 1966, as the 1960s political and cultural revolution was getting into full swing, I left yeshiva and went to public school, where I spent my last two years of high school. There I made friends with the hippies in the school (still a small but growing minority), and generally threw myself into the LA's 1960s countercultural scene. Needless to say, my formerly strict observance of Jewish law lapsed quite a bit during this period.

That might have been the end of the story, but instead of just going on to college and leaving the Torah tradition behind me, I decided to return to yeshiva to study full-time. Though during my public high school years I had strayed considerably from the Torah path, I never really gave up my fundamental beliefs that this was the right way to live. I felt the need to give it another chance. I began by studying with the rabbi who had first taught me Talmud when a youngster, Rabbi Simcha Wasserman. I again began to observe all the laws strictly and now spent all day studying Talmud. I still kept the leftish political views that developed during my time in public high school, and continued my friendships with a number of my close friends from that period (though I saw them only rarely), but mostly I became immersed in the Torah–yeshiva world much more deeply than before. I moved in to the school's dormitory, and lived and breathed Torah constantly.

I made significant progress, and in the middle of my second year there, Rabbi Wasserman suggested that it was time for me to go to a bigger yeshiva in Israel. So, I left for Jerusalem, where I studied for almost two years. By this time I had decided that I would pursue Torah study as my life's work and become a yeshiva rabbi myself. While in Jerusalem I experienced profound but conflicting emotions regarding this life choice. For instance, the first time I went to the Wailing Wall in the Old City of Jerusalem, I truly believed that I experienced something like a personal revelation, though of course I couldn't really describe what I felt (and can't to this day). Also, I found the high level and intensity of study at the yeshiva exhilarating and fulfilling.

On the other hand, storm clouds of doubt and discontent were also forming on the horizon. I began to have anxiety attacks that shook me and made me reflect on aspects of my life that I had been hiding from myself. Moral and intellectual objections to Torah doctrines began to intrude more and more on my thinking, and I found less and less personal satisfaction in the yeshiva atmosphere, to the point that I experienced it as extremely stifling. I began to seek contacts outside the yeshiva and gradually realized that I wanted to leave and attend university. After much internal turmoil, I decided to return to Los Angeles, where I enrolled at UCLA, became a philosophy major, and never really looked back. I suppose it took a few more years before I realized that I had lost all of my religious beliefs and indeed classified myself as a secular atheist. I also lost interest in continuing my involvement with the Jewish community, even on a purely cultural level. While never denying my past life as a yeshiva bochur, indeed treasuring it in many ways, I did definitively leave it, and Judaism more generally, behind.

Torah Judaism and TCA

So much for the bare-bones narrative of my life as a Torah Jew; now to put some flesh on those bones and get into some detail. For this purpose, I want to organize my discussion around three key ideas that I think illuminate the structure of Torah Jewish life, and perhaps many other forms of religious life: transcendence, community, and Aristotelian flourishing. By "transcendence" I intend a connection with forces and purposes beyond one's personal concerns and the details of one's own life. By "Aristotelian" flourishing I intend the ability to develop and exercise one's peculiarly human capabilities, as for instance through intellectual or artistic endeavors. "Community" is self-explanatory. To a very rough first approximation, one could say that God provides the transcendence, the Jewish people the sense of community, and Torah study the Aristotelian flourishing.

These three aspects of Torah Jewish life are, however, interwoven in a very complicated way, which I'll try to convey in what follows.

I'll begin with Torah study. Torah Judaism has a feature I've always admired, and, from my own limited knowledge of other religions, seems unique to it. This is the idea that what is essentially a kind of scholarly research, Torah study, counts as a form of religious devotion. In fact, study of the Torah (which normally means the Talmud) is considered a duty (for men, of course), and this duty is taken so seriously that it gives rise to a corresponding sin that served in my youth as one of the principal sources of guilt, the sin of "bitul Torah." You commit the sin of "bitul Torah" when you are awake, not actively involved in "learning" (which meant thinking about, reading, or discussing some aspect of the Torah), and have no good excuse for not doing so. Possible excuses are: you're eating, at work, or in the bathroom, or fulfilling some other religious obligation or some social obligation, or engaging in necessary leisure. But the default is, if you're awake and have no other pressing need, you should be learning Torah. What an amazing constant source of guilt, and yet also a tremendous affirmation of the significance of intellectual activity.

What is so engaging in Talmud study, especially for anyone with a philosophical bent, is the emphasis on subtle conceptual distinctions and complicated inferences. You start with a passage of Talmud that doesn't make sense on the face of it, or apparently contradicts another passage. Enter the commentaries to explain it, or explain away the contradiction. Usually this involves introducing a distinction. But then the commentaries disagree with each other, and then you search among further commentaries to find even more subtle distinctions, and on it goes. One passage of a few lines of Talmud can involve one in days of scholarly research and complex reasoning on one's own part. What's beautiful about it is that though there is on the one hand a rigid structure of authority—in the end we're trying to figure out God's word, so it has to be right—there is always room for one's own original contribution, thanks to the complexity of the dialectic.

A word about the authority structure. In the yeshiva world, one's heroes are Talmudic scholars. Greatness in learning is the key to membership in the rabbinic "hall of fame." There are two dimensions along which "greatness," and thus authority, is measured: one that applies within a particular era, and the other that applies across time. With regard to the former, relative authority is determined by the judgments of peers concerning one's scholarly achievement, just as this is done in secular academic professions. With regard to the latter, the idea is that the farther back in time, the greater the scholar, and thus the more authority (this is a rough approximation). Moses is at the pinnacle, having talked directly to God and received the Torah directly from Him. It's significant that though Moses is the one who led the Jews out of slavery and performed all those miracles in Egypt, he is known by the name "Moshe Rabeinu," which means "Moses our teacher." The prophets and judges come next, then the authors of the Mishna, the authors of Gomorrah, the early commentaries (the "Rishonim"), the later commentaries (the "Acharonim"), and then finally the scholars of the last couple of centuries. Though the most subtle intellectual work you see is by later authors, the idea is that all these distinctions and nuances were known by the early scholars and either handed down orally or forgotten and then rediscovered. So one could always introduce a new distinction that solved a tricky problem but have faith that this idea, too, was known to Moshe Rabeinu. Through this mechanism, much latitude for individual creativity was allowed while maintaining the structure of authority.

The rabbi with whom I first studied Talmud, and with whom I studied immediately after high school, was perhaps the most significant influence on me during my youth. Rabbi Simcha Wasserman was the youngest son of Rav Elchanan Wasserman, who right before World War II was perhaps the most important Talmudic scholar in Eastern Europe. It's extremely hard to explain what it was like to be in the presence of a man like Rabbi Wasserman as he lectured on a passage of Talmud. Of course, he had the appearance one expected from any yeshiva rabbi—beard, black yarmulke, worn suit, general Eastern European facial features. But the really special ones, like Rabbi Wasserman, had a sparkle in their eyes, and exuded a warmth and spiritual joy that, combined with penetrating intellectual power and a keen sense of irony and humor, was spellbinding. Even as a small child I could see what distinguished him from others who looked the look and talked the talk but didn't really have that something special that made them stand out. Having this encounter with the genuine article at this age, someone who instantiated what was best about the tradition that produced him—as it were, the "form" of the yeshiva rabbinical scholar—left an indelible impression on me. In a way that I'll try to make clear later, it was precisely this appreciation of authenticity, instilled in me by my exposure to figures like Rabbi Wasserman, that eventually played a major role in causing me to lose my faith in the doctrines they taught me.

Of course, what makes all of this intellectual activity a form of religious devotion is the fact that God commands us to engage in it and that what we are studying is His law. Belief in God is central to Torah Judaism. For one thing, there is the biblical fundamentalism. It is a tenet of faith that God literally created the world from nothing in six days. The waters of the Red Sea were parted by God, using Moses as his agent. In fact, every word of the Pentateuch is believed to be dictated by God to Moses. Then there's the constant praying and saying blessings and the injunction not to take God's name in vain. The point of wearing a yarmulke, I was told when a child, is to have a constant reminder that God is above you in heaven. One even thanks God with a special blessing after going to the bathroom, because He allows your body to function properly. Nothing in one's daily life, in other words, escapes some reminder of God's authority and majesty.

Earlier I identified the source of transcendence in Torah Judaism with belief in God. In a way this is obvious, and doesn't distinguish Torah Judaism from other forms of Judeo-Christian belief. A search for transcendence, as I understand it, is a search for significance in one's life, lasting significance in particular. Well, what could be more significant than the fact that the creator of the universe, its most powerful, beneficent, and wise actor, takes an interest in you, and somehow your activity contributes to His purposes? Clearly it's also of utmost importance that belief in God turns death from an ultimate end into merely another stage in one's journey. As a Torah Jew I felt this sense of transcendence quite palpably, especially in such moments as my first trip to the Wailing Wall. Here I am, I thought, where God's divine presence is most intensely located.

But there is a particular way that Torah Judaism links the transcendence afforded by connection to God both to Torah study and to the Jewish people, the embodiment of our third theme, community. Within Torah Judaism, world history is represented as the history of the Jewish people, which in turn is understood as the chronicle of the complicated relationship between God and his often errant, but at bottom, deeply loved children. The Jewish people constitute God's agent in the world, the instrument through which His own agency is expressed. And perhaps the most important way that Torah Jews carry out this mission is through the study of Torah. Torah study literally, on this view, makes the world go around.[3]

A story I heard in yeshiva illustrates this point nicely. The story involves Rav Chaim Volozhin, the most eminent pupil of the Vilna Gaon, himself the most important rabbinic authority in Europe of his time (and for a century or two before, probably). Rav Chaim was giving a lecture on some Talmudic point when all of a sudden the students in the room began running over to the window. It turns out that Napoleon's soldiers had just entered the town and were marching down the main street. The students were witnessing a small part of what was clearly a world-historical process, and it's not surprising that they interrupted their study to get a good look. Rav Chaim upbraided them by saying they had their priorities reversed. What's going on in here, in this room where we are studying Torah, he said, is what's of world-historical importance, not what's going on out there.

One could, of course, just write this off as a not-very-convincing attempt by a frustrated professor to get his students to pay attention. I never did hear whether or not the students stopped gawking at the soldiers; probably the force of Rav Chaim's personality was enough to get them to stop. But the story survived two hundred years for a reason. It expresses a very deeply held belief that studying Torah is not only a religious obligation, not only something that binds you personally to God and the Jewish people, but something that actually contributes to God's plan for the universe. The idea that pure intellectual activity brings you most closely in contact with the spiritual essence of the world I found, and still find, very powerful, and it shows how closely interwoven are transcendence and Aristotelian flourishing in Torah Judaism.

Let me return now to what I said above was the complex relationship between God and the Jewish people. What makes it complicated is the fact that the Jewish people are not represented as merely God's instrument and servant, but also, as mentioned above, his often-badly-behaved children, and this tension between God and the Jewish people is crucial to the dynamic of Torah life. Reading the chronicles in the Bible and the Midrashic commentaries makes it clear that the parent–child relation is precisely the right model. It's a commonplace that many parents attempt to realize themselves through their children's lives, and then are brought up short by the fact that their children are independent people with projects and lives of their own. Similarly, God lays out a plan for the role of the Jewish People in history, and damned if His children aren't constantly rebelling and going their own way. Now of course, rebelling is "sinning," and the ideology of Torah Judaism is that we should be "good" children and follow the plan, but one can't help noticing that the streak of rebellion—as it's put in one biblical passage, we are a "stiff-necked" people—is often celebrated, though surreptitiously—it's the "subtext," as it were.

There are instances where standing up to God is openly celebrated, though this is officially clothed in the idea that this is also what God wants. One such event, of paramount significance, is the moment when Moses defied God at Mount Sinai in the incident of the Golden Calf. Moses, returning from his forty-nine days on Mount Sinai to receive the Torah, discovers the people's rebellion in building the Golden Calf. God says in anger, "Moses, leave me to pour out my wrath on them and destroy them; I will then start a new nation from your children." Amazingly, according to the Midrashic commentary, Moshe Rabeinu (himself quite furious with the people, of course) replies to God, "If You will forgive their sin, fine, but if not, blot me out of the book that You have written." God relents, and the people are saved. The idea that Moses could speak this boldly to God, for the purpose of saving his people, has always moved me greatly, and it still does. In particular, what comes across is not just Moses's daring rescue attempt, but the sense that in his view the Jewish People matter more than God and His law. What's more, God endorses this judgment.[4]

There is a widely cited story from the Talmud that also illustrates how the People take precedence. During the days of the Sanhedrin, the rabbinic court that decided points of Jewish law during the period when Israel was still a political entity and the Temple was extant, the legal disputes that arose would be decided by majority, as in our Supreme Court. One such debate featured a particularly eminent scholar on one side, and everyone else on the other. He was so sure of his stand that he said, "If I'm right, let that tree over there uproot itself and jump to another spot." Damned if it didn't do just that. The other sages replied, "We don't take instruction from trees." "Okay," he said, "if I'm right let that river change course." Again, the river changed course. They replied, "we don't take instruction from rivers." "Well then," he finally said, exasperated with their stubbornness, no doubt, "if I'm right let a voice from Heaven proclaim that. 'Sure enough, a voice from Heaven proclaimed that he was right in his interpretation of the law. At this point the others replied, "We don't take instruction from You (i.e., God) either. You gave us the Torah, and with it the rules for its interpretation, and now it's our job. So You keep out of it." According to the Talmud, Elijah the prophet was visiting with a scholar from the era after the destruction of the Temple, and was asked how God reacted when defied by the members of the Sanhedrin in this way.[5] Elijah replied that God laughed and said, "My children have bested me."

It's this background understanding of the nature of the relationship between God and the Jewish people that has always made me feel alienated from "progressive" Passover Seders. Despite the fact that I now lead a totally secular life and endorse leftist political views, I've never been able to see the story of the exodus from Egypt as a celebration of all human liberation from oppression. For me, Passover is too personal. As I see it, Passover is the story of a volatile love affair between two very particular characters—God and the Jewish people. While I understand the urge to universalize it, it just doesn't work for me.

Despite the crucial roles played by God and Torah study in the worldview of Torah Judaism, I think it's clear that it is the people—community—that plays the most significant role. True, the source of the Jewish people's significance is the idea that we were chosen by God to do his holy work—mainly, study his Torah. But in the end, loyalty and connection to the people becomes the most important duty in Torah Judaism; and in this sense, in Judaism more widely.

One manifestation of the primacy of community is the fact that it is common to find Jews who keep up their (relatively) strict observance of the laws of Kashrut and the Sabbath but proclaim that they do not believe in a lot of the doctrine. I remember quite well that I "came out" to my parents in stages. First I told them I didn't believe in God, then I told them I didn't keep the Sabbath anymore, and finally I told them I was going to marry a non-Jew. Well, the first stage made almost no impression, the second caused quite a fuss, and the third, well, you just have to see *Fiddler on the Roof* to imagine their reaction.

The idea, I think, is that ritual practice and observance, even more than a matter of obeying God, is a sign of one's commitment to community membership. The preservation of the community is of paramount importance, which is why one of the worst sins you can commit, in the eyes of most Torah Jews, is to marry a non-Jew. Sure, you are supposed to maintain your faith in God and obey His commands, but the bottom line is that you don't break with the community.

During my life as a yeshiva bochur I was completely sold on God and Torah study. I believed in God wholeheartedly and threw myself into the study of Talmud. I also found the idea of God's relationship with the Jewish People to be a profoundly moving idea, and it was certainly important to me that I was contributing to the People's fulfillment of their divinely ordained role. Yet, I must admit, there was always a part of the community aspect of Torah Judaism that didn't sit well with me.

It's not that I didn't share in the sense of community loyalty that all my friends and I grew up with. As the children of the Holocaust generation—many of my childhood friends were children of survivors—the idea of loyalty to the People was ingrained very deeply. Yet I never really fully internalized the sense that just because someone was Jewish I had some special connection with him or her. I mostly only knew Jews when I was very young, and I certainly felt strong bonds with my friends. But this visceral sense that many Jews have of a need to associate with other Jews was never very strong in me. Participation in many community functions was often a chore for me, something I did out of obligation. I found myself interested in and wondering about the world outside and drawn to people with different backgrounds. Strong emotional bonds were always for me a function of actual connections, not a matter of ethnic identification. My sense of community identification was more ideological than it was for many of my peers and therefore more easily weakened when the structure of Torah beliefs was dismantled, a topic to which I now turn.

Leaving It All Behind

In my brief biographical narrative above I told how, after significant internal struggle, I came to abandon my life as a yeshiva bochur. A lot of elements went into that sea change, and it's difficult, especially now after so many years, to present a clear and coherent picture of that process. So I'm not going to try. Rather, I'm going to indulge in some reconstructive history, telling the story unabashedly from my current perspective, relying on memory, of course, but also on insight gained years after that process was completed. So what were (are) my objections to the Torah life, and to what extent do the three elements of transcendence, community, and Aristotelian flourishing play a role in my current secular life?

I'll begin with the more intellectual, or philosophical problems, though I don't want to spend much time on these. It's not that they weren't important for me, but anti-theistic arguments can be found lots of places, and it isn't the focus of my concern in this paper. Suffice it to say that I came to believe (and still believe) that the metaphysics of theism generally, and Torah Judaism in particular, along with the fundamentalist narrative about the Bible and all that implied concerning the status of modern scientific theories, is just untenable. For many familiar reasons, which I find utterly convincing, the idea that there is a supernatural, omnipotent, omniscient, and omni-benevolent deity that created and watches over the world, is one I can't now take seriously.[6]

However, one aspect of the process by which I came to this conclusion does bear elaboration. Talmud study, as I've said a number of times, involves acute and subtle forms of reasoning. As my admiration for Rabbi Wasserman makes clear,

I was especially sensitive to signs of intellectual honesty and authenticity, values I saw embodied in him and other Talmudic scholars I encountered. But there was always a tension between this value of intellectual honesty and the constraint that the Torah had to be right and you couldn't question God's word. That even Jewish scholars felt the tension is evident, I believe, from the way that the People's rebelliousness was celebrated. Still, in the end, the principle that the Torah, as the divine word of God, had to be right constituted an absolute constraint on intellectual pursuit, one that for me stood in stark conflict with the values of intellectual honesty and authenticity. I chose the latter.

But the interesting question for my purposes is not really why I can't take Torah Jewish theism seriously, but why it should matter. As I mentioned above, there are many Jews who maintain varying degrees of connection with traditional practice who don't espouse the fundamentalist beliefs definitive of Torah Judaism. It was certainly an option for me to join their ranks. Maybe I couldn't really be a full-fledged Torah Jew anymore, since that really does involve buying the fundamentalism, but I might have maintained a somewhat traditional Jewish life nevertheless. It certainly would have allowed me to maintain a normal relationship with my family, which was a pretty strong incentive. So why didn't I choose this option? This gets to the heart of the matter that I think this entire volume is about. What kind of life have we given up and why, and what kind of life have we chosen instead?

The reason I couldn't really choose the "cultural Torah-Jew" option had to do with certain deep moral objections to that way of life, together with the realization that it just wasn't personally fulfilling. I spoke above of how essential the role of the Jewish People, its special status, is to Torah Jewish life. In many prayers, the phrase "and You chose us from among all the other nations" occurs, and the claim that we are the Chosen People is one of the principal tenets of Torah Jewish faith. The spirit of that claim pervades much cultural Jewish life, even for those who don't strictly believe it. Well, I just couldn't buy the Chosen People idea anymore. For one thing, it just didn't seem true. I looked around at my fellow Jews and at the other people I knew, and also thought carefully about the histories of various peoples, and this special divine spark that supposedly attached to the Jewish people just didn't seem evident. I came to the conclusion, something I believe to this day, that all peoples—not all people, because there certainly are individual differences—are pretty much the same.

But the main problem was that the doctrine of the Chosen People conflicts with very basic moral principles I had internalized concerning the value of every human life, and the general egalitarian ideals that attend a modern Western democratic culture. I had also never really abandoned the leftist political views I had acquired while in public high school, which were more radically egalitarian in nature. Torah Judaism is actually not consistent in this regard, since one can also find sources for this more egalitarian ethic, but the emphasis is clearly on our inherent special nature, and I could no longer abide that form of chauvinism.

Though just at the level of ideology this insistence on Jewish specialness bothered me, it wasn't until I lived in Israel that it began to cause serious internal conflict. It was there that I saw firsthand how Jews treated Arabs the way Jews were themselves treated in Eastern Europe. It took time for this to sink in, but the seeds of future moral outrage were planted then. I could no longer ignore how the ideology of special divine favor was being realized in practice.

I remember years ago talking with a friend of my parents about the relative virtues of various religious traditions. One virtue he maintained for Judaism was its disdain for proselytizing. "Well," I said, "this can go two ways. It might easily be seen as an expression of racial or ethnic superiority; we are the 'chosen people' and won't encourage others to join us." He responded that whatever sense of superiority or exclusivity there was in Jewish sensibility was nothing for others to fear, as historically Jews have not been responsible for any of the kinds of crimes against other peoples that have been perpetrated by others, especially against us. I replied, "Perhaps historically this has been true, but then we haven't had any power for two thousand years. Just look what happened once we got some, in Israel."

Let's be clear about what founding the Jewish State of Israel involved and continues to involve. We came into another people's land—admittedly, after enduring centuries of oppression ourselves—kicked them out brutally, and treated those who remained like dirt. We continue to oppress Palestinians horribly, and shamelessly exploit our own history of oppression and guilt-trip the rest of the world into letting us get away with it. *This* is how God's people act? Not any God I wanted to have anything to do with.

Of course, any people, even God's "chosen people," can act badly, and this alone might not be enough to undermine the doctrine. What bothered me in particular, however, was that this didn't seem to be an aberration. Both the role of Torah Jewry in actively participating in the oppression and subjugation of Palestinians, and the way that Torah doctrines lent themselves to be exploited for that purpose, made this evident. God gave the land to us, it's a sin to give any of it back, Arab lives don't have the same value as Jewish lives—all of these claims have Torah sources. It's just too natural and easy to slide from thinking of one's own kind as distinguished by God to thinking of others as beneath contempt.

I want to emphasize that this isn't just a matter of how the government of Israel behaves. Unfortunately, today, especially in the United States, Jewish communal life has been largely hijacked by the Zionist project. Though there are finally some cracks in the wall of defiant support for anything Israel does, the kinds of vicious accusations leveled at anyone who shows concern for Palestinian suffering has made the organized Jewish community an unwelcome place for many who might otherwise seek fellowship there. Though there are many factors that explain this unhappy state of affairs—and again, Jews' history of oppression is clearly among them—I do believe that the chauvinistic emphasis on the People that is deeply rooted in Torah Judaism is also among them.[7]

I certainly don't mean to say that I think this problem is peculiar to Torah Judaism. It seems to me history has shown all too well that when community is made a fundamental value around which a form of life is organized, there is a large risk that in circumstances of conflict with other groups things will get very ugly. Jews are no better or worse than others in this regard. My point is just that the Torah, to which I used to look for moral guidance, seemed to be part of the problem here, not the solution.

As I mentioned earlier, there were also personal issues. As long as I believed in the basic tenets of Torah doctrine and was immersed in the yeshiva world, with its intellectual fulfillment, feeling connected, indeed feeling obligated to feel connected, to the Jewish People wasn't a problem. But once the special nature of the Jewish People was no longer underwritten by divine writ, I found the communal sensibility stifling and in conflict with a sense of my own autonomy. Continuing to live as a member of the Jewish community, even those portions of it not infected by Zionist zealotry, just wasn't for me.

Why? It's not that I see no need for community or that I can't understand how people who share a tradition might find fulfillment in association with each other. I certainly see nothing wrong with the idea of a modernized Jewish communal life that sheds both those chauvinistic elements to which I morally object along with the fundamentalist beliefs. But to me there isn't much point. For one thing, what kept me deeply engaged in Jewish life was so tied up with the beauty and grandeur of genuine Torah Judaism that the available modernized replacements seem frankly shallow and lifeless to me. For another, I just don't find the kind of connection to others built on history and tradition very sustaining.

I feel very close to my friends and family and certainly recognize special obligations to those with whom I've developed various relationships, as well as to my community more broadly speaking. Indeed, my participation in the Palestinian support movement does have something to do with my being Jewish, because it seems to me that when your community makes a mess one has a special obligation to help clean it up. But in the end I mostly define myself as an individual, with my own projects and interests, and cherish the ability to associate with those who share what I value in one way or another.

I remember well one of the arguments that was often made to me for why I shouldn't marry my non-Jewish wife. "But what will your children be? They won't know who they are," relatives would say, in a self-satisfied tone that expressed their confidence that finally they had an unassailable argument. "What will they be? People," I would respond; "they'll be people and know that's what they are." I suppose that's not enough for some. But for me, having spent so much of my youth tied to a community by God's command and now finally set free, this suited me just fine.

Torah Judaism provided transcendence through God, community through the Jewish People, and Aristotelian flourishing through Torah study. My chosen profession, philosophy, clearly provides ample opportunity for Aristotelian flourishing. What's more, I'm no longer constrained by a dogmatic bottom line, so it fulfills that need even better than Torah study. Community for me is something that must be constructed on a more voluntary basis. It's hard, no doubt, and of course, no one has found a really good substitute for age-old traditions to provide people with the means to express their fellow-feeling in structured ways. It's hard to just make up holidays and rituals, and therefore my own communal life with friends and family relies heavily on those we were bequeathed by our traditions. Still, we can choose what we want to take from that past and with whom we choose to experience it, and to me this is crucial.

So what about transcendence? If there's no God in my life, how do I deal with the loss of connection to what's beyond, the feeling that my projects and concerns lack significance? My attitude toward this question was influenced early on in my college career when I encountered Nietzsche. In fact, it was reading Nietzsche that finally put the nail in the coffin of my belief in God. From Nietzsche I got the idea that aside from the fact that it's false, belief in God might actually be morally wrong.[8] This meant that you couldn't try to hedge your bets by maintaining your belief, or going agnostic (that great cop-out); you really had to take a stand. It had never occurred to me before that it could be wrong to believe in God, so intent had I been on defending myself against the charge that it was wrong to lose my faith. This was a real eye-opener.

So how could it be wrong? Well, of course, not wrong in the stealing/murdering/raping sense of wrong. Rather, it's wrong in the sense that belief in God expresses a rejection, or denial, or perhaps subjugation of one's humanity. It involves turning one's back on the human will to overcome challenges, to create, and instead makes servility to authority the ultimate aim of human life. It projects onto an unapproachable and incomprehensible Other all that is good and magnificent in human experience and achievement. Why is it wrong? It's a sin against ourselves, that's why.

An interesting example of the kind of self-denying projection I'm talking about can be seen in the framework of Torah study itself. As I described earlier, a crucial element in Talmud study is the recognition of the authority of historically earlier scholars and sages. Every new distinction we come up with, every new argument, is supposedly just a matter of rediscovering what was there from the beginning and was known to Moshe Rabeinu, to boot. But, of course, this is all inverted. The Torah, like every other human endeavor, develops and grows. It's the most recent scholars, building on those who came before them, who have honed it to its finest and subtlest shape. But rather than take credit for this ever-developing body of thought, we belittle ourselves as unworthy descendants of those who had genuine wisdom and insight.

The very idea that we require salvation from above is an idea I now find quite offensive. It's not that I see only good in human nature. Far from it. As a species we seem particularly prone to acts of savagery that distinguish us on the planet. But we must take responsibility for ourselves, and while taking responsibility for our dark side also take pride in our achievements. Theists of all (traditional) kinds often make human hubris—the urge, as it is sometimes called, to "play God"—into the source of much evil in the world. I side with (my understanding of) Nietzsche here in seeing this as the great inversion of reality that it is. For it is our unique capacity as rational beings with a moral sense to transcend mere nature. Rather than acknowledge that fundamental fact and take responsibility for it, theists re-describe it as "playing God." No, as I see it, it's God who's playing us.

In the end, I do think one loses something significant when one loses belief in God. I admit that the idea that my life was somehow a matter of concern to the ultimate power of the universe provided me with a sense of my own significance that I lost when I lost that belief. I also miss the comforting thought that however dark the world seems, the bright light of redemption may be just around the corner. (Of course, we may have to do our share to attain it, but the point is we have a powerful ally on our side.) Finally, with God gone, so is eternal life. I've had to confront the reality of death in a new way.

To that sense of loss just described I have two responses. First, I say, "Welcome to life as it is rather than how it only seemed to be in your fantasy." For human beings, growing up is often a matter of facing painful truths, and the loss of this sort of transcendence and moral guarantee must be swallowed and dealt with along with many other aspects of reality; in particular, as mentioned, the ultimate nature of death. This is one way to read the story of Adam and Eve, of course. Human innocence can no longer be sustained, now that we've eaten from the "tree of knowledge." So be it. The Nietzschean in me says, "Deal with it."

But then, as with the tree of knowledge story, I think there's a way in which this loss of theological transcendence can be seen as an opportunity as well. In line with what I take to be a common theme of both Nietzsche and Kant, we can turn this indifference of the universe to our lives and projects into the opportunity to make ourselves the ground of our own significance. As rational intentional agents we can see meaning and significance where we ourselves make it. To quote Kant, "Two things fill the mind with ever new and increasing wonder and awe: the starry heavens above me and the moral law within me." What's within us needs no validation from the starry heavens—its significance is internally certified.

So there's no guarantee good will triumph over evil, and we must be the authors and creators of our own significance. That we can be the ground of our own significance—and, I would argue, have always been, though we hid it from ourselves behind a veil of mythology—is really a profound miracle in its own right, worthy of Kant's wonder and awe. Once we rid ourselves of the veil imposed by religious ideology and practice, we face formidable challenges: We must face our own death without comfort of an afterlife; we must endow our projects with significance from within; we must find it in ourselves to fight for justice though the odds may be against us; and we must self-consciously build a new sense of community based on recognition of our and others' autonomous choices. Can we succeed? I don't know, that's the whole point. Still, it's all we have, and it's a noble project to try.

THREE

Religio Philosophi

Daniel Garber

As I write these words, I am sitting in a hotel room in the Latin Quarter of Paris. Three hundred and fifty years ago or so this area was frequented by my people. I don't mean my ancestors, who were in an altogether different part of Europe, doing very different things. I mean the people I study. In early- and mid-seventeenth-century Paris you could find many of the people who made science and philosophy what it is today. Descartes lived here for a while; though he moved away, he came back from time to time, and his spirit (immaterial, of course) haunted these streets for many years. Pascal lived here, around the corner, actually. Mersenne lived across the river, in a neighborhood to which one could walk in thirty or forty-five minutes. I don't know where Hobbes lived during the crucial decade of his life that he spent here, but it must have been close; Paris wasn't that big back then. Ditto for Gassendi. A few years later Leibniz was to visit for three short years that shaped the rest of his intellectual life.

These people, whose life work has become my own, were shaped by the religion and the religious controversies of the societies in which they lived. They lived in a world where religion and faith were everyday presences, almost as real as the streets they walked and the buildings they passed. Mersenne and Gassendi were priests. Mersenne, at least, took it very seriously. Although later he was known for his scientific and mathematical work, in his early years, he was known for slim devotional works and fat, indigestible tomes in which he defended the world against atheism, deists, and heresy in general. While less obviously connected with theology, Gassendi also had a kind of theological program; his project could be construed as making Epicurus and Epicureanism safe for a Christian society. Pascal wasn't a priest, but his name became associated with the Catholic theological movement of Jansenism, which sought to bring Catholicism back to its spiritual roots in Augustinian thought. Though he was an important mathematician and physicist, he is now best known for his *Pensées,* the notes he left for an apology for Christianity that he was working on at the time of his death. Descartes did his best to avoid genuine theological issues, such as the Eucharist, something that he was not entirely successful at doing. But his own philosophy proper bristles with appeals to God: his benevolence, his infinity, the way in which he sustains the world from moment to moment. Leibniz directed his philosophy at learned Europe, of course, but he also directed it at the communities of the faithful (or, at least, at their leaders). His reform of philosophy was intended to be a reform of the religious life of Europe as well, giving it the basis for a reunification of the churches that had been torn asunder during the Reformation. And one can even say about Hobbes, almost certainly an atheist, that his philosophy was largely shaped by religious concerns. His central problem as a political theorist was the stability of society. And the central thing undermining the stability of society was religion in one guise or another, from the gaggle of sects that arose during the period of instability in early-seventeenth-century England, to the Catholic Church, whose pope undermined the sovereignty of secular rulers.

And the list goes on and on and on. Religion was a fundamental fact of life for people in the seventeenth century: you could not ignore it and its effects. It penetrated intellectual life, social life, political life, daily life.

Something draws me to study these people. I know that many who study the philosophers of the past do their best to make them as much like us as possible, to clean them up and try to show that their philosophy need not depend on the kinds of religious and theological assumptions that many contemporary philosophers now have trouble taking seriously. Others study some of these figures precisely because they are connected with religious themes. Indeed, in an age when religion and philosophy have come apart, there must be a certain attractiveness to going back to a time when they weren't, at least for those who now take religion seriously. But I don't fall into either of those camps. I am not a believer, and my interest in these historical figures is not increased by the fact that they took religion seriously. But, at the same time, I am not at all put off by the fact that they did. Indeed, it is one of the things that interests me most about them.

One of the ways that I sometimes think about what drew me into the kind of historical work that I do is that it allows me to live in other possible worlds, other possible philosophical worlds. The fascination with the past is precisely that it isn't the present. People were different, and they believed differently from what we do now about themselves, about the world, about what philosophy is and how one should pursue it. I find it interesting to explore those worlds, and try to understand how they looked from the point of view of the people who inhabited them. I think that there is something that we can learn as philosophers from doing this; for that reason I feel comfortable teaching in a department of philosophy, and feel that I have something to contribute to my students and to my colleagues. But there is also an almost aesthetic side to my fascination with the past, the almost visceral pleasure I get from being a visitor in another intellectual world. And part of that is the fact that religion was so important in that world. I am drawn to these people for whom faith was so central, and I get great pleasure from trying to figure out what it was like to live in their world.

But I am a voyeur in that world, and I cannot pretend otherwise. I find that I simply cannot share their theological viewpoint. Much as I try, much as I may want to, I cannot be a believer.

This is something that seems to divide me from most of my atheist friends. Most of the people I know at the university are cheerful atheists. Theism is simply not an issue for them. When we talk about the question (which we don't often) they express extreme puzzlement at my curious position. They don't understand why people might be theists, and certainly don't understand why someone who isn't a theist might *want to be* one, but can't. The only person I have talked with about this who shares my own curious view is a man who started his academic life in a Catholic seminary preparing to be a priest, before he lost his faith. I have the feeling that he is still looking for it, in a way. Odd company for a secular Jew like me.

I was brought up in a secular Jewish household. We belonged to a local synagogue, and I was sent to Hebrew school and had a bar mitzvah. I was particularly close to my mother's father, a socialist-Zionist who took being Jewish very seriously. Though he had been to a yeshiva in Vilna (Vilnius), he had rejected much of that world and was very proud to have been associated with the Jewish Enlightenment. On his shelves were the traditional Jewish texts. But there were also copies of Darwin and Marx and Spinoza (in Yiddish, of course), and the classics of more recent Yiddish and Hebrew literature, which were echoed in the poems and essays he wrote. He had faith, though it was not an altogether traditional kind, and he felt little need to participate in religious activities at the synagogue. He was a major influence on me, a kind of model. When I was an adolescent, I spent time with him, helping him put his writings into English, talking about ideas with him.

I had faith then, when I was an adolescent. It was, perhaps, part of a deep desire to be attached to the culture in which I was raised, to the people with whom I felt connected. Religion has an enormously important social function. It is something that binds people to one another, gives them a community of like-minded people with whom they can be associated, a very clear meaning to their lives. It did that for me. But at some point in my late teens, I found myself losing faith. Part of it was, perhaps, my increasing distance from the traditional Jewish community. I found myself more and more uncomfortable with the narrow and chauvinistic kind of education that I had received from the synagogue. Our own faith was presented as the only possible one, the only reasonable one. The Christianity of my next-door neighbors was presented as ridiculous and unreasonable ("How could *anyone* believe..."). This came to offend me. Also, I found the knee-jerk support of Israel more and more questionable as I learned more and more about the complexities of Middle Eastern politics. I felt betrayed. All of this is perfectly compatible with continued faith, of course: one can reject the institutions of organized religion without, at the same time, rejecting the religious impulse. But something else changed: I no longer felt moved by appeals to God. Not that I discovered any new reasons not to believe, or any arguments for the non-existence of God. God just became irrelevant to me and to my life.

I don't pretend to have an argument *against* the existence of God; that seems no more possible to me than an argument *for* his existence. It is, as Pascal puts it, something that is beyond the ability of reason to prove or to disprove: "If there is a God, he is infinitely beyond our comprehension, since, being indivisible and without limits, he bears no relation to us. We are therefore incapable of knowing either what he is or whether he is. ... 'Either God is or he is not.' But to which view shall we be inclined? Reason cannot decide this question" (§ 418).[1]

Pascal, in fact, comes as close as anyone does to convincing me to believe in God–not just the wager, but the whole program of the *Pensées* in which the wager is embedded. Pascal understands me, and the *Pensées* speak to me. They are addressed to the libertine of his day, the person who lives in the larger world, who likes to drink, gamble, carouse with loose women, stay out late at night, and live the life of pleasure. As a closet libertine, that speaks to me. Pascal then shows me that underneath my cheerful and fun-loving exterior, I'm really deeply miserable. He convinces me, in fact, that my frantic seeking after pleasure is a sign of my deeper misery and fear about what will eventually become of me. But, at the same time, he argues that the very fact that I am miserable and that I am aware of being miserable is evidence that I am something more, that I was once in a better state and that I can hope to attain that better state again some day. And he makes me want to attain that better state: he makes it attractive to me and makes me think that I can attain it. It is at this moment that the famous wager argument enters.

When I told one of my younger colleagues that I found Pascal attractive, almost persuasive, he looked at me very strangely: as someone who had had a certain amount of philosophical training (and whom he thought was at least minimally competent), didn't I know of the dozens of fatal flaws in the argument? Of course. But read in the context of the *Pensées*, many (though not all) of the problems with the argument are addressed. After a careful preparation in which your desire to believe is discovered, and then cultivated, and in which all alternatives but the Christian God that Pascal wants to lead us toward are eliminated, the wager argument has real force for me. It harnesses the very libertinism that seems to lead toward the world of pleasure, and redirects it toward God and eternal life. Pascal treats the existence of God as a gambling problem: "Infinite chaos separates us. At the far end of this infinite distance a coin is being spun which will come down heads or tails. How will you wager?" (§ 418) As every good libertine knows, you bet on that which has the greater expected utility. If God exists and you believe in him, then you win infinite happiness; if he exists and you don't bet on him, then you lose. If he doesn't exist, then it doesn't matter whether you bet on him or not. So, Pascal concludes: "If you win, you win everything; if you lose, you lose nothing. Do not hesitate then; wager that he does exist." (§ 418) Of course, things get a bit more complicated when you consider the value of your present life of dissolution and (what you think of as) pleasure, and when you consider the probability that God actually exists. But in the end he makes at least an initially plausible case that the good gambler, the one who wants to maximize his gain, will bet on God, that is, choose to believe that God exists.

Pascal, of course, knows full well that belief is not a matter of decision and will; I cannot just choose to believe. What he recommends is that you act as a believer would. What that would mean is to go to mass and take holy water, and eventually, God will move your heart and genuine faith will come. I'm sure that he would understand (though perhaps not approve) if I chose instead to go to synagogue, light the candles on Friday evening, and observe kashruth.

But I can't do it. I get to the last step, and I just can't cross the line and commit myself to doing what I can be sure will lead to faith. I keep asking myself why not. My inability to make the commitment to something I find so attractive has caused me to think hard about the curious epistemic situation that religion involves us in.

Although I do recognize the benefits of being a believer, that is not enough to move me to do that which would produce in me the belief. Pascal has given good reasons for believing, but he has given me no reasons for belief, reasons for thinking that it is true that God exists. And that is what I need to take the step: the kind of belief that Pascal leads us to would seem to be a fraud, a belief we hold simply because we want to live in a world in which God exists. To believe for such reasons would seem to be pathological.

Pascal himself saw matters as somewhat more complicated than that. It is interesting to see how he maneuvers the libertine into the position where God moves his heart, and he acquires real faith. But it is also interesting to consider what happens afterward. It is very important to understand that Pascal is not a straightforward fideist: he does not think that belief is simply a matter of receiving God's gift. After faith is acquired, the story continues. Speaking in the voice of God here, Pascal writes:

> "I do not demand of you blind faith.
>
> "I do not mean you to believe me submissively and without reason; I do not claim to subdue you by tyranny. Nor do I claim to account to you for everything. To reconcile these contradictions I mean to show you clearly, by convincing proofs, marks of divinity within me which will

convince you of what I am, and establish my authority by miracles and proofs that you cannot reject, so that you will then believe the things I teach, finding no reason to reject them except for the fact that you cannot *by yourselves* [i.e., with reason unaided by faith] know whether or not they are true." (§ 149)

Here things get a bit unclear to me. Sometimes Pascal speaks as if the evidence is open to those who genuinely seek God, who want to find him. The last passage continues as follows:

> God's will has been to redeem men and open the way of salvation to those who seek it, but men have shown themselves so unworthy that it is right for God to refuse to some, for their hardness of heart, what he grants to others by a mercy they have not earned.
>
> . . .Thus wishing to appear openly to those who seek him with all their heart and hidden from those who shun him with all their heart, he has qualified our knowledge of him by giving signs which can be seen by those who seek him and not by those who do not.
>
> There is enough light for those who desire only to see, and enough darkness for those of a contrary disposition. (§ 149; cf. § 427)

Elsewhere, though, he suggests that the evidence is available only to those whose hearts have been moved by the grace of God, that is, those who have been given faith by having their hearts moved:

> The prophecies, even the miracles and proofs of our religion, are not of such a kind that they can be said to be absolutely convincing, but they are at the same time such that it cannot be said to be unreasonable to believe in them. There is thus evidence and obscurity, to enlighten some and obfuscate others. But the evidence is such as to exceed, or at least equal, the evidence to the contrary, so that it cannot be reason that decides us against following it, and can therefore only be concupiscence and wickedness of heart. Thus, there is enough evidence to condemn and not enough to convince, so that it should be apparent that those who follow it are prompted to do so by grace and not by reason, and those who evade it are prompted by concupiscence and not by reason. (§ 835)

This is what Pascal seems to have had in mind in the following somewhat puzzling passage: " 'Why, do you not say yourself that the sky and the birds prove God?' "—'No.'—'Does your religion not say so?' 'No. For though it is true in a sense for some souls whom God has enlightened in this way, yet it is untrue for the majority' "(§ 3).

Now, this is an interesting and very powerful idea. Pascal's God doesn't ask for a blind faith: it is a faith supported by reasons. But these reasons can be appreciated only *after we are in a particular state of mind: only after we are committed to him, in a way, after we have already dedicated ourselves to the search for God, only after God has moved our hearts.* Without divine grace, reason and experience are impotent, they are unable to give us real knowledge. But *after* we have attained a state of genuine belief, we are in a position to recognize the validity of the arguments for God's existence, the miracles and prophesies, the experience of nature itself. Only after the conversion can the believer appreciate the rational grounds of his or her faith.

And so, if Pascal is right, after I engage in the practices that he recommends, I will have not just faith, but a faith that is grounded in reason. After attaining faith I will be in a state in which I believe and in which I think that it is fully rational to believe.

This is obviously an attractive end point. But I still find myself resisting it. I don't entirely understand why I resist, but perhaps an analogy will help me explain. The situation is, in a way, not unlike a Kuhnian paradigm shift. The issues are vastly more complicated than I can discuss in the short space I have here, but, to be irresponsibly brief, on Kuhn's conception, a paradigm embodies a way of looking at the world. Changing paradigms thus involves changing the way we look at the world. In this connection Kuhn uses the Gestalt psychologist's duck–rabbit, a figure that can look like either a duck or a rabbit, depending on the way we look at it, but not both. The shift from one paradigm to another is like the way the figure shifts from the duck to the rabbit. And so, for example, when we move from the Ptolemaic Earth-centered universe to the Copernican universe, we see the world differently. In the Ptolemaic paradigm, it is evident that we are located on a stable platform around which the rest of the universe revolves. But when we switch to the Copernican universe, the considerations that once counted in favor of the stability of the Earth no longer move us, and the harmony and simplicity in planetary astronomy that results from placing the sun at the center of the planetary system make us wonder how we ever tolerated the complex system of epicycles that the Ptolemaic system required. Of course, the Kuhnian machinery of paradigm and incommensurability is vastly more complicated than this simple presentation suggests, as is the particular example of the move from a Ptolemaic to a Copernican cosmology. But it is suggestive. The move from atheism into Pascal's version of a theistic universe seems very similar to this kind of paradigm shift: we move from one rational system into another.

So why won't I do it? When the Ptolemaic astronomer imaginatively puts himself into the Copernican's position, he sees the world in the way that the Copernican does, he sees it as a rabbit and no longer as a duck. In that situation, he presumably feels the weight of the arguments in favor of Copernicanism. And it is this that enables him to move from the one paradigm to the other. This is how scientific revolutions happen for Kuhn. I can put myself into the theist's position, in a sense: I can, in a way, imagine what it is like to be a believer. But

I can't put myself in that position in the way the Ptolemaic astronomer can look at the world from a Copernican point of view. Even when I try to imagine what it is like to be a believer, the reasons that Pascal says move a believer don't move me. If they did, then I wouldn't have to go through the motions the way Pascal says I must in order to attain the state of belief that I seek. If they did, then my conversion would be rational, the way the conversion from the Ptolemaic universe to the Copernican is. But it isn't. I may know that *if* I subject myself to a certain regimen (i.e., engage in religious practices), then eventually I will attain a state in which I will believe in God, and I will believe that my belief is rational. But that isn't good enough. From my present point of view, it looks too much like intentional self-delusion.

It is important to see that it is not a question of resisting belief because I have no evidence or other reason to believe in God. That doesn't bother me a lot. The fact is that the epistemological notion of evidence or reason to believe is greatly overrated, in my opinion. There are lots of things that I believe without necessarily having a reason for them. I believe that I am the age I am; that I grew up in Schenectady, New York; that my mother's name is Laura and my father's is William; that New York is north of Washington; and on and on and on, not because of any evidence. I just know these things, and the fact that I don't believe them because of any "evidence" I might have for them (in the philosophical sense) doesn't trouble me in the least. Of course, if challenged, I could produce evidence—my birth certificate, my high school diploma, the testimony of my parents, and so on. If this weren't enough, I could probably go back further and get more, though depending on how skeptical those inquiring are, they may or may not be satisfied. (If they were convinced that I was trying to falsify my age for some reason, they might always remain at least somewhat unconvinced.) For some people, belief in God might well be like that: they just *know,* and that's that. If required, they might well be able to produce reasons. But these reasons may or may not be able to satisfy the atheist. And if they didn't, so much the worse for the atheist, from the point of view of the believer. The fact that he or she can't always convince what might appear to be a stubborn opponent might not make any difference to the believer at all. Nor, perhaps, should it.

My worry is different. If I follow Pascal's program, I will, indeed, land in a state in which I believe, and in which I am genuinely convinced that I can give a good reason for what I believe, if challenged. But am I entitled to trust my confidence when I am in that state? After all, I deliberately performed a series of steps that I knew would, if I followed them, put me into exactly that state. Now, it is one thing if, in the course of events, I find myself in that epistemic state. But it would seem to be quite another if I deliberately put myself into that state. In that case, it looks as if I am deliberately going about deceiving myself, believing because I *want* to believe. The process by which I attain the rational belief would seem to undermine the rationality of the final outcome. Truth and rationality are too important for me to give up, even for the possibility of eternal salvation, not to mention the pleasures that come with being a believer in this life.

But even so, I find myself fascinated by the way the world looks to the believer. I can visit it, explore it as a tourist, participate in some of its pleasures, but never live there. I feel destined continue as a passionately interested observer of other people's faith, but never a genuine participant.

I would like to thank the students in my Workshop in Philosophy and Religion at the University of Chicago in spring 2002, where we worked through Pascal's text and many of the issues in this paper. I would also like to thank Ana Maria Pascal, who corresponded with me over the last couple of years, trying to convince me to take the final step I continue to resist. Though she did not succeed, I learned a great deal from our exchanges.

FOUR

For the Love of Reason

Louise M. Antony

I always had trouble with Limbo. Limbo, I was taught, is a place where good but unbaptized people go when they die. We are all born carrying the stain of original sin on our souls, and unless the stain is washed away through baptism, we are unfit to be in the presence of God.[1]

There was no part of this doctrine that made any sense to me. For starters, there was the whole idea of "original" sin. The *original* original sin, of course, was the one committed by Adam when he disobeyed God's commandment not to eat from the tree of knowledge of good and evil.[2] Adam himself was punished—fair enough—but then somehow, this sin that *Adam* committed got "passed down," besmirching the soul of every one of Adam's descendants. I found it repugnant, the idea that a crime committed by one of my ancestors could sully *my* personal soul. It was an idea quite at odds with the liberal, meritocratic principles to which my parents seemed otherwise to subscribe.

This concept of original sin was often presented to me in terms of natural law–like gravity, it's just the way things are. But the analogy seemed inapt; gravity had nothing to do with what you *deserved.* And anyway, I'd protest, didn't God *make* the laws? If so, why did He choose to make things so that you inherited your parents' guilt? Why make the laws of spiritual heredity Lamarckian rather than Darwinian?[3]

I was also troubled by the idea of a soul's being "unfit" to be in the presence of God, irrespective of the rectitude of its owner. It made sense to me that the souls of unrepentant sinners would be unfit, but the people in Limbo could have been as saintly as Gandhi—could even *be* Gandhi—and God still wouldn't have them. This "fitness" sounded almost aesthetic–as if the unbaptized righteous had body odor, or weren't dressed properly. Maybe God was allergic . . . ? At the very least, if something made baptism a condition of entrance into heaven, why didn't He see to it that the sacrament was a little more widely available?

Now my mother felt the force of this consideration, and as a consequence was a great supporter of the Maryknoll missionaries. (This was long before they became associated with radical liberation theology.) She would write them a small check every month and encourage me to make a contribution as well. She impressed upon me the cosmic importance of bringing the Word of God and, crucially, the sacrament of baptism to the innocents of the African jungles. "This is the work that God wants us to do for Him," she'd explain. But wait a minute, I thought. Now you're telling me that the eternal fate of some poor child in Africa depends on what *I* do? This was a heavy burden to bear for a youngster with twenty-five cents in her pocket and a new issue of *Action Comics* beckoning from the news rack. It would only be much later that I'd come to realize that the setup presumed by my mother's creed, whereby the spiritual fates of millions of others is made precarious in order to provide me with opportunities to practice virtue, was at least as repugnant as the original injustice.

But there was something that bothered me almost as much as Limbo itself: the way grownups reacted to my questions about it. First they'd offer a perfunctory, stock, and utterly impertinent response. "The souls in Limbo don't suffer," they'd all say. Huh? Maybe they're not in actual pain, like the souls in Hell, and or even the ones in Purgatory, but these poor souls are being deprived of the Beatific Vision, an experience of which, it was emphasized in other contexts, is the final purpose and goal of human existence!

So the next move would be "but they don't *know* they're being deprived of anything." Double huh. It's OK not to share your chocolate with your sister as long as she never finds out you have it? This "ignorance is bliss" reasoning seemed specious to me even as a small child. And it was, once again, inconsistent with the messages I got in every other, non-religious context. My father, for example, was an elementary school administrator, and he was passionate in his support for public education. He would go on and on about the need to cultivate in children—to *inculcate* in children—the "desire to learn." He would have been incensed had anyone suggested that as long as an illiterate child had no conception of the pleasures of reading, it was fine to leave well enough alone.

Not many adults were willing to go on to round three. They would grow impatient. "Louise," my mother would say, "you just think too much." Sometimes they'd get positively angry. What was the matter with me? Why did I have to argue about everything? Didn't I realize that some things just had to be taken on *faith*? In general, I was informed, I should concentrate more on loving my neighbor and less on being a smarty-pants.

None of the nuns or priests from whom I received religious instruction were of any help on the matter of Limbo, nor, for that matter, on any of the other issues that troubled me. There was also the Trinity: how could there be "three persons in one God"? I remember trying to wrap my childish head around this "holy mystery" in the classes preparatory to my receiving my First Communion. For several months running, I would go home from religious education one week, think hard about the whole thing, then return the next week with a new idea to offer Sister. It was always wrong. Maybe God was like a family, I suggested. There was, after all, a Father, a Son, and (remember, now, I was only six-and-a-half, and He was usually depicted as a bird) the family pet, Holy Ghost. No, said Sister, God is not like a family. OK—maybe God is like a three-leafed clover (I had just been taught that this was how St. Patrick explained the Trinity to the heathen Celts in Ireland)—the Father is one leaf, the Son is another, the Holy Ghost is a third, and they're all parts of God. No, said Sister, God is not like a three-leafed clover, St. Patrick notwithstanding. Well, maybe each person is like a different mood of God—God the Father is the angry mood, God the Son is the loving mood, and the Holy Ghost is some other kind of mood. No, said Sister, not moods, either. Finally Sister, clearly exhausted, told me that I'd never understand the Trinity because it was a *mystery of faith*. Mysteries of faith are, by their nature, incomprehensible. We must simply believe them. But how can I believe something I don't understand, I asked? "Just memorize your Catechism," was Sister's reply. "Belief will come."

Now it wasn't just religion. Limbo wasn't the only mystery with which I was preoccupied. I also had problems with Santa Claus. I had no trouble with flying reindeer—remember that my world was amply stocked with miraculous violations of physical law. The difficulty again was moral. Barbara Perkins, my friend who lived at the top of the hill near the bus stop, always got loads of presents "from Santa Claus" at Christmas time. We're talking play kitchens, bicycles, puppies, Barbie dolls *with* Dream Houses—major loot. I, on the other hand, generally received one present from Santa, carefully selected and duly solicited from one of Santa's department store "helpers" (I had asked about the baffling proliferation of Santas early on, and had received and accepted the standard answer), and this one present was never very grand.

Now this was curious, I thought. I understood that there were well-off families in the world, and not-so-well-off families, and I understood that mine was one of the not-so-well-off ones. But why did *Santa Claus* respect these distinctions? Why did he bring more toys to the rich kids than to the poor ones? Apparently, in the cases of really indigent kids, he planned to bring nothing at all—why else the "toys for tots" drives at our church every Christmas? If anything, you'd think that Santa would try to *rectify* economic inequities—that he'd give that play kitchen to the little girl whose parents couldn't afford to buy her anything. Was Santa Claus a supply-sider?

I made the enormous social blunder of bringing this up with other kids, indeed, with Barbara Perkins herself. (I'm pretty sure I suggested that she could do a little to bring moral order to the universe by giving me her play kitchen.) They were not interested—reasonably enough: one's not a kid forever, and there are cartoons to be watched. But adults didn't appreciate my questions, either. I'd get a little patronizing approval for asking "such a serious question!" but once they saw that I really meant to know what was going on, they'd get irritated. I don't know how I described their reactions to myself at the time, but as I remember them now, it seems clear that they, no less than their kids, thought I was being a colossal drag.

What I got from all of this was that thinking was fine and good, but only in its place. A little learning might be a dangerous thing, but a lot of thinking was worse. Today I am a parent, and I know firsthand the tedium and frustration of dealing with a child who won't stop asking "why." I also know that the questions of an inquiring child may be more motivated by the hope of delaying bedtime than by the love of knowledge. And finally, I know there are children who relish making their superiors squirm; I surely was one of them. But with all that said, I still, to this day, resent the way I was made to feel as a child—that my questioning was *inherently* bad, that there was something wrong with *me* for wanting things to make sense.

As I've said, the reactions of grownups to my questions about religion were doubly distressing to me because of their dissonance with the principles adults were explicitly promoting in other contexts. In school, a broadly libertarian and individualistic ethos prevailed. We were always being exhorted to "think for ourselves." In reading, we were urged to "sound out the words instead of just asking," and in arithmetic to figure out the problems on our own. Science teachers and science books agreed heartily that curiosity is a marvelous thing, the engine of all scientific achievement. One must not take things for granted; one must always ask "why." The best scientists, it was stressed, are the ones who see mystery in the everyday, who press for deeper and deeper understanding. In the biographies of Marie Curie I devoured, she was praised for seeing questions no one else did and for persisting in her work until she got her answers. (My mother, by the way, got me these books. She was a secret feminist. She kept the secret even from herself.) In my elementary school citizenship classes, democracy was praised as the most perfect political form because it allowed every citizen to "follow his own conscience." My parents and teachers, counseling me about personal behavior, stressed the importance of doing what *I* knew was right, regardless of what other people thought. Why in religion was I supposed to dumbly accept whatever the authorities told me?

Somewhere along the line, I came to the conclusion that my inquisitiveness was sinful. It was not just that it was prideful—I'd been told that explicitly, and often enough. This new idea was that the questions had been put into my head by the devil, and that, indeed, the whole world had been mined with dangerous ideas, ideas that could threaten my faith if I indulged them. No one ever told me such a thing in so many words, but it seemed to me a good explanation for the taboo against thinking in religion, together with my apparent inability to respect it.

My little theory kept me in a pretty constant state of anxiety, lest I take seriously something that turned out to be incompatible with religious teachings. I was pretty interested in biology and genetics as a kid and read everything I could get my hands on. Before very long, I encountered the theory of evolution. It seemed really plausible to me, and ingenious. But I didn't see where in the theory souls were supposed to come in. It's not that I had ever been told that evolution was inconsistent with Catholicism—the Church in which I was raised was not fundamentalist, and condoned metaphorical readings of Scripture. The conflict was more of my own making. It seemed to me that if evolutionary theory was correct, then biological differences were matters of degree: apes just gradually became people. But that seemed parlously at odds with the religious picture: that human beings, in virtue of possessing immortal souls, were fundamentally different from everything else in nature. I decided that I should try not to believe in evolution.

I remember, too, being terrified by a particular cover on *Time* magazine that posed, in huge red letters against a black background, the shocking question: "Is God Dead?"[4] It's hard for me, to this day, to explain just what I found so profoundly unsettling about this question—I certainly wasn't simply shocked that anyone would think such a thing. It was rather the elemental uncanniness of the concept of God's dying—of the end of an eternal, all-powerful being. (Obviously, I never read the article—I might have been reassured to learn that the "death of God" was just a particularly provocative way of expressing disbelief.)

You might think, given all these complaints, that I resented my religion and wanted nothing more than to be free of it. But that's not the way it was. Despite my frustrations, I was passionately devout. I tried really hard to say my prayers mindfully, to pay attention at Mass, and to obey the Ten Commandments, especially the fourth, which apparently covered not teasing the cat. I failed regularly in these efforts, but made regular Confessions. I didn't particularly like candy, so I would make a point of giving up comic books for Lent. (Although I must admit this was sly of me, since Sundays were not part of Lent, and Sundays were when we went to the drugstore where comic books were sold.) I memorized prayers that no one else knew, and read unassigned books about saints. I took seriously all the rules of observance, never missing Mass on Sundays, and strictly following the more obscure requirements of Lenten abstinence (I was told frequently that I took things *too* seriously). I respected and trusted my parents: if they told me all this stuff was true, then I was pretty sure it had to be true. I just couldn't figure out *how* it could be true.

I think I identified being religious with being good. Most of my charitable acts, such as they were, were carried out under church auspices, though probably not for the right reasons. I found the idea of martyrdom really exciting and prayed that I might someday give my life for Christ. (My mother's suggestion—that God's plan for me might have more to do with dusting and table setting than with famished lions or flaming stakes—was ill received.) But I also heard in the Sunday sermons, and in the Gospel readings, two consistent moral messages that moved me deeply—first, that every human being had an immortal soul of surpassing moral value, and second, that our overarching duty on Earth was to demonstrate our love of God through our acts of love for humankind. I would be martyred, I decided, while teaching deaf and blind leukemia victims in Africa.

Because I was usually in the minority, being a Catholic made me feel special. In the Upstate New York suburb where I spent some of my childhood, and later in Western Massachusetts, nearly everyone I knew was some sort of Protestant (exception: my best friend in Vestal, New York, who attended the Polish American Catholic church. She's also now a philosopher—go figure). There was one Jew that I knew of in Vestal, and one who attended my high school in Sheffield, but all I knew about Jews or their religion was that they didn't believe in Jesus, and so did not celebrate Christmas. My mother assured me that they could, nonetheless, be Very Good People. (Swelling the population of Limbo, I thought.) Protestantism was very mysterious to me. I could tell anyone who wanted to know exactly what my theological beliefs were—they could have the short version, in the form of the Apostle's Creed, or the long—very long—version codified in the Baltimore Catechism, which I had memorized. But if I asked my Protestant friends what they believed, they seemed not to have a clue. In some cases, they were unclear even as to which denomination they belonged. Several of my friends reported that they attended the church they did because their parents liked the minister there. What with fasting Sunday mornings before Communion, abstaining from meat on Fridays, and giving up candy for Lent, I felt smugly superior to these Protestant friends, whose religions, it seemed to me, required very little of them.

My religion was with me every day. I said my prayers in the morning on waking, and again before I went to bed at night. I reminded myself that it was my religious duty to treat my elderly Great-Aunt Louise—an imperious and stentorian woman who had come to live with us upon the death of her husband—with respect. (Not that I was very successful.) Minor medical discomforts, like my weekly gamma globulin shot, were offered up for the poor souls in Purgatory. (Purgatory is not the same as Limbo. The souls in Purgatory will eventually enter heaven, once they've done their time.) I made it a practice to receive Holy Communion every Sunday (unless I was ill, and excused from attending Mass).

Another daily reminder of my religion—not a pleasant one—was my almost continual sense of guilt. I have already mentioned my failures with respect to Aunt Louise. I was no better about teasing the cat, or about fighting with my sister. The worst attack of guilt I ever suffered, however, came one time when I yielded to the temptation to preserve my Communion record, and received the sacrament without being sure that it had really been sixty full minutes since I had eaten. I had been spending the night with friends who owned a small boat, and while my mother had extracted from them a promise to get me to mass as a condition of my being allowed to stay, they were themselves freethinkers and not terribly enthusiastic about the whole enterprise. The only Catholic church in the area was about a half-hour drive from the marina, and we needed to get to the earliest service—8:30 a.m.—in order to preserve a reasonable chunk of the day for boating. Despite the early hour, my friends insisted that I eat something before we left. I must not have had a watch; I remember calculating that if it took us half an hour to get to the church, then by the time the priest actually distributed Communion, it might possibly be an hour later than my last bite. I knew perfectly well that if I wasn't sure I had completed the required period of fast then I ought not to receive Communion. It was a mortal sin to take the sacrament if one was not "properly prepared"—a condition that also precluded being in a state of mortal sin. Nonetheless, I was fetishistic about my record, and persuaded myself—for the moment at least—that I was in the clear.

The second after I received the host, however, the scruples set in. By the middle of the brilliantly sunny and perfectly still afternoon, I was stricken with nausea and the shakes. I refused to go swimming, terrified that I might drown in a state of mortal sin and go straight to Hell. I told my hosts that I was seasick. They favored the more plausible diagnosis, given the circumstances, that I'd contracted some stomach virus, and cut short the day to get me home. Once there, I burst into tears, confessed the whole story to my mother, and demanded that she call the church and arrange for me to make a confession. Now, my mother, while very devout and scrupulously observant, was also a sensible and loving parent and tried her best to persuade me that no one as obviously sorry as I was (for an offense she was not even convinced I'd committed) was destined for Hell, and that I could just wait until the regularly scheduled confessions the next Saturday. Nothing for it—I was hysterical at the thought that I would have to carry the weight of my blackened soul all through the week. So she called the rectory and reached our young assistant pastor, who agreed to hear my confession over the phone.

This worked in the end, but the rescue was nearly derailed by the earnest young priest's attempts to convince me that I was too young (I was eleven) to have really, knowingly, and willingly committed a mortal sin. I was righteously insulted by this suggestion. I knew the definition of a mortal sin, I exclaimed, and every clause was fulfilled: 1) it *was* a grievous wrong, 2) I *knew* it was a grievous wrong, and 3) *I wanted to do it anyway*. (Now, at some level, I surprised myself. I had earlier argued to Sister that no one could possibly satisfy all these conditions at the same time—that you couldn't really, really want to do something that you, at the very same time, really, really believed was wrong. But now, suddenly, talking to Father, I saw that yes, you really, really could!)

Most of my youth, I did not look forward to Sunday mass. When I was a girl, it was still said in Latin, and though I'd follow along in my missal (once I learned how to read), I found most of the ritual pretty boring. There was no singing, unless it was a high mass, and then it was the priest who sang (so much the worse!). I did, for the most part, rather like the sermons, and the Gospel and Epistle readings. And I did find my religious education classes interesting (although, as I've been at pains to explain, often for the wrong reasons).

A great deal changed, though, once the Second Vatican Council reforms were implemented—mass in the vernacular, responses recited and hymns sung by the congregation—my concentration, and consequently my piety, were much improved. I loved the "folk mass." Like all good flower children, I knew two separate chord progressions on the guitar and was thus amply equipped to strum accompaniments to "Hear O Lord" and "Sons of God." (Accustomed as I was to staring at a bloodied body while I prayed, I was taken aback by a non-Catholic friend's horrified reaction to the cheerful exhortation to cannibalism in the chorus of the latter hymn: "Eat His body / Drink His blood / Allelu-, allelu-, allelu-, allelu-u-ia . . .") I began attending a teen discussion group in a neighboring parish run by an inspiring young priest from the seminary up in Lenox, a student (I now surmise) of liberation theology. Doctrinal difficulties began to recede, and my religious practice began to resonate with the calls for justice and liberation sounding throughout U.S. society.

Thus I continued to consider myself a devout Catholic all during high school. (Leave aside the odd mortal sin. Many non-Catholics I talk to are certain that my loss of faith had to do with sex, but this just reflects their prejudice. Like many, many of my Catholic peers, I found it pretty easy to dismiss the Church's teachings about premarital sex and contraception as inessential, old-fashioned, and not to be taken seriously.) But while I carried my religious identity with me to college, I carried right along with it a still-unsated curiosity about matters theological and moral. The one was about to come crashing into conflict with the other.

I knew absolutely nothing about the subject when I sat down in my first philosophy class. I was taking it to fulfill a distribution requirement and was dimly apprehensive that the readings would be incomprehensible and would somehow require knowledge of ancient history. Imagine my delight, then, when I discovered that philosophy was all about arguing! Not only was my constant questioning tolerated; it was positively encouraged. Finally, finally—a place where reasons had to be given, a place where no one would tell you it was impertinent to ask. I could scarcely believe that I could earn credits just for doing what (to me) came naturally.

So the good news was that everything could be questioned; everything was up for debate. But that, it turned out, was also the bad news. It was one thing, I discovered, to raise my questions about the nature of the afterlife and the justice of the Creator from a background of religious commitment, and quite another to raise such questions in the context of a no-holds-barred debate. I began to realize that in all my childhood worrying, it had never occurred to me that my questions might just not have answers. I certainly had never really considered what it would mean for my own religious faith if that turned out to be the case. But now I found myself in the company of people who saw religious commitment itself as open to challenge, who were asking a question I had never, ever dared to even formulate: is there a God?

The first rumblings of distress arose with our survey of the traditional arguments for the existence of God. I fought tooth and nail to make one of them work, but I had to admit in the end that none of them seemed fully convincing. First came the a priori arguments, the arguments that were supposed to proceed from self-evident principles. Anselm's argument seemed like verbal sleight of hand. Each of Aquinas's five ways depended on premises that seemed far from self-evident to me. Descartes's argument involved the puzzling claim that an idea could contain no more "reality" than its source, but how do you measure "amounts" of reality? Much as I hated to admit it, these arguments seemed frivolous, more suited to *Alice in Wonderland* than the New Testament. The arguments that appealed to empirical evidence seemed more promising, at least initially. But William James's argument, based on his own religious experience, finally failed to convince. Far too many of my friends had had "religious experiences" of the chemical type (it was, after all, 1971) for me to trust any "insights" gleaned on that basis. The argument from design—wherein God is posited to explain the intricate orderliness of nature—seemed, despite its problems, the last hope.

But then came the day that literally changed my life—the day when I first heard the "argument from evil." The reasoning is easy to state: Suffering exists. If God can do anything, He must not want to prevent suffering; but if He does not want to prevent suffering, He cannot be perfectly good. Therefore, there is no all-powerful, perfectly good Being. The argument has been known for centuries, and many replies have been attempted. For example, many theists point out that a great deal of the suffering in the world is the result of human beings' exercising their freedom. We must be free, they argue, if we are to be capable of virtuous actions, but free will carries with it, necessarily, the possibility for vicious action as well. Since God cannot intervene to prevent human actions that He knows will cause suffering without compromising the freedom of the actors, He must acquiesce. With respect to the rest of the world's suffering—that due to droughts and floods and earthquakes and disease—the most popular explanation is that it is simply the necessary consequence of God's enacting what is, in fact, the best of all possible systems of natural law.

I was not satisfied with the proffered explanations of natural evil. I saw no particular reason to believe, other than the mere desire to do so, that an *omnipotent* God could not devise a better way of organizing the world than the plan currently in evidence. (Voltaire, of course, satirizes the suggestion in the person of the ridiculous Dr. Pangloss.) The free will defense, on the other hand, I found not merely unpersuasive, but morally disturbing. It's fine and good that God should afford me the opportunity to practice virtue, but why should innocent others be allowed to suffer if I choose to practice vice instead? Also, is there no limit to the amount of suffering that must be permitted under this justification? The U.S. Constitution enshrines freedom as a societal value, but our civic institutions ensure that my freedom is consistent with equal freedom for everyone else. If I perform an act that infringes upon your rights, then I am subject to punishment and to restraint. Why, then, couldn't God have set things up similarly, with serious criminals being whisked away to Hell before they did too much harm? As things stand, there are apparently no limits on the nature and scope of atrocities that God will allow some human beings to perpetrate against others. Didn't Hitler show his true colors pretty decisively after—I don't know—the first million?

My childhood worries about Limbo returned with new significance, and new urgency. How could a just God design such a system, a system that doomed innocent people, before they were even born, to an eternity of deprivation? Hurricanes and plagues might come with an otherwise functional network of natural law. Murder might be the regrettable cost of giving human beings free will. But Limbo seemed to be utterly and profoundly *optional.* I could find no connection between it and any otherwise desirable purpose. The only possible response I could think of was the one I had spent all of my short life hitherto resisting: "It's a mystery."

By the middle of my first semester, I was experiencing a full-blown crisis of faith. I could not accept the possibility that my religious belief had no rational defense, especially not now after I'd fallen in love with a discipline devoted to rational defenses. But neither could I relinquish my belief. A world without God seemed literally unimaginable; everything would be changed. I was frightened, in contradictory ways: there is no God, and surely He'll punish me for thinking this. At the same time, I was angry: *why* were there no good answers? Why had God made it so difficult to make sense of His will? If He wanted us to believe, why had He made all the reason and evidence work against belief? Indeed, I achieved a few days' respite from my struggles when I considered that if God had given me the faculty of reason, He must have expected me to use it, and so couldn't reasonably fault me for giving up my belief. But this expedient didn't work for long. Limbo, after all, wasn't reasonable, either, but there it was.

In the end, it was more philosophy that saved me. My class had moved on from the existence of God (even if I hadn't, quite) and was studying the basis of moral value. One theory we considered was called "divine command theory," the view that it is God who puts moral value into the world, that what is morally good is whatever He wants to happen. Initially, I thought that this was the view that I did and ought to hold, indeed, that all religious people must hold. But an argument from Plato changed my mind. In his dialogue *Euthyphro,* Socrates asks the eponymous character to define "piety." Euthyphro responds that pious acts are those that are beloved by the gods. Fine, says Socrates—that tells us which acts are the pious ones, but it doesn't tell us what makes them pious: is it the gods' loving them that make them pious, or is it their being pious that accounts for the gods' loving them? In familiar terms: are acts of kindness, courage, and so forth good only because they are the kinds of things God happens to like? Or is it rather that God, being perfectly good, likes such acts because they are also good?

The first possibility struck me as morally repugnant: it made God's preferences morally arbitrary. God *happens* to dislike murder, but had He liked it, then it would have been morally OK. In contrast, on the second option, God dislikes murder *because* it is morally wrong: it doesn't become wrong *only* because He chooses to prohibit it. On this alternative view, His prescriptions and prohibitions do not *constitute* moral goodness; they are, rather, *manifestations* of it. The more I considered the matter, the more convinced I became that this second view was really the more religious—indeed the more pious. So the Euthyphro argument did not, in itself, aggravate the threat to my faith: had I discovered it before I acquired my doubts, it would not have occasioned any. In the context of my growing skepticism, however, the discovery of this argument liberated me from any felt *need* for faith. Once I realized that God was not necessary for there to be objective moral value, I also realized that religious *belief* was not necessary for anyone to be a good person. The objectivity of moral value is simply independent of God's existence. All that is lost, if there is no God, is a divine enforcer. In a world without God, there is no guarantee that the virtuous will ever be rewarded, nor that the vicious will ever be punished. We must do what is right simply *because* it is right.

At last I was ready to admit to myself that I no longer believed in God. I'll never forget the sudden upsurge of relief when I finally acknowledged that my faith was gone. I felt suddenly free—free of the obligation to avow propositions I didn't understand, free of the struggle to make sense of doctrines that couldn't be made sensible, and free of the need to square everything I learned with Catholic dogma. My only doxastic obligations henceforth would be to reason and evidence. "Now," I thought to myself, "all I have to believe is what I think is true."

OK, OK. I said that's where my *obligations* lay; I didn't say I always discharged them. As I pursued my philosophical interests, and as I began to take a more serious interest in politics, I came to realize that intellectual integrity is pretty hard to achieve. Time and again, I fell prey (and still do, of course) to nonrational influences. I wanted to sound smart, and I wanted to agree with my smart friends. I wanted to defend the views of favorite teachers, and I wanted people I didn't like to be wrong. Once I began committing my own philosophical views to paper, and eventually, to print, I found that I felt constrained by what I'd already said, whether or not I still believed it was right. So I can hardly claim that by giving up religious commitments I had freed myself of dogmatism and wishful thinking. Still, there was a big difference. The little voice inside my head that used to whisper warnings when I ventured onto doctrinally dangerous ground ("Catholics don't read that book") had now become reason's agent ("You don't really believe that," "You know she's right about that," "What's your evidence?") While I earlier strove to reconcile disturbing facts with Catholic teachings—or indeed, to avoid encountering the disturbances in the first place—I now tried to keep my belief apportioned to the strength of the argument.

Equal in importance to what I now assigned as the *having* of reasons was my explicit commitment to the *providing* of reasons. I came to understand that my earlier frustrations had been as much with my teachers' and parents' refusal to engage in rational discussion as with my inability to discover what I wanted to know. And I saw clearly the nature of the conflict between the rhetoric of individual worth inherent in my childhood education and the grownups' retreat to dogmatism and authoritarianism in response to my questions: the refusal to give reasons is *disrespectful* to the person who asks for them. We will not all agree with each other, and given that, we cannot all be right. But if we are to treat each other properly as equals, we must be willing to explain ourselves. I *owe* it to someone with whom I disagree to show her the basis of my position, so that she can evaluate it for herself.

Simply announcing one's reasons is, of course, merely the beginning of rational engagement. "God (or Marx or George W. Bush) said it, I believe it, and that's the end of it" is not what I have in mind. Commitment to the practice of reason giving entails a willingness to continue the chain of reason giving until common ground is reached. Nowhere is this principle more important than in the political realm. Philosophy holds it to be an intellectual duty to provide arguments for one's positions, but when we are talking about the establishment and implementation of public policy, the duty becomes civic as well. My friend's reasons for opposing abortion may be religious in nature; it is certainly her right to be moved by her church's teachings, or by her reading of the books she regards as Holy Scripture. But if I am to acquiesce in a prohibition on the practice, I'm entitled to a reason that moves *me.*

Looking back on my development from devout Catholic girl to adamant atheist, I think that it was its bottom-line dogmatism that drove me away from the Church, and indeed, from the very possibility of religious faith. "Faith" presents a paradox: if a doctrine can be defended on rational grounds, then it needn't be taken on faith. But if it *cannot* be defended on rational grounds, why should you believe it?

I've often heard people quote approvingly the aphorism that "faith is believing where you cannot prove." The idea seems to be that since matters of great importance outstrip the human power to know, we must jump in and simply commit ourselves to certain ideas. The question, though, is *which ones*? There's very, very little that can literally be *proven*, that is, shown to be true without any possibility of doubt—only the propositions of logic and mathematics, and some philosophers will dispute even those! Nothing about the world of experience can be demonstrated with complete certainty. The evidence of our senses is partial, and we sometimes make mistakes. We must rely every day on memory and the testimony of others—both fallible—for a great deal of the information we need to make our way in the world. If we had to foreswear all these less-than-perfect sources, we'd know virtually nothing. But the aphorism, when taken as an endorsement of faith, suggests that, once we leave the realm of certainty, no distinctions can be made—that it's as rational to believe in unicorns as it is to believe in bacteria. The occurrence of the Holocaust cannot be *proven*, in this strict sense; must we therefore take deniers seriously? Lack of proof cannot entitle one to believe, or else anyone would be warranted in believing anything she wanted to.

Now, in truth, few people would explicitly endorse an inference of the form "there's no proof that *p;* therefore, I am entitled to believe that *p*." But I've encountered many who accept a related, and equally fallacious, pattern of reasoning: "There's no proof that *p* is false; therefore it's not irrational to believe that *p* is true." So people will say, "Since no one can prove there is no God, I'm not irrational if I believe in Him." But once again, "proof" is a red herring. I cannot *prove* that aliens have never visited Earth, but given all the considerations against it, I'd be irrational not to reject the proposition. Reason makes demands in two directions.

Of course everyone has a moral and, at least in the United States, at least so far, a political right to believe whatever she wants. As a card-carrying member of the ACLU,[5] and insofar as I have the courage, I will defend this right to the death. But this gets us back to the point I was insisting on above. You are certainly entitled to believe whatever you like, if the matter affects you alone. But if what you believe is supposed to have bearing on what happens to someone else, then you had better have good grounds for your opinion. Majority rule is a kind of tyranny when people don't respect each other enough to form their opinions responsibly. More and more I hear people in my own country speaking about matters of social policy and foreign affairs with the same blithe fideism they evince when expressing their religious views. "Bush will keep us more secure." Really? What makes you say so? "Oh, it's just what I believe." And so thousands must die in Iraq.

Throughout contemporary U.S. society, reason is denigrated as cold, mechanical, and sterile, while irreason is celebrated. Inspirational posters cite the authority of Einstein in elevating supposedly irrational "creativity" over rational thought: "Logic will get you from A to B; imagination will take you everywhere" or "'Imagination is more important than knowledge." Right—there's our problem: too much logic, not enough fantasy. Have you met my president?

The human interest stories in my local paper (on the front page of the "Faith" section—there is no "Reason" section) regularly honor the fidelity of people suffering the most appalling depredations: debilitating accidents, ruthless illnesses, spouses and children lost to senseless wars—all consistent, in the minds of these latter-day Jobs, with the limitless goodness of God. Likely as not, there will be featured, in the same edition, people who have prevailed against astonishing odds—the woman who survived the cancer that all the medical experts said would kill her, the husband who survived the landmine that killed all his buddies—all cheerfully attributing their own good fortune to God's great love for *them.* Never mind the quick paradox (He loved you enough to get you through chemotherapy, just not enough not to spare you the cancer in the first place)—what about the illogic of divine responsibility? God is to be thanked for the good things that happen but never blamed for the bad.

A college friend born and raised in a reformed Jewish household, never very religious, suddenly surprised all his childhood and college friends—not to mention his Jewish wife—by converting to messianic Judaism, becoming a "Jew for Jesus." One evening a few months after his conversion, my husband and I visited for dinner. My friend was recounting an incredible story from his hellion adolescence: he had failed to see a "road out" sign and driven his motorcycle over a fifteen-foot cliff, tumbling off the bike, and landing, "miraculously" unhurt, at the bottom of the ravine. At this point in the story, he suddenly stopped, looked off into the distance, and announced solemnly, "I see now that Christ was saving me for something." Oh, I thought to myself, so I guess He was just all finished with my father, who died suddenly of a heart attack at the age of fifty-three, leaving behind a homemaker wife, her elderly aunt, one daughter just starting graduate school, and another (me) only eleven years old.

After a deadly plane crash in North Carolina, I was contacted by a reporter at the local paper, who asked me to comment on a series of striking coincidences and tragic ironies. One young woman had been scheduled to fly into Charlotte aboard the doomed flight for a family reunion but became ill and canceled four hours before takeoff. A honeymooning couple had been awarded, by sentimental airline personnel, a complementary upgrade to first-class and were both killed. What did it all mean? the reporter wanted to know. Could I, as a philosopher, make sense of all this? Well, no, I couldn't "make sense of it," I said, which didn't stop me from blathering on for a good five minutes. My immortal words, quoted in full: "There are an infinite number of things that happen, and they all have causes. Some of the causes are evident and some are not. Some of the things are preventable; some are not. Some of them are things that we are happy happened. Some are not."[6] You'll not be surprised to hear that they didn't call me much after that.

More edifying, presumably, were the also-quoted remarks of a local rabbi, reflecting on the significance of the patterns of destruction wielded by Hurricane Fran. She saw the Hand of God in the fact that a large, expensive, and recently installed stained-glass window in the synagogue had been spared, despite a tree's having come down right next to the building. But then in the same breath, as it were, she cautioned the faithful not to yield to the temptation to blame God for damages they had suffered. God's plan is mysterious, she reminded everyone. (No kidding–stained glass windows are more important than people's lives!) Apparently, in her world, God gets the credit if the outcome is good, but need take no responsibility if it's bad. We expect our politicians to behave like that, but God?

I see the celebration of irrationality everywhere in popular culture. In movies and TV shows, reason and respect for science are almost invariably characteristic of arrogant and closed-minded villains; good guys have "imagination" and rely on "faith." Consider, just for starters, the 1947 "feel-good movie" *Miracle on 34th Street* (remade in 1994). The plot concerns Doris Walker, a no-nonsense single mother (played by Maureen O'Hara) working as a public relations executive at Macy's. She has raised her daughter, Susan (Natalie Wood), in accordance with her belief that "we should be realistic and completely truthful with our children, and not have them growing up believing in a lot of legends and myths. . . . Like Santa Claus, for example."[7] Susan's preternatural gravity shows us that a childhood shaped by such principles is devoid of color and joy. Doris herself is all business and has no time for either Susan or romance. (Is it her ruthless realism that unsexes her, or her professional ambition? The movie manages to trash working moms and clear thinking in one fell swoop.)

Doris is finally redeemed—and Susan's childhood restored—when she is won over to the cause of Kris Kringle, the jolly old gent she hires to be the Macy's store Santa. Kind and generous (though awful in his rage against crass materialism), the man has one quirk: he believes he is the *real* Santa Claus. This is patently impossible, defying all fact and all logic, and is, for just that reason, the very thing that must be accepted by all sympathetic characters before the gratifying denouement. Doris is a hard nut to crack, but finally, conquered by the patient equanimity of the wise old Kris—not to mention the romantic attentions of his handsome lawyer—Doris finally abandons her "silly common sense."[8]

It's a little tricky to figure out what the real message of this film is supposed to be. It's not that we all should really believe in Santa Claus (although why not?). Rather, it's that we should believe *in something*. But why use the figure of Santa Claus to make this point? Is it that commitment to moral values is on a par, rationally speaking, with belief in fairies, that the one is no more rationally defensible than the other? What's going on, I think, is a linkage—one I'm eager to sever—between two kinds of rationality. One is the human capacity for logical reflection; the other is the construct of classical economics, the coldly calculating self-interest that eschews values and affection. It is this latter kind of "rationality" that has commercialized Christmas, not the former. We are supposed to read Doris's skepticism about Kris as cynicism about the possibility of disinterested virtue—Kris is just too good to be true. But why yoke idealism to credulity?

One needn't subscribe to the central dogma of Christianity to appreciate the moral value of charity. Nor must one be a theist to regret and resist the exploitation and commodification of every laudable impulse human beings possess. Indeed, if one judges by trends in the United States, the relationship between materialism and religiosity is precisely the reverse. Today's most enthusiastic cheerleaders for free market capitalism—that juggernaut of commercialization—are also the most vociferously "Christian." On the other hand, you'll find no more eloquent critic of commodification than the atheist Karl Marx.

I know that many people (including many of the authors in this volume) experienced a deep sense of loss when they left the religious communities in which they had been reared. I must say that, for me, the feeling of relief was paramount, eclipsing any glimmer of regret. If I have any regrets at all, they are ones that have emerged since I became a parent. I am sorry that I was not able to provide my children with the kind of structured moral community that churches and synagogues can offer. My husband and I have both been active in progressive movements, and we've made sure that our kids logged plenty of time at demonstrations and political meetings ("Yes, you have to come; this is 'church' for us," I'd explain.). But there simply are no secular institutions that can serve the myriad psychological, social, and moral purposes that religious institutions currently do. However, I see this fact as a challenge to secular moralists, not a reason to pretend to believe something I don't.

In fact, it hardly matters whether I have any regrets or not. The pragmatic argument for religion—"believe and all this can be yours"—is bound to fail, at least for me. I find it impossible to believe things that make no sense to me or that I have profound reasons for thinking are false. Given the number of times this pragmatic line has been urged upon me ("for your *children's* sake, if not for your own!"), I'm inclined to think that I'm anomalous in this regard. Or maybe not. Maybe many people don't actually believe the tenets of their religion but rather collectively agree—in some subtle and wholly implicit way—just to say they do.[9] I have good reason to think that many people don't actually know what tenets their denominational affiliation commits them to. I know for a fact that many Catholics simply ignore doctrines they find unpalatable and disregard injunctions they find inconvenient. But even if this kind of doublethink makes religion possible for some, it's not a strategy I could adopt. There would be no "doubleness" in my case; there would be only pretense.

Some people have told me that they feel safer in a universe watched over by a benevolent God, and suggested that I would, too, if I could just recover my faith. I beg to differ. The world of my childhood, a world in which the supernatural intruded regularly into daily life, was a frightening world, a world in which *anything* could happen: the sun could stop, the dead could rise, virgins could give birth. Angels were real, but so were demons, and demons could take over your soul. As a child, I had been morbidly fascinated by the story of St. Jean Vianney, the "Curé d'Ars," a humble parish priest who was said to have struggled for years with demonic possession, until finally cured by exorcism. (Or so I remember.) I had not thought about the Curé until many years later when I attended the London premiere of *The Exorcist.* Despite the fact that I had been, at that point, an atheist for two years—or maybe *because* of that—I found the film utterly terrifying. For months afterward, I was beset with unwanted memories of the demon-dominated child. I couldn't sleep in the dark and I couldn't remain in a room if the stupid theme music came on over the radio.[10]

In contrast, my children's world is governed by natural law, which is extremely strict. The sun does *not* stop (at least not in my lifetime) and the dead do not rise (without cardio-pulmonary resuscitation). It's true that this means one must abandon hope for miraculous interventions. After a car accident during my first year of graduate school, I remember looking in the rear view mirror at my horrifically bloodied face (broken nose—don't worry) and thinking with profound distress that my fate lay entirely in the hands of merely human doctors. But the upside of a thoroughly natural world is that you know what you're dealing with. You can have confidence, for example, that your newborn is not a demon in human form, come to prepare the way for a satanic invasion. (It's hard enough being a parent without having to worry about *that.*) And don't tell me that praying protects you from anything. The Jewish and Christian traditions are replete with stories of righteous and holy people, from Job to St. John Vianney, tempted and tortured by God, always for His own mysterious purposes.

My children, in fact, are pretty unflappable where ghosts and monsters are concerned. When my husband and I took them to the Museum of the Moving Image, it just so happened that the museum was featuring an exhibit on special effects in my old nemesis, *The Exorcist.* As I was trying to warn the children—then about seven and eleven—that the pictures might be too scary for them, they rushed past me to scrutinize a life-sized model of Linda Blair (the actress who portrayed the possessed child), fully demonic, levitated above her bed. They watched the outtakes from the infamous head-spinning scene with clinical dispassion, and pored over the various devices and prostheses required for the magic of projectile vomit. The final verdict on this totemic film of my youth: OK for how old it was, but pretty clunky. I was incredulous (if relieved): didn't they find it *scary*? "Mom," said my son, rolling his eyes. "Stuff like that isn't *real.*" Right on, son.

I have no trouble calling myself an atheist, but if I had to choose a designation, analogous to "Catholic" or "Christian," that might convey something about my positive commitments, I would choose "humanist." I would connect myself with thinkers like Aristotle, Descartes, Hume, Kant, and Marx, who were awed and inspired by human capacities: for thought, for creation, and for sympathy. As they appreciated, our value as persons does not depend upon and cannot be secured by the patronage of any external being. It emanates from within.

Human dignity is not, and should not be thought to be, hostage to any myth. Ironically, this may be the message of at least one story in a sacred text. Early in my career, I was asked to teach a course on theories of human nature; the syllabus began with the creation story in the second and third chapters of *Genesis.* I had never read the Hebrew Bible as a child and was familiar with the story of Adam and Eve only from retellings. I was fascinated to read the actual text (albeit in translation), which differed in many significant ways from the narrative I remembered. God, for example, appears more calculating than loving: He creates

Adam for the express purpose of tending His garden (Gen. 2:15), and Eve for the express purpose of helping Adam in his work, no other beast being suitable for this task (Gen. 2:18–23). And He lies: He tells Adam that if he eats from the Tree of Knowledge of Good and Evil, "in the day that thou eatest, thou shalt surely die" (Gen. 2:17). The serpent (who is never identified as evil, only as "more subtil than any beast of the field"—Gen. 3:1) is the one who actually tells the truth: that they won't die if they eat from the tree and that the reason God has forbidden them from doing so is that He is afraid of their becoming "as gods, knowing good and evil" (Gen. 3:5). This is confirmed when God, in consultation with unidentified others, expels Adam and Eve from the garden—not, mind you, as part of their punishment, but to keep them away from the Tree of Life: "Behold, the man has become as one of us, to know good and evil, and now, lest he put forth his hand, and take also of the tree of life, and eat, and live for ever: Therefore the Lord God sent him forth from the garden of Eden" (Gen. 3:22–23).

I am no Bible scholar but note only that the story, taken at face value, renders a trope familiar from many ancient mythologies: the stealing of a divine prerogative by the presumptuous human. Always such thefts are punished: Prometheus is sentenced to eternal torment, Pandora releases pain and sadness into the world, and Adam and Eve, with all their descendants, must toil and suffer. What's the lesson? Well, it could be that it's prudent to do what powerful divinities tell you to do—in Adam and Eve's case, to remain in a state of childlike ignorance, devoid of conscience or principle, dependent but safe. Or one could extract a different, more noble message: that knowledge and reason, those godlike powers, are so valuable that having them is worth enduring the wrath of the most powerful being in the universe. On this reading, Adam and Eve did not "fall from grace," they ascended into moral responsibility. This is how I choose to read the story, and how I conceive our struggle as a species—to claim our rationality, to confront the harsh realities that constrain us, and to acknowledge our own responsibility, in spite of the cost—therein to make ourselves "as gods."

My thanks to Judith Ferster and Joseph Levine for their comments on an earlier draft of this essay.

FIVE

Life without God: Some Personal Costs

Daniel M. Farrell

I'm damned if I know where I got the idea, but there it was, as clear and firm in my five-year-old mind as any idea could possibly be: all I had to do to get to heaven was somehow get into our parish church when no one else was around, climb up onto the high altar, open the door to the tabernacle, which seemed to me to be the focal point of the Mass (it didn't occur to me that doing this might be difficult), enter (on my hands and knees, since it looked just big enough to admit me in that posture), and slowly make my way, still on hands and knees, to heaven. (I never worried, for some reason, that it might take a very long time to get there.)

I was not a stupid child: it puzzled me, intensely, that no one else seemed ever to have thought of this easy route to our common goal—family and friends weren't gradually disappearing, at any rate, as one might have expected, had they known what I thought I knew—and this in turn made me worry that there must be something problematical about my plan. But for the life of me I couldn't think what it was, and so I bided my time, confident that it would not be long before I would be with God and our Lord, his Son, in heaven.

If I really believed all this, why did I never actually take steps to get into that tabernacle and begin my journey? I don't know the answer to this question—most likely, I sensed that it would be cheating and also that it would be grievously wrong to do such a thing, since it would involve touching something that only a priest was allowed to touch. But I feel certain that I really did believe I could get to heaven in this way, partly because I remember spending so much time thinking about it and puzzling over the fact, already noted, that no one else seemed to be planning the same trip.

I don't know when, exactly, I learned that my plan was ill conceived, but I do remember how profoundly dismayed I was—indeed, how deeply depressed I was—when I learned or somehow figured this out. As I've said, though, I was not a stupid child. And so, after a while, I began to think seriously about alternatives. And, of course, knowing what I knew, and being situated in the sort of family I was situated in, it wasn't long before I realized that what I had to do was to become a priest. This, after all, was what our Lord had himself told us, at least implicitly, when he said "If you would be perfect, then go, sell what you have, give what you get to the poor, and come, follow me." This was an invitation to the priesthood, I had been repeatedly told, and though I knew that, of the many called, only a few were chosen, I felt certain that I would be one of those few.

Why did I take Christ to be talking about how to get to heaven, when what he'd actually been talking about was how to achieve perfection? I'm not sure, but my guess is that I simply willfully misinterpreted him and that I did this, however unselfconsciously, because I really was intent on figuring out how to get to heaven. Heaven, after all, and its alternative, was forever, while this life—well, everyone knew how little *it* mattered and how short it was.

It saddens me, when I think about these things, to realize that I was a child who cared so little about this life and so much about that imagined life to come. But the peculiarities of my own early psyche are not to the point here. The point here is to ask a question that, while surely not unrelated to what might have been going on in my five-year-old mind all those years ago, is, in any case, a not uninteresting question in its own right: namely, *why is this world not enough for some of us, and what does believing in God do to mitigate this sense of the world's not being enough on its own*?

The simplest answer to the first part of this question, of course, is that the thought that *this is it*, and that we ourselves will exist no more when our bodies fall apart, is a very hard thought to accept, at least for many of us. So we invent another world, and a "soul" that will travel to that world when the body dies, and we thereby come to feel a lot better about our bodily mortality. God comes in, on this way of thinking, as that which makes both this world and the other world possible.

There's surely a lot to be said for this answer. But there's also something rather overly simple about it, I think, at least as a diagnosis of my own case and of the cases of many former believers I have known. For if I ask myself what I felt was the most important thing I lost, when I stopped believing in God, "The possibility of eternal life" is not the answer that immediately comes to mind. That may well be what I *ought* to have felt was the most important thing I'd lost, but it was not in fact what I would have said—nor is it what I would say now, as I look back at the very difficult period that ensued after I left the seminary because I could no longer believe in God.

Here I need to return to autobiography for a moment. I've said that when I realized the road to heaven was not quite so easily found as my childish mind had initially supposed, I turned to another, less literal road, by misinterpreting Christ's New Testament invitation to follow him in a life as a priest. But, of course, there were eventually some changes in my thinking about this road as well. For I did eventually come to see that Christ was really not talking about (heavenly) *rewards* but, rather, about what is required if one would be perfect, where perfection had clearly to do with fitting oneself in some way into some sort of divine plan.

This is admittedly rather vague, but the important point for present purposes is that when, at the age of nineteen, I left the seminary, after almost six years, because I had ceased to believe in God, what was most difficult for me, and what constituted by far the most serious loss, was not the loss of that hoped-for paradise, nor was it the loss of an important relationship with a Very Important Friend; rather, it was the loss of the clarity I'd had about what I should do with my life.

Initially, my new, post-God, post-seminary state felt more like uncertainty, and confusion, than like some major crisis—after all, I was young, I was fairly smart, and I had a whole new world of opportunities ahead of me. All I had to do was figure out what to do with myself and the rest of my life.

But here begins, and for me began, the problem. For it turned out to be very difficult to adjust to a world in which the decision as to what to do with my life had to be made by me, alone, and without the help of the man-God who had, I thought, invited me to follow him in a life of good works. In fact, it gradually came to seem that it would be *impossible* to make a rational decision about what to do with my life, since, without God, and the sense of a decision that was backed by a divine plan, no decision about what to do with my life seemed to be any more compelling than any other.

Of course, I knew that some such decisions would be more appropriate to my talents and inclinations than others, and I sensed, fairly confidently, that some were decisions I'd be more likely to be comfortable with than others as time went by. And in that sense, I knew that some such decisions would indeed be more rational or "sensible" than others. But from another perspective, it just didn't seem to me to *matter* what I did with my life, given that there was no longer the possibility of the kind of divine "certification" my earlier plan had had. I was, in short, suddenly facing the sort of existential "crisis of meaning" that so many others have faced when they realized they could no longer believe in God.

What's behind this sort of crisis, with which I shall assume at least some of my readers are familiar? Why, that is to say, would anyone feel they can't make meaningful life-altering decisions, and live a truly meaningful life, if they no longer believe in God?

One answer has to do with the idea, mooted above, that nothing can really *matter* if we live in a godless universe. The idea, perhaps, is that things that might have been *worthwhile,* because possessing some sort of intrinsic value, cannot reasonably be thought to be worthwhile, or to have value, if there is no God.

Why, though, would someone think this? Is the idea, perhaps, that something can have value only if God *pronounces* it valuable? Suppose this is right—suppose, that is, that the view that nothing would or could be worthwhile in a world without God rests on the view that things that are worth doing, or that have value, *have* their value, or are worth doing, because, and only because, God has pronounced them valuable or said they are worth doing. Certainly, something like this was lurking somewhere in my own mind, I think, all those years ago.

I wish I could say that something like Socrates' argument in Plato's *Euthyphro* disabused me of this idea, but I'm afraid I can't. At most, I think I can say that I somehow saw instinctively, or intuitively, what I now think that argument shows so elegantly: namely, that if one has a certain conception of God and of his relation to The Good, one has to grant that what one actually believes is not that God's pronouncements *make* things worthwhile or valuable—things that otherwise would *not* be worthwhile or valuable—but, rather, that God, if we believe in him, is our best source of reliable knowledge of what is worthwhile or of value.

Losing God as a source of this sort of knowledge is itself a very big loss, of course, and in fact I think that some of what I was feeling in those post-seminary years of late-adolescent confusion was the effect of this loss: I had to figure out what was worthwhile, or of value, *on my own,* and this was not something I had been well trained by my teachers to do. But I did learn to do it, and my seminary training was not irrelevant as I gradually learned to do it. After all, many of the things I had formerly thought to be valuable or worthwhile, because I had been told God had pronounced them to be of value, were things that it still seemed quite reasonable to think were valuable, even without God to reassure me about my judgments: things like the importance of honesty and respect for others; kindness, both to friends and non-friends alike, but especially to those less well-off than I am; and development of my native abilities and talents, both for my own sake and for the sake of the good I might thereby be able to do for others. These things, I saw, could well be thought to be important or worthwhile in their own right, quite apart from their certification by a God in whose existence I no longer believed.

But, then, why, after I'd come to see this, did my "crisis of meaning" not suddenly, or at least eventually, abate? Why did I still suffer from a sense of the futility or meaninglessness of it all, even after realizing that things of value had their value, and in fact had to have their value, even for God, independently of the fact that God approved of them? And why do I have the sense, even now, that something like this is also true of many others who once believed in a personal God but now no longer do?

One possibility, I suppose, is that, while able to see things as valuable without God and God's will, I felt that without God I had no reason to promote or pursue those things. I had a list of things that I considered worthwhile, but I no longer had any reason to promote or pursue them.

I think there may have been a period where something like this was in my mind; but, if there was, it was short-lived. For I'm certain that, even without philosophical training, I was able to see, as others in similar circumstances have surely seen, that it would be incoherent to believe that something has value, or is worthwhile, and at the very same time believe that one nonetheless has no reason whatsoever, given that one no longer believes in God, to promote or pursue that thing. For surely, to believe that something has value is to be at least *disposed* to promote or pursue it and to be disposed to see promoting or pursuing it as reasonable, and even a confused adolescent unschooled in the theory of value would have been able to see this.

But, of course, seeing and granting *this* does not ensure that, in cases of conflicting values, one will see oneself as having any more reason for pursuing one value than for pursuing another. The realization that to value something is, *inter alia,* to be disposed to promote or pursue it, and to see promoting and pursuing it as reasonable, is not itself enough to motivate one to promote or pursue any *particular* thing one deems valuable, over any of the other things one deems to be of value as well, when one cannot pursue or promote all of them at the same time. One still has decision problems, that is to say, even when one thinks one knows what is, at least for oneself, valuable or worthwhile. But, now, how can *God* have provided—or provide, for those who believe in him—an answer to *this* problem: the problem of how to choose among, or "order," the various things, including ways of living one's life, that one considers valuable or worthwhile? And why, whatever we suppose believing in God does in this connection for those who believe in him, might it appear to some people to be impossible, or at least impossibly difficult, to deal with this problem in a world without God?

The simplest answer to the first of these questions is to suppose that, for many believers, at least, God himself instructs them, directly or indirectly—that is, personally or via intermediaries—on how to order the values they have gotten from him and how to make the difficult decisions that having a multiplicity of values entails, especially when, among these latter, they face important and very difficult decisions about what to do with their lives. Certainly, as I have intimated above, this was true for me: all sorts of "advisers" were available to me, from my earliest years, to tell me what God wanted me to do with my life.

I'll return to this question about how believing in God might help with the sorts of decisions we're thinking about. Here, by way of anticipation, I want to note the obvious point that not every answer to the question of how belief in God might help with such decisions needs to be as simple-minded as the answer I have just sketched. The paths to wisdom about these matters, as many religions conceive those paths, and conceive the relevant notion of wisdom, are quite varied—and in some cases extremely subtle.

At this point, though, I want to briefly address the second question above: how might someone try to deal with the decision problems we're concerned with here *without* having recourse to help from God, or religion, and what sorts of problems and challenges might he or she face?

Begin with the question of how such a person might proceed, leaving difficulties with her procedure until later. Even this is not an easy question, and it would of course be ludicrous to suppose there is only one plausible answer. I can think of one answer, though, that strikes me as not only plausible but also as an answer that might help us with the question of why answers that are not based in some way on belief in God do not work for all of us. This is an answer that tells us to address the questions that concern us here by engaging in a certain kind of imaginative enterprise—by engaging in what we might call "thought experiments" of a certain sort. Specifically, it suggests that we should deal with the relevant questions—about how to arrange or "order" the things we value into some sort of life or life plan—by addressing such questions in a way in which many people in fact actually address them in everyday life: namely, by *picturing* or *imagining* one's life as it might go, if one were to make certain choices over others, and then tentatively *settling* on the one that feels best.

"Settling," on what basis? On the basis, quite literally in some cases, of considering how we *feel* about ourselves and our lives as we look at them or imagine them unfolding in any given scenario, and asking whether or not, as we contemplate a given scenario, we feel we can endorse it. Thus, I, for example, after leaving the seminary and enrolling in a secular university, had to decide whether to pursue a degree in philosophy, hoping to move on to graduate school once I finished college, and from there to a career in college teaching, or to instead pursue a degree in social work, then move on after college to professional school and a career as a social worker. And I made this decision, once I had reassured myself that both options had a great deal of appeal for me, by imagining myself in each career and asking myself how I felt about the life I would have if in fact I chose that career and it went reasonably well by the standards of those already engaged in such careers.

This is, of course, a terribly sketchy and unnuanced characterization of the imaginative process I have in mind here, and on another occasion I would be anxious to say more about it. For present purposes, though, I want to assume that my description of this process is not entirely unintelligible and that something *like* what I have described is something people actually do, and perhaps not infrequently, to address the question of how to choose, from among the many lives they might have and might value, one over another. And I want to assume this because, in the end, the problem I want to identify with this approach is a problem for this approach regardless of exactly how the approach is elaborated and is, moreover, a problem that plagues most—though not all—*other* "God-free" approaches to decision making in the relevant contexts.

That problem is easily stated: this way of making the relevant decisions ensures that one must ultimately view them as, in a straightforward and very important sense, radically *subjective* decisions. To be sure, these "second-order" value-decisions, as we might call them, about how to choose among, or "order," what we might call our "first-order" values, are, in the view I'm considering, *no more* "subjective" than are our decisions about what those first-order values *themselves* are. Thus, my choice of philosophy over social work, while certainly a straightforwardly subjective choice, was surely no more subjective than my decision to include both of these areas on my list of possible final choices, while not including geography, say, or biology, which didn't interest me at all, at least as potential majors and bases for an eventual career. But, for some reason, I found what appeared to me to be the radical subjectivity of the former decision, about how to weigh one first-order value of mine against another, much more disconcerting than what I had to grant was the equally clear subjectivity of the latter decision (about what my first-order values *were,* at least for the purposes at hand). Indeed, "decisions" of the latter sort did not, and still do not, present themselves to me as *decisions* at all. Certain things simply seemed (and now seem) more valuable or worthwhile to me than other things, and eventually I accepted the fact that they were more valuable or worthwhile to me, even as I recognized that I could not, even if my life depended on it, give an account of their actually *being* more valuable or worthwhile than any of the other things I might have valued.

Hold aside for a moment the worry that there is a kind of inconsistency in being concerned about the subjectivity of one's second-order value-decisions while not being at all concerned about the admitted subjectivity of one's first-order value-decisions (or *values,* as I would prefer to say). Why, in any case, should the realization that one's second-order value-decisions are no more objectively grounded than one's first-order values create a "crisis of meaning" of the sort I've described above?

Recall that, as I am conceiving them, second-order value-decisions are decisions about how to choose, from among one's first-order values, the values that one wants to make central to one's life plan. While such decisions can sometimes be revoked, they are, at least when made self-consciously, quite clearly *momentous* decisions for most people. And, of course, this sense of their momentousness, or seriousness, is only augmented—sometimes quite intensely—when they are decisions that one knows are *not* easily or readily revoked. (Note that "decisions" about one's first-order values, wherein one comes to see that one values some thing or some activity without having to order it relative to one's other first-order values, are not nearly so momentous, at least for most of us. This alone, it seems to me, may be enough to explain why one might, without inconsistency, have certain views about or attitudes toward the former that one does not have, at least to the same extent, toward the latter.)

But how does their momentousness, as I am terming it, explain how such decisions could be in some clear sense especially *difficult* for some people and especially fraught with the kind of significance they have for some of us? The answer, it seems to me, is fairly obvious: it's not their momentousness *as such* that makes such decisions so difficult and so fraught with cosmic significance for some of us but, rather, their momentousness coupled with the special psychological needs of those of us who think of and experience these decisions in the ways I have been describing. After all, there are plenty of non-believers who do not find it as difficult to deal with these questions as do people like me, and this is surely not because they do not see them as momentous decisions, nor is it (always) because they do not see such decisions as ultimately radically subjective decisions. Rather, it is, I think, because they do not have a need, relative to such decisions, for something others of us seem so clearly to need—namely, some sense that in making them we are not merely relying on how we *feel* about the life they will constitute but are also somehow making decisions that are the *right* decisions, at least for us.

Why might one need something like this? Why might one need to have this kind of reassurance about the relevant sorts of decisions? I'm not sure I can answer this question, even for myself, but I think the answer surely has something to do with a related need some of us have—namely, a need to be able to believe that, when all is said and done, our lives will have had some sort of special *significance* when they are over. If this is right, it will be clear that at this point we have in a sense come back to where we started, since an obvious question is why one should suppose one's life can't have that special significance if one's second-order value-decisions are no more objectively grounded than one's first-order value-decisions. For this question I have no answer. So far as I can see, the fact is simply that some of us do seem clearly to believe that our need for a life that matters cannot be met without some sort of (objective) standard of correctness, or success, for the making of basic decisions about how to shape our lives and live them out.

What about the other part of our question—the part that concerns how believing in God renders the making of the relevant sorts of decisions easier for those of us who have the kinds of needs and related beliefs I have been describing? Clearly, for those of us who accept the argument of Plato's *Euthyphro,* to which I have alluded above, the help that God gives us in making such decisions cannot consist in the fact that his wanting or telling us to make a certain decision (in the relevant context) *itself makes* that decision the right decision for us. Rather, if we accept the argument of the *Euthyphro,* God will be helpful to us in making such decisions because, or insofar as, he is someone we believe we can count on to know what the right decision would be for us—or, at any rate, to know which decisions are not clearly the *wrong* decisions for us—and to communicate that knowledge to us, or otherwise help us attain it, in some way or other. This, of course, is because, if one accepts the argument of the *Euthyphro,* one believes not that God *makes* what we call "right" or "good" decisions right or good, but, rather, that God *sees* what's right or good for us, perhaps on the basis of considerations that only he can see, and tells us, in light of what he sees, how to proceed. But this, of course, is quite enough for many people, especially those with the sorts of needs (for reassurance) that I have described above. For provided only that one has confidence in God's wisdom and love, one will be confident, given appropriate assumptions about one's access to God's preferences for oneself, that one is doing the right thing or making the right decision when one makes the sorts of decisions that concern us here in accordance with God's instructions.

If I may assume that the preceding remarks have identified at least one significant loss some of us might understandably feel we have sustained when we lose our ability to believe in God, two points seem worth mentioning as we conclude.

First, it is worth noting, I think, that agnostics and atheists with the kind of psychological needs I have been discussing, but who also accept the basic thrust of the argument of Plato's *Euthyphro,* can certainly *hope,* at least in principle, to find a source of "objective value" on which to base their decisions about how to order or choose among their second-order values. For, as we have noted, someone who accepts Plato's argument believes not that God *creates* objective values but, rather, that he *identifies* them for us. Given this fact, we should not be surprised if we find that at least some of the sorts of freethinkers I have been discussing eventually find what they believe is an adequate God-free account of objective value on which to base the relevant choices and decisions since, in theory, belief in the existence of such an account is not dependent on belief in the existence of God. And, in fact, this is, at least in my experience, something we often enough find when we look closely at the lives and beliefs of individuals of the relevant sort: they sometimes *have* found a secular equivalent to one part of their former theistic faith—in a moral theory like Utilitarianism, for example, which tells us that happiness is the supreme human good and that morally defensible decisions are decisions that promise at least as much happiness as any of the other possible decisions open to one when one acts.

A second point that's worth noting as we conclude is the following: it's curious, if the reflections above are at all useful in understanding the enormous sense of loss some of us feel when we cease to believe in God, and that we continue to feel even as we otherwise become comfortable with our new, nontheistic worldview, that former believers with the sorts of psychological needs I've been discussing so seldom choose an obvious alternative to a search for godless objective values—I mean the alternative wherein one *repudiates* the need for objective values and accepts, instead, the possibility of a meaningful life without them. Why, for example, does not some updated version of Existentialism appeal to the sorts of people we're talking about—a twenty-first-century version of the Existentialism of de Beauvoir, say, or Sartre, with its insistence on the importance of choice *without* a background of transcendent, independent moral values and on the "bad faith" involved in convincing oneself that such values are even possible? It's almost as though, once the idea of objective value gets a hold on a certain kind of person, via the grip of belief in God as revealed in some particular religion, giving up belief in God is easier than giving up the belief in the need for objective value if one's life is to make any sense. And surely this is rather odd and makes one wish for an account of these matters that cuts considerably more deeply than I have been able to manage here.

Thanks to Louise Antony, and to an anonymous editor at Oxford University Press, for helpful comments on an earlier draft.

SIX

Overcoming Christianity

Walter Sinnott-Armstrong

Old-time Religion

My childhood was inundated with Christianity. It's not that my family was especially religious. They weren't. It was just that I grew up in Memphis. Like most southern U.S. cities in the 1960s, Memphis was overflowing with Christianity. There was more Christianity in Memphis than water in the Mississippi River. Just as the Mississippi was hard to escape when it flooded, so Christianity was unavoidable in Memphis, especially around Christmas, Easter, and Thanksgiving. Anyway, I didn't try to avoid it. I went along, like any good child would.

My family attended church together every Sunday morning. After the service, I went to Sunday school. I sang in the church choir and later served as an acolyte. My parents made sure that I prayed every night. I went to religious kindergarten and elementary school. We memorized Bible verses and put on Christmas pageants year after year. Pictures on the walls reminded me of Jesus even when I was not paying attention to the lesson in daily chapel. While riding a bus or walking down any street, I could see church spires all over town, and I could hear a regular refrain of "Praise the Lord." I'm not complaining. Religion did not bother me at the time. My point is just that Christianity was so pervasive that any child who grew up in such an environment would be susceptible. Religious thoughts would become automatic. If someone had asked me if I believed in God, I would have answered, "Of course," not because I had thought about it, but because I had not thought about it.

Religion surrounded me in the air I breathed. Just as you don't notice the air until it gets polluted, so I barely thought about religion until controversy arose.

One controversy came in the form of a new preacher. I'll never forget his sermon on alcohol. Lots of people in the church drank a lot of alcohol. The new preacher saw this as a problem, so he spoke about the need for moderation—not even abstinence. He argued that too much alcohol could ruin your family and your life. I found him persuasive. The alcoholics in the congregation were not so receptive. In their view, he was a foreigner (a Yankee!) who had no business telling them how to live their lives. He was gone before long. What struck me about this brief encounter had nothing to do with whether or not the congregation really did drink too much or the new preacher should have been more diplomatic. What struck me was that nobody listened to him or faced his arguments. As soon as they realized he was saying something they did not want to hear, they shut their minds tight and got rid of him. I started to fear that religious people listened only to what they liked.

Another incident reveals how sheltered and naive I was. Almost every week, we saw another family whose son was a close friend of mine and whose parents were the closest of friends with my parents. They were not, however, members of our country club. One day I asked my parents why. The answer was straightforward: "Because they are Jewish." "So what?" I thought. Of course (!), our country club did not allow Jewish members. Later I found out that the club did not allow Catholics either. Why not? It was hard to get an answer, because nobody wanted to talk about it, but the reason seemed to have something to do with rumors that the Jews got Jesus killed and the Catholics believe whatever the Pope says. These reasons did not make sense to me. It wasn't my Jewish friend who got Jesus killed, and the Catholics I knew did not slavishly follow the Pope. I was young but not stupid. I could already see that religious beliefs were dividing people and making it harder for me to play with my good friend at the country club.

On a larger scale, the civil rights movement was growing, and Memphis was in the midst of the action. Some churches supported the movement by providing places to meet and to sing stirring religious protest songs. Still, the churches I knew best—the lily-white ones—stood in the way. One day a black couple walked into the back of a large white church, and more than half of the congregation stood up and walked out. I knew some of the people who walked out and who did not see anything wrong with what they did. They even claimed to have God on their side. Of course, these were abuses of religion. Liberals said (and still say) that true religion supports civil rights. Nonetheless, the tendency to accept religious traditions without questioning seemed closely allied with the conservative tendency to accept the Southern tradition of segregation without questioning. The religious mind-set—the willingness to accept tradition on faith—looked dangerous because it enabled injustice.

Evangelical Christianity

Despite my growing qualms, I was not ready to give up religion yet. I still liked the songs and the spectacle. I've always had a weakness for stained glass and Bible stories. The people in church were friendly to me. If I had renounced or denounced religion in Memphis, my family would have been shocked. So I stayed silent.

About this time, I left Memphis for prep school in Connecticut. The Hotchkiss School was the greatest academic experience of my life. I learned so much so quickly. Probably the most important thing that I learned was to work hard. But one reason I worked so hard and learned so much was that I was terribly lonely in my first years. My southern accent was as strong as they come, so my origins were obvious every time I opened my mouth. The other students laughed at me. I learned to laugh at myself. It is hard for the butt of jokes to make close friends. When I returned to Memphis for vacations, my old friends were too busy and some seemed to see me as a traitor to the South or, even worse, an intellectual. I did retain a few close friends in Memphis, and I eventually made some good friends at Hotchkiss, but the first years away were rough. In those tough times, there was one group that always welcomed me warmly and seemed genuinely glad to see me—the Christian fellowship. They also sang beautiful songs and talked about important issues. So I went to their meetings more and more. During meetings, I had several religious experiences, where I really felt as if God touched me, and then I committed and recommitted myself to Christ. By the time I entered my first year at Amherst College, I was going to a religious service twice a week, attending meetings in between, taking religion courses, and looking up to my sister, who had become head of the Brown Christian fellowship.

This new brand of Christianity at college seemed much better than what I had seen in Memphis and elsewhere. The Amherst Christian fellowship was nondenominational, so they seemed less divisive than old-time religion. As evangelicals, they welcomed everyone into their churches. They also used arguments to persuade people to become Christians, so they seemed to listen to reason. I thought that I had found a form of religion that posed none of the problems that created my earlier doubts.

I was especially impressed by Josh McDowell, an evangelical speaker I heard early in my first year of college. McDowell claimed that Jesus had fulfilled hundreds of prophecies in the Old Testament. He laid out the details of each one, then calculated the probability that all of these prophecies could have been fulfilled by chance. His calculation made it look extremely improbable that all of this could have happened without a divine plan. He (and I) concluded that Jesus was sent by God to save us, just as the Bible said.

This line of thought made me want to learn more about the Bible. I was convinced that studying the Bible would enable me to argue better for my Christian beliefs. It had the opposite effect. When I looked closely at the Bible, it began to seem confused and arbitrary. Nobody had ever told me that other stories about Jesus did not make it into the canonical Bible merely because they were rejected by a church council centuries after Jesus. I could not stop myself from asking why we should take their word about which stories were true. Even when I limited my attention to the canonical books of the Bible, I saw more and more inconsistencies. Not all four gospels can be literally true. You don't have to be a professional logician to see that. The Old Testament also began to look questionable, not only because its historical accounts were implausible in light of available records, but also because many of its moral teachings were repulsive. I could not see any reason to drown so many innocent children in Noah's flood. Why didn't God tell Noah to take some children along with the animals on his ark?

Although convinced that the Bible had been corrupted by human authors, I still held out hope that *parts* of it were divinely inspired. It seemed natural to seek those passages that came directly from Jesus, so I studied the parables in a course at Smith College. (I took the course at Smith instead of at my own college because the Bible teacher at Amherst was reputed to be an atheist, so he obviously could not be trusted.) My term paper might be the most scholarly piece I have ever written: For each parable, I calculated the percentage of Greek words that could be traced to roots in Aramaic, the language of Jesus. Before I finished my calculations, I did structural and stylistic analyses of each parable. It turned out that eleven of the parables shared a similar structure and style, and the same eleven parables had significantly higher percentages of words with Aramaic roots. I concluded that these parables probably came from a single author who spoke Aramaic. Of course, I could not prove that the author was Jesus, but who else could it be? I thought I had proven that these passages came almost straight from Jesus.

I was ecstatic, so I told all of my friends in the Christian fellowship. Most of them responded in the same way: "What about the other parables? Are you saying that those did not come from Jesus? That must be wrong." Their reactions were horribly disappointing. I was ready to have my study criticized in a rational way, but they did not uncover any problems in my argument. They rejected it simply because they did not like my conclusion. What could be more dishonest? I wanted to get the facts straight. I wanted arguments and evidence. I thought they shared my goals. They didn't. They pretended to base their religious beliefs on arguments, but it was all a sham. They were just as close-minded as the congregation in Memphis, and they were also hypocritical, because they pretended to be seeking the truth.

Another incident nurtured my budding skepticism. My sister was a strong person who never backed down just because she was a woman. Then she began to attend a new church near her college where they took the Bible literally. They interpreted a passage in Paul's Epistle to the Corinthians to dictate that women should not speak in church. She went to their services and remained dutifully silent while men spoke. I was shocked and dismayed. It was obviously unfair, yet she conformed. Of course, I could reinterpret the passages so that they would not reach such an obnoxious conclusion. But it was, again, the mind-set that bothered me. You had to go along with whatever the Bible said, even when it was puerile. If you reinterpreted the Bible to avoid its clear meaning, then you were dishonest, since your interpretation was distorted by your desire to make the text say something plausible. Neither option was attractive to me.

The final straw came when the Christian fellowship decided to send a group out to try to convert people to Christianity. They pressured me to go along, and I caved in to their pressure. It was one of the most uncomfortable positions I have ever been in. I stopped people as they walked by, and I asked them whether they wanted to hear about Jesus. Most were annoyed. Some uttered obscenities. They did not bother me much. It bothered me more when people wanted to talk with me. As I was giving the stock arguments that I knew so well, I could hear myself as if I were a bystander listening to what I was saying. It sounded shallow. I had doubts and could see problems in my arguments, but I did not tell them. I felt dirty.

This reaction was due in part to my philosophical training. After studying great philosophers, such as Plato, Descartes, Hume, Kant, and Wittgenstein, it became easy to see gaping holes in arguments for Christianity. It also seemed distasteful to hide these holes in order to gain followers. Good philosophers face objections and admit uncertainties. They follow where arguments lead, even when their conclusions are surprising and disturbing. Intellectual honesty is also required of scholars who interpret philosophical texts. If I had distorted Kant's views to make him reach a conclusion that I preferred, then my philosophy professor would have failed me. The contrast with religious reasoning was stark. My Christian friends seemed happy to hide serious problems in the Bible and in their arguments. They preferred comfort to intellectual honesty. I couldn't.

Philosophy did make me uncomfortable. Life is much simpler when you trust a book to guide you. I also had many dear Christian friends whom I did not want to lose. So I still might never have found the courage to give up Christianity if I had not met Liz. We met during my first year of college, but we did not fall in love until my second year. By my third year, we were spending most of our free time together. (We have now been married for over twenty-five years.) Liz was not a Christian, but I could not understand how such a wonderful person could be sent to hell by a good God. Moreover, as I was courting Liz, I did not need my Christian friends as much. I was free to look at Christian doctrines more impartially. It became clearer to me that I had no reason to hold my Christian beliefs. Of course, many people believe with no reason, but usually only if they have some ulterior motive. With Liz by my side, I did not have as much motivation to remain Christian. Because I had no motive or reason, my faith waned.

New-Age Christianity

By the end of college, I had no real interest left in religion. I did take one course in the philosophy of religion during graduate school, but the topic seemed distant, almost like studying a strange culture. During this period, I fiddled with religious claims, trying to make them compatible with science and common sense. Maybe God was not all-powerful or not all-good. Maybe God was not a person but only an impersonal force or all of nature. Maybe religious language should be understood not as making truth-claims but merely as expressions of hope (or fear?) or in terms of pragmatic effects on people's lives.

Such reconstructions of religion all seemed to avoid the issues by changing the subject or by robbing religious claims of all content. Once religion becomes so wishy-washy, you can't refute it, but you also have no reason to believe it. It might make some people feel good to talk about "a higher level of existence" or a "guiding force," but there is no evidence for anything of the sort. I couldn't (and still can't) even figure out what such quasi-religious humbug means.

These liberal reconstructions also struck me as too far from what most people in churches believe. The kind of religious beliefs that control people's lives and lead them to take stands on political and moral issues cannot be the watery spirituality that is vague enough to avoid conflicting with anything. There is no point in going to Church or praying to something so indeterminate. No "higher level of existence" could save believers or help them get to heaven or perform miracles or create the world. I tasted many flavors of low-fat and low-carb Christianity, but none was even close to satisfying either intellectually or personally.

Quietism

That's how I overcame Christianity in my personal life. For the next twenty years, I almost never thought about it, except as a waste of time. Religion was not as pervasive in New Haven (where I went to graduate school) or in Hanover (where I have lived since 1981). So it was easy to avoid, most of the time.

I did have to lecture in my department's Introduction to Philosophy class. The course was team-taught with other professors, and sometimes my co-teachers did not want to lecture on the existence of God. The students wanted to discuss this topic, so someone had to do it. That someone was me. It was easy to get a good lesson out of arguments for God's existence. The classic arguments are relatively simple and make good examples of common fallacies that I wanted to teach students to avoid. To balance the arguments for God, we looked at arguments against God. That was easy, too. There is so much suffering in the world that I could pick my examples. Many children have been born with horrible birth defects that caused them tremendous pain and early death. An all-good God *would* prevent these harms if he could. An all-powerful God *could* prevent them. It follows that there is no God who is both all-good and all-powerful, as traditional Judaism, Christianity, and Islam claim. The argument was so obvious that beginning students had no trouble appreciating its force.

To be even-handed, I also presented various responses by theists. That was the hardest part of my lectures to prepare, because I really wanted to make some responses look plausible, but my main goal was to teach students critical thinking, and every response to the problem of evil has glaring defects. Maybe free will is more important than any amount of suffering, but what does free will have to do with natural evils, such as birth defects? Maybe God repaid the child's suffering with a ticket to heaven, but then why didn't God send him straight to heaven without the suffering? Maybe God was teaching a lesson to the child's parents, but isn't it unfair to use one person's suffering to teach others (especially when you could use better teaching methods)? Maybe we mere mortals are too feeble and ignorant to see the justification for suffering, but then why should we believe that there is any justification? Maybe God is not subject to our lowly human moral standards, but then why should we love or worship such a God (except out of fear or confusion)? Maybe we need some suffering to make us appreciate the good things in life, but why do we need so much, and why must it be distributed so unevenly? It was hard for me to stand up in front of my students and try to make such feeble responses look good when I really wanted to teach them how to evaluate arguments critically.

My dilemma got worse when it came to grading students. I wanted to be totally fair, and I fear that I might have gone too far at times. I felt sorry for students who had to defend their beliefs in God. It was hard for them to give any decent argument. To compensate for their disadvantage, I graded them more easily than I did students who adopted the more-plausible positions that God does not exist or that we do not know whether or not God exists.

While teaching my students, I had plenty of time to think about where I stood on religion. No proof is possible in this area, but the evidence clearly led to atheism, so my views solidified. No longer was I an agnostic. I had found good reasons to believe that God does not exist.

I still wasn't ready to speak out. Why would I want to make a big deal out of my atheism? This was bound to alienate friends and family. It might have scared away good students who happened to be religious. What good would it do? Not much; I could tell that from reactions by religious people. They never seemed to get the point of the problem of evil, even though it was hard to imagine any more obvious refutation. So I saw no reason to stick out my neck.

Evangelical Atheism

My quietism ended when current events taught me the dangers of religion. I had always known how religions, including Christianity, led to wars in the Middle East, Ireland, and so on. Many wars, of course, are not based on religion. Even religious wars result from non-religious forces as well. Nonetheless, it is hard to deny that many wars have been and continue to be fueled in large part by religious beliefs. It is no coincidence that terrorists are so often motivated by religion, since it is harder to get non-religious people to volunteer as suicide bombers.

On a more personal level, I was not prepared for the death of Matthew Shepard. When bigots kill defenseless homosexuals, they do not always cite religion as their reasons. Christianity still fuels their bigotry. If Christians did not broadcast their condemnation of homosexuals, then the bigots would be less likely to kill. Christianity is at least part of the cause. I came to see why Christianity should be held responsible for these deaths. The dangers of religion are even more evident when abortion doctors are killed by openly religious groups.

Of course, atheists kill, too. Russian and Chinese communist governments are famous examples. However, these atheists killed in the name of communism, not atheism. There are other ideologies besides religions that produce killers. But that does not change the fact that religions, including Christianity, play a large role in causing many people to kill.

Other deaths are caused by religious views in less obvious ways. One such case was brought to my attention by a conference at Dartmouth College on stem-cell research. Scientists talked about the prospects for medical advances from stem-cell research, and then some speakers replied that it was immoral on openly religious grounds. It seemed like an easy case to me, but maybe I was just not seeing the secular reasons for opposition. So I asked one speaker who had been on a government commission that had heard well over a hundred witnesses for and against restrictions on stem-cell research. He reported that not one single witness had spoken against stem-cell research other than witnesses who had come specifically to represent an openly religious group. This confirmed my view that there were no non-religious reasons against stem-cell research. Yet our government was restricting it. "Doesn't that conflict with our Constitution's clauses on religion?" I asked. His answer was clear, "Yes." This exchange brought home how harmful religion is. Stem-cell research could help cure or alleviate a host of ills from paralysis to juvenile diabetes, but religions slow down the research. (They won't stop it, although they might move it outside the United States temporarily.) Such religions are, thus, responsible for all the harms these patients suffer that could be alleviated if the religions stopped controlling the U.S. government.

As I saw more and more instances of religion's controlling politics in disreputable ways, I grew angry. It seemed so unfair for people to suffer because others held indefensible views. I wanted to do something about it, but what? My question was answered by a student whom I did not know was religious. He asked me to debate William Lane Craig in an open forum at Dartmouth. I agreed. I knew that Craig had been studying these issues full-time for many years, and he was known as a master debater. Still, if I did not try to articulate my views, I would see myself as a coward. So I accepted. Nervously, I prepared by looking at Craig's Web site, where I found his standard arguments. Then I checked with colleagues at Dartmouth about each point. I was ready. The debate went well for me. For weeks afterward, atheists came out of their closets to congratulate me. One student said that I was doomed to hell, which was upsetting, but he was obviously troubled.

Not much later, I received an invitation to debate Craig again. I was told that this time he insisted that I go first. Fine. So I constructed my three arguments against the existence of God, went to Minnesota, and debated him in a large evangelical church. This one went pretty well, too.

I felt as if I was doing something important. At least I was trying to do something about an important problem, and I had fun doing it. By now I had my comments on Craig's opening statement at Dartmouth and my opening statement in Minnesota, so I found a publisher, and Craig and I published a debate book together, after adding responses to each other's criticisms.[1]

Some of my Christian friends do not appreciate our book. They tell me that their brand of Christianity is nothing like the kind that Craig defends or the kind that kills abortion doctors and homosexuals. I'm glad of that. Still, by calling themselves Christians, they associate themselves with certain institutions and views. That association buttresses those institutions and views by allowing true believers to claim more support than they really have. It would be clearer and better to emphasize the differences between their "spiritual" views and traditional religion. If true religion is as harmful as I think, then we all should want to dissociate ourselves from it.

Despite some opposition, our book's reviews and reactions have been generally gratifying. To help advertise it, I agreed to publish a short piece in the Dartmouth alumni magazine. I knew that Dartmouth alumni included many religious fanatics. I expected many negative reactions. I got them. My favorite (because it was so amusing) was an e-mail that called me a "small minded" "egotist," "an arrogant fool," and a "pompous PhD," then added "it is pathetic that the College allows you in a classroom," and "That you don't [believe in God], I am sorry to have to inform you, calls into question your intelligence." Then it concluded, "Please be assured that this theist will impartially consider any persuasive response you can offer and, as such, I look forward to continuing this dialogue with you." Did he really think I wanted to have a dialogue with someone who would say such things about me in response to a short opinion piece? The letter writer had not even bothered to read my book.

This exchange indicates a larger problem: Many theists feel perfectly justified in abusing atheists. I would never consider writing such a diatribe against a theist who argued for belief in God. I would remain calm even if a theist misrepresented atheism. Most atheists I know let ridiculous religious views go unchallenged. This might be because they have been taught by theists that it is somehow impolite or unconstitutional to criticize religion. Whatever the reason, theists speak out, but atheists remain silent.

As a result, people constantly underestimate the number of atheists and agnostics, as well as those people who don't care enough about religious issues to form any opinion. This tendency to discount atheism was illustrated when I recently visited a top prep school with my teenage daughter. In front of all the visitors, the principal proudly announced that his school is open to *all* religious views. As evidence, he reported that about forty percent of his students are Catholic, forty percent Protestant, and fifteen percent Jewish, with the remainder believing in various other religions, including Buddhism. He didn't even mention atheism. Apparently, he did not take atheism to be a significant position on religious issues. Another possibility is that none of his students are atheists, but that's unlikely. Many of my students (and colleagues) at Dartmouth are atheists now and were atheists in high school. Or maybe the atheists at this prep school hide their views from their teachers (and from their parents), so there are many more atheists than theists imagine.

Why would atheists hide? Many atheists avoid religion because they find it boring. Evangelicals often hound atheists, who don't want to spend their lives talking about God any more than they want to spend their lives talking about UFOs or the Loch Ness monster. For such myths, their motto is "Get over it!" Another reason is that criticism of religious beliefs is often considered impolite or even unconstitutional (although it isn't). Religion is treated like a senile relative whose bizarre statements are not to be questioned. But there is also a darker side to atheists' silence: Atheists fear that their views will alienate friends and family, not to mention prospective clients and employers. Preachers often saddle atheists with the slogan, "Everything is permitted." Who would want to befriend or hire or vote for anyone with no morals? Of course, very few atheists really believe that everything is permitted. Still, as long as this parody of atheism is widespread, it takes courage to admit that you are an atheist.

Moreover, most atheists see little to be gained by broadcasting their beliefs. Theists won't listen, and atheists don't need to listen. This defeatist attitude means that fundamentalists get away with spouting harmful nonsense. They gain confidence, and many undecided people with open minds hear only one side of this important issue. If atheists let themselves be cowed, our country's policies will continue to be distorted by ancient religious myths. More religious wars will arise. And there will be more suffering among people who need abortions or stem-cell treatments or just sexual freedom. Our best hope for progress is for atheists to speak out and (as politely as possible) tell any theists who will listen why religious beliefs are ridiculous.

I admit that religion has some personal benefits for some people. Religious beliefs help many people get through their daily lives. They also motivate some people to help others. But that is sad. If people cannot face their lives without illusions, and if they are not motivated to help others apart from the commands of a fictional God, then we are all in deep trouble. We should all care about each other and try to help each other regardless of whether or not any God tells us to do so.

Of course, when I am teaching, I do not force my atheistic views on vulnerable students. I present both sides as fairly as I can, and I encourage students to think about the issues for themselves. Still, I wonder whether it might be better to teach the truth. Professors don't put up with beliefs in ghosts, even in student papers. Why should we have to treat religion differently?

But we do. When a friend needs to believe in God in order to be able to face life, it feels cruel to announce your atheism and argue that such religious views are bunk. It might also be cruel to hold students responsible for their religious views by giving them the grades they deserve. Nonetheless, there remain many occasions when atheists can and should speak out. We should not let politicians, in particular, base their policies on religion without being questioned. We should not let religion distort academic and popular discussions. When such occasions arise, atheists need to speak out. This is the only way to overcome Christianity in society and to pave the way for real progress.

SEVEN 

On Becoming a Heretic

Edwin Curley

When I was a child, I did what children do: I accepted the view of the world that the more vocal adults around me taught me to accept. My mother—and my maternal grandmother, who had lived with us from my infancy—were Episcopalians. They saw to it that I went to the Episcopal church and Sunday school, and rejoiced when I became an acolyte. For a while my mother cherished the hope that I might become a minister. My father, whose mother's attempt to raise him as a Christian Scientist had alienated him from organized religion, was an agnostic. But for a long time I did not know this. In the interest of family harmony, he kept quiet about religious matters until many years later, after my mother had died.

As I became an adult, I began to have doubts about the religion in which I had been raised. Partly this came from the failure of my attempts to pray for my grandmother's recovery from a debilitating illness. Partly it came from my reading Somerset Maugham's *The Razor's Edge,* which posed the problem of evil in a powerful way. But probably the most crucial factor was the prayer book my mother gave me when I was sixteen.

At the back of the prayer book were printed the articles of religion, which, it seemed, members of the Episcopal Church were expected to accept.[1] I had not thought much about them when I was preparing for confirmation. I was only thirteen then, and there was much I did not understand. Our minister was an admirable man: highly intelligent, cultured, and humane. At thirteen I was content to accept what he told me, simply on his authority.

But at sixteen I read those articles of religion, carefully and critically, for the first time. I was disturbed that my church accepted predestination. Before the foundations of the world were laid, the articles said, God had chosen some vessels for honor and others for dishonor, that is, some of his human creatures for salvation and others for damnation. This did not seem fair. But one of the first principles of my church was that no one should be required to believe, as necessary for salvation, any doctrine that could not be proved from scripture. So far as I could see, there was as good scriptural foundation for this teaching as there was for any doctrine my church taught. Paul's Epistle to the Romans seemed pretty unequivocal on this score.[2]

There also seemed to be strong philosophical reasons for accepting predestination. If God is omniscient, if he knows everything, he must have foreknowledge of the future, including his creatures' ultimate destiny.[3] So before they are born there must be a fact of the matter about what their fate will be, a fact that would seem to be unalterable, unless we suppose that God can be mistaken in his beliefs. So our belief that we might determine our destiny by the choices we have yet to make, choices that might go either way, must be an illusion.

Moreover, if God is omnipotent, if he can do anything he wants to do (or any logically possible thing he wants to do), then nothing can happen except by his will. If I wind up going to hell, God must have willed that I go to hell. This takes it out of my hands. How can I prevent what an omnipotent being wills?

Theologians sometimes try to save God from responsibility for our sins by saying that he merely permits them. But to permit something to happen when you could have prevented it, and when you knew what would happen if you didn't act, is not to escape responsibility for it. In Lillian Hellman's *Little Foxes,* Regina is having a quarrel with her husband when he suffers a heart attack. He asks her to bring him his medicine, and she refuses to do so. She has it in her power to bring him the medicine, and she knows what will happen if she does not. Her decision not to bring him the medicine makes her as much responsible for his death as if she had shot him.

Some Christian philosophers will no doubt object that, although God *could* prevent me from committing the sins that will justly cause my damnation, he *cannot* do so in a way that would entitle me to moral credit for refraining. If he causes me to refrain from sin, then by a proper definition of freedom my refraining will no longer be a free act; the freedom required for moral responsibility also requires that the free act not be caused. His inability to cause me not to sin is a consequence of his inability to do what is logically impossible, an inability that does not detract from his omnipotence.

Even if we accept the libertarian conception of freedom that this reply presupposes, it doesn't seem to work. It doesn't show that God can't cause me not to perform the act that, if done freely, would be a sin. It just shows that he can't do this without depriving me of the libertarian freedom necessary for my refraining to accrue moral credit. It's the value he places on human freedom that prevents him from causing me not to sin, and that value may seem, on reflection, too high.

Christian philosophers sometimes invoke, in this context, the analogy of a mother raising her child. Wanting him to learn to be a responsible adult, she refrains, after a certain age, from interfering in his decisions, believing that she needs to let him make his own mistakes. But parents who act this way rarely have certain knowledge of what their children will decide in the absence of their intervention. And presumably, a loving parent would act differently if she *knew* that her child were going to make a decision that would have catastrophic and irrevocable consequences, if she knew, for example, that it would lead inescapably to his death.

If I am destined to go to Hell, God will not only have known that from eternity, he will also have willed it from eternity. The scriptural texts supporting predestination seem to do no more than endorse the implications of deeper theological commitments to God's omnipotence and omniscience. Sometimes Christians claim that the acceptance of predestination—or as they may say, *double predestination*, the predestination not only of the elect, but also of the damned—is an example of Calvinist excess. It's well to remember that the chief theologian of the Roman Catholic Church also accepted double predestination.[4]

Another doctrine of my church that disturbed me as an adolescent was the doctrine that we are all sinners, who require God's grace if we are to be saved. If we define "being a sinner" in a very inclusive way, so that it's enough, to be a sinner, that once in your life you did something seriously wrong, no doubt all adults are sinners. I don't think many of us get very far in life without doing something we are (and should be) ashamed of. But it's absurd to claim that infants in their cribs are sinners. Nevertheless, in the Christian tradition it is normal to baptize infants at an early age because it is believed that they come into the world tainted by the sin of Adam and Eve. This is the doctrine of original sin. I cannot believe in original sin. Original sin is less widely accepted now than when my church was founded. I find many Christians who reject original sin. I sympathize with them. Their hearts are in the right place, certainly. But Christians can reject original sin only at the cost of a substantial reinterpretation of their scriptures and traditions.

Consistently with the doctrine of original sin, it is common among Christians to believe that we cannot earn salvation by our works. If we are to be "justified," that is, to achieve salvation, it must be by our faith in Jesus. Not that this is an action that is in our power to perform or not, an alternative to obeying God's commandments, which is beyond our power. Rather, God is merciful; he may forgive us and treat us *as if* we were righteous. The mark of our having been forgiven is that God, by an act of grace, gives us faith (Rom. 3:21–26).

This doctrine has implications I find appalling. It implies that those among us who lack faith in Jesus have not received grace, have not been forgiven, and will, if we continue in that state, go to Hell. So the doctrine of justification by faith, which has strong support in the Christian scriptures, leads to *exclusivism*, to the idea that all who reject Christian doctrine must be damned, no matter how good they may be by ordinary standards. If God chose the beneficiaries of his grace on the ground of some distinctive merit they possessed, this might not be unfair to those he didn't choose, whom we would presume to lack that merit. But that would be contrary to the idea of grace, which implies a free gift, not something given to someone who deserves it on account of merit.

So usually it is held that God has no reason for choosing some and not others. He acts quite arbitrarily. It's a hard and ugly business, this doctrine of grace. I suppose that if you have already accepted Hell and original sin, you may be grateful for having a shot at salvation—even if it does seem to be a lottery in which the odds are not on your side. Of course, if you think you have faith, then you may also think you have won the lottery and you may set aside thoughts about the unlucky losers.

I was also troubled by my growing realization that, although everyone in the little town in which I lived gave the appearance, at least, of being a Christian, globally there were millions of people who were not Christians, or even, as I learned, theists of any sort.[5] I didn't know any of these people, but I guessed that many of them must be at least as good as the people I did know. Yet my church taught that these people could not be saved, no matter how good they might otherwise be, if they did not believe in Jesus. While there might not be any philosophical reason to believe this, there certainly seemed to be ample scriptural support for it, as illustrated most clearly by the Gospel of John, though also by other texts.[6] Could a just and loving God condemn so many of his creatures to eternal torment simply because he had not willed that they be born into a community in which they would have the opportunity to be taught the right religion?

For that matter, could the doctrine of eternal torment as a punishment for sin be justified even for those who have sinned in their acts as well as in their beliefs? Perhaps some people have sinned on such a grand scale that they deserve the most awful punishment we can imagine. Plausible candidates would be Hitler, Stalin, and others who have been responsible for the torture and murder of millions of people. But the scriptures that my church pronounced sacred seemed to teach that *most* of us will go to hell: "The gate is wide and the road easy that leads to destruction, and there are many who take it. . . the gate is narrow and the road is hard that leads to life, and there are few who find it" (Matt. 7:13–14). Another passage reads: "Many are called, but few are chosen" (Matt. 22:14).

So far as I could see, most people, whatever their shortcomings, had not sinned so extravagantly that they deserved eternal punishment. One lesson I had learned in my childhood was that the punishment for an offense should be proportionate to its gravity. My sense of justice rebelled against the idea that the vast majority of mankind would receive a punishment that only a few, at most, could have sinned grievously enough to deserve.

I had other moral objections to Christianity, objections to some of what seemed to be its most central moral teachings, the doctrines of the Sermon on the Mount. Jesus' attitude toward sexuality seemed repressive. By the time I was in my late teens, I had looked at many a woman with lust in my heart. But I did not think that desiring a woman was in itself a sin, not when I was not acting on those desires (Matt. 5:27–28). Nor did I think that divorce ought to be impermissible (Matt. 5:31–32). Nor did it make sense to me that we ought always to turn the other cheek (Matt. 5:38–41). Sometimes, I thought, we must resist evil. Like most young men brought up in the forties and fifties, I accepted the war against Germany and Japan as necessary, and thought of military service in such a cause as a source of honor, not a violation of my duty to God.

By the time I was in college, I called myself an agnostic, and my doubts led me to the study of philosophy and its history. Among the philosophers I studied were Christians, like Augustine, Aquinas, and Descartes, for whom the rational defense of their religion was very important. Others, like Hobbes, Spinoza, and Hume, were critics of Christianity. These studies did not lessen my doubts; they increased them. But living, as I did, in a predominantly Christian society, I discovered that, even in the relative tolerance of our day, you could not openly reject the majority religion without incurring some costs.

When I was in graduate school at Duke, after I had completed two years of course work, I got a call asking if I would be interested in a one year job at a small liberal arts college in the Shenandoah Valley of Virginia. It was the summer of 1961; the one member of their philosophy department had just suffered a nervous breakdown; and they needed someone in a hurry for the coming year and didn't mind the fact that I did not yet have my PhD. They did, though, mind the fact that I did not have the religious beliefs they would have preferred. When I visited the campus for my interview, the dean asked what my religious views were. I replied that I was an agnostic, whereupon he asked: "You'll keep quiet about that, won't you?" By this stage, I had a wife and a one-year-old child. We had been struggling to get along on a graduate student stipend for two years. The thought of making a visiting lecturer's salary—$4,800 for the year!—was too enticing to pass up. So I did not let that condition deter me from accepting his offer. I would not accept a job on those conditions now.

At that college it was traditional for the dean's wife to pay a social call on new faculty. We had been warned to expect a call but not told *when* to expect it. So when the dean's wife rang our doorbell one Sunday morning, we were not prepared. We had slept in and were having a late breakfast; the house was a mess, and no one was dressed to receive company. The dean's wife explained cheerfully that she had been in church but had developed a cough. Not wanting to disturb the other worshippers, she had decided to call on us; she added, "I knew you'd be home." If you were not in church on a Sunday morning in that town, there was no place else to be. Sometimes it is not enough for Christians to let their non-Christian neighbors disagree in silence. They need to make it clear to us that we are aliens in a Christian society.

Of course, things used to be much, much worse. In the historical period I have mainly studied, you could be put to death for rejecting far less of traditional Christianity than I reject. Just questioning the doctrine of the Trinity was enough, in England in the 1650s, to incur the death penalty.[7] But my personal experience of the hostility some Christians have toward non-believers—even in twentieth-century America, with its tradition of religious freedom—has inclined me to be skeptical when the historical figures I've studied profess orthodoxy. It's a matter for debate among Hobbes scholars, for example, whether he was a Christian, as he claimed, or an atheist, as his critics claimed. No doubt we will never settle this issue. But we should, at least, be able to agree that when the cost of candor is high, we should not be surprised to find people not practicing it.

So far, my objections have been mainly theological; they are objections to teachings whose basis is primarily scriptural rather than philosophical. The main exception to that generalization is the doctrine of predestination, which has philosophical grounds as well as scriptural grounds. I know many Christians will not feel that their understanding of Christianity requires them to accept all these doctrines, either because they have a different interpretation of scripture or because they do not regard the Christian scriptures as absolutely authoritative in determining their beliefs and conduct. I think those Christians who adopt a freer attitude toward scripture—and do not feel that their acceptance of Christianity commits them to predestination, or Hell, or original sin, or justification by faith, or exclusivism—those Christians have their hearts in the right place, I say. But I also think their feet may be planted on the slippery slope to heresy, and that more conservative Christians, who would accord greater authority to scripture, have a clearer right to call themselves Christians. How much of traditional Christianity can you reject and still be a Christian?

Let's turn now to objections not so scripturally based. It is common among Christians to believe that God is a personal being, who created the universe and who is omnipotent, omniscient, and perfectly good. Indeed, it is commonly said that God must possess all perfections. Yet we observe that the world this perfect being has created includes many imperfections: there is much joy in the world, but there is also much suffering—much of it apparently undeserved; and there is sin. We call these things evil. How can they exist in a world that owes its origin to a God with the attributes Christians believe their God to possess?

The usual response now is to say that though God *could have* created a world without evil, it was better for him to have created the world he did, in spite of the evils it contains. The occurrence of those evils was necessary for goods that are even greater. If God had so created the world that it contained no evil at all, that world would have been less good, all things considered, than it is even with all the evil it contains. This is called *the greater goods defense.*[8]

The Christian may say we humans rightly do many things we expect to cause avoidable harm. We build a bridge from San Francisco to Marin County, knowing that in the construction some workmen will fall into the water and drown. We could avoid their deaths by not building the bridge. But the bridge is a great good. Given our human limitations, we cannot build it without some people dying a result. So we build it and accept their deaths as part of the cost of bridging those waters. And God's permission of evil may also be justified by the greater goods to which it leads.

An omnipotent being, of course, does not face all the hard choices we do. If he wants a bridge across those waters, he need only say "Let there be a bridge" and there will be a bridge. One question the greater-goods defense raises is: what kind of good could be so intimately connected with evil that even an omnipotent being would have to accept the evil as the price of realizing that good? And what good could be so great that it would justify such a being's accepting the amount of evil there is in the world as the price of attaining that good?

The usual answer these days is freedom. There must be freedom if there is to be moral goodness. And the price of giving humans freedom is that sometimes they will misuse it. Even an omnipotent being can't cause a person to *freely* do good. And freedom, with the moral goodness that sometimes results from it, is a good sufficiently great that it makes the evils that also result worth accepting. This is what is called *the free will defense*.

There is a problem, of course, about appealing to human freedom to solve the problem of evil when you also believe in predestination and divine foreknowledge. This is a problem of long standing, with which many philosophers have wrestled. No solution has gained general acceptance. And until Christian philosophers have worked out an acceptable solution to that problem, I think non-Christian philosophers are entitled to regard the free-will defense as very problematic.

But there are other problems about the appeal to freedom. There are evils whose occurrence has no discernible connection with freedom. Theologians call them natural evils, meaning such things as earthquakes, floods, tornadoes, diseases, and so on. If a deer dies in a forest fire, suffering horribly as it does so, that is an evil. It is not only human suffering we must take into account when we are weighing good against evil in this world.

Now, if you accept the theory of evolution, you will believe there were other animals on this planet long before humans appeared on the scene.[9] Humans evolved from other species through a long and gradual process during which many of their ancestor species died out. This is how new species are born, through the death of old species weeded out by natural selection, the elimination of living beings that are less well adapted to compete in the struggle for survival in their environment. When the less well-adapted species die out, many of their members die of starvation, or disease, or predation, all methods that involve considerable pain and suffering for the animals less able to compete. None of that suffering can be justified as a necessary consequence of permitting humans freedom. We weren't around then. So none of it seems beyond the power of omnipotence to prevent without the loss of that good.

Here's another objection. The greater-goods defense can easily lead to a kind of cost-benefit analysis that is deeply repugnant to our moral sense. Consider the kind of case that troubled Ivan in Dostoevsky's great novel, *The Brothers Karamazov.* A little girl is treated quite brutally by her parents, who beat her because she has done something that made them angry. Perhaps she wets the bed repeatedly, and they think she ought to be old enough to control her bladder. Or perhaps the father is an alcoholic who abuses his daughter sexually. *The Brothers Karamazov* is fiction, but to hear about real cases like this, you need only listen regularly to the eleven o'clock news.

The free-will defense seems to say, in cases of this kind: well, it's all very unfortunate, of course, but this is the price we must pay for having freedom. For the father to have the opportunity to display moral goodness, God must give him the opportunity to choose evil. You can't have the one opportunity without the other. And the father's having the opportunity to display moral goodness is such a great good that it outweighs the fact that he chooses evil.

But who gets the good here? It's the father. And who suffers the evil? It's the little girl. Let us grant, for the sake of argument, the questionable assumption that the benefit outweighs the cost. Freedom, we'll concede, is a very great good, even when it isn't properly exercised. Still, it makes some difference who pays the cost. Freedom may be a great good, even a good so great that it would outweigh really horrendous suffering. But justice requires some attention, not only to the net amount of good, after you have subtracted the evil, but also to the way the goods and evils are distributed. Some distributions just aren't fair.[10]

The mention of Ivan Karamazov brings me to my final point. Ivan claims that if God does not exist, everything is permissible. Dostoevsky, speaking through Ivan, may have stated the problem of evil as powerfully as any atheist; but he was himself a Christian, who believed that God must exist if we are to make sense of morality.

I think the opposite is true. I think Christian belief makes morality, as we normally think of it, unintelligible. Consider the story of Abraham and Isaac in Genesis 22. One day God put Abraham to the test. He said to Abraham: "Take your son, Isaac, whom you love, and go to the land of Moriah, and offer him there as a burnt offering." God gives no reason for this horrifying command. And Abraham asks none. He simply sets out to obey. And he nearly does obey. He has the knife raised to kill his son, when God sends down an angel to stay his hand. God then says he is satisfied with Abraham: "Now I know that you fear God, since you have not withheld your son, your favored one, from me." In the end, God does not actually require the sacrifice. But he does require that Abraham demonstrate his willingness to carry out the sacrifice.

What's the moral of this story? I suggest it's this: as God's creatures, our highest loyalty must be to God, even if this requires the sacrifice of our deepest human loyalties; God is our creator, our Lord, and we owe him absolute obedience, no matter what he commands—and he might command anything. There are no constraints on his will, so we might be required to do anything. There is no predicting what he might require, and there is nothing to say that his commands will not change from one moment to the next. At the beginning of the story, God commands Abraham to kill Isaac; in the middle he commands Abraham not to kill Isaac.

If there is a God who is liable to command anything, and if our highest loyalty must be to this God, there is no act—save disobedience to God—that we can safely say is out of bounds, no act of a kind that simply must not be done, not even genocide, to use a crime I think most of us would shrink from committing, even if we believed God had commanded it. If this God exists and we must obey him unconditionally, then anything whatever might turn out to be permissible. This view is destructive of morality.

From this line of thought there seem to be only two possible escapes. One is to say, as Robert Adams does, that the God he believes in is a loving God, who simply *would not* issue a command as brutal as one which required the killing of an innocent child, or of entire people—men, women and children.[11] Anyone who claims that he has issued such a command must be rejected as speaking falsehoods about God. This line leads, I think, to a deep skepticism about the validity of scripture as a record of God's revelation to his human creatures, since scriptural passages that report that God did in fact issue such commands are not hard to find; for example,

> When the Lord your God brings you into the land which you are about to enter and occupy, and he clears away many nations before you, the Hittites, the Girgashites, the Amorites, the Canaanites, the Perizzites, the Hivites, and the Jubusites, seven nations mightier and more numerous than you, and when the Lord your God gives them over to you, and you defeat them, then you must utterly destroy them; you shall make no covenant with them, and show them no mercy.[12]

If the Christian scriptures are at all accurate in their portrayal of God, then he has frequently acted in a way that did not display love toward *all* his creatures. We can avoid this conclusion only by being deeply skeptical about the accuracy of the scriptural portrayal of God.

The alternative, I think, is to say yes, the scriptures are generally accurate in their portrayal of God. He does frequently command things apt to *seem* to us abominable. But if he has commanded them, they must *be* right, however they seem to us. This alternative leads to a deep skepticism about our ability to make moral judgments. If the mass slaughter of the innocent is not wrong, then we don't know how to tell the difference between right and wrong, even in what would appear to be the clearest cases. We must either give up Christianity or give up morality. I choose heresy.

This essay is a revised version of my opening statement in the debate I had with William Lane Craig on the existence of the Christian God, at the University of Michigan in February 1998.

EIGHT

Mere Stranger

Marvin Belzer

> For Christ plays in ten thousand places,
> Lovely in limbs, and lovely in eyes not his . . .
> —Gerard Manley Hopkins
> "As Kingfishers Catch Fire"

My story is grounded in the good religious experiences I had as a child, for I was brought up in a strong evangelical Christian home, and I loved the religion, which was the center of my life until I was well into my twenties. I believed that I and all other human beings need to be *saved,* where salvation requires a special connection with God through faith in Christ. These beliefs gradually dissolved and, as I will explain, they did so because of my faith itself.

Heart-Warming Experiences, Reflection, and Faith

We sang a simple song in Sunday School when I was five or six years old:

> Into my heart, into my heart,
> come into my heart, Lord Jesus—

It made perfect sense to invite Jesus into my heart. I knew my heart was located roughly in the middle of my chest. Inviting Jesus there had palpable effects—pleasant physical sensations and emotions in that part of my body–warm, open, and peaceful feelings.

By the time I was eight or nine years old, I had a sense of taking responsibility for myself when there was a message in church about sin and the need for repentance. I accepted my own sinful nature and my need to be forgiven. Sometimes there were specific sins to repent (and I would always be on the lookout for flaws in myself), but usually I was connecting more generally with whatever it may be that gives the idea of original sin its power for people. I could differentiate between the open, peaceful heart and the burdened, closed heart, the sinful heart. I was attracted to the idea of escaping the sinful nature. And so in response to the call to repentance, I would pray and express remorse for my own sins, and often I would surrender into peace, joy, lightness, relief, calm, and confidence. I had ecstatic heart-based experiences of letting go, of surrender to Jesus and to the whole world beyond me. I would emerge feeling love and acceptance and interest in other people.

Since these experiences were powerful and not uncommon, it was easy enough to believe that I'd been *saved.* The experiences were grounded in the belief in a magnanimous and personal source of the universe. *God.* It is a vast thought, and yet my mind as a child encompassed that thought; at least I gestured in its direction in a liberating way. I definitely believed in God, and I believed that God cared about me personally. These beliefs were grounded in the good experiences, just as those experiences were grounded in the beliefs—the beliefs and experiences were mutually supporting. Belief in God was a core belief at the center of my web of belief. The belief was abstract, similar to my beliefs about numbers, and it was as central for me as were the basic truths of arithmetic. Yet it was grounded and personal because the experiences were interpreted as making for a connection with God, and given my situation I had no salient reasons to doubt any of it.

The heart-warming emotions I experienced in the church meetings gradually faded away after a few days. A calm clean thread persisted, nourished by daily prayer and Bible reading, but the ecstatic states would disappear. So what then? Was I no longer saved? What had happened? What did it mean? It made sense to me, as my parents and others advised, that the reality of being saved persisted even after the experiences had faded. I am still saved; I can have *faith* in that because our faith was in God, not in the experiences themselves. So I learned early that experiences might come and go, but one's faith could be stable and continuous. One shouldn't rely on the experiences very much. One enjoys and appreciates them, but when the strong emotions disappear one still has faith that something good persists. It did not matter very much exactly how I felt on any given day. This insight was based on my ability to reflect on the religious experiences and emotions. *I had to reflect on them.* Without thought I easily could get stuck in a depressed state when the good feelings faded. So when I was young this sort of rational reflection supported my faith in a clear and definite way.

Belief in God was linked to actions and attitudes toward other people. My parents were generally very kind. The kindness of my parents was understood to be the kindness of Jesus, a part of the whole package that was a source of wonder and joy, and it definitely was the center of our lives. My parents often showed interest in strangers; they were often helping somebody with problems, and this was interesting to me. So I was often in the presence of people who were in trouble, and my folks were trying to help them (especially to help them get saved), and the motivation was a sense of profound connection with the center and source of everything that exists. Often somebody strange was sitting at the dinner table. *Who is this person?* It was engaging and liberating to grow up around this. I experienced the normal problems we encountered as a family in a wide context due to my participation in my parents' generosity and kindness to people outside the family. (Admittedly, there also was pity intermixed—where pity, a "near enemy" of compassion, includes subtle arrogance, a quiet sense of one's being superior to those being helped.)

I never developed the idea that there was an inherent conflict between our religious life and rational thought. For Wesleyans (we were Nazarenes, a branch of Methodism), science and philosophy are not regarded as bad (so far as I know; I am not writing here as an expert in Wesleyan theology, only the way it came to me as a young person). One *should* endeavor to think clearly and honestly about things. As noted, it was important for me to make sense of the ecstatic experiences after they faded, and it was there I'd begun thinking abstractly and seriously about things in my own life. John Wesley was part of the English Enlightenment and not, strictly speaking, a fundamentalist. I never was told that the Bible is literally true. The Bible has to be *interpreted,* just as you have to interpret ecstatic experiences, and interpreting passages in the Bible requires thinking about them. More generally, science is one thing, salvation another, and while the Bible is a guide to salvation and is infallible concerning questions about our salvation, it is not necessarily the final word about historical or scientific matters of fact unrelated to salvation. God created the world; science can tell us what the world is like and how the creation came about. The theory of evolution by natural selection, for example, never presented itself as a problem for me or my Christian faith. Science is about what can be observed; it is about the nature of this world, and (as it still seems to me now) there is no serious conflict between science and religion. It is not difficult to find ways to reconcile any scientific theory with speculative beliefs about what is beyond direct observation just so long as one does not claim that the religious speculation is based on the science or assume that science is the only source of knowledge or insight about things.

Thinking also was important for us in acting correctly. We internalized high standards for behavior, and going beyond mere rules, we should be kind like Jesus. My mental life included patterns of continuous self-evaluation. Are my actions right? *What would Jesus do?* Are my thoughts right? Consistency was an important concept because we shouldn't be hypocrites, saying one thing while doing or thinking another. These points were part and parcel of my own Christian orientation, not foreign elements.

Reflection was especially important to help us share the good news of the Gospel effectively. We need to think seriously about the situations of other people. Sharing the Gospel was important to me because, from day one, I'd taken seriously the idea *everyone* needs to be saved. We accepted the "exclusivist" idea that the Christian faith is the only way to salvation—the only way to avoid going to hell—and so it is crucially important for the ultimate well-being of everyone. *What Jesus would do is get people saved!* I understood why people are motivated to become missionaries, and I always loved it when missionaries visited our church. They invariably brought photographs and slides of people from all over the world, and I was aware that there is tremendous diversity among people on our planet. This diversity was shocking and delightful to me when I was young—*Some people hardly wear clothes!*—But, alas, this raised a question. Wouldn't they go to hell for that?

A missionary named Donald Owens made a good point about this sort of question. To be effective as a missionary when going into another culture to evangelize people, Owens said, one needs to distinguish between what we believe and do that is essentially Christian and genuinely necessary for salvation, on the one hand, and what we believe and do that is only part of our own culture and not essential for salvation, on the other. What is genuinely necessary is what one really needs to be saved, and what is superfluous is merely part of our own limited culture. Clothing styles more or less fall on the superfluous side of this sensible distinction. So also, for example, would the language one speaks. One needs to profess faith in Christ but not necessarily using English.

The Essential and the Superfluous

What then *is* essential for being saved? What does one need to do, regardless of one's particular culture and upbringing, to ensure that one goes to heaven after death and avoids hell? We believed people would end up in hell if they did not become Christians like us. But just as clothing styles and languages differ, so also do beliefs, and many people have lived and died without having Christian beliefs, and this has happened through no obvious faults of their own. They were simply living their lives in situations where they never had a fair opportunity to become Christians. Missionaries had not yet reached them with the good news of the Gospel. *Would a fair and powerful God permit even those people to suffer in hell after death?*

Evangelical Christians do not take this question very seriously, and I can understand from my own experience why this is so. The idea of hell for distant unbelievers was not on my mind very much as a child except as part of the imperative to go assist them. While I believed that hell is real and while this belief mixed an element of fear, even terror, into the more positive emotions, the idea of hell was not all that salient because my good experiences had established me securely on the side of joy. I understood that the Old Testament's aggressive message of a wrathful and vengeful God had been superceded by the New Testament's message of love: "There is no fear in love. But perfect love drives out fear, because fear has to do with punishment. The one who fears is not made perfect in love."[1] I believed this message, and so I did not worry much about myself going to hell when I was young, or, at least, these fears were not consciously on my mind. And the satisfying aspects of the religion and my experiences obscured the implications of saying that anybody who is not a Christian ends up in hell.

I had read C. S. Lewis's discussion of the problem in *Mere Christianity.* His discussion illustrates how superficial treatments of the problem can lead one to suspect there is a serious problem for evangelical Christians: "Here is another thing that used to puzzle me. Is it not frightfully unfair that this new life should be confined to people who have heard of Christ and been able to believe in Him?"[2] Lewis uses the phrase "new life" for the Christian life both in this world and beyond, and whatever may be the details about sin and redemption, the idea of a *new life* sums it up. The underlying assumption is that if you do not have this *new life,* you will end up in hell. Given his clear expression of the problem, one expects him to solve the puzzle concerning people who have never heard of Christ or been able to believe in him, and here is how he does it: "The truth is God has not told us what His arrangements about the other people are. We do know that no man can be saved except through Christ; we do not know that only those who know Him can be saved through Him."[3] Lewis asserts explicitly that nobody can be saved except through Christ, so he does not quite reject exclusivism. But his answer to the puzzle is that we don't really know what God is doing in detail. *It is a mystery to us.* Aspects of the story about salvation are unknown to us. So even if we assume Christ is essential for salvation, as Lewis says, we do not know that *only those who know Him* can be saved through Him.

This means that explicit Christian belief is *superfluous*—at least for some people. For all we know, there are people who do not in fact need to become Christians in this life in order to be saved. Anyone claiming that Christian faith in this life is necessary to avoid hell is going beyond what they honestly can be said to know. Indeed, they display a sort of arrogance that actually must be insulting to God because it flies flat in the face of the fairness of God because many people do not have a fair chance to develop Christian faith.[4]

The realization that explicit Christian faith has to have been superfluous to the salvation of many human beings did not by itself unravel my own Christian beliefs. But it was a first step because it defused the urgency of spreading the Gospel based on the idea that people really need it in order to avoid hell. And it naturally opened other questions–if explicit Christian faith is superfluous for some people, why isn't it superfluous for all? If we don't really know what God is doing relative to the central issue of salvation, perhaps we should not be so confident about our other basic beliefs.

But isn't that the whole point of Christianity, that God is *revealed publicly* in Jesus? So this question came into focus. To clarify it, we can look at another widely quoted passage in *Mere Christianity,* where Lewis discusses the core Christian idea that Jesus is divine:

> A man who was merely a man and said the sort of things Jesus said would not be a great moral teacher. He would either be a lunatic—on a level with the man who says he is a poached egg—or else he would be the Devil of Hell. You must make your choice. Either this man was, and is, the Son of God: or else a madman or something worse. You can shut Him up for a fool, you can spit at Him and kill Him as a demon; or you can fall at His feet and call Him Lord and God. But let us not come with any patronising nonsense about His being a great human teacher. He has not left that open to us. He did not intend to.[5]

Does this make sense? Is it responsive to reasonable questions about special revelation through Jesus Christ?

No, it did not make sense to me. It is not an adequate reply to serious questions about what human beings can know generally about the divinity of Jesus; for what Lewis himself had said in response to the puzzle about salvation applied here as well—*we actually don't know*. We do not really know what Lewis claims to know about Jesus, about his intentions, and so forth. The past is irretrievably gone, and there is much that no one living now can ever know about what happened concerning Jesus, especially concerning the relatively few passages in the New Testament to which Lewis is referring. We don't really know exactly what Jesus said, as opposed to what was added later by people who were excited generally by his life and teachings and who read things into his life story. People debate these points in detail, but it will always remain speculative. Looking into those debates, it was clear to me that I was never going to know very much about what Jesus intended to do or imply, certainly not enough to have definitive support for what Lewis claims.

There is no reason to accept Lewis's claim that any reasonable person has to accept literal claims about Jesus' divinity. If unbelievers really needed to be saved by accepting the Gospel revealed in Jesus, then other explanations had better be available to them. The "lunatic or God or worse" premise is false. If you already believe in Jesus' divinity, it might sound good, but otherwise it just falls flat. It was clear to me that I really did not know what Lewis claimed to know about Jesus—and that Lewis did not know it either, despite his claims. Lewis's type of argument might work to persuade some people, but nonetheless it is purely rhetorical and manipulative, and it does not take seriously the epistemic situations of unbelievers. I was beginning to see how speculative were my own Christian beliefs. It was obvious that I would always remain largely ignorant about relevant details concerning the past—about what Jesus actually claimed, what he meant by his claims, and so forth—and dogmatic claims like Lewis's definitely were not helpful.

Looking at this world as best I could, then, was it clear to me that the basic claims of revelation made within Christianity *are* true? No, not really. I began to realize that my own grounds for believing in the things Lewis was defending were not much better than those of people who had never even heard about it, or for whom the Gospel was not a live alternative. And such people were not only far away in the jungles of South America, they were near me, the strangers in whom my family had always shown interest. And it became clear that, given the facts of *their* lives, most of them had not really had anything like a fair chance to become sincere Christian believers. There wasn't anything necessarily wrong with them even when they were not Christians. I was identifying with them more fully, seeing things more clearly from their perspectives, and I was not merely seeing them as beings I was supposed to help save. I was seeing that what I had to say to them about my own religion—and what anybody had to say, putting the best spin on it—was not all that convincing. It certainly wasn't like lightning hitting them, and so no wonder they didn't or couldn't muster the faith.

The Superfluity of Core Beliefs

None of this mattered very much at first to my own beliefs since I was aware that the whole thing is based on faith and, as noted, *I had faith!* I was looking into these issues seriously *because* of my faith, because I was serious about its role in human life. And I was not naive about how Christian faith works. Obviously, it is not based on having some sort of demonstrative proof about the basic historical claims. The past is irretrievably gone, and many questions will simply remain unanswered. *But God is alive now, as am I, and I am related to God now. There isn't a vast separation from God.* On the contrary, as Protestants, we believed that there is immediacy in the relation with God, and this immediate and personal dynamic relationship could not possibly be dependent on our ability to peer with certainty into the distant past. Spiritual life was not dependent upon unknowable information and mere speculation about the past. The details about the historical Jesus were not all that relevant to my living relationship *now* with God.

But my access to this relationship with God was through my connection with Christianity, so what does it mean if others reasonably do not or cannot make this connection? Now, this question turned out to be important to me. I was accustomed to assuming a sort of absolute common ground between me and all other human beings—the need for salvation through Christ and the possibility of being saved and having the new life in Christ about which Lewis speaks. The assumption of common ground with others was a basic aspect of my faith. *And I had no interest in a more private religion.* I knew that other Christians, such as Calvinists, did not assume there is common ground with others on the outside—they believe, for example, that some people (such as themselves) are "chosen" or predestined for salvation, and others would simply be left out through no fault of their own. Salvation is an act of grace, and nobody deserves it, so even those left out have no grounds for complaint. But such Calvinist views were not relevant to my own Wesleyan beliefs—I regarded such views as absurd; they are inconsistent with the New Testament conception of a fair and universally loving God—and in any case they were no more relevant to me than were the weird views of Mormons or Buddhists.[6]

But I was aware, of course, that there existed competing religious views, and it gradually began to dawn on me that none of the religious views could be uniquely important. What I have in common with others who have never heard of or accepted Christ, or who may hold different views about the meaning of Christ, is more important to God than what makes us different. My own views may well appear absurd to other people, just as their views seem absurd to me. It really could not matter much to God whether or not one was a Christian or what one believed about Jesus. God must want us to think about things other than specifically religious beliefs and practices, otherwise God certainly would have made it more obvious, in a general way accessible to everyone, what we all should believe and do about religion. *Pay attention to this world; don't be fixated on some other world.* Even the story of the Incarnation can be seen as signifying that we should embrace our physical lives as well as the spiritual. Instead of focusing on abstract religious doctrines and personal status, we should dive into human life with all its complications and messiness and sexiness and sorrows and joys. St. Paul says that Christ, in becoming human, *did not consider equality with God something to be grasped!*[7] If equality with God is not worth grasping, what is? Certainly not my own religious ideas and preoccupations. In a similar spirit, Dietrich Bonhoeffer writes from a Nazi prison in 1944:

> During the last year or so, I have come to appreciate the "worldliness" of Christianity as never before. The Christian is not a *homo religious* [sic] but a man, pure and simple, just as Jesus became man . . . . It is only by living completely in this world that one learns to believe. One must abandon every attempt to make something of oneself, whether it be a saint, a converted sinner, a churchman, a righteous man, or an unrighteous one, a sick man or a healthy one . . . . This is what I mean by worldliness—taking life in one's stride, with all its duties and problems, its successes and failures, its experiences and helplessness . . . . How can success make us arrogant or failure lead us astray, when we participate in the sufferings of God by living in this world?[8]

Whereas St. Paul describes Christ as letting go of the Godhead in order to participate in created life, Bonhoeffer describes living fully in this world as a way of participating in the suffering of God.

In any case, these sorts of thoughts began to influence my views about God's relationship to the world. Many of my beliefs about God began to seem superfluous from God's point of view, and not only those pertaining to the evangelical message about hell. God doesn't really care what we believe—*about God!* And this point doesn't apply merely to those who have never had the chance to hear the

Christian Gospel. It pertains to me as well. God couldn't possibly want me, or any of us, to spend our lives in this amazing world preoccupied with specific abstract religious issues or clinging to our own practices that cannot be shared by all. Life is not trivial, and it is not a pointless game. We are in a startling and mysterious situation. There is a great deal of suffering in the world, yet (as it seemed to me) happiness is possible. The real problems of people should be addressed—surely this is God's view!—and we should not be obsessed with any of the secondary religious stuff.

It was my faith that made possible these types of thoughts; indeed, they were emerging from deep within the faith. *Do not make divisions between those who are saved and those who are not saved.* This distinction cannot go very deep in actual practice because in acting upon beliefs based on this distinction my actions will be based upon my own limited assumptions about what is important. Just as Jesus transcended the Old Testament distinction between a specially chosen people and those who are not specially chosen (the Christian Gospel is universal) so also the distinction that I had accepted between *being saved* and *not being saved* isn't *a propos*. The difference between one's being inside and outside the religion is itself superficial.

My faith in God and interest in other people gave rise to these thoughts, just as the moving ecstatic experiences had led me when I was young into reflection about the role of those experiences relative to an ongoing faith in God from day to day. Without a strong faith, I might not have bothered to look into these things in the way that I did look into them. I might have remained in a sort of dull hazy state about these matters. Nonetheless, at that time my faith in God was gradually eroding the conceptual framework of specifically evangelical Christian beliefs about God because that framework was too rigid and too confining for the expansive nature of the faith itself.

Two Wagers

And then a new wrinkle appeared because I connected for a while with the fear of hell myself.—*But wait! What about me?*—I am not living deep in the jungles of South America. I have had many privileges, including acquaintance with the Christian Gospel. Sending me to hell for not believing in the Christian religion, were I not to believe, would hardly be unfair given all the positive advantages I have had, at least compared with many other people. After all, one fact that motivated my questions was the contrast between the information I had and that which others lacked! So maybe I was going to end up in hell myself if I stopped professing the specific Christian beliefs, even if South American aborigines and Muslims and my friends from non-Christian families were going to get some sort of exemption or get more chances later on in some future life to accept Christ.

The fear that engendered these types of thoughts was deep in my pysche. Lewis expresses it well when he talks about the idea that God is going to *invade* the world again: "Christians think He is going to land in force; we do not know when. But we can guess why He is delaying. He wants to give us the chance of joining His side freely. . . . God will invade . . . . It will be too late then to choose your side."[9] True, this comment is not in the spirit of his milder comments that "we don't really know how" the mechanics of salvation is going to work out. But I certainly understand his aggressive all-or-nothing evangelical stance, for the fear of being on the wrong side—the fear that Lewis is expressing and inciting—was deeply engrained within me, even though for me the fear usually had been overshadowed by the message and experience of divine love.

So there was a period of time when it still seemed possible that I myself could be destined for hell, were I not to be a professing Christian in this life, even if it turned out that everybody else would be getting an exemption or another chance later on. *Perhaps I already had had my fair chance!* But by then I was not willing to identify myself as a Christian because it seemed too trivial; it seemed false to the central core of faith in God itself to cling to the superfluous, for the reasons I have explained. I didn't want to have some sort of inherently private faith, since the aspirations for the faith itself were higher. And so during this period of time I was willing to risk going to hell myself, sort of for the sake of the integrity of this faith, and it was my faith itself that was making it possible. I was risking hell rather than accept a position that God surely could see is superfluous and therefore unworthy of acceptance.

I know this is an odd claim more suited to fiction than real life (von Strassburg's Tristan is willing to go to hell for the sake of romantic love), and I suppose it should be embarrassing to say so, but all the same there was a period of my life when I consciously was willing to go to hell after death rather than compromise and accept a sort of private religion in this life.[10] Consciously, even vividly, I was risking hell for myself in abandoning specifically Christian beliefs and practices, and I was doing so because it seemed with all my heart that God could not possibly value our focusing on such things in the way that I had been doing all my life until then.

My thoughts and feelings contrasted markedly with those behind Pascal's wager. Pascal reasons that even if the odds of God's existing seem very small, hell would be an infinitely horrible outcome compared with what one gives up to devote oneself to God in this life, so one should strive to believe in God just to be safe. His gamble, it seems to me, is grounded in fear and pessimism. My own gamble was grounded in joy and optimism. From within my own faith, I looked with contempt upon Pascal's ridiculous trivialization of the basis for religious life. What I got from my folks and the Nazarenes, from Wesley, from the New Testament Jesus, and from my own heart-based experiences was life affirming, not life denying. It was grounded in love, not fear. And it wasn't merely an intellectual pose or exercise, for it was the central issue in my life as I conceived it. In any case, I was risking hell, and I saw vividly what was at stake, including what I was risking if God is the way Pascal assumed. But basically my faith in the love of God also was optimistic enough not to settle into a sort of depressed and frightened state of mind. My roots in Wesleyanism came to the rescue. Things should make sense. *God cannot be that dumb! God surely can see what my own situation is, God can see that I am sincere, that I am trying to be true to what is genuine and essential—and that I am simply letting go of the superfluous.* My ability to think this way was an expression of my faith in a fair and loving God, whereas Pascal's wager presupposes that God is a complete moral idiot.

Unraveling of the Theistic Conceptual Framework

And then something completely unexpected happened. I totally stopped thinking about God. Not all at once, but over a relatively brief period of time, thoughts about God stopped occurring in the normal flow of things as they had been doing ever since I could remember anything at all. I was not thinking about *God* at all, and not merely orienting my thoughts to other things because God wanted me to think about other things. The theistic framework simply unraveled and completely disappeared from my mind. The concept of God became idle. It was not a live concept any longer. Questions about God or rebirth or afterlife or, generally, about the propositional content of the various religions are no longer serious questions. My faith in God led to the dissolution of the specific Christian beliefs, and then the theistic faith itself disappeared as well.

A pattern had begun when I was eight or nine years old. I found that rational reflection supported my faith when I needed to make sense of the ephemeral nature of the good experiences. I continued to think about things, including how to connect with people who needed to know about Jesus in order to get saved. And it was my faith that animated the entire process. I cared about strangers who would end up in hell if they did not get saved, which meant that I better think seriously about their predicament and about how to communicate with them in order to help them. And I had enough faith in God and in my relationship with God to trust the process that took place.

I realize it may seem odd to say that my faith in God led to the unraveling of my religious beliefs, for I definitely do not have any substantive beliefs now about God or rebirth or any other speculative religious issues. If the religion was so important to me, why didn't I simply make some revisions in the framework of beliefs rather than let it dissolve? Because from the beginning my faith was conceived as part of something much vaster than me, potentially shared by all, and it was of extreme importance within this life. This reflects the evangelical side of me. It was extremely urgent to know Christ, and the need was universal. Even a revision along the lines of universal salvation would still posit a basic division in this world between those with access to the special knowledge—the personal relationship with God through knowing about and accepting Christ, and those on the outside. Even if it eventually it is universally shared in some other life (or there is at least fair access), here and now in this world the conditions are not universal, and this means that faith cannot be of utmost importance in this life. One can avoid hell even without knowing about Christ at all in this life—even Lewis has to admit it (although, as noted, he seems to forget it soon after admitting it). The simple fact is that there is a deep incoherence in the evangelical Christian guidance for living in this world: it says its message is essential, but obvious facts about the world are such that it cannot possibly be essential. It would be easier, in a way, if its message were that God is cruel and unfair, in which case Pascal's wager would make more sense. But that isn't the message at all. We are talking about the God of Jesus, the God of Love.

My response was not a simple switch to the outside. The difference between inside and outside disappeared, and this came to seem the deep core of what I'd been accepting all along. Or if there is a difference, it cannot be characterized in terms of the religious beliefs and practices that had been central to my life. It has to be common ground that is universal and shared in this life. Probably Bonhoeffer's letters from prison had (and still have) a strong influence on me. *It is only by living completely in this world that one learns to believe. One must abandon every attempt to make something of oneself.*

Some Christian believers may want to dismiss my own interpretation of what happened as a sort of rationalization for leaving the religion. And admittedly there certainly was (and is) plenty of anger, fear, arrogance, self-absorption, and greed lurking in my mind. These states tend to be deeply suppressed in me, since it was always wrong for us to be angry or greedy and so forth (and so I became pretty good at not even recognizing these states in myself so that I would be able to evaluate myself overall as good). And such states unconsciously may indeed have been at work to undercut my religious beliefs. Maybe I was just plain angry in a suppressed way about having to be good all the time (not to mention having to worry about saving people all over the world) or about having lived in a sort of deprived way sexually or in other ways compared with those in the wider culture. Maybe my story is indeed some sort of rationalization for getting out of the narrow views. Or perhaps my obsession with the abstract stuff about God and salvation just got boring compared with living more fully without the filter of the religion.

Maybe so. But this was not what was consciously on my mind. For example, I didn't (and don't) *feel* angry or bitter—and the story I have told here is what was consciously in mind. The conscious process for me was driven by faith. My faith was guiding me. There is a persistent and discernible thread of love and joy, care and trust, going all the way back, and this definitely is the heart of it. The story of my shadow side probably would be more exciting than the conscious one, but my goal here has been to tell the story as it has unfolded so far in consciousness. Whatever unconscious forces may have been in play, they have been in complete harmony with the conscious process I have described.

Continuity

When the concept of God became idle, I would still sit quietly, sort of praying but without trying to formulate words or thoughts, simply listening in silence. So I started meditating in this way on my own several years before I had any idea about what was known about formal meditation methods in various cultures. I was in graduate school, doing work in logic and analytic philosophy. At the same time, I was beginning to learn to relax and communicate in sexual relationships. A hatha yoga class opened my body to the smooth flow of pleasurable, fine sensations of which we can be aware throughout our bodies. It was a natural step to become serious about mindfulness meditation (*vipassana*). All of this that came into my life—analytic philosophy, sexual opening, connecting with sensations in the body, intensive vipassana meditation retreats—all of these have, for me, been forms of waking up, and as such they are expansions of the process that began with the heart-opening experiences as a child.

There is quite a lot of continuity between my life now and my earlier practices as a Christian. John Wesley developed *methods* (which is why his followers are called Methodists) for developing a spiritual life through regular Bible study, reflection, and prayer. There is continuity between my praying each day as a child and the fact that I find it easy and natural to dive into new forms of meditation practice and check them out to see what value there might be. I did a solitary yearlong retreat a few years ago. I have explored many forms of meditation, including focused concentration, body-based mindfulness, vipassana, open awareness, loving-kindness, sharing joy, and many others.[11] There are even forms of meditation (Tibetan *deity* or *guru yoga*) that turn out to be similar in form to what I was doing in Sunday School when I was inviting Jesus into my heart![12]

An openness to what is real within my experience has been my path all along. I did not choose this path any more than I chose my body. My early heartwarming experiences drew me in deeply. These led to serious rational reflection about what is really going on. *It is so much better to unmask, to feel, than to pretend and pose. . . . It is only by living completely in this world. . . .* I cannot imagine my life as one in which I am clinging to the comforting thought that I am saved or chosen or otherwise safe as determined from some external perspective. Even though I was content with my own Christian faith, I could never have been comfortable or complacent within it because of the overwhelming imperative to convert people who were otherwise bound for hell, and, as I have explained, this urgency is what ultimately guided my own movement out of the formal religion. The specifically religious concepts definitely fell away completely, and I am not trying to reconceptualize any of it.

When I teach meditation methods, I have little to say about how meditative experience relates to metaphysics or salvation or enlightenment or future life fantasies or any of the other usual themes. *Well, if you are interested, see for yourself!* I am drawn to accounts of the Buddha that make him sound worldly and down to earth, much like Bonhoeffer, making his own radical break with the dogmatic forms of otherworld religiosity of the Indian culture of his time.[13] There was something in my own early religious practice that I have not lost, and I am grateful for it. I feel fortunate to have maintained this connection rather than have gone numb. The process of letting go of the beliefs was probably inevitable for me from the beginning since the propositional content is trivial in the light of the heart-warming experiences and other experiences that have come my way.

NINE 

An Atheist's Fundamentalism

James Tappenden

I am an atheist. In particular, I don't accept the truth of the Christian religion. Nor do I believe any other doctrine positing the existence of a supremely powerful intelligent being that intervenes in the course of nature, but I will be solely concerned with Christianity here. In fact, when I consider the truth of (say) the story of the resurrection as a factual question to be assessed according to the canons of evidence we use with more worldly questions of fact, I find it hard to take the question seriously. That's not, however, what this essay is about. The essay *is* about a different point that I learned about myself, somewhat to my surprise: I am a fundamentalist. What I mean by that is that I have a firm, though not altogether clear, conception of what it is that I am refraining from believing when I refrain from belief in the Christian religion. My aim in this essay is to indicate why I think it is important to pay Christianity the respect of rejecting precisely *that* conception rather than some hermeneutically cleansed, ecumenical surrogate.

A Story

There was a specific moment when I realized I was a fundamentalist in the sense I want to explain. I had suspected it previously, but this was a defining moment when it became clear that my belief had enough depth to unexpectedly take charge of my actions. I was surprised at the depth of feeling I discovered. I tell this story somewhat sheepishly, as one will when looking back over decades to recall the youthful naïveté that prompts one's better instincts to overrule one's sense of one's own interests. (I assure you I was a completely different person back then.)

Because of a complicated set of circumstances, including a rare intrusion of Fijian politics in my life, a new minister needed to be found at the last moment to officiate my wedding. Neither my fiancée, Michele, nor I had ever met the new minister, and so the day before the wedding we entered the minister's office for our first ever meeting and a required session of premarital counseling. In principle, though no doubt rarely in practice, this session could prompt the minister to refuse to officiate, if the couple appeared insufficiently Christian, by the standards of that parish or diocese, to participate in the sacrament of marriage. It was not a small wedding, and all the guests were in town, so a last-minute rescheduling was out of the question. Michele knew me well enough to anticipate complications, and so she had extracted assurances from me that I would be on my best behavior. (In the sense of "best behavior" of course, which means not "honest" or even "moral" but rather "tractable.")

The discussion began well enough. I kept my own counsel as Michele answered the questions about our expectations concerning the spiritual life of our family. On a couple of occasions I could feel the familiar stirring in my throat and tensing of my hand as the urge to express and punctuate an opinion suffused me, but I swallowed the urge. At some point, though, the minister asked me directly some variation on the question "Are you a Christian?" Michele had just answered the same question flawlessly, and in her case sincerely, by expanding on her enthusiasm for the social teachings that a politically committed reader might extract from the gospels, so I had the benefit of a crib. But I just couldn't keep myself from acknowledging what I took to be an obstacle. (A stumbling block, I might have said, though I retained at least the shred of prudence needed to keep scriptural allusions out of it.) To be a Christian, I suggested, required a belief that Christ was divine: that he was God incarnate, or at least that Christ's life represented a divine intercession that miraculously altered the course of nature. And (I felt I had to add) I didn't really believe that. To my surprise, and Michele's relief, the minister disagreed: it was the broader spiritual message of the gospels that mattered—the social teachings of Christ. I began to reply, but a few sentences into with what might have turned into an unintended conversion of our pastor, I noticed Michele's horrified look and felt her nudge. So I reverted to bland agreeableness—yes, of course, the social teachings—but it took an effort of will.

So the episode ended anticlimactically, but it did set me reflecting. What was it that surged up in me so powerfully when the question was put directly? It wasn't just a reluctance to identify myself as a Christian, because there was a sense of "Christian" that was offered and I'm sure with some ingenuity I could have found several variations on the liberal doctrine that I actually embrace, if they were sufficiently God-free. Part of my response involved not only a bedrock sense that I'm not a Christian, but also a visceral sense that secularized Christianity is fundamentally untrue to what it is to be a Christian. That was the moment when I realized I am a fundamentalist. There are very firm limits to the doctrine that I am not believing when I say I am not a believing Christian, and I take it to be very important that my decision should be the decision not to believe this rather than something else. Furthermore, it is important to me that this sense of what it is to be a Christian should not be obscured by a substitution of morality or social justice or generic spirituality for acceptance of the divinity of Christ. To accept such a substitute would be to fail to accord Christianity the respect it deserves.

The challenge I faced was to explain what—if anything—fundamentalism as I understood it amounted to. The negative doctrine of "no secular Christianity" is insufficient to give the stance content. But I found that as I attempted to give positive content to fundamentalism as I understood it, I came up either with views that deserved respect for reasons that are not unique to Christianity or else with views that I didn't regard as respectable. So I set out to clarify just what it was I took myself not to be believing when I rejected belief in Christianity, and why I took it that it was important to disbelieve precisely that rather than something else.

As often happens when we try to articulate the basis of a powerful but vaguely articulated reaction, I found the job more complex than I had anticipated, with many interwoven threads. One of the threads seemed easy for me to identify by superficial reflection: I've known and respected many sincere Christians, and at a visceral level I thought it disrespectful of those beliefs to shuffle them away by some hermeneutic trick. A large part of my reaction derived from the high regard I've had for many people in my life who embraced a sincere faith, and my recognition of the importance of this faith in their lives.

But my reaction couldn't be solely explained by a desire to be true to the beliefs of people I hold dear, since I had the opposite reaction to secular Christianity. I've also known and cared for many people whose emotional world was bound up with the kind of hermeneutically filtered religious view that interprets away benchmark doctrines like the divinity of Christ, replacing them with a progressive social message and an undifferentiated spirituality largely obliterating differences among religions. I also have a genuine respect and affection for many proponents of the *liberal* vision. But as my pre-wedding reaction witnessed, the fact that I know and respect many adherents of a liberal theology doesn't prompt me to take them to have gotten Christianity right, even when the incentive of narrow self-interest was nudged onto the scale. Indeed, I couldn't throw the sense that such ecumenical exercises in de-deification were missing what was important in Christian belief in particular. As Kierkegaard has put it, these hermeneutic exercises "leave everything standing but drain it of significance." Indeed, it seemed—and seems—to me that this sort of secular theology represents a kind of cheating and a slight to humanist morality: an effort to dress up a humanist moral vision in grander, blandly spiritual garb, with the implicit suggestion that the humanist moral vision alone is inadequate without the dressing. Perhaps this stance is ill considered, and in any event I'll not be defending it here. I mention it only to help bring out my attitude to fundamentalism by contrast.

My attitude toward a secularizing liberal theology—my sense of how it misrepresents something genuinely important—can be clarified with a couple of examples. Consider a loving parent who loses a child. Even though there is something universal in the experience, which is shared by all grieving parents, what matters to the parent is that specific child. To suggest that the grief is exhausted by what is universal in the experience is to miss what is most important. The same can be said when what is lost is not a beloved person or real thing but rather a motivating idea. Consider an aspiring athlete or artist who finally comes to acknowledge that he simply lacks the talent to attain the goal that has driven his life for a decade or more. Of course, we fail to respect the power of this loss if we treat it as just another career change or change of habits, but we also disrespect the loss if we acknowledge its force but are blithely neglectful of the specifics.

Of course, we don't always respect powerful emotional reactions: sometimes we take them as frivolous. If someone were to become distraught for weeks over the loss of a newspaper, we would take this to be an overreaction, unless the reaction turned out to be indirectly channeling some other emotion we take to be more serious. (Perhaps the paper was a last memento of a beloved, deceased relative.) Such distinctions of serious and frivolous are not sharp and are no doubt matters of degree, but we can make enough sense of them for the purposes of this paper. At bottom, my reaction derived from a sense that fundamentalist Christianity as I understand it addresses a serious psychological need and that we owe it to those who turn to it to at least properly characterize what it is that is addressing this need.

Atheistic Fundamentalism

Certainly, the label "fundamentalism" is tossed around frequently these days, and I'm using it in a somewhat nonstandard way. Since I don't have any other useful term ready to hand, I'll stick with "fundamentalism," but I should ward off misunderstandings from the outset. Fundamentalism as I understand it requires 1) a belief in the actual divinity of Christ, 2) acceptance of the view that Christ's life and divinity represent a miraculous intervention of divine causation to change the course of nature, and 3) that acceptance of the divinity of Christ (perhaps combined with other conditions) can prompt a divine act of transformation in the individual's moral status or character. I could add more, but I'll stick to these three tenets in this paper.

"Fundamentalism" about Christianity, as I understand the position, does not require belief in the literal truth of every line of the Old and New Testaments. I find such a view difficult to take seriously, and in fact I think that nearly nobody in practice adheres to fundamentalism so understood, though many people trumpet their embrace of some form of it. Let's consider for a moment what such a position would actually entail. One would need to embrace the divine inspiration of not only the original written scripture—including even notoriously suspicious bits like the complete shifting of gears at Mark 16:8—but also the infallibility of those who sifted the canon from the apocrypha, and perhaps even those who transmitted and copied the documents, and so on. Even the issue of "literal truth" hasn't been thought through with care. I dare say that we will find few defenders of the claim that when Christ says "I am the door" (John 10:9) he means he is, in fact, a door, through which people can literally walk in and out to (non-figuratively) find pastures. Rather, the literalist wants to maintain that a specific range of contested passages must be read literally: the question then becomes the one I'm addressing, that of finding the core that is not to be interpreted away.

Even if we set aside issues arising from the division of literal and figurative and the collation of canon and apocrypha, "fundamentalism" in the "every sentence literally true" sense is an empty label. The scriptures as they stand simply contain too much that no one today would be willing to defend (at least not publicly). Literalism also faces the moral reservations laid out compellingly in my colleague Elizabeth Anderson's contribution to this volume: to accept every jot and tittle of scripture requires an acceptance of the moral acceptability of genocide, among other things. I'll refer to Liz Anderson's paper for chapter and verse; I'll just observe that in the practice of those who proffer scriptural passages as resolving public policy questions, a variety of recorded divine instructions are quietly ignored, while favored texts are prominently advertised. On occasion, there are actual arguments presented for shrugging off (say) the texts advocating the stoning of adulterers just after the ones condemning homosexuals. (And indeed, combined with the unequivocal, wiggle-room-free injunction against divorce and remarriage (Matt. 19:9, Mark 10:11, etc.) this instructs us to stone to death the legion of multiply-married members of congress who fatuously presume to "defend" my marriage with silly, mean-spirited and irrelevant (to my marriage) legislation.) But such arguments are invariably embarrassingly weak and are clearly driven by a desire to conjure up anything resembling a reason to condemn homosexual activity, rather than being a distanced reflection on the message of scripture.

In other words, the illusion of a plausible "literalism" can be sustained only by a studious failure to notice all the picking and choosing that keeps it viable. There are no (or almost no) genuine fundamentalists in the "literal truth of every jot and tittle" sense, though there are many people who—by means of various kinds of double-think—think of themselves as fundamentalists in this sense, and appeal to such literalism for lazy rhetorical advantage.

It is crucial to distinguish how many different stances are bundled together in popular discussions of a "fundamentalism" set in opposition to the interpretative activity characteristic of liberal theology. One could hold, as I do, that belief in certain facts about the course of history must be embraced for one to be a Christian. The opposition to liberal theology consists in the view that these facts cannot be explained away, treated as figurative, or somehow interpreted out of the doctrine. The facts at issue are "hard" facts, so to speak. It is important to distinguish this core position from extensions of it. One could hold further that not only the facts but also some specific presentation of those facts is basic and does not admit further interpretation. For example, one might not only accept the existence and divinity of Christ but also that the presentation in (some version of) the gospels is true in all its particulars. It could further be held that the canonical presentation in scripture is complete—in that it leaves no significant moral dilemma unresolved. This additional step might be combined with the suggestion that the canonical presentation of the religious doctrine is a part of a simple moral algorithm: if you have a moral question, consult the canonical text, find the relevant instruction (which is in there somewhere), and act according to its unambiguous meaning. Extensions of the core position are often associated with the label "fundamentalism," but they go beyond what I'm discussing here.

A particular motive is often attributed to adherents of religious doctrines to which the label "fundamentalism" is attached: a discomfort with uncertainty, vagueness, or ambiguity. I have no doubt that such a psychological impulse drives some literalists. But it's important to see that one can be a fundamentalist in the sense I intend while tolerating a great deal of unclarity and even vagueness concerning what moral principles the core religious belief entails. It need not be that fundamentalism in this sense denigrates human reason to a simple pragmatic instrument for computing consequences from given principles. A fundamentalist in the admittedly perhaps nonstandard sense in which I'm using the term can believe that many moral decisions are underdetermined by the core factual beliefs about Christ's existence and divinity, and that substantive human reasoning is capable of ascertaining correct moral and even religious conclusions that go beyond the core beliefs.

The Human Importance of Christian Belief

There are many reasons that one might want to treat a religious belief with deference, even though one regards it as false. Many of these reasons apply to fundamentalist Christianity as I understand it. However, most of the reasons apply to secular beliefs as well; what I am aiming for is an indication of why fundamentalist Christianity as I understand it is worth respect for reasons distinctive to fundamentalist Christianity. For orientation, I'll separate out some generic reasons before proceeding.

There is, for example, a general social custom of adopting a certain hands-off attitude toward religion, both as a matter of good manners and a principle of public policy. Disdainful jokes about specific religions are seen as in bad taste. Conversations between penitent and confessor are legally privileged. Churches are exempted from taxes, a citizen can be forgiven certain social obligations like military service when the obligations conflict with his religious principles, and so on.

But these norms represent a deference to religion in general; both as a way to keep peace in society, and as an acknowledgment of the importance of religion in many people's lives, we make this special allowance.

On a more personal level, we may respect and defer to religious faith because we acknowledge the ways that many people draw strength from their faith, even under circumstances that might seem unbearable. We all recognize that it is no easy thing to cope with anguish, or to infuse one's life with a sense of purpose and value in the face of tragedy. Not surprisingly, ideas like the existence of an afterlife where we can rejoin loved ones, or the existence of a God who, in this afterlife, rewards the just and punishes the unjust in accordance with their merits (to mention just the two Kant deduced) have an uncommon power to console. If religious faith can play such a role in someone's life, it's only decent to leave well enough alone, even if one takes it to be obvious that the relevant beliefs are false. But of course, this is a consideration we're inclined to extend to false beliefs generally, even prosaic, non-miraculous ones with no religious import. If a grieving parent believes their child died a hero on the battlefield to whom hundreds of soldiers owed their lives and they find this belief to provide their only solace, it would be despicable to convince them otherwise, even if the overwhelming evidence suggested that his death was the result of cowardice and incompetence, or that he had poisoned himself and several of his comrades with toxic self-brewed moonshine. (These special free passes, of course, govern religious faith as a private matter. When specific details of religious doctrines are appealed to as justification for public policy decisions, or more generally as the basis for the treatment of others, the claims should be evaluated with the same standards of evidence we use for other factual claims in the public domain.)

One of the ways that Christianity, of course, gives emotional support to people is by providing the hope of a miracle. Naturally, this is true of many religions, but an apparently distinctive feature of Christianity is the cast it gives to miracles involving personal transformation, including some that are *conceptually* impossible. The point I'm aiming at has to be delineated carefully. The idea that we can receive divine aid to become different people is a staple of a variety of religious doctrines as well as the formless appeals to a "higher power" found in twelve-step therapies. Typically, these are quite straightforward hopes. For example, perhaps there is an ingrained and powerful habit or desire—such as a compulsion to drink or gamble, or a propensity to rage—that the believer needs to be free of and despairs of his ability to free himself by his own devices. (This particular hope for divine assistance isn't even a hope for a miracle in that it need not involve a violation of the laws of nature.) However, there are other times when the believer is not despairing of himself as he is made up but rather wishes to wash away some moral stain. This sort of desire, too, has many different forms and manifestations. In some cases a person may have done something shameful and now regrets it. If it were possible to change the past, the person would undo what was done, but this is not going to happen, and the person knows this. The desire for forgiveness involves a regret over the inescapability of the past. There is a variation on this scene that is more complicated: say that among the ramifications of the shameful act or acts are things that the despairing penitent *doesn't* want undone. In particular: what if the penitent has changed—become a different and better person—as a result of the actions he now is ashamed of?

This last possibility turns on the way that our past experiences and actions contribute to who we are. You can come to appreciate more deeply the importance of kindness by coming face to face with the aftermath of one of your own cruel acts, for example. People gain instruction in the value of truthfulness by dealing with the damage caused by the lies they tell. It is a recognized truism that we become practically competent by learning from our mistakes, but it is also true that moral maturity can draw from this source. In cases like this—if the penitent is clear-headed about the matter—repentance doesn't involve a simple wish that what had been done could be undone. Rather, it is a wish that the results of what was done should be *preserved* (at least those aspects of what was done that involve personal character) but that these specific bad actions should have a transformed moral significance.

Guilt and regret become especially complicated when what is regretted was a necessary condition for something that you don't—and shouldn't—want to give up, like a better character or ethical wisdom. An unjustly acquired fortune can be given away as part of an effort to make amends, but it would be strange to want to forgo deeper moral knowledge as part of an act of spiritual improvement. (Augustine is a compelling exemplar in part for this reason: though repenting of his libertine past, he didn't want to turn his back on the lessons it had taught him.) It is a recipe for an especially insidious kind of despair when you feel well-founded shame at actions whose very wrongness you recognize to have been indispensable in bringing about some of what you regard as the best part of yourself. In the face of this sort of despair, the message of Christian redemption is especially powerful. God intervenes in the course of history, in ways that include a divine transfiguration of the physical world: Christ, though manifestly human, was, in addition, divine. An analogous transformation—a washing away of sin—is offered to the sincere penitent who requests it. What is offered is a special kind of miracle: not a change in the physical events of the world, but a metaphysical change in the moral significance of one's own inner nature.

This kind of response to despairing over the self—as Kierkegaard might have put it—is a crucial feature of the Christian moral vision as I understand it (I don't want to assert dogmatically that it is distinctly Christian religion since I don't understand other religions well enough to say). This message of redemption by faith in a divine Christ addresses a serious psychological need, a need that is unaffected by alternatives that share the moral and social vision but lack the component of divine grace. Sometimes what we despair about requires not just a miracle, but a miracle of this specific type. As an atheist, I choose a different path. I can't choose to believe this, and so I find different ways to cope. But I understand why someone might be driven to choose differently.

Summing Up

Obviously, I haven't begun to give an exhaustive account of the motives for believing in the divinity of Christ: I've only gestured at one. But my aim has been to bring out why even someone who doesn't just disbelieve the core story of Christianity but finds it literally incredible might nonetheless want to make sure we get the story right. The doctrine of the miraculous divinity of Christ draws power from deep human needs that are untouched by secularized variations on Christian themes. The imperative to accurately present the doctrine that addresses these needs arises simply from a humanist's respect for human life and experience.

TEN 

Thank Goodness!

Daniel C. Dennett

There are no atheists in foxholes, according to an old but dubious saying, and there is at least a little anecdotal evidence in favor of it in the notorious cases of famous atheists who have emerged from near-death experiences to announce to the world that they have changed their minds. The British philosopher Sir A. J. Ayer, who died in 1989, is a fairly recent example. Here is another anecdote to ponder.

Two weeks ago, I was rushed by ambulance to a hospital, where it was determined by CT scan that I had a "dissection of the aorta"—the lining of the main output vessel carrying blood from my heart had been torn up, creating a two-channel pipe where there should only be one. Fortunately for me, the fact that I'd had a coronary artery bypass graft seven years ago probably saved my life, since the tangle of scar tissue that had grown like ivy around my heart in the intervening years reinforced the aorta, preventing catastrophic leakage from the tear in the aorta itself. After a nine-hour surgery, in which my heart was stopped entirely and my body and brain were chilled down to about forty-five degrees to prevent brain damage from lack of oxygen until they could get the heart–lung machine pumping, I am now the proud possessor of a new aorta and aortic arch, made of strong Dacron fabric tubing sewn into shape on the spot by the surgeon, attached to my heart by a carbon-fiber valve that makes a reassuring little click every time my heart beats.

As I now enter a gentle period of recuperation, I have much to reflect on about the harrowing experience itself and even more about the flood of supporting messages I've received since word got out about my latest adventure. Friends were anxious to learn if I had had a near-death experience, and if so, what effect it had had on my longstanding public atheism. Had I had an epiphany? Was I going to follow in the footsteps of Ayer (who recovered his aplomb and, in an article in the *Spectator,* insisted a few days later "what I should have said is that my experiences have weakened, not my belief that there is no life after death, but my inflexible attitude towards that belief"), or was my atheism still intact and unchanged?

Yes, I did have an epiphany. I saw with greater clarity than ever before in my life that when I say "Thank goodness!" this is not merely a euphemism for "Thank God!" (We atheists don't believe that there is any God to thank.) I really do mean *thank goodness!* There is a lot of goodness in this world, and more goodness every day, and this fantastic human-made fabric of excellence is genuinely responsible for the fact that I am alive today. It is a worthy recipient of the gratitude I feel today, and I want to celebrate that fact here and now.

To whom, then, do I owe a debt of gratitude? To the cardiologist who has kept me alive and ticking for years and who swiftly and confidently rejected the original diagnosis of nothing worse than pneumonia. To the surgeons, neurologists, anesthesiologists, and perfusionist who kept my systems going for many hours under daunting circumstances. To the dozen or so physician assistants, and to nurses and physical therapists and x-ray technicians and a small army of phlebotomists so deft that you hardly know they are drawing your blood, and the people who brought the meals, kept my room clean, did the mountains of laundry generated by such a messy case, wheel-chaired me to x-ray, and so forth. These people came from Uganda, Kenya, Liberia, Haiti, the Philippines, Croatia, Russia, China, Korea, India–and the United States, of course–and I have never seen more impressive mutual respect, as they helped each other out and checked each other's work. But for all their teamwork, this local gang could not have done their jobs without the huge background of contributions from others. I remember with gratitude my late friend and Tufts colleague, the physicist Allan Cormack, who shared the Nobel Prize for his invention of the CT scanner. Allan—you have posthumously saved yet another life, but who's counting? The world is better for the work you did. Thank goodness. Then there is the whole system of medicine, both the science and the technology, without which the best-intentioned efforts of individuals would be roughly useless. So I am grateful to the editorial boards and referees, past and present, of *Science, Nature, Journal of the American Medical Association, Lancet,* and all the other institutions of science and medicine that keep churning out improvements, detecting and correcting flaws.

Do I *worship* modern medicine? Is science my *religion*? Not at all; there is no aspect of modern medicine or science that I would exempt from the most rigorous scrutiny, and I can readily identify a host of serious problems that still need to be fixed. That's easy to do, of course, because the worlds of medicine and science are already engaged in the most obsessive, intensive, and humble self-assessments yet known to human institutions, and they regularly make public the results of their self-examinations. Moreover, this open-ended rational criticism, imperfect as it is, is the secret of the astounding success of these human enterprises. There are measurable improvements every day. Had I had my blasted aorta a decade ago, there would have been no prayer of saving me. It's hardly routine today, but the odds of my survival were actually not so bad (these days, roughly 33 percent of aortic dissection patients die in the first twenty-four hours after onset without treatment, and the odds get worse by the hour thereafter).

One thing in particular struck me when I compared the medical world on which my life now depended with the religious institutions I have been studying so intensively in recent years. One of the gentler, more supportive themes to be found in every religion (so far as I know) is the idea that what really matters is what is in your heart: if you have good intentions, and are trying to do what (God says) is right, that is all anyone can ask. Not so in medicine! If you are wrong—especially if you should have known better—your good intentions count for almost nothing. And whereas taking a leap of faith and acting without further scrutiny of one's options is often celebrated by religions, it is considered a grave sin in medicine. A doctor whose devout faith in his personal revelations about how to treat aortic aneurysm led him to engage in untested trials with human patients would be severely reprimanded if not driven out of medicine altogether. There are exceptions, of course. A few swashbuckling, risk-taking pioneers are tolerated and (if they prove to be right) eventually honored, but they can exist only as rare exceptions to the ideal of the methodical investigator who scrupulously rules out alternative theories before putting his own into practice. Good intentions and inspiration are simply not enough.

In other words, whereas religions may serve a benign purpose by letting many people feel comfortable with the level of morality they themselves can attain, no religion holds its members to the high standards of moral responsibility that the secular world of science and medicine does! And I'm not just talking about the standards "at the top"—among the surgeons and doctors who make life or death decisions every day. I'm talking about the standards of conscientiousness endorsed by the lab technicians and meal preparers, too. This tradition puts its faith in the *unlimited* application of reason and empirical inquiry, checking and re-checking, and getting in the habit of asking, "What if I'm wrong?" Appeals to faith or membership are never tolerated. Imagine the reception a scientist would get if he tried to suggest that others couldn't replicate his results because they just didn't share the faith of the people in his lab! And, to return to my main point, it is the goodness of this tradition of reason and open inquiry that I thank for my being alive today.

What, though, do I say to those of my religious friends (and yes, I have quite a few religious friends) who have had the courage and honesty to tell me that they have been praying for me? I have gladly forgiven them, for there are few circumstances more frustrating than not being able to help a loved one in any more direct way. I confess to regretting that I could not pray (sincerely) for my friends and family in time of need, so I appreciate the urge, however clearly I recognize its futility. I translate my religious friends' remarks readily enough into one version or another of what my fellow brights have been telling me: "I've been thinking about you, and wishing with all my heart (another ineffective but irresistible self-indulgence) that you come through this OK."[1] The fact that these dear friends *have* been thinking of me in this way, and have taken an effort to let me know, is in itself, without any need for a supernatural supplement, a wonderful tonic. These messages from my family and from friends around the world have been literally heartwarming in my case, and I am grateful for the boost in morale (to truly manic heights, I fear!) that it has produced in me. But I am not joking when I say that I have had to forgive my friends who said that they were *praying* for me. I have resisted the temptation to respond, "Thanks, I appreciate it, but did you also sacrifice a goat?" I feel about this the same way I would feel if one of them said, "I just paid a voodoo doctor to cast a spell for your health." What a gullible waste of money that could have been spent on more important projects! Don't expect me to be grateful, or even indifferent. I do appreciate the affection and generosity of spirit that motivated you but wish you had found a more reasonable way of expressing it.

But isn't this awfully harsh? Surely, it does the world no harm if those who can honestly do so pray for me! No, I'm not at all sure about that. For one thing, if they *really* wanted to do something useful, they could devote their prayer time and energy to some pressing project that they *can* do something about. For another, we now have quite solid grounds (e.g., the recently released Benson study at Harvard) for believing that intercessory prayer simply doesn't work. Anybody whose practice shrugs off that research is subtly undermining respect for the very goodness I am thanking. If you insist on keeping the myth of the effectiveness of prayer alive, you owe the rest of us a justification in the face of the evidence. Pending such a justification, I will excuse you for indulging in your tradition; I know how comforting tradition can be. But I want you to recognize that what you are doing is morally problematic at best. If you would even *consider* filing a malpractice suit against a doctor who made a mistake in treating you, or suing a pharmaceutical company that didn't conduct all the proper control tests before selling you a drug that harmed you, you must acknowledge your tacit appreciation of the high standards of rational inquiry to which the medical world holds itself, and yet you continue to indulge in a practice for which there is no known rational justification at all and take yourself to be actually making a contribution. (Try to imagine your outrage if Pfizer responded to your suit by blithely replying, "But we prayed good and hard for the success of the drug! What more do you want?")

The best thing about saying *thank goodness* in place of *thank God* is that there really are lots of ways of repaying your debt to goodness—by setting out to create more of it, for the benefit of those to come. Goodness comes in many forms, not just medicine and science. Thank goodness for the music of, say, Randy Newman, which could not exist without all those wonderful pianos and recording studios, to say nothing of the musical contributions of every great composer from Bach through Wagner to Scott Joplin and the Beatles. Thank goodness for fresh drinking water in the tap, and food on our table. Thank goodness for fair elections and truthful journalism. If you want to express your gratitude to goodness, you can plant a tree, feed an orphan, buy books for schoolgirls in the Islamic world, or contribute in thousands of other ways to the manifest improvement of life on this planet now and in the near future.

Or you can thank God—but the very idea of repaying God is ludicrous. What could an omniscient, omnipotent Being (the Man Who has Everything?) do with any paltry repayments from you? (And besides, according to the Christian tradition, God has already redeemed the debt for all time, by sacrificing his own son. Try to repay *that* loan!) Yes, I know, those themes are not to be understood *literally;* they are symbolic. I grant it, but then the idea that by thanking God you are actually doing some good has got to be understood to be just symbolic, too. I prefer real good to symbolic good.

Still, I excuse those who pray for me. I see them as like tenacious scientists who resist the evidence for theories they don't like long after a graceful concession would have been the appropriate response. I applaud you for your loyalty to your own position—but remember: loyalty to tradition is not enough. You've got to keep asking yourself: What if I'm wrong? In the long run, I think religious people can be asked to live up to the same moral standards as secular people in science and medicine.

PART TWO

Reflections

ELEVEN

Transcendence without God: On Atheism and Invisibility

Anthony Simon Laden

> "Feare of power invisible, feigned by the mind, or imagined from tales publicly allowed, Religion; not allowed, Superstition."
> —Thomas Hobbes, *Leviathan,* chapter 6

> "I am invisible, understand, simply because people refuse to see me."
> —Ralph Ellison, *Invisible Man*

This essay is about seeing, about what to look for, and what difference that might make. I start, however, with a story that helps explain the nature of my own atheism.

At the heart of Aristotle's *Nicomachean Ethics* lies a puzzle that no one who wishes to teach it can ignore. Aristotle tells us that the aim of his book is to investigate what form of life is the "best for man." He then devotes almost the entire book to a discussion of the life of moral virtue, seemingly arguing that such a life is the best life. In the final sections of the book, however, he appears to change his mind and very quickly concludes that a life of contemplation, of the exercise of intellectual virtue, is in fact the best life, better than the active life of moral virtue. The puzzle, then, is how to make sense of these final pages. Were they a mistake, not meant to appear in a text that, after all, was assembled by his students and has had a complex and not unbroken history? Was it a merely self-serving but essentially ad hoc addition that allows the author to put himself at the top of the heap, claiming with satisfaction that the philosopher leads the best life? Or can one find hints that this is what was coming all along, so that the discussion of moral virtue is, after all, merely a preparation and a prelude to the final conclusion in favor of philosophy? Clearly, this final alternative would make the text more coherent, not to mention more interesting, but it can be hard work figuring out how to make that case. It was not until I was in the middle of teaching the *Ethics* for the third time that I came upon a strategy that I liked for solving this problem.

To understand what any of this has to do with atheism, you need to know two more points about Aristotle's *Ethics.* First, Aristotle argues that the best life for a human being will be a life that is also the most human life, the life that exhibits to the highest degree whatever it is that makes us human. So, if the life of contemplation is going to win out over the life of moral virtue, it must express our humanity in a deeper or more accurate way. Second, to say that a particular kind of life is the best life is not meant to be taken in a stuffy, morally uptight, righteous kind of way. Aristotle thinks that the best life will also be the most pleasant. So making the case for the life of contemplation as the best life requires showing what would be so great about it. And in my case, it required making that case to a bunch of undergraduates at the end of a long and difficult term. That is, to people who were not terribly well positioned to feel the attractions of the life of the mind.

As I have come to understand Aristotle's *Ethics,* a key idea that runs through the entire work is that of attention. What turns out to distinguish virtuous from less exalted forms of activity has to do with the way a virtuous person pays attention to his surroundings and what he is doing. Part of what makes temperance or moderation in eating and drinking a virtue, according to this reading of Aristotle, is that the temperate person attends to the right qualities of what he eats and drinks. He notices the qualities that make good food good, and that make fine dining experiences truly enjoyable. Since these do not include excess, gluttony does not even tempt him. Similarly, the courageous or just person or the virtuous friend attends to the right aspects of his interactions with others, acting on the basis of the properly salient characteristics of the situation. His excellence, therefore, lies in large part in what Aristotle describes as his perception. Note, however, that the ability to pay attention to the right things in the right ways is a good candidate for a distinctively human capacity. It involves reflection, not merely the registering of external stimuli. To attend to certain details, I must see them in a certain way, I must direct my attention toward them, and do so under a certain conception of why they matter, why they are the right details to be taking notice of. We can then begin to understand what is so wonderful about the virtuous life in terms of the attention it involves. In particular, a life of moral virtue gets its excellence from two directions. The morally virtuous person exercises his capacity for attention excellently. That is, he does what humans do, and does it well. In addition, those things to which his attention is drawn repay such excellent attentiveness. They are, we might say, worthy of even the excellent attention of the virtuous person. To see what this characteristic comes to, think of the difference between a fine meal and a fast-food burger and fries, between great music and a commercial jingle, between a friendship and a mere acquaintance.

Understanding the value of a life of moral virtue in terms of attention allows us to see why a life of contemplation would be even better. Basically, what Aristotle calls a life of contemplation involves attending to those things that are most perfect, most beautiful, most worthy of and able to hold our attention. And this is where my own atheism enters the picture. The first time I came to understand

Aristotle in this manner was while teaching him. Standing in front of a dozen undergraduates, I laid out the argument above and then tried to get them to feel its pull. I told them to imagine something of inexhaustible beauty and interest, something you could think about and pay attention to constantly and for your whole life without ever finding it boring or uninteresting, something whose interest for you would continually unfold and reveal new aspects and details and delights. As sometimes happens when I am really in the grip of a point, I went into a kind of rapture, trying with my words to call forth in front of them something that would give them an inkling of the joys that could be had in its contemplation. In my own mind, as perhaps in Aristotle's, the objects that held that space were the objects of philosophy: the mysteries of reality, the human condition, the universe. To drive home the point that a life of contemplation could really be the most pleasant, I told them to imagine that, having found something to which you could devote infinite and ever-increasing and ever more pleasant attention, you were told that you were being given the option of spending your entire life contemplating it. "Wouldn't that be the best life?" I asked.

Later that day, one of my students came by my office to talk to me about a paper. Before he left, though, he said that my lecture had really struck a chord with him. His mother, he said, was a religious Christian, and he said that my description of Aristotle's contemplative life reminded him of her understanding of what paradise would be like: an eternity spent gazing on the face of God.

Until he spoke those words, God had not entered my thoughts, had not been on my radar screen, and yet the moment he said that, it was clear to me that he was right: the rapture I had tried to make real for my students with a description of a life of intellectual activity and contemplation was, in essence, no different from the rapture that many religious believers imagine await them in heaven: an eternity contemplating the face of God.

I take this story to capture something central to my atheism: it is neither a conscious rejection of belief in God, nor a rejection of the possibility or desirability of a form of transcendence or rapture that takes me outside of myself or beyond myself. It is merely the absence of God on my imaginative landscape as a possible source of such things. God, for me, as perhaps for Hobbes, is invisible in a very particular sense: God plays no role in my imaginative, reflective, or even emotional understanding of or engagement with the world around me. God, I might say, never seriously occurs to me. Later that same week, I told this story to a friend and colleague of mine who is a very observant Jew. I told it to him as a story about the depth of my atheism. Upon hearing it, however, he told me that he thought it showed the depth of my religiosity. Though the thought of God had not been the source of my rapture, it was my capacity to feel that way and find the importance of that idea in Aristotle that he took to be the central moral of the story. According to him, I was a kind of religious atheist.

Because "religious atheist" has too much of the ring of the paradoxical about it, and because I don't want the meaning of religion to be a topic of discussion here, I'll rephrase this by saying that I am an atheist who nonetheless values transcendence and thinks that experiences of transcendence are one of the things that make life worth living. Sorting out exactly what this means, how it is possible, and why it leads me to atheism rather than to God will be the work of the rest of this essay, and bring me back to the two quotes that serve as its epigraphs.

Let me start by distinguishing between transcendence as a property of objects (possibly including beings like gods or persons) and transcendence as a property of experiences. An object has the property of transcendence insofar as it exceeds, in some way or other, the ordinary human realm. Similarly, experiences have the property of transcendence when they somehow go beyond our ordinary experiences, when they somehow draw us out of and beyond ourselves. We can then pose the question about the relationship of religious belief and transcendence more precisely as follows: Is it possible to have a genuinely transcendent experience (the sort that gives value and meaning to your life) without experiencing a transcendent object? Now, the natural answer to this question is no. The assumption that transcendent experiences must involve experiences of transcendent objects leads to what I will call the proximity view of transcendence. The proximity view holds that our lives gain meaning and value from the experience of transcendent objects, be they divine beings, vistas of extraordinary natural beauty or transcendentally beautiful works of art. Now, on the proximity view, it should be obvious why belief in God, and the various religious and moral and life-orienting actions that flow from that belief will lend value to one's life. Gods are by definition greater than us, beyond the realm of ordinary human experience; and the God of Judaism, Christianity and Islam is not merely better than us, but is a kind of incarnation of perfection itself. What could be more transcendent than that? A fervent belief in God, the sort that is intimately tied to religious devotion, is then a sure-fire path to transcendence on the proximity view. Moreover, if this is your conception of the path to and value of transcendence in human life, then any other attempt to move beyond the confines of a single ordinary human life will pale in comparison.

But the proximity view can seem mysterious when we start to think about it. If what we are looking for is a way to lead our lives that infuses them with meaning and purpose, then it can seem odd that the experience of something bigger and better than ourselves will do that. To see this point, take something short of divinity that is nevertheless beyond the ordinarily human: some great vista of natural beauty, or some work of art of extraordinary power and beauty. Now imagine that you lived close to it, so you experienced it daily: it was the view you saw when you looked out your bedroom window, the sounds you heard as you went about your daily routine. This regular experience would make your life go better in all sorts of non-trivial ways, no doubt. But why should the mere experience of extraordinary objects infuse your life with meaning in a way that would be inconceivable without it?

One natural response is to say that the proximity of such a thing to your ordinary routines would change those routines, and those changes would be the source of the added value and meaning of your life. There are at least two ways this might happen. First, it might be that what is transcendent about the experience of transcendent objects is something about the quality of the experience itself. What you actually experience when, opening your bedroom curtains each morning, you are confronted with the beautiful vista is different from what you would experience if confronted with a more ordinary view. The quality of your attention changes, develops. Second, the changes might extend beyond the quality of the experience itself. You might be moved to preserve the breathtaking natural vista just outside your front door, and this commitment to conservation would give your life meaning. You might be moved to study and reflect on the great work of art or architecture, and this investigation and contemplation would give your life meaning. Coming close to God through fervent belief would similarly move you to a life of religious commitment, to ordering your life around His commandments, or spreading His message, and it is these activities that would add meaning to your life. We might describe such activities, as some religious believers do, as being pursued in the light of God. On this line of thinking, our activity takes on a kind of heightened significance because of its (and our) relation to God.

Notice, however, that both of these responses move us away from the proximity view. If what adds meaning to my life are the actions and endeavors I am led to undertake as a result of my proximity to some transcendent object, even when those centrally involve the activity of experiencing itself, then the mere proximity is not what adds value to my life. The added value my life takes on comes from how I live it, not what lies in its neighborhood. This thought, however, leads to the second conception of the relation of transcendent experience to transcendent objects.

I will call this second conception of the value of transcendence the activity view. Here the thought is that the experiences of transcendence that give meaning to our lives are not experiences of something outside of ourselves to which we can be closer or further away, but a kind of activity that results from our orientation to the world around us. The activity view brings us back to the opening quotes about invisibility and back to Aristotle. I will argue that the activity view rests on the thought that the transcendent experiences that can infuse a life with meaning and value involve seeing what is otherwise invisible, yet nevertheless worthy of our attention. This claim requires some clarification. In particular, we need to distinguish two senses of invisibility.

First, an object can be invisible to me if it is somehow hidden from my view, either because I am physically blocked from seeing it or because of what Ellison describes as the construction of my "inner eye." In either of these cases, the object's invisibility is a fact about my vision, not its ontological status. Second, an object can be invisible to me if it isn't really there. In this case, its invisibility is primarily a fact about it, not my capacity to see it. Of course, from my point of view, these two sources of invisibility look the same. And this poses an ongoing problem. We learn at an early age that the mere fact that something is hidden from sight does not imply that it is not there. Rather young infants continue to focus their attention on an object even after it has been hidden behind a parent's back, and they even alter their perspective so as to bring it back into view. So we know that sometimes, looking for invisible objects is a worthwhile task. At the same time, however, the invisibility of an object is a powerful reason to doubt its existence, and often a good one. I can be pretty sure that my failure to see a pink elephant sitting on my desk sipping a lemonade means that there is no such elephant there, not that he has merely decided to be invisible so as not to disturb my concentration. Whereas the infant's craning her neck to look behind her father's back to see what became of the teddy bear is a sign of dawning comprehension of the world and a tenacious will to understand, my attempt to see that pesky elephant on my desk, to make him visible, will likely be taken by those around me as a sign of just the opposite: my increasingly unsteady grip on reality.

But the realm of invisible objects is a whole lot richer and more complex than the hidden teddy bear and the non-existent pink elephant might indicate. To a large degree, we see what we are conditioned to see, what we expect to see, and this is a result of the "construction of our inner eyes." And this means that part of the invisible realm includes that which is somehow beyond our ordinary experience, the mundane sights and sounds of our ordinary day-to-day lives. In other words, among the things that are normally invisible to us are all those things that I described above as transcendent objects, as being beyond the scope of ordinary human experience. Since, once seen, these objects are able to pull us out of ourselves, to lead us beyond the confines of our everyday lives, to give meaning to our lives, it makes sense to describe the activity view in terms of coming to see that which is invisible. In the case of transcendent objects, it is clear that the struggle to see in this way is just the struggle to move beyond the borders of our ordinary experience and tap into something extraordinary.

But such transcendent objects make up only part of the invisible realm. A great deal of that which is invisible to us is hidden from view while nevertheless being right there in plain sight. The infant learns to move her head to the side to see the teddy bear again. But something different is needed if I am to see the hidden beauty in a stranger's kind expression, or the full humanity of those I pass by casually everyday. In such cases, seeing the invisible will require something closer to understanding. I will have to learn to see differently, in part by training myself to pay attention to aspects of what I see that have been invisible, to see them as worthy of my attention. According to the activity view, it is this activity itself that yields the transcendent experience insofar as engaging in it pulls me out of and beyond my ordinary experience. I can learn to see my ordinary life and its ordinary surroundings as extraordinary. If there are non-transcendent objects that are both invisible and worthy of my attention, then this transcendent experience need not be an experience of transcendent objects.

Of course, it can. The activity view also suggests that a fervent belief in God will be a path to transcendent experience. After all, it is the fervent believer who strives to see in the world around her the manifestations of God's existence, to make what Hobbes described as a "power Invisible" visible. It is also the fervent believer in God who tries to make God manifest through her actions, to bring about the kingdom of heaven, to fulfill the commandments, and thus to make God visible. Sometimes, these connections go in reverse: one comes to a fervent belief in God by coming to see some occurrence as miraculous, not merely extraordinary: as a manifestation of God's existence. Whatever the direction of causation, such examples suggest that the fervent believer in God gives meaning to her life not because she is close to a transcendent being, but because she struggles to see what is invisible yet worthy of her attention, to see what is revealed by looking at the world in the light of God.

My point, however, is that the activity view suggests that religious belief is neither the only path to transcendent experience nor one that is obviously superior to its rivals. As the quote from Ellison reminds us, God is not the only "invisible" entity in our universe that is worthy of our attention. There are lots more who are closer to hand. And if the activity view is correct, then the attempt to see such invisible entities can also give the same kind of meaning and value to our life that the fervent believer gets from her religious devotion. We have already seen one path to such transcendent experience in the form of Aristotle's life of contemplation, and I think Aristotle does have something like the activity view in the back of his mind when he concludes that the life of contemplation is the best life. After all, he also claimed that philosophy begins in wonder, and this suggests that he would be happy with a description of philosophy as the practice of seeing the hitherto invisible. But in the rest of this essay I want to focus on a different path, suggested by the quote from Ellison.

Here, we need to take a detour into recent critical race theory. Ellison's metaphor of invisibility continues to resonate with people who try to describe the effects of oppressive social systems on both their victims and those in the oppressor class, and it is common for scholars of critical race theory to invoke the image of invisibility. Ellison claimed that in a racist society, those classified as black were made invisible. In particular, their personality, their status as persons, as those who were owed certain forms of respect, was not seen by whites. Those who are thus made invisible by their society are, in the words of the philosopher Charles Mills, "sub-persons": "the peculiar status of a sub-person is that it is an entity which, because of phenotype, seems (from, of course, the perspective of the categorizer) human in some respects but not in others. It is a human . . . who, though adult, is not fully a person."[1] The invisibility of the sub-person means that her suffering does not count, that her lack of freedom is not oppression, that her expression is not speech that needs to be protected or art worthy of celebration and admittance into the ranks of culture. The depth and meaning and pathos of the lives of invisible people are thus hidden from the view of the visible people, the full persons, and also, very often, from other invisible people and even from themselves; they thus escape the normal attention of people; they lie beyond their ordinary experience.

In the case of systematic oppression on the basis of race, gender, class, or other broad categories, the invisibility of the oppressed group is deeply built into the variety of cultural and social attitudes and expectations that set the horizons of what is considered ordinary and normal. Thus, to stay with the case of race, part of what is meant by saying that those classified as black are invisible is that white people implicitly equate being human with being white, producing art or culture or history or meaning as doing things the way they do them (and non-white people are taught or encouraged or forced to follow suit). So, people with dark skin can be acknowledged as being human, or producing culture, as long as what they do fits within the familiar confines of the ordinary experience of white folk. The meaning of the invisibility of members of oppressed groups is that those of their behaviors, expressions, feelings, thoughts, theories, and experiences that fall outside the boundaries of the ordinary (white) world are not seen as, understood as, being worthy of the attention that human activity merits.

Striving to make visible those people who are rendered invisible by our society, then, can be a path to transcendent experience. It involves seeing personality, subjectivity, and all the vast interest that a human life can contain in people and places where we have been trained not to expect to find them. It thus involves a broadening of our vision, a widening of the world of interest and attention for us. Through such efforts, we can make the ordinary world around us light up with its extraordinary qualities. We do this, however, not merely by widening the domain of beings to whom we pay attention in the way we have learned to pay attention to those we regard as persons. We also need to broaden our understanding of what it means to be a person. Seeing the invisible involves seeing the heretofore invisible on their own terms, understanding their ways of being human as ways of being human, even when these are perhaps radically different from what is defined as familiar by our society, and which we have learned to take as the standard of humanity. It thus leads us to an appreciation of perhaps radical difference as something to be embraced and attended to, as something worth looking out for and learning to see. In so doing, it may lead us to see ourselves and our lives in a new light as well. A life that is oriented around developing this kind of sight, then, can be as imbued with transcendent experience and thus with meaning and value as one devoted to making manifest the presence of God in the world.

At this point, however, the astute and skeptical reader will have many worries. Let me try to assuage some of them. First, it may look as if I have smuggled back in the idea of transcendent objects lying at the root of transcendent experiences insofar as I have focused on seeing invisible *people.* If, as Kant argued, persons have infinite worth, then they too will count as transcendent objects, and the transcendence of the experience of seeing invisible persons can be explained on the proximity view. Whether or not persons count as transcendent objects, however, my claim is that the transcendent experience that comes from learning to see invisible people arises from the activity itself, and not directly from the properties of what is seen. All that has to be true in order for the activity of seeing invisible persons to afford those who engage in it a transcendent experience is that invisible people are worthy of our attention.

It is important to note at this point that I am not trying to argue about how or why to be moral. I am interested, rather, in showing how a life without God can nevertheless be infused with transcendent experiences that give it value and meaning. I do think that other persons are particularly worthy of our attention and that attending to them leads to moral action, but neither of those beliefs need be true to establish the point I want to make in this essay.

Second, the last several paragraphs have talked about the value that might be added to a life by striving to see invisible people. One might wonder, however, whether this is a path open only to the oppressors. That is, as described above, it is primarily members of the oppressor class who are blind, and whose lack of vision condemns the oppressed group to invisibility. If transcendence is to be gained through an effort to see, is it a path open only to the dominant group?

I don't think so. The social systems that render some people invisible work on the invisible people themselves. Part of what it means to be invisible, then, is to doubt your own status as a person, to doubt, in Ellison's words, "your own existence." So the work of making visible the invisible can involve finding ways to make yourself visible to others, and this may involve learning to see yourself and your action as visible, or perhaps as not naturally invisible, but rendered that way by a society in need of change. Such work can also be a path to transcendent experience. Coming to see yourself and your actions as fully human, whether or not you are oppressed, involves seeing them as connected to the whole complex tapestry of collective human life and history. It involves understanding that you fit into something larger than yourself, that you are not just an isolated individual, existentially cut off from those other instantiations of your species. It involves, for instance, showing that your speech is speech, has meaning, and is not just mere noise. But speech has meaning because others understand it, because it partakes of and (re)-constructs an irreducibly social system of language.

A slightly different worry might be expressed thus: even if the path to transcendence is open to both oppressor and oppressed, it does seem to involve some pre-existing invisibility, and that seems to suggest that humans could only pursue this secular path to transcendence in a world marked by severe injustice. If that were true, it would make this project dodgy at best, self-defeating at worst. Once again, however, this worry misses the mark. While the sorts of systematic oppression that Ellison describes bring out the role of invisibility in human interaction most starkly, the underlying problem of others' invisibility to us, and our invisibility to ourselves are permanent features of the human condition, independent of whether that condition is also marked by oppression. First, part of what renders people invisible to others is their mere anonymity. In the course of our daily lives, we may treat most other people we encounter as invisible, failing to fully attend to their humanity. So part of the work of seeing invisible people does not depend on overcoming systematic oppression and the forms of attention it leads us to develop. Part of the work just involves opening ourselves up to the full humanity of all those around us. But I think the quest to see invisible people goes deeper than this, and that the connection with oppression is important to make this further aspect clear.

To see this further point, note the connection between the problem of invisibility and two more-standard philosophical problems: alienation and skepticism. Someone who is socially visible in a world where others are socially invisible will be perennially faced with skepticism. How does he know there isn't more out there than he is seeing? And if that is a possibility, then how does he even know that what he sees is what is out there, and not merely his own projection? In the face of the terror that can come from unbridled skepticism, some will turn to faith, to an insistence that the invisible is there, whether or not it will reveal itself in plain sight. But another response to skepticism is a turn to a kind of Aristotelian training and effort to improve our capacity for seeing, for attending to that which is around us. Learning to trust our vision will require an act of faith, and faith always involves a leap, but that leap can be made more manageable if we work to train and develop our senses, if we work to see what was once invisible.

On the other hand, someone who is socially invisible will be faced with alienation. He will doubt his own existence because nothing and no one around him will provide him evidence of that existence. No one will treat him as if he matters, no one will recognize his speech as speech, his cries as signs of pain or suffering or injustice, his productions as part of culture. But a world that fails to reflect us in any way is a world in which we are doomed to feel always foreign, a stranger, as if we do not belong. It is a world from which we are alienated. Once again, the terror of alienation can lead to faith, the comforting faith that our pain is part of a larger plan, or that it is but a vale of tears to be passed through on the way to an eternity where we will have a place. But it can also lead to an effort at both seeing the world anew and working to change it.

A world in which people are divided into oppressed and oppressor is a world where some people are socially positioned to fall prey to alienation and others are socially positioned to fall prey to skepticism. But in a more just world, these problems do not disappear; they merely get mixed up. Part of the human condition involves both being alone and being with others. We are each single persons, locked in our bodies, looking out at the world and at others. From that perspective, the world and other people can seem very far away, impossibly out of reach, beyond our vision, our actions, our words. That is the root of skepticism. But we are also social creatures, existing in a complex web of relationships structured by language and reason and common action. From that perspective, we can sometimes get lost in the flood of humanity of which we form but an insignificant part. That is the root of alienation.

On that description, then, combating the problems of alienation and skepticism is part and parcel of being human. The struggle to see that which is invisible, and in particular, to see the sometimes invisible humanity of ourselves and others, is one way of responding to these inextricably human problems, and so it is not dependent on oppressive social systems to have meaning. In making this argument, which moves from the special condition of racially oppressed people to general features of the human condition, we need to exercise care. The argument above claims that an analysis of the condition of the racially oppressed can throw general aspects of the human condition into relief. It does not claim that it is a general feature of the human condition to be racially oppressed, that racism thus oppresses us all. Racism harms us all, but it does not oppress us all.

So far I have claimed that we can imbue our lives with purpose and meaning through transcendent experience that arises from the activity of trying to see what would otherwise be invisible, and I have suggested that this can be done in a theistic way, when the invisible entity we strive to see is God; and in a secular way, when the invisible entities we strive to see are our fellow human beings. Now, clearly, these two projects can overlap. The theistic effort to see God often translates into a moral effort to treat the humanity of others properly, to see our fellow human beings as also made in God's image, or as one of God's creatures. My point, though, is that the transcendence of each pathway is independent of the other, and so the secular path need not rely on the theistic one for its underlying value.

But I have also said that I am an atheist, and to the extent I strive to give my life meaning via one of these paths, it is the secular one that guides me. Is this merely a matter of taste or biographical experience? Is it a rationally defensible choice? Perhaps neither. But having found myself traveling the secular path, and having reflected on the reasons for its value and entertained the value of a theistic path, I have never found reason to abandon my atheism. So I'll close this essay by highlighting two related reasons I have for not regretting my lack of belief in God.

The first involves what is created by the secular struggle to make visible the invisible humanity of others, and that is something that is often romanticized under the name "community." The struggle to make the humanity of others visible is, in essence, a reciprocal project. In seeing your humanity, I need to make mine manifest to you. In part, I do this by showing you that I am making the effort to see your humanity. That is, after all, the act of a human being, of someone capable of directing his attention in a certain way, and caring about how he does it. So the result of this struggle is that we together come to see something we might not have seen before. Furthermore, through this reciprocal action we come to find ourselves acting together, not merely side-by-side. We are now engaged in a joint project of reciprocal recognition of one another's humanity, and this further ties us together, not as wholly isolated selves impossibly reaching across the void that separates us, but into a kind of whole, what I like to call a "we." Now, I take it that a similar sort of unification is part of the aim of the religious quest to make God visible. It, too, will involve making oneself visible to God, baring one's soul, as it were. And through one's unification with the divine in this way, one is also thereby united with other believers, with whom one also forms a community. But it strikes me that there is a key difference between a community united under the guise of a supreme power, and a community of equals who form themselves through collective action and recognition. It is, to put the point in the language of politics and political philosophy, the difference between a monarchy and a democracy, between the social contract of Hobbes and that of Rousseau. Many people find democracy too messy and find Rousseau a bit scary. I am not one of them.

And this brings me to the second reason. What makes Rousseau scary to some is the thought that without a real, external sovereign to anchor them, the people working as a collective will devolve into a kind of mass tyranny. What, I think, makes the thought that we could give ourselves a form of transcendence in the absence of some external transcendent power scary is a similar worry. In the absence of God, all there is left to human life is human action and interaction with ourselves and each other and other aspects of the natural world, and the only meaning any of it has is the meaning we manage to give it. Our existence is thus one long walk on a tightrope over a yawning abyss and there is nothing to catch us should we fall into meaninglessness or isolation or even mere ordinariness. But that is exactly what I find so exhilarating about being an atheist. Life is up to us; there are no safety nets. That's a bracing thought. It's also a reason to live.

Thanks to Charles Mills, Tamar Schapiro, Samuel Fleischacker, David Owen, and Caroline Guindon for helpful comments on earlier drafts.

TWELVE

An Aristotelian Life

Marcia Homiak

I know many good people who are religious. I consider them to be good people because they are disposed to respond with kindness, comfort, and help when others are in distress or in need. They are warm, outgoing, and compassionate, taking a genuine interest in others' lives. They are optimistic, disposed to see the good in others and to see what's right with the world. They are resilient, able to bounce back from setbacks, disappointments, or personal tragedy. And because they are warm, cheerful, resilient, and kind, others appreciate them, admire them, and love them. They have strong ties of connection with other people, in their families, in their religious communities, and with friends. And I know that their fine qualities of character are forged in their religious involvement. There are many other religious people whom I have never met but whom I deeply admire. I think of many, both famous and obscure, who fought in the civil rights struggles of the 1960s in the American South. I know that their fight for justice and equality, their fight against bigotry and hatred, was motivated by a sense of purpose that is properly described as religious. For they fought for an ideal—the values of freedom and justice—that they saw as a sacred, Judeo-Christian ideal. Their devotion to this ideal gave them the courage and determination to face jeering and hostile mobs, to suffer imprisonment and beatings.

My friends who are religious are not heroes. They have not endangered their own lives to make the world a more just and equitable place. Still, I think they share important qualities of character with the civil rights workers. Both my friends and the civil rights workers are genuinely concerned about the welfare of others, both those they know and those who are strangers. They are decent and caring people, who ungrudgingly help others. I think both they and the civil rights workers share this religious perspective: that we are, after all, God's creatures, God's children, and so no one should be excluded from the comfort of community, mutuality, and love.

So, taking these kinds of life as exemplars, I'd say there are great benefits to the religious life. A way of life inspired by religious values (i) can provide direction for how to live, (ii) can offer the love and compassion of friendship and community, (iii) can motivate acts of human decency, and (iv) can motivate acts of great courage and determination. And for all these reasons, (v) it can provide comfort in difficult times. Now, some people might think that only a religious life can provide these benefits, for only a religious life, they think, can provide proper moral direction, and only God's eternal love can ground human kindness, decency, and courage. And perhaps only God's love can provide the comfort we need when all seems lost. But in my view, there are non-religious ways of life that are equally admirable and that contain these same great benefits. These ways of life are principled and coherent. Their values offer sound practical guidance for how to live. These ways of life provide for the important goods of human community, friendship, and love. They are not self-centered. They explain how kindness, courage, and other admirable traits of character are not only possible, but also probable. And they provide the resources for great psychological strength that will carry us beyond desperation and despair.

In this essay, I will describe one kind of non-religious life that I find admirable and worthwhile. My sense of what it looks like is based largely on the writings of Aristotle, a pre-Christian philosopher who lived and taught in Athens in the fourth century BCE. When Aristotle wrote of the life he found most admirable, he knew he was describing an ideal that did not exist in his world. It does not exist in the modern world either. But that doesn't mean we can't live in ways that express its most important values. At the end of my essay, I'll return to the benefits of the religious life, and I'll ask whether an Aristotelian life can provide for these benefits. I think it can. If that's right, we don't need religion to be good friends or good neighbors or to have moral strength.

Aristotle's Picture of a Flourishing Human Life

Aristotle begins the *Nicomachean Ethics,* his most famous work in ethics, by asking: what is the best life for human beings? He thinks most people will agree that the best human life is a happy or flourishing life. But he doesn't think it is at all obvious what a happy or flourishing life is. He knows that some people will think a happy life is focused on material and sensual gratification. But Aristotle thinks that's too superficial. Happiness can't be just a continuous stream of good feeling. That, he says, would be a passive life, fit only for grazing animals. Nor is a life of political power and status the best life for a human being. For that kind of life can easily be taken away (as we know from every election cycle). So whatever happiness is, Aristotle thinks it must be a life that is distinctively human and hard to take from us. It must be a life that we create and that is enduring and stable. Happiness is a human achievement. It does not come from the gods, he says in book 1, chapter 8, but results from the exercise of abilities that are distinctively human. So what are these abilities?[1]

The abilities distinctive of human beings, in Aristotle's view, are rational or cognitive abilities—the abilities to think and to know, to figure things out, on the basis of reasons. Aristotle doesn't mean that only human beings think and learn. But he thinks that only human beings think in ways such as these: we deliberate about what to do, about what kind of life to lead, and about what sort of person to be. We look for reasons for acting or living one way rather than another. The same thing goes on in more-ordinary experiences, such as when we participate in sports. A well-played game is often one that requires players to make smart decisions, quickly, about which strategies to use to win a point. These various ways of thinking are examples of reasoning about practical or personal life. We also think on a more theoretical level. We think about the nature of the world and why it seems to behave as it does, and we construct theories (again looking for reasons in favor of one theory or another) to explain how the world works. Like practical reasoning, theoretical reasoning also occurs in ordinary life. When we listen to music or watch a cultural performance or stop to look at a picture, we are often exploring complex relationships among forms and sounds. Sometimes we are rewarded by gaining some insight about what we hear or see. In all these ways, both ordinary and grand, we deliberate, form theories and explanations, and reflect about our own lives and the lives of others. We make reasoned judgments among alternatives. When Aristotle sets out in the first book of the *Nicomachean Ethics* to sketch what the best human life is, he is doing the kind of thinking and deliberating that only human beings do.

However intelligent animals may be, they don't engage in these forms of thinking. I have, I think, quite an intelligent cat, who is very good at capturing live food in the backyard and also very good at communicating with me about what she at any moment wants to do. But my cat cannot decide to forego mice in favor of birds. She cannot decide what kind of feline life she wants to lead, and she cannot make changes in her own life based on that reflection. She is not that kind of creature. But I can decide to live differently from the way I do.

Aristotle's key idea is that the best life for a human being (the most human of human lives) consists in the full realization of these distinctive human powers. What is it to realize them fully? Aristotle doesn't mean that we must become adept at every kind of activity in which deliberating and judging on the basis of reasons is called for. That would mean we'd have to master all forms of cultural, scientific, and philosophical activity, and that is not possible for any human being. He means, rather, that we develop them to the extent that we enjoy their exercise in whatever specific activities we choose to do. When that happens, we are what Aristotle calls "self-lovers"—we love that distinctively human feature of us that sets us apart from other creatures. Aristotle thinks it is natural—part of human psychology—for us to enjoy the exercise of our realized human powers. This means in part that we don't love just some specific activity or activities that call upon our human powers, such as baseball or tennis or sports in general. Rather, if we are lovers of our rational powers, we will enjoy their realized use in a wide variety of different and even seemingly unconnected activities: in managing a softball game, in identifying an unusual bird on a hike, in solving a crossword puzzle, in determining the right present for a friend.

Why is it important that a self-lover love the exercise of her rational powers in general, rather than that she love them as they are realized in a specific activity? Remember that Aristotle thinks that a well-lived life is stable and enduring, that human happiness is an achievement that cannot easily be taken away. If we loved only one or a few types of activity in which we use our rational powers, then if it should turn out that we can no longer perform these activities (say we are injured and can no longer play baseball or tennis), our happiness disappears and our life seems to lack zest and meaning.

For Aristotle, happiness is a human accomplishment (it's not given to us by a god or by fate or by chance). But that doesn't mean happiness is an individual accomplishment. Rather, Aristotle thinks happiness is a group achievement. We can see what he means if we consider his idea of self-love in more detail. Aristotle thinks that we cannot become self-lovers on our own, because we cannot realize our human powers on our own. To realize our own powers, we need the company of others who are also realizing their powers, and, ideally, we also need a political community or state that acts to promote and protect the realization of these powers.

Let's consider the idea that we need the company of others who are realizing their powers if we are to realize our own. In book 9, chapter 9, of the *Nicomachean Ethics,* Aristotle writes: "It is thought that the happy person must live pleasantly. But the solitary person's life is hard, since it is not easy for him to be continuously active all by himself; but in relation to others and in their company it is easier. Hence his activity will be more continuous."[2] What does Aristotle mean by "in relation to others"? One interpretation (with which I agree) is that to realize our powers we need to engage in activities in which we, along with the other participants, each contribute to a mutually recognized goal.[3] The participants share a commitment to the goal and understand the parts played by different individuals in reaching the goal. Good examples of what Aristotle has in mind are cooperative activities like team sports and orchestras. In baseball games and orchestral performances, we can see ourselves as parts of a larger enterprise. When we do, we identify with the other members of the team or the orchestra. That is, our conception of who we are is broadened to cover the activities of others who play different parts in the overall goal. We can see others as realizing specific capacities that we have chosen not to realize. Then, when others act, it is as though we are acting, too. By expanding our conception of who "we" are, these shared activities make the use of "our" powers more continuous and more stable.

Most of us are parts of several cooperative enterprises. We are usually members of families, we are often members of amateur sports teams, we often belong to social clubs or religious associations, we are sometimes members of professional associations in connection with our work, and so on. Aristotle thought there were many such cooperative activities in the communities he knew. Finally, there is another cooperative enterprise that is extremely important to Aristotle—that is the political community or state that organizes all these other cooperative ventures.

Aristotle thinks that as we engage in these cooperative relations with others and come to enjoy them, we don't simply *identify* with our cooperative partners. We will also develop feelings of *friendship* for them. Aristotle means that we develop a concern for the good of our partners for our partners' sakes. This is an extremely important point for Aristotle, for it means that cooperative activity of the kind we've described succeeds in giving individuals new, different desires and motivations from the ones they had when they first took up the cooperative enterprise. Individuals may have begun these activities with no interest in the good of their partners. (They may not know anyone else in the orchestra.) They may have started out only for their own individual advantage. Think of neighbors who clear away a nearby vacant lot to plant a vegetable garden. Each person may initially participate only because she wants her share of the fresh garden produce. But as the cooperative venture develops, as individuals play their appropriate roles in the attainment of the shared goal, and as individuals demonstrate their realized abilities, other-directed feelings and desires emerge. Aristotle will go even further and say that we come to *enjoy* the realization of our partners' powers and also that we come to recognize the good of our cooperative partners as our own good. This follows from our seeing our cooperative partners as expressing aspects of ourselves that we have chosen not to develop. If when they act, it is as though we are acting too, their pleasure is a pleasure for us and their good is our good. In short, engaging in shared activity with others transforms us—our "I" becomes "we."

Now to Aristotle's view about the political community. Aristotle thinks that human beings cannot live the best possible lives—they cannot completely flourish—unless they live in the right kind of political community. One of the most famous phrases from Aristotle's *Nicomachean Ethics* is that the human being is "by nature a political animal" (book 1, ch. 7). Aristotle means that the best life for a human being is lived not only with family and friends and associates in the kinds of groups we've already described but also with fellow citizens in political activity in a special type of state.

What kind of state does Aristotle think is necessary? First, Aristotle proposes a public education system (a radical idea for his time, as no Greek city to this point had ever provided education to all its citizens) whose aim is to develop citizens' cognitive powers. Children learn not only to read and write but also to appreciate the order and beauty of the world around them. They learn music and literature, science and mathematics, all so that they can develop a rudimentary knowledge and appreciation of how the world works. Because their education is devoted to the recognition and appreciation of both truth and beauty, Aristotle thinks that young people will develop a taste for active, rather than passive, leisure activities. They will want to use their powers in music, theater, and athletics. They won't simply be interested in consumption. In effect, Aristotle thinks that, like cooperative activities, education is also transformative. It gives young people the desire and motivation to use their human powers rather than to be couch potatoes.

Aristotle's city provides for its citizens in other ways as well. Aristotle sees that citizens can't live flourishing lives if they are impoverished and that they can live flourishing lives without being wealthy. So the city distributes parcels of land to all, in such a way that citizens have the material resources they need in order to participate fully in public life. In this way, the state guarantees that citizens are publicly equal, even if some are wealthier than others.

Finally, consider the government itself. Aristotle thinks that the public education all citizens receive serves them in good stead when it comes to governing the city. Everyone is equal in his ability to deliberate about what is good for the entire city, so all citizens will take turns ruling and being ruled. That citizens take turns ruling means quite a bit for Aristotle. First, all citizens belong to an assembly that meets regularly to determine what is advantageous and just for the city. Second, all citizens have an equal chance to participate at other levels of government because the various officials are chosen by lot. Moreover, there is no way for groups of especially powerful citizens to emerge because officials yield their spots to others after short periods of time through a system of rotation. So citizens are politically equal: they are all members of the citizen assembly, and they all have an equal chance of being chosen by lot to serve even in the most powerful offices. In contrast to other ancient political ideals such as Plato's Republic, which is ruled by an elite, Aristotle's city is ruled by ordinary citizens. No special skill or elevated status (of wealth or power) is required for political office. All that is needed is ordinary reasoning ability and a solid general education.

But here's a problem with Aristotle's picture of the flourishing human life. Aristotle's citizens grow up under a public education system whose aim is to realize their rational powers and to develop in them a love of the activities of thinking and knowing and figuring things out, whether their subjects of thought are theatrical performances, sporting events, physics, philosophy, or political science. The more citizens develop their powers, the more enjoyable their lives become. But doesn't that mean that citizens just care about themselves and their own pleasures? We already know that Aristotle's answer is no. For he thinks that as we develop and exercise our powers, we will do so along with others who are developing and exercising their powers. These associations will produce friendly relations, and so we will develop a concern for others for their own sakes. So we won't just be interested in our own flourishing. But he has something else to say that shows even more clearly that a flourishing person won't be self-centered. He thinks that we can't fully develop our powers without being morally virtuous—that is, to flourish we must be courageous, good-tempered, and generous; and to flourish we can't be self-indulgent, irascible, boorish, and timid.

To see what his argument is, let's think back briefly to Aristotle's views about education. We've already seen that he thinks a proper education will transform us. We will become people who prefer activities that call upon our developed abilities rather than people who prefer mindless or undemanding activities. For Aristotle, that shows that we won't be people who over-indulge in easy pleasures such as eating and drinking (or watching TV). Aristotle thinks that over-indulgence in the easy pleasures shows that someone is unhappy with his life and wants to escape from himself. But Aristotle's self-lover is someone who enjoys her life.

Or think about courage. Someone who comes to love the exercise of the rational powers will recognize the role they play in a flourishing life. Such a person enjoys her life, she is confident that it has meaning and worth, and she does not want to lose it. If she is fortunate enough to live in the kind of political community that is needed to sustain a flourishing life, she will want to defend those institutions against danger and attack. She fights for the right reasons—in that she fights to defend a way of life that is good, that she values, and to which she is committed. So Aristotle's picture of the courageous person fits our picture of courage, in that we think the courageous person is prepared to die for what she believes in.

A pattern is emerging to Aristotle's explanations of virtuous and vicious behavior. Some people have too little confidence in their own value. They don't love themselves enough. As a result they don't have the strength and determination to act in ways befitting a human being. This is the problem with many of Aristotle's morally vicious types, including people who are self-indulgent, cowardly, and irascible (they don't get angry enough). These people prefer to do what's easy or what doesn't make appropriate demands on the use of their cognitive powers. In other cases, because individuals don't sufficiently enjoy the exercise of their own powers, they find their pleasure in what others think of them. So, obsequious flatterers want most the favor of the more privileged, and vain people want most the honor others can bestow. On the other hand, if people think too highly of themselves, they will act in ways that endanger the pleasures of friendship and social life. These are the churlish, cantankerous, and insensible types.

But Aristotle thinks that self-lovers won't be motivated to act in these vicious ways. For they have a strong sense of their own worth that is based on their own achievements as evidenced in the exercise of their developed abilities. Their self-worth is not overly dependent on the opinions or achievements of others. Nor is it contemptuously independent of others' views and others' activities. For proper self-worth is not an individual accomplishment. To be preserved over time, it requires that we cooperate with other self-lovers in shared activity in a specific type of political community. These activities produce stable ties of friendship and affection. The self-lover's positive view of herself and her ability to identify with the goals of others enables her to be trustful and generous in her dealings with others. She does not feel threatened by or hostile to others and is not afraid of being left unaided by them.

Finally, it's important to remember that, for Aristotle, if proper institutions are in place, these attitudes and behaviors emerge naturally, as a result of psychological tendencies we experience in the course of ordinary life. For, other things being equal, Aristotle thinks it is natural for us (it is part of our psychology) to enjoy the exercise of our realized powers, and it is natural for us to enjoy the realization of others' powers, too. So if we are fortunate enough to live in a community that provides us with an educational system that develops our abilities to think and to know, that offers us opportunities to use our developed abilities in shared activities with others, and that provides the material goods we need for realizing our powers and for participating in civic life, we will develop a healthy self-love and attachments to others in which we care about them for their own sakes. Self-love and friendly associations will be the psychological foundation of virtue and of a life lived well and happily.

Is Aristotle's Ideal Realizable?

Now clearly part of the reason Aristotle's self-lovers are able to be virtuous is that their political community provides the material conditions they need for this kind of life. Their community provides the proper public education system; it guarantees a level of material well-being (in the form of private property ownership); it subsidizes community activities (such as dramatic and athletic competitions) that promote social ties and that further develop the human powers; it guarantees an equal level of participation in community decision making and in the implementation of those decisions. It is in many ways a deeply democratic and egalitarian political community that recognizes the value of having a broadly educated citizenry. Aristotle thinks that serious inequalities in wealth or position or background will create vicious tendencies (such as animosity and envy) in the city among those less advantaged, which will then lead to division and civil unrest. So it is crucial for the city to provide the institutional support that will enable citizens to become self-lovers. This explains his insistence on meaningful citizen participation in government. The aim in part was to keep government in the hands of ordinary people and to prevent the formation of elite groups who would serve only in their own interests.

But here is a problem. Aristotle did not think that any city close to this one existed in his lifetime. He knew he was describing an ideal. But if this city is only an ideal, why bother to think about it at all? This question is even more pressing for us at the beginning of the twenty-first century than it was for Aristotle's contemporaries. In Aristotle's day, one could gather regularly in an assembly of citizens. But now there are too many of us. To take turns ruling and being ruled, we'd have to drastically reorganize our working lives and our economic lives. In addition to these practical difficulties involved in implementation, there are other serious defects in Aristotle's community that I haven't yet mentioned. Although Aristotle argued for radical departures from some of the traditional practices of his time, he did not see beyond all of the deep prejudices of his time. Aristotle thought that some individuals were not capable of becoming proper lovers of self, because they lacked the requisite rational powers. In this group he placed women and "natural" slaves. And because he thought that most forms of paid work served to diminish the exercise of the human powers, he banned craftspeople, tradespersons, and farmers from the citizenry of his ideal state.

If there are so many obstacles to implementing Aristotle's ideal, and if it has such serious moral defects, the question again is, why think about it? Because, first, Aristotle's prejudices are just that, prejudices. He has no good argument to show that women and "natural" slaves don't have the same cognitive powers as free men. And he has no good argument to show that citizenship should be limited to free men who do non-manual work. His denigration of women, "natural" slaves, and manual laborers doesn't follow from his philosophical views. Second, ideals are important. Aristotle understood that good political leaders must study the nature of human good and how it can be embodied in political organization. For how else will they know which political arrangements succeed or fail at promoting human good? Aristotle saw that even if his students could not succeed in creating an ideal community, their understanding of it could serve as a guide as they strove to come closer to that ideal. The same applies to us. We, too, need ideals to guide us, both in our personal lives and in our political lives. Third, and finally, though Aristotle's ideal may look unrealistic, it is at least partially realizable for many of us, and so it fares remarkably well, as ideals go.

How is it (at least partially) realizable? To answer this question, I will begin by considering my own situation.

To flourish in the Aristotelian sense, one needs to have developed one's cognitive powers to some degree. One doesn't have to be a genius or even an intellectual. But one has to take some joy in the activity of figuring things out, whether these things happen to be the best strategy to use in a tennis match, the best approach to realizing a character on stage, or the best way to remove nine layers of paint from an old bookcase. Usually, we develop our cognitive powers as we grow up, with the help of family members and teachers at school. Sometimes we are self-taught.

Equally important, we need some way of exercising these realized abilities in ordinary life. Sometimes we are fortunate enough to have paid work that calls upon our developed abilities and allows us some control and decision making power over the nature of our work and how it is done. But even if we don't have paid work that makes appropriate demands on our cognitive powers, we often participate in recreational or avocational activities that do. Many of us regularly participate in sports or games. Many of us attend cultural performances. Many of us garden or do home repair. All these activities are demanding and challenging and engage us in trying to figure things out.

To flourish, we need to participate in cooperative activity with others who have developed their cognitive powers. For we need the stimulation and challenge, the support and esteem, of others who are competent to judge us. Without others' encouragement, admiration, and support, our own confidence in who we are and in what we do will gradually disappear. Team sports provide this kind of stimulation and support as an integral part of what they are. Other activities, such as home gardening, seem less social, less cooperative. But the gardener who has developed her abilities will be reasonably knowledgeable about how to cultivate her garden, and she will want the advice of other competent gardeners and their reactions to what she has done or is planning to do. If other competent gardeners respond favorably to what she has accomplished, her sense of her own value and competence will rise.

In my own case, the second and third elements of a flourishing life have proven more important than the formal education I received. My parents died when I was young, so I did not have any adult family members to encourage and guide me in the course of my development. My primary and secondary schools, even my college education, were not particularly stimulating. I really did not begin to learn the craft for which I had officially been trained until I began to teach my own courses. Then I had to figure things out more thoroughly, and more quickly, than I ever had before. I was aided in this effort by my work environment. I am fortunate to have work that satisfies reasonably well Aristotle's picture of activity that supports, rather than undermines, self-love. In this regard I am not unusual. I imagine that what I go on to say about my own work can be replicated, with appropriate alterations in detail, for many different kinds of work.

The most obvious Aristotelian feature of my work is that it makes continuing demands on my rational powers. I teach the great texts in the history of moral and political philosophy to undergraduate students, most of whom have never had any exposure to philosophical thinking and writing. These texts are challenging—and thrilling—to teach. Like Aristotle's ethical and political writings, they endure for a reason—they all have something important to say about how human beings should live and treat each other. Even if we disagree with these texts, they force us to confront the reasonableness of our own views. Can we find good arguments to pose in response to them? The texts pose a challenge for me personally, and the teaching of them poses a different challenge for me personally. When I meet these challenges sufficiently well, I have a sense of satisfaction that contributes to my enjoyment of my work and to my self-esteem and self-confidence.

But I don't work alone. The college offers me a community of teachers and thinkers who share my interests not only in teaching effectively but also in figuring things out. This is clear in the frequency with which professors from different departments create and organize team-taught, interdisciplinary courses of their own choosing. These courses offer extremely clear examples of what Aristotle meant by "shared activity." First of all, they expose one to areas of study that are unfamiliar, that one hasn't chosen to study oneself. If the courses work well, they broaden one's sense of what is interesting, and they increase one's understanding of the nature of the world—of what is beautiful, insightful, and different. Professors share the aim of creating and implementing a course that works intellectually, both for the students and for themselves. And as each professor contributes to the course in her lectures and assignments, the others feel that they are contributing at the same time, though indirectly through the actions of another. If the course works and the team meets its challenges sufficiently well, then each member of the team gains a sense of accomplishment that contributes to her enjoyment and her self-esteem. For these reasons and others, ties of affection and camaraderie are formed.

In addition to my shared activity with colleagues at my college, I also participate in shared activity with philosophical colleagues at other colleges and universities. Whenever I participate in a conference or publish an essay, I am contributing to ongoing studies to which I am jointly attached with other philosophers. These activities bring the same psychological benefits as the more local forms of shared activity at my specific institution.

Finally, there is another form of shared activity that my specific institution offers me that brings a slightly different set of psychological benefits. These benefits aren't usually duplicated in other forms of work. My college has two publicly acknowledged goals. One is to provide an excellent education in the liberal arts and sciences. The second goal is broader in scope. The college sees itself as contributing to the wider shared activity of making the world better. My college explicitly recognizes the ethical and political importance of developing one's cognitive powers, and it explicitly recognizes that many of the college-age students in the United States aren't able to take advantage of the formal opportunities for education that exist. So it actively recruits students who have been disadvantaged by poverty and prejudice. And it actively recruits faculty members who can effectively mentor non-traditional students. More than twenty-five percent of the faculty are people of color; more than thirty-six percent of the student body are from minority and/or disadvantaged backgrounds; approximately seventy-five percent of the students receive financial aid; and more than sixteen percent are first-generation college students.

This sense of what the college is about drives many of the decisions departments and individual faculty members make about what courses to offer, what kind of faculty appointments to make, and how courses are taught. For example, the college's urban and environmental policy major recently established formal ties with a community-oriented advocacy organization, whose explicit aim is to promote justice and democracy in the Los Angeles area. Students have the opportunity to work with this organization to address local issues of housing, transportation, immigration, land use, and so on.[4] Through these forms of "community-based learning," students, faculty, and the college itself enlarge their conception of learning to include community action and political policies. And by sharing a commitment to the goals of justice and democracy, individual faculty and students gain a sense that they are acting to do their part in making their society a more just and equitable place. Many of the faculty are energized by working toward this goal, and as they see the progress their institution has made in implementing it, they feel more optimistic about their own lives and about the future of their country.

Of course, my work environment doesn't replicate all of the desirable features of a flourishing life. There is still a great deal of mind-deadening work (such as the grading of most exams and the writing of most department and committee reports) that must be done. But the unpleasant aspects of my work are in part mitigated by the fact that there are no elite groups among the faculty. Everyone has the same teaching load and roughly the same department and committee responsibilities. Department chairships are rotated in a regular and fair way. But I don't have control over all the decision-making processes that affect me. Although I can contribute to these processes (to the process, for example, by which college-wide administrators are hired), many of the most important decisions the college makes are in the hands of a few administrators, and there seem clearly to be limits to administrative tolerance of non-administrative involvement in decision making. Finally, although faculty, administrators, and administrative staff work under reasonably self-expressive conditions, the most-unskilled work at the college is done by a group of low-wage facilities and food service workers, who cook, clean, and maintain the campus. In this way, the college mirrors the moral defects of the wider society.[5]

The wider society is in some ways very far from Aristotle's ideal, for it promotes what Aristotle would call passive, rather than active, enjoyment. That is, it promotes the ownership and accumulation of material goods for their own sake, rather than the creative use of material goods to develop one's own rational powers or the powers of others. Although the wider society speaks eloquently of fairness and equal opportunity, by denying citizens the guarantee of a decent standard of material well-being, it falls far short of promoting the conditions and sustaining the institutions that are needed for a full realization of the rational powers. However, although I don't live in the kind of society Aristotle admired, I do live in a society that gives me many opportunities to work to make it better. These efforts are often publicly permitted as part of the democratic process. For example, during election cycles, I can work for political candidates (assuming there are some, which is not always the case) who I believe recognize the value and significance of providing the general conditions under which individuals can learn to develop and then to exercise their cognitive powers. So I can work for candidates who aim to ensure that all citizens are covered by health insurance, that our public education system is adequate and available to all, that steps be taken to reduce the disparity in the ownership of property and wealth, that public cultural events be funded, that the environment be protected as a source of great beauty, and so on. Aristotle's vision of the best society gives me something toward which to strive, just as he intended.

A Comparison with a Religious Life

Now I want to return to my comments at the beginning of this essay. There I described the many good people I know (or know of) who are religious. They are good in that they have many fine qualities of character and because they act for morally admirable ends. They are deeply connected to other human beings. One can see that this is so in their family ties, in their friendships, in the strength of their religious communities, and in their willingness to comfort and aid those in need, especially those whom they don't know. Because they see all of us as God's children, they are not disposed to be stingy and ungenerous, to be contemptuous and disdainful of others, to be puffed up by a sense that they are better than others. They recognize others' dignity and worth. Their love of God, their commitment to religious ideals, gives them direction in their personal lives. Sometimes their commitment to these ideals—of justice and equality, of human dignity and worth—is so powerful that they are prepared to sacrifice their own lives to fight against hatred, bigotry, injustice, and evil.

So it strikes me that religious commitment can bring great benefits: (i) it can provide a guide for how to live one's life, a guide for what is important, valuable, and worth pursuing; (ii) it can provide motivation for acts of human decency, for generosity and beneficence; (iii) it can provide the psychological strength to do what is right against great odds and in great peril; (iv) it ties people together, into relationships of love, friendship, and affection; and (v) it can provide comfort in difficult times.

Now, I think that a life inspired by Aristotle's views can provide these same great benefits. Let me explain.

Consider the first benefit of a religious life—having a guide for how to live. As we've seen, Aristotle explicitly presents his view of the flourishing life as a guide to help us in making practical decisions, whether these are small personal decisions or large political decisions. When he argues that one political community is better for human well-being than another, he makes those decisions in terms of how, and the extent to which, communities are able to provide the resources and institutions needed for human flourishing. The main recommendations he makes for how to achieve the human good (that the community must provide for the education of its citizens, that it must provide citizens with a level of material resources that enables them to participate in the life of the community, that political offices must not be a reflection of relative power or wealth) give us a reasonably good sense of an ideal that is worth pursuing and toward which we can realistically strive.[6]

Aristotle's views can also be a guide in matters of daily life. As I write this essay, the unionized employees of many Los Angeles area supermarkets have been on strike for months. They are demanding adequate healthcare benefits, not only for themselves but also for future employees. Their employers are threatening to reduce the benefits package already in place, claiming that they must protect themselves against impending competition from a superstore chain that is poised to establish itself in the Los Angeles area. Should I cross the picket line at my neighborhood grocery store? I think Aristotle would conclude that the human costs of denying the workers their demands outweighs whatever loss in profits the grocery stores might incur. For, like education and a decent level of material well-being, we need adequate medical care in order to develop our cognitive powers. That means he would probably think that it is the responsibility of the political community to provide for it. But setting that issue aside and working within the parameters of Los Angeles life as it exists, it seems clear that Aristotle's views imply that I ought not cross the picket line. Now, if the superstore chain succeeds in establishing itself in the Los Angeles area, should I patronize it? People say that the prices at the superstore chain are the lowest one will find anywhere. Again, I think, the Aristotelian answer is no. For the superstore chain survives by denying proper benefits to its workers (both in the United States and overseas), by actively discouraging any efforts by workers to join unions to improve their working conditions, and by organizing most of the paid work in such a way that it becomes monotonous and routine, thereby making few, if any, demands on the human powers. Yes, economic costs matter, but what is more important for Aristotle is the cost to the development of the human powers. One does not have to agree with these Aristotelian answers. The point is that one can see that they are Aristotelian answers to the problems of modern life.

The second great strength of a commitment to religious values (of justice, equality, dignity, and worth) is that we recognize the value of other human beings and are disposed to treat them with warmth and compassion. A religious commitment can prevent us from developing a false sense of our own value and can explain our willingness to perform acts of human decency to help others in distress and in need.

Now Aristotle's self-lover, like the admirable religious person, is also disposed to treat others decently. Aristotle's self-lover has the proper attitude toward her own value and worth that is based on her own achievements as evidenced in the exercise of her developed abilities. But, as we've seen, self-love is not an individual accomplishment. To be preserved over time, the self-lover must cooperate with others in shared activity. In doing so, she will develop stable ties of friendship and affection. She will become concerned about the good of others and will be trustful and generous in her dealings with them. She values these ties of affection, which shows that, like the person with religious commitment, she doesn't overestimate her own value and worth. But nor does she underestimate it. She values herself enough to have the strength and the determination to act on her vision of the human good. Aristotle's self-lover loves what is most human in herself, and as a result she acts generously, in good temper, with care and concern for the good of others.

The third benefit of religious commitment is that it can give one the strength and determination to go beyond acts of ordinary moral decency, to do what is right against great odds and in the face of great danger. I think Aristotle expects that the institutions of his ideal state will promote in citizens a similar strength and determination. For citizens will grow up appreciating their education and their developed powers, and they will value the city as the institution that preserves and makes possible the lives they enjoy. They know that if their government is destroyed, the institutions that promote human good are lost. So Aristotle expects that if the Persians, Spartans, or other acknowledged enemies attack, citizens will be inclined to fight to defend their city. They will be willing to risk their lives for what they take to be of greatest value and worth. Like the person of religious commitment, Aristotle's virtuous person is prepared to die for what she believes in.

I'll consider the fourth and fifth benefits of a religious life together. Sometimes things go badly in our personal lives, and we are despondent and want to give up. The need then is not for political courage. It's not a matter of fighting those who threaten us with injustice and tyranny. Rather, we need personal courage, the courage to see ourselves through sadness or despair, the courage to pull ourselves up and keep going. In situations like these, we seek comfort from others who care about us and share our values. We look to our family and friends. It's in part because a religious life promotes ties of friendship, love, and community that it can provide comfort. But a religious life provides comfort in another way as well. For if we are religious, we can take comfort from our conviction that God loves us, that no matter what happens, no matter how much pain we may suffer, that God sees what we are going through and that God cares. And it will help to know that no matter what we do, God will always love us. For God is always there.

Now there is no wholly dependable, totally continuous, eternal source of unconstrained and unconditional love in Aristotle's view. For in Aristotle's view there is no God who loves and cares about human beings. But that doesn't mean Aristotle's self-lover doesn't have the other psychological resources that are available to the religious person for getting through difficult personal times. In particular, the self-lover will have the comfort of family and friends. For, as we have seen, Aristotle thinks that concern for another's well-being that is typical of friendships and family relationships will arise naturally, as a result of experiences that we have in the course of ordinary life. And when someone becomes our friend, she cares about us for our own sake. So Aristotelian friendship certainly is other-directed, as a love grounded in religion is, but it is a response to specific qualities in individuals or to actions that individuals perform.

In addition to thinking that friendship is a natural part of human life, we know that Aristotle also thinks it is necessary if we are to flourish and become self-lovers. We need the confirmation of others, and without sharing activity with others, we can't fully develop our rational powers. Without friends (whether these are friendships among baseball lovers, among teaching colleagues, among business associates, among family members, or among romantic partners) we cannot live well. Moreover, as we've seen, Aristotle thinks that wider social relations are also crucial to the development of our rational powers. Communities are critical—both the small variety that we find in our professional lives and the larger variety whose aim is to secure and sustain the material conditions needed for a flourishing life. A flourishing human being is without question connected to other persons, as family members, as friends, as colleagues, as political citizens. So the fourth benefit of a religious life (that it gives a central place to family, friends, and community) is a critical ingredient of an Aristotelian life.

Yet there is no external source of continuous and unconditional love in Aristotle's view. So does this mean that the psychological resources available to the Aristotelian are too weak to sustain us in difficult times? I think not, for I think that the Aristotelian has an internal source of great strength. Because it is internal and does not have its source in God, I think religious views tend to overlook it. Indeed, sometimes religious views disparage it. The internal source of strength for Aristotle lies in the exercise of our developed powers and in the further development of those powers. Why? It is because the exercise of our powers is enjoyable, and as we develop our powers more fully, more and more of the world becomes comprehensible to us, and this is thrilling. One could put it very simply: learning can carry us through. Learning anything that is interesting or stimulating. It needn't be a conventionally intellectual activity. Learning how to fix a car can carry us through. Learning how to strip paint from woodwork can carry us through. Learning to speak Spanish can carry us through. Each time we learn something, we feel that our own life is more enjoyable, and that is precisely what we need to feel if we are going to conquer sadness and despair. I don't think Aristotle would be much in favor of psychotherapy. He'd be more inclined to support pragmatic changes in an individual's life, changes that would ultimately strengthen the individual's sense of accomplishment and worth by providing new opportunities for the use of her developed skills in creative and challenging contexts. For the determination and courage that we need to take us through difficult times comes, in Aristotle's view, from within. Although this healthy sense of one's own value is not invulnerable to the features of the larger world (because one does need friends and community to develop and secure it), once established under reasonably favorable circumstances, it is, in Aristotle's view, as stable and enduring a source of confidence and strength as anything else available to us in human life.

Conclusion

In this essay I've described a non-religious view of a well-lived life. It offers a reasonably clear guideline for how to live. It gives a central place to intimacy, love, and friendship. It explains the importance of living as citizens in a politically progressive community. It is a source of strength and courage in difficult times. And because it gives pride of place to a healthy self-esteem, a confidence that emerges from the development of our cognitive powers, it provides an additional benefit: it offers a life that is a continuous source of confidence and joy. One could add a god to this picture. But I don't see what is gained by it.

I am thankful to Louise Antony and Peter Dreier for helpful comments on earlier versions, and I am especially grateful to Janet Levin, who provided insightful guidance at every stage of the writing of this essay.

THIRTEEN

Without the Net of Providence: Atheism and the Human Adventure

Kenneth A. Taylor

Against Providence

At first glance, it may appear that those who believe in divine providence have a happier lot and are much less prone to despair than those who reject god and divine providence altogether. That alone may seem to give us good reason to prefer belief to non-belief. I shall argue in this essay that there is almost nothing to be said for either the view that belief in providence provides invincible armor against despair or for the view that the atheist who rejects providence need surrender to a paralyzing despair.

Many theists evidently do take comfort in the belief that there exists a god who both loves humanity and who guarantees, through divine providence, that human history will ultimately culminate in an unqualifiedly good outcome. Such comfort is not entirely unreasonable. If history is guided by divine providence, then whatever apparent ills may befall us along the way, we may be assured that moral darkness will not ultimately triumph over light and that the innocent are not destined to suffer injustice at the hands of their persecutors for eternity.

To be sure, the long run of history may be a very long run indeed. Already, entire epochs have known far more oppression than liberty, far more war than peace, far more famine than plenty. Of the roughly 106 billion human beings who have so far lived on the Earth, it seems a fair estimate that an extraordinary percentage have lived in circumstances of considerable material, political, and/or spiritual deprivation. Not even the providential theist can be certain that many more millennia of moral darkness do not still await us. To acknowledge this is to acknowledge that the belief in divine providence need not be a sufficient guard against deep despair about the likely course of any particular span of human history or the course of any particular human life. Indeed, to the extent that the theist concedes, and even insists upon, the inscrutability to human reason of god's divine plan, it would seem to follow that nothing merely in the world as we cognize and experience it can directly ground or justify a belief in providence. Nor is it merely a matter of the currently unfinished state of the human drama. For all we know, the culmination of god's divine plan may come only in the great hereafter, once human history has run its entire earthly course. But just because the culmination of god's plan might take place outside of history, there is no reason to suppose that even if we could survey in one glance the entire earthly course of the human adventure, we would ipso facto have sufficient grounds for the providential hypothesis.

Advocates of the providential hypothesis typically do not, of course, profess to believe it on entirely rational grounds. The belief in providence involves a faith that is supposed to transcend mere reason. But it would be hasty to conclude, for that reason alone, that there can be no rational grounds for adopting the providential hypothesis. Suppose we execute a Pascalian gestalt shift and consider not the "upstream" evidential support, or lack thereof, for the providential hypothesis, but the "downstream" practical consequences of accepting or rejecting it. Suppose we ask not what we rationally ought to believe, but how, all things considered, we should rationally prefer to live. The answer cannot be that we should always rationally prefer to live a life guided by beliefs that are rationally grounded in the evidence or even that we should always prefer that our beliefs be true rather than false. Some beliefs, even if they are both true and rationally grounded in the evidence, may serve only to undermine our deepest, most identity-constituting projects and thus to undermine our very being in the world. Whatever else beliefs are, they are instruments for guiding and supporting our practical projects. If holding a belief would be instrumental to the success of a practical project, then that by itself may give us sufficient reason, in particular sufficient *practical* reason, for adopting that belief, even if that belief is false or unwarranted by the evidence. There is, to be sure, a legitimate fear that by considering the instrumental value of holding a belief *to constitute* rational grounds for adopting it, we may slide off into rationalizing self-deception or willful neglect of the evidence. Think here of the spouse who, desperate to save a marriage, is willfully blind to all evidence of betrayal. Though belief in the straying spouse's fidelity may be instrumental to keeping the marriage alive, self-deception of this sort seems hardly to be a cognitive virtue.

We need not, however, go all the way to endorsing the practical rationality of self-deception to appreciate that we can have reasons for believing, even where epistemic warrant of the purest sort falters. Sometimes good evidence is simply not to be had. We may believe, and be rational in believing, nonetheless. A thoroughgoing skeptic might well insist that the very conviction that we believe without warrant should itself undercut the rationality of believing. In believing, after all, we stake out commitments with respect to how things are. If we are convinced that we merely believe and do not know or that we believe groundlessly, we must thereby acknowledge that things may not be as we have committed ourselves to their being. But then, the skeptic will ask, in what sense can we be rational in believing? The answer rests on the necessity of acting, of getting on with our practical projects. For creatures like ourselves, belief, or belief-like commitment, is often required to carry us "all the way to action." If we did not have to act, we might remain in a state of suspended judgment. But the exigencies of life often require us to act and so to place our doxastic bets on how things are in the world. We do sometimes hedge our bets when the evidence provides us less than full warrant. Sometimes, for example, belief is accompanied by a preparedness to find out that things are other than we have committed ourselves to their being. But we should not suppose that this preparedness entails that we are not really committed, that we do not really believe, but only surmise or suppose or provisionally accept without making a flat-out commitment.

If we look at matters this way, it seems perfectly reasonable to wonder whether the exigencies of life as a human being on Earth might not give us a kind of practical ground for placing our doxastic bets with divine providence, despite the fact that the world as we experience it provides no decisive epistemic warrant for that hypothesis and provides ample grounds for doubting it. Just because the providentialist already believes in providence, she may contemplate the entire course of human history and even the ultimate course of her own or another's life with a confidence that no atheist can muster. Even in her most despairing moments, the providentialist may face all the ills that may come her way with equanimity and a quiet confidence. And that equanimity and confidence may lend the providentialist an inevitable determination and steadfastness in the face of what might otherwise be a paralyzing despair. Armed with the belief that history is directed by divine providence, she need only content herself with playing the part that it has been given to her to play. The rest is in the hands of one whose wisdom is superior to her own.

Many theists, including those who believe in providence, believe in a freedom of the will so complete that we may simply choose not to cooperate with the divine plan. Such thoroughgoing freedom is no doubt metaphysically problematic on its own terms. But let us grant the possibility for the sake of the present argument. A question immediately arises. If our freedom is so thoroughgoing that we may introduce departures from god's plan into the created universe, does it not follow that god's entire plan is hostage to our choices? But if that is so, it is hard to see how the providential hypothesis can provide the promised invincible armor against a potentially paralyzing despair. If we, with our merely finite wills and intellects, may divert creation from its divinely decreed course, then it would seem to follow that history is not after all guaranteed to culminate in a perfectly good outcome. Only if the outcome of history is guaranteed by god in a way that is beyond our capacity to undermine can the providential hypothesis even purport to provide invincible armor against despair.

I do not mean to suggest that the providentialist must view human will and agency as entirely irrelevant to the course of history. One can imagine a universe in which god keeps history on course by making compensating adjustments for departures from the plan that would otherwise be brought about through the exercise of human will. In effect, god creates a universe that simultaneously meets his own providential aims and responds to the free exercise of human will. God may "intervene" in this way either "in" time or "all at once" from outside of time. On either way of looking at matters, god is to be understood as being prepared to "respond" to all contingencies. The Christian Bible, with its long narrative of the fall from Eden, centuries of alienation, and ultimate reconciliation through the Christ, is plausibly understood as telling the story of a god who is in constant interaction with humankind over the long course of human history, directing all toward the good in a way that respects the ultimate freedom of humanity to choose its own destiny.

I will resist the temptation to plumb the alluring metaphysical depths of a universe in which human will and agency compete with divine providence to determine the course of human history. However exactly we resolve or attempt to resolve our metaphysical puzzlement about the workings of providence, it should be clear, I think, that no real security can be purchased with the coin of providence in the first place. God has a plan for the universe. Assuming our freedom, we may either cooperate with that plan or fail to cooperate with it. But if god foresees and prepares for all contingencies, then history will culminate in a state of god's intending, no matter our choices. Consequently, it is hard to see how it *matters* to god's plan what *we* do. Our freedom and our choices are entirely irrelevant to the outcome of history. Because god is prepared for all contingencies, god evidently has no particular need that we perform any particular action, no particular need that we make one choice rather than another. Rather than supporting and validating our practical projects, the belief in divine providence would seem to undercut the very significance of them.

The theist may respond that what matters to god is not the particular outcome—which, after all, god himself guarantees—but the particular *path* that history must travel in order to reach that outcome. Perhaps that is why god rewards those who "cooperate" with his plans and condemns those who fail to do so. But just why god should punish those who fail in this way to cooperate with his plans is itself something of a mystery. His plans are, after all, inscrutable to us, by the theist's own concession. It is not as though we can discern though our ordinary cognitive means *which* path is the path that will put us in solidarity with god's will. Moreover, whatever path we choose, we can do nothing that can possibly interfere with the ultimate fulfillment of god's divine plan. The universe will be as god wills it to be, whatever we do. To be sure, in Dante's *Inferno* we read that the gates of Hell were forged with divine love, rather than with divine wrath.

Dante's thought, I think, is that god wills, from an abundance of love, that we choose freely at least our own destinies, whatever we will that they be. If we choose for ourselves eternal damnation, then it is an expression of god's love that we in fact endure such damnation. So here is at least one place in god's creation in which our own choices make an absolute difference, according to the theist. But that reply still leaves it a mystery just what it is to "side" with god, to "cooperate" with his inscrutable plan. That mystery is only deepened when we add the Socratic question of whether anyone would knowingly choose her own eternal damnation.

Against Secular Stand-ins for Providence

I have been arguing that it is neither epistemically nor practically rational to take solace either for oneself or for humanity at large in the providential hypothesis. But where does the rejection of providence leave us? How shall we live in a material universe "guided" by nothing but the unyielding laws of blind nature? What confidence can we have in a social world founded on nothing but the finite and all too fallible wisdom of humankind? With what degree of hope shall we contemplate the long sweep of human history or even the course of our own lives? I ask these questions as one who lives in circumstances of relative plenty, freedom, and security, as a member of a privileged elite in a powerful, wealthy, and consequential nation. I do not ask them from the gulag or the concentration camp or on the field of battle in some fruitless, forlorn war. Still, they strike me with an urgency borne of a deep sense of the contingency and fragility of all merely human arrangements. The prestige and influence of my consequential and powerful nation will someday diminish as surely as did that of Rome or the Soviet Union. The elite to which I belong may be supplanted by another, hostile perhaps to all that I value. My own individual life projects may run aground and come to naught. My deepest loves may end in betrayal and recrimination. I may endure loss upon loss of those I hold most dear. If, in the face of such real possibilities, I contemplate the future, confident only that there is no god who cares for and guides human history toward the good and no god who has loving concern for my own being in the world, what but a blind and blithe trust that the good will win out, that my projects will not come to naught, that my loves will endure, could shield me against a paralyzing despair?

Many take comfort in one or another secular vision of the historical inevitability of a broadly encompassing moral community. Some see history as culminating in the realization of the manifest destiny of one or more nation–states, or in the transnational triumph of global capitalism or in the worldwide revolution of the proletariat or in the triumph of reason or of sympathy and fellow feeling. To live one's life under the banner of some such vision is to imagine a life spent advancing the cause of the morally right and winning side. Living under such a banner is no doubt as tempting for some atheists as the providential hypothesis is for some theists. But nothing in the world as we cognize and experience it could convince a clear-eyed person that there is any guarantee. From where we now stand, it seems no more likely that history will culminate in thoroughgoing moral community and fellow feeling than that history will culminate in moral fragmentation and mutual enmity. Indeed, the long sweep of human history bears ample witness to the darkness that has been spread under the banner of one totalizing fantasy or another of an all-encompassing moral community. Empire, subjugation, and exploitation of every variety, even genocide and murder on massive scales, have been "justified" by appeal to such visions.

I do not mean to gainsay the very possibility of our ever achieving a global moral community in which the dignity of all is equally affirmed and respected. In fact, I take the building of such a community to be an urgent project, a project that largely defines the grandest hopes of the liberal, secular modernity to which I find in myself a deep allegiance. But the hope of an all-encompassing and all-affirming moral community is merely a project, a project barely begun and far from completion. Between where we now stand and where we may hope to end, there lies a yawning chasm. And nothing in our experience of the world warrants great confidence in our collective ability to cross that chasm without falling into fragmentation and discord. My point here is that all totalizing secular fantasies heretofore on offer about the inevitable moral dynamic of human history are no more grounded in the facts of human life and history as we experience them than are the transcendental fantasies of the providentialist. Indeed, to the extent that such secular fantasies merely represent an attempt to find an immanent and secular stand-in for providence and divine command, this is not an entirely surprising outcome. The world we cognize and experience no more warrants belief in a grand secular narrative about the inevitable moral dynamic of the human adventure than it warrants belief in the proposition that history is providentially guided by a supremely good and loving being.

Creation of Value Ex Nihilo

I intend these last remarks to be sobering. But it would be to misunderstand the true nature and source of value, meaning, and morality to take then as a counsel of despair. Many religious believers maintain that only divine fiat could possibly be the source of universal or absolute morality and objective value. They believe with Dostoyevsky's Ivan Karamazov that if god is dead, then everything is permitted. But if everything is permitted, then there really is no distinction at all between what is permitted and what is forbidden, no distinction between right and wrong. In the absence of god, we live in a universe utterly devoid of meaning, purpose, and value. Correlatively, if we acknowledge that there really and truly are moral absolutes and objective value in the universe, it is supposed to follow immediately that we must also acknowledge the god who is their sole possible source and author. We simply cannot have it both ways, the theist maintains. Either we view our lives and the universe as governed by moral absolutes and suffused with objective value—and thereby acknowledge the god who is the author of all value and all morality—or we deny the existence of god, and resign ourselves to lives utterly devoid of meaning and value, in a universe governed by no moral law.

This supposed dichotomy is a false one. The universe might possibly contain both absolute morality and objective value, even if there is no god to decree what these shall be. To say this is not to deny that settling just what these might be and just where they might come from in the absence of a divine author is a philosophically daunting task. Philosophers have devoted considerable energy and great ingenuity to just that daunting task. I will not, however, undertake a review of the prodigious fruits of those efforts here. The mistake to which I intend to draw attention is not the mistake of denying even the possibility that absolute morality and objective value might somehow subsist in a universe not authored by any supreme being. The mistake on which I focus is more fundamental and occurs one step earlier in the chain of reasoning we have just been considering. Theists may be particularly prone to it, but they are not alone in making it. The mistake I have in mind is the mistake of supposing that if the universe contains nothing of objective value and no moral absolutes, then human life must, as a consequence, be utterly devoid of meaning and purpose.

Suppose we grant that we live in a finite, merely material universe, containing at its core nothing of intrinsic or objective value, governed by no purpose and no universal or absolute moral law. Still, whatever else the universe does or does not contain, *we* exist in it and through it. And we are creatures who value things. We do not *find* or *discover* value in the universe, as if values were antecedently present in the universe, independently of anything that we do or are. Value and meaning are not hidden in some deep reaches of the order of things, waiting merely to be uncovered by the inquiring human mind. We *create* values. And we create them more or less ex nihilo. We do so simply by engaging in the merely human and entirely natural activity of *taking* things to matter *to us*. By *taking* things to matter, we thereby *make* them matter. We make them really and truly matter, at least to ourselves.

Now, there is not and need not be anything either within or without the merely material universe to "vindicate" our merely human valuing—not god, not a transcendental realm of objective goodness, not a realm of natural rights, not a system of categorically binding commandments of reason. We may cry out with longing and despair to the cold uncaring universe to embrace our value, to vindicate our *right* to value what we value. But we will hear only silence in return. The universe is mute, devoid of all power to either affirm or deny the worth we place on either ourselves or on others. So be it. We do not matter *to* the universe. Still, we matter to *ourselves* and sometimes to others who sometimes matter to us in return. And that is all the mattering that it is worth our while to concern ourselves about.

It is often claimed that if value and morality are nothing but merely human creations, grounded in nothing but merely contingent facts about what we merely happen to value, we are left with a relativism that is destructive of all morality and values. What matters to one may fail to matter to others. If there is no external authority to which we may appeal to decide what is really and truly worthy of valuing, then each person becomes the creator and arbiter of her own values. Such an outcome, it is often thought, is really the end of all morality and of all mattering, rather than a vindication of them. But moral relativism in fact reflects deep and inescapable facts about the human situation. Though those facts may be unsettling to many of our most cherished dreams, if we are to confront the challenges that human beings collectively face in a clear eyed and life-affirming manner, we must accept and not recoil from them.

Each person is indeed the ultimate creator and arbiter of her own values. But it does not follow that one's own values and normative lights are destined to remain always and only lights of one's own, as if each of us were always destined to be and remain a moral community of one. Human beings collectively have the capacity to constitute moral communities, communities held together by systems of reciprocal obligations and commitments. Indeed, there has never been a time when human beings did not find themselves distributed in moral communities of varying scope and complexity. Our ancient progenitors formed themselves into normative communities encompassing only small circles, drawn around kin, clan, or tribe. The rough general trend of human history has been haltingly toward normative communities of ever-increasing scope so much so that we are now able to conceive of something barely dreamt of in many ages of the past—the real possibility of a global moral community.

But let neither the rough general trend of history nor our current capacity to imagine alternative realities tempt us into the conclusion that an all-encompassing moral community is either rationally or historically inevitable. If we survey the long sweep of human history, we find that one, then another moral community has taken its stand, flourished for a while, then run aground. To be sure, though moral communities are one and all equally creations of human beings, they are not, from our current point of view, all created equal. Some moral communities have been instrumental to what we, here and now, by our own lights, take to be progress. Some have not been. Moral communities are often contested and always contestable. What one moral community regards as moral progress, another may regard as moral decline. There is no privileged stance, fixed once and for all, outside of history and culture, from which we may determine by which normative lights the "truth" is to be measured in such disputes. This is not to deny that we typically do measure by our own current lights. And we take ourselves to be justified in so doing. But as dear as our own lights may be to us, they enjoy no antecedent privilege except that of being our own. There may come a time when our own lights are entirely extinguished and when we are viewed by those who follow as having undertaken merely one more failed experiment in collective existence. With what right shall we then protest the verdict of history?

If each person is really an ultimate arbiter of values and a moral authority entirely unto herself, how have we escaped the Dostoyevskian predicament that everything is permitted and nothing forbidden? The answer is already ready to hand. Though there is no external normative authority, either in heaven or on Earth, that supercedes our own, there is genuine normative authority in the world—the authority that lies within each of us. Each fully mature, intact, and reflective human being has the power to bind him or herself to a norm and thereby to commit to living up to those norms in ways that may even entitle others to hold him or her to the relevant norm. Once one has committed oneself, it is no longer the case that everything is permitted and nothing forbidden. Some things are forbidden to one simply because one forbids them to oneself.

There is an intricate story to tell about the normative authority that lies within each one of us. That story explains the source and nature of our normative powers, articulates the factors that constrain and govern the exercise of that authority, and outlines the consequences for individual and social life that flow from the exercise of that capacity. I lack the space to tell that story in detail here. But I need to tell a small bit of the story, if I am to be able to say why the rejection of providence and of every totalizing secular stand-in for providence need not lead to a paralyzing despair.

I begin by saying a bit more about what it takes for a person to be really and truly bound by a norm. The key lies with our powers of rational reflection. An agent is rationally bound by a norm *N*, if she would endorse *N* upon culminated competent reflection. To a rough first approximation, culminated competent reflection is a kind of "ideal" rational reflection. Talk of "ideal" reflection is prone, however, to carry certain unwarranted connotations. For example, some philosophers tend to think of ideal rational reflection as reflection that tracks the "objectively good," whatever exactly that is. Others believe that under "ideal" reflection, rational agents are guaranteed to converge on endorsements of the same standards or norms. As used here, the phrase "ideal" reflection is intended to carry no such connotations. There is, on my view, nothing in the universe that merits the title "objective goodness." Nor do I find it plausible that moral convergence is guaranteed to us. Even at some imagined ideal limit of moral inquiry, and even assuming the full reflective rationality of all, the norms that one endorses, and by which her life is thereby governed, may not be endorsed by any other. That is part of what I meant earlier when I said that it is a real possibility that human adventure will culminate in thoroughgoing moral fragmentation and enmity.

Not just any form of reflection can bind an agent to a norm, however. Excessive emotion, illicit substances, mental dysfunction, and immaturity may all disrupt or distort reflection. Under such circumstances, reflective endorsement of a norm would constitute no rational commitment to that norm. Reflection is "competent" only if no such disruptions or distortions exist. Competent reflection is thus the kind of reflection, whatever it is, that is more or less characteristic of mature, intact, well-functioning human minds. Only competent reflection about the course of our lives could suffice to bind us to norms. To be sure, standards of competence are subject to a certain variability. What counts as "competent" reflection in a pre-scientific, pre-literate, pre-philosophical age may differ radically from what counts as competent reflection in a scientific, literate, and philosophical age. But we need not explore such complications in depth here.

The reflection that binds us to norms must be not only competent but must also "culminate." Intuitively, the culmination of reflection is a matter of reflection coming to a stopping point, at least temporarily. We may reflect and reflect, but until reflection culminates, we have not bound ourselves to any determinate norm. Very roughly, reflection culminates when it produces an endorsement that is "stable" in light of all currently relevant inputs. Reflection culminates, that is, when further reflection would yield the same endorsement, at least given the same input. Now the stability in which reflection culminates is typically merely a local and temporary stability. The inputs to reflection change in myriad ways and for a plethora of reasons. They change in response to social and personal upheaval; in response to new voices, demanding recognition and respect; in response to new discoveries about either our individual lives or about our collective places in the order of things. Reflection is practically inexhaustible. We are subject to constant moral testing, to constant opportunities for discovery, for growth, for failure, for success. What stability and fixity reflection achieves, in light of the constant churning of the moral whirlwind, is likely to be but the fixity and stability of the dialectical moment. Still, when reflection achieves a stable and fixed endorsement, even if only for a dialectical moment, we have *decisively* committed to govern our lives by the endorsed norm. For at least this, we have given that norm our full rational backing. Giving a norm one's full rational backing amounts to decisively undertaking to govern one's life by the relevant norm. It is through such decisive rational commitments that we escape the Dostoyevskian predicament.

Now, I alone have the power to decisively commit myself to governing my life in accordance with a norm. Others may attempt to coerce me into living in accordance with some norm. Such coercion may even play a role in causing me to "obey" the relevant norm. That does not, however, make the norm rationally binding on me. I am bound—really and truly bound—only to norms of my own culminated competent reflective endorsement. Yet, despite the fact that another cannot bind me to a norm, she may nonetheless be *entitled* to *hold* me to a norm, even to a norm by which I am not bound. We must distinguish, that is, between being bound by a norm and another's being entitled to hold one to a norm. In particular, it is important that entitlements to hold another to a norm can arise in two different ways. They can be *self-generated* or *granted by the subject*. When *x* entitles herself to hold *y* to *N*, *x* has a self-generated entitlement to hold *y* to *N*. When *y* entitles *x* to hold *y* to *N*, *x* has a *y*-granted entitlement to hold *y* to *N*.

We endow ourselves with self-generated entitlements to hold another to a norm when we endorse that norm not merely as a norm for ourselves but as a norm for others as well, perhaps as a norm for the entire rational order. In endowing oneself with a self-generated entitlement, one takes one's own normative authority as a normative authority for all. Now, the urge to take what is merely one's own normative authority as an authority for all is both a blessing and a curse. Giving into such urges often leads us into moral conflict. But moral conflict is often a mere way station on the path toward more-encompassing moral community. Moral conflict arises when I entitle myself, through purely self-generated entitlements, to hold you to norms by which you are not bound and that you may even abhor. When I do so, you may entitle yourself to resist my attempts to so bind you. For example, I may endorse a norm that requires the abolition of slavery everywhere, while you endorse a norm that permits slavery. I may thereby entitle myself to hold you, by whatever means necessary, to my abolitionist norm. You may entitle yourself to resist my so holding you. When that happens, we have deep moral conflict.

I do not mean to say that agents are never mutually and reciprocally bound by a system of norms. When we self-generate an entitlement to hold the entire rational order to a norm, we may, in effect, offer that norm up to others as candidates for their endorsement as well. We ask others to ratify our self-generated entitlement by granting us entitlement in return. When agents do ratify each others' self-generated entitlements by granting entitlement, they thereby achieve *mutual ratification* of a system of norms. They thereby make the system of norms mutually and reciprocally binding on one another. They no longer enjoy merely self-generated entitlements. They have granted one another *mutual and reciprocal entitlements* to hold one another to the norms by which they are now mutually and reciprocally bound. They have acknowledged each other as full and equal partners in a normative community. To acknowledge one another in this way is for each to say to the other that the normative authority of one is also a normative authority for the other.

None of this is automatic. It grows haltingly and dialectically from an initial tension generated by agents' competing self-generated entitlements. These self-generated entitlements reflect first and foremost our self-recognition and self-valuing. Each fully reflective, intact, rational being recognizes herself to be an original, non-derivative source of reasons for herself. But almost without hesitation we sometimes take what are merely reasons of our own as reasons for other rational beings. Our tendency to extend our own reasons beyond our own domain is brought short by the recognition that other reflective rational agents value and esteem themselves in just thc ways that we value and esteem our own dear selves. To recognize another as a fellow reflective rational being is to recognize that the other is an original and non-derivative source of reasons for herself. In this mere recognition, we have already elevated the other rational being above the whole of non-rational nature. Non-rational beings, who lack the power of reflection, are nothing at all either to themselves or for themselves. They are at best a derivative source of reasons for any rational being. Non-rational beings can indeed be sources of reasons for us, but only in virtue of the rationally optional interests that we happen to take in them. We may esteem non-rational beings as instruments, as objects of wonder and awe, even as objects of a peculiar kind of sympathy or love. But they are not the kinds of beings for which even the possibility of normative community arises.

But the mere recognition of another as a fellow rational being, a being capable of the deepest sort self-valuing and highest self-estimation, is not yet the achievement of normative community. In the bare recognition of another as a fellow rational being, one has not thereby reflectively owned the other as a non-derivative rational source for oneself. Nor has one thereby limited the presumed reach of one's own normative authority. Recognition does, however, pose the question, "What, if anything, shall we do, be, or believe together as fellow rational beings?" This happens when we confront each other with concrete demands for respect and recognition of the normative authority that lies within. I claim here and now a right to what I take to be mine. I demand recognition and respect of my claim from you. Correlatively, you claim rights to what you take to be yours. Our claims may conflict. We are confronted with a question. How, if at all, shall we be reconciled? How, if at all, shall we live together? The struggle to arrive at mutually acceptable answers to such questions, a struggle in which we sometimes succeed and sometimes fail, is what I mean by the dialectic of ratification.

Through the dialectic of ratification, I try to get you to ratify me and my norms. I try thereby to make it the case that me and my norms govern your life. Simultaneously, you try to get me to ratify you and your norms. You try thereby to make it the case that you and your norms govern my life. When we are each governed by the other, we constitute a normative community. We have made ourselves into original normative authorities and non-derivative sources of reasons for each other.

Normative communities are among humanity's highest achievements. Through the constitution of normative communities, we extend the reach of our own rational powers. For example, through the mediation of mutually ratified norms of inquiry and communication that direct the truth to be sought and told, my having reasons for believing a certain proposition may give you a non-derivative reason for believing that proposition as well. Through the mediation of mutually ratified norms of conduct calling for mutual aid and cooperation, my having a reason for pursuing some good may give you a non-derivative reason to refrain from interfering with my attempts to pursue that good and perhaps even a reason for aiding me in my attempts to achieve that good. Mutually ratified norms are thus the rails along which reasons may be transmitted from cognizing agent to cognizing agent. Within a normative community, the rational powers of one become rational resources for all. Normative community thus makes possible the emergence of complex cooperative rational activity, including shared forms of inquiry, deliberation, and argument.

I stress again, however, that contrary to the dreams of, say, Kant, an all-encompassing community of reasons is not an a priori, rationally mandatory imperative categorically binding on all rational beings as such. Indeed, there are myriad ways in which we might fail, despite the full rationality of all who are party to the failure. The norms by which I would see the world governed, that I most urgently offer up for mutual acceptance to the entire rational order, may simply be rejected. That would make them an insufficient basis for normative community. But it need not make them any less dear to me nor in any way weaken my commitment to them. Not out of mere hubris or self-love, but out of deep concern for the entire rational order, one may self-generate an entitlement to shape the unyielding world by one's own normative lights. One may prefer to shape the world by the force of argument, if argument will suffice. But by what imperative must one abandon one's deepest convictions about the governance of the world, if argument should fail? Yet, were one to succeed through mere coercion in imposing norms upon a reluctant world, one would not have achieved true normative community, but the mere domination of one over another. With fellow rational beings who succeed through coercion in holding me to norms of their own endorsing, despite my abhorrence of those norms, there can only be rational enmity and a discord of reasons. Even if I appear to endorse their domination over me through incompetent or non-culminating reflection, that amounts to a mere semblance of normative community, not its reality.

Conclusion

I do not mean to say that discord and domination are inevitable. I mean to insist only that the building of normative community is always an achievement—a local, rationally optional, historically contingent, and politically precarious achievement. With this understanding of normative community in hand, it is time to face our final challenge. If we reject not only the providential hypothesis but also all totalizing secular moral fantasies about the historical or rational inevitability of an all-encompassing moral community, how might we rationally orient ourselves toward the human adventure? How can we avoid a paralyzing despair in the face of such utter fragility and contingency?

We must begin by acknowledging forthrightly and without hesitation that we are left with no simplemindedly uplifting alternative narrative of human history.

The voice of human reason speaks throughout history in a cacophony of competing ends that may never be reconciled. It is a real possibility that the human adventure may end in discord and thoroughgoing enmity or in the domination of some over others. But we modern secularists should take this real possibility not as a counsel of despair but as an urgent call to arms. The moral order is an order entirely of our own constituting. If we would build a world in which all stand equal before all, in which all are equally valued, then it falls entirely on our shoulders, and on the shoulders of no one else, to constitute that world. The work of building from the bottom up an all-encompassing moral order is heroic work, invigorating work, work that calls upon the best of ourselves.

There are, to be sure, many with whom we would achieve normative community who will reject from the depths of their own rational self-valuing the defining dreams of a secular liberal modernity. That very fact sets up a dilemma. If all-encompassing normative community is neither historically inevitable nor rationally mandatory, with what right do we seek to impose that vision on a reluctant world? Down the path of forceful imposition lie Stalin's gulag, Mao's Cultural Revolution, George Bush's misbegotten invasion of Iraq, and the dark dreams of Al-Qaeda. But if we abandon the dream of an all-encompassing moral community in the face of resistance, we open the door to unending discord and division. One might seek a middle ground in a tolerant relativism that acknowledges that each person lives by her own normative lights, that recognizes that normative lights may vary from person to person or culture to culture but refuses the very idea of self-generated entitlements to hold others to norms they do not themselves endorse. Though I count myself a relativist of the deepest kind, such tolerance is no option in our times. The contingencies of history have guaranteed that there are no peoples of the world with whom we can escape asking the question what, if anything, should we do, think, or be together as fellow rational beings? We are enmeshed with all rational beings in the struggle to constitute ourselves as beings in the world. We are brought into fraught contact through the relentless globalizing of commerce, through the worldwide degradation of the environment caused by our thirst for ever greater consumption, through the imperial hubris of the world's leading military powers, through the power of the media to bring the suffering and poverty of the world's teeming masses to the attention of distant and indifferent elites and the corresponding power to make that indifference manifest to all.

So what is the answer? How shall we orient ourselves in a world where nothing is guaranteed to us, where the pursuit of even our deepest most life-affirming aspirations may lead us into moral darkness? How shall we live in the face of utter moral contingency? I suggest that where the providentialist recoils from contingency, we atheists should embrace it. What could be more exhilarating than to know that it falls entirely in our hands to make the world as we would have it be? If Nazism or Stalinism or Islamic fundamentalism or American imperialism are to be beaten back, only we all-too-fallible humans can beat them back. If there is to be progress and moral harmony, only we humans, divided and as at odds as we find ourselves, can bring them about. Is humanity really capable of building an all-encompassing moral order, in which all are valued and respected? Let us try it and see.

FOURTEEN

Disenchantment

David Owens

The tension between religion and intellectual knowledge definitely comes to the fore wherever rational, empirical knowledge has consistently worked through to the disenchantment of the world and its transformation into a causal mechanism. For then science encounters the claims of the ethical postulate that the world is a God-ordained, and hence somehow a *meaningfully* and ethically oriented cosmos.[1]

Weber speaks of a tension, but for many, science's disenchantment of the world is instead a liberation. Science empowers us; it gets us what we want. Two things stand in the way of our getting what we want: technical obstacles and superstitions. Science eliminates them both. It removes the technical obstacles by giving us a *technology,* a recipe for constructing machines that help us get what we want. Beyond that, science conquers superstitions; it gives us a picture of the world, a theory of how the world works, which *disenchants* that world. The scientific picture of the world leaves out much that used to prevent us from doing what we want. It excludes from reality all sorts of imaginary beings, forces, and powers that used to constrain us. Once these mind-forged manacles are broken, we can take advantage of the technology science provides.

This essay is not about whether or not science gives us the whole truth about our world. I shall not ask if there is meaning in the cosmos or if, on the contrary, all meaning, all purpose comes from ourselves. My worry is that the truth of science would not be liberating. To empower, science must extend our ability to act; yet by draining the cosmos of meaning or purpose, science threatens to undermine this very capacity. And that should make us wonder if we can live in a disenchanted world. Religious worldviews may not be true, but we may not be able to do without them unless we can find some other way of imbuing the cosmos with meaning.

I'll trace the process of disenchantment, starting with the natural world, moving onto the human body, and finally arriving at the human mind. Science's claim to liberate is most plausible when confined to the natural world. But once we include ourselves in the scientific worldview, the worries begin.

Disenchanting the Natural World

The disenchanting power of science, its conquest of superstition, is what interests me. But first let us take a brief look at technology, science's other great gift to the human race. Technical obstacles prevent our actions' having the effects we desire: the car doesn't start when we turn the ignition, taking the remedy doesn't cure the cold. Once we understand how cars and colds work, we can surmount these obstacles. Science teaches us how these things work and, knowing how they work, we can build auto-ignitions and design cold cures that produce the right results. Science tells us how to manipulate the world around us, how to bend it to our will.

Technology is science's most tangible product. In the last four hundred years, a comprehensive theory of the physical world has been devised. During the late eighteenth century and the nineteenth century, this theory was applied to all aspects of human life in that great social transformation known as the Industrial Revolution. Prior to that revolution, people knew how to construct simple machines for specific purposes, but they didn't have a systematic recipe for matching any given human need with a machine that could satisfy it. They didn't have a proper technology. Science has changed all that.

During the nineteenth and twentieth centuries, our scientific understanding was extended first to the biological and then into the psychological realm. We figured out how living things evolve and replicate; we discovered the biochemistry of the body. Biotechnology in all its forms swiftly followed. In the eighteenth century there was a smallpox vaccine, but no one understood how it worked. Now we have conquered many of the major diseases that threaten mankind; we have a plethora of surgical procedures for repairing, or simply improving, the body; and the techniques of genetic engineering offer us new ways of manipulating both ourselves and the rest of the living world.

True, the human mind has proved recalcitrant, but even here there is some progress to report. Our understanding of the physiology of the brain is clearly in its infancy, and this shows in the crudity of our technology of the mind. We are good at handling relatively uncomplicated phenomena like pain and sleep loss. We are less good at coping with mental illness. Still, science has recently put new weapons into our hands. Prozac and Ritalin change the psychology of human beings in ways we think desirable. A comprehensive technology of the mind, a technology of our more complex beliefs, desires, and emotions seems feasible in principle. One day we might be able to transform ourselves as we can now transform our bodies and the physical world around us.

Technology is no good to us unless we are prepared to use it. One thing that stops our using it is superstitious doubt about whether or not it will work. Our battle plan demands action, but the horoscope looks bad; the plane is air-worthy but we are heading into the Bermuda triangle; AIDS can't be cured until its victims repent of their sins. Science tells us that these doubts are unfounded: they rest on a belief in supernatural forces and magical influences that have no reality. A superstitious belief in these forces might affect what happens in the physical world by influencing the way *we* behave in it, but the forces themselves have no impact whatsoever.

These superstitions prevent our taking advantage of technology by making us doubt its efficacy or reliability. There are other nonscientific beliefs that stop our using technology without questioning its power. Say there is an ancient oak in my garden, in just the place I would like to build a little crazy golf course for the kids. I decide to cut the oak down with my chainsaw. Many of us would have qualms about this, but not because we have any doubts about the reliability of the chainsaw. Wouldn't it be wrong to cut down such a magnificent tree just to build a crazy golf course? We might think this wrong because other people, my neighbors and future generations, would be deprived of the sight of this grand old tree. But, some say, it is wrong to destroy this tree for a quite different reason, a reason that has nothing to do with the interests of human beings, present or future. In their view, living things like an oak have a certain place in the natural order. They grow leaves, produce acorns, and become gnarled. In so doing, they discharge their natural function. We have no right to interfere with the natural functioning of the oak just because we want another crazy golf course. We have no right to frustrate the aims implicit in the oak's activities and terminate its existence. To cut the oak down and burn it in order to make way for a crazy golf course would be to misuse that bit of nature, to pervert its natural functioning. Here, the application of technology must be curbed.

There is nothing in the scientific picture of the world to support this line of thought. The scientist acknowledges that we human beings have purposes and we impose those purposes on the world: we fix our environment to suit ourselves. But the things we work on, our physical material, has no purpose of its own. I may make some sticks of wood into a chair and thus give them a function. But, apart from me, these sticks have no function. They could be used as a seat, as a doorstop, or as a bludgeon. Anything these sticks can do I could use them to do and that would become their function. It is people who determine what parts of the natural world are for: in themselves they have no purpose.

Of course, science acknowledges that trees have evolved, and it offers an explanation of their existence and characteristic activities. Oaks, like all other species of living things, are not designed; rather they are a product of random mutation and natural selection. By observing oak trees, we can distinguish those processes that aid the survival and reproduction of this species—putting down roots, shedding acorns, even fueling the occasional forest fire—from those that do not. But there is nothing here to support the idea that the tree's shedding its acorns is a more natural event than my applying a chain saw to its trunk. Our species has been destroying trees since the dawn of time: burning forests to make way for agriculture is one of humanity's most characteristic activities.[2] By doing such things, our species increased and multiplied. If that is all it means for an activity to be natural, how can I be upsetting the natural order by cutting down a tree?

In recent years, scientists have criticized the destruction of the Amazonian rainforests by logging companies. They point out that the destruction will have serious side effects—it will alter the composition of the Earth's atmosphere, for example—and the bad consequences of upsetting our ecosystem may outweigh the benefits of having more paper, fuel, agricultural land, and so forth. Here the scientists are appealing to the needs and interests of human beings; they object to the logging on the grounds that it will be bad for *us*. They are not saying that the logging somehow perverts the natural order, that it is intrinsically wrong because it fails to respect the life of a forest. That thought would make no sense to them.

The Industrial Revolution could not have occurred without the technical know-how science gave us. But, by itself, this technical know-how was useless; science also needed to disenchant the natural world, to strip it of any purpose that might conflict with our aims; once that had happened, we felt entitled to apply this technology everywhere. The Industrial Revolution required us to exploit the natural world, to interfere with its workings on a scale never before imagined: we had to dig up fossil fuels, create canals, divert rivers, build factories and cities on virgin land, and that was only the beginning. Those who did all this viewed nature as a resource, there to be used by humanity for its own ends and, with the aid of genetic technology, these people are now redesigning our crops and our livestock. For them, nature has no purposes of its own, it is dumb material waiting to be made into something useful.

When I speak of science's disenchantment of the world, I mean science's removal of natural purpose and meaning from the world. In many people's view, this disenchantment is liberating: it enables us to mold our natural environment to suit ourselves. How could we live without using modern technology? Who would seriously contemplate forgoing the benefits of industrialization? And why should we deny these benefits to those who don't already have them? Perhaps the scientific attitude is the right attitude to take toward the natural world, or at least the only feasible attitude for us to adopt. But science's powers of disenchantment now affect our understanding of human beings themselves. It is our turn to be disenchanted.

Disenchanting the Human Body

> It is impious, says the old Roman superstition, to divert rivers from their course, or invade the prerogatives of nature. 'Tis impious, says the French superstition, to inoculate for the small-pox, or usurp the business of providence, by voluntarily producing distempers or maladies. 'Tis impious, says the modern European superstition, to put a period on our own life, and thereby rebel against our creator. And why not impious, say I, to build houses, cultivate the ground, and sail upon the ocean? In all these actions, we employ our powers of mind and body to produce some innovation in the course of nature; and in none of them do we any more. They are all of them, therefore, equally innocent or equally criminal.[3]

Science treats human beings as a part of the natural world; it tells us how we work. Once we know how we work, we can devise technologies of self-transformation, ways of making body and mind more pleasing to ourselves. There have always been such ways: primitive forms of surgery (like circumcision) and primitive drugs (like opium). But, until recently, our knowledge was too slight to support any systematic technology of the self. Not understanding human physiology, we had to take disease, handicap, and physical appearance as givens, as brute facts that we must somehow come to terms with. Not understanding human psychology, we were subject to mental illness and mental defects of all kinds.

But, at least with regard to the human body, it is no longer so. Once our ignorance of the human body was dispelled, it fell under our control: we can cure disease, overcome handicap, and remove physical deformities. And now that we are in control of the body, why should we limit ourselves to curing illness? Why shouldn't we improve the body, mold it at will? Breast enlargements, pectoral implants, and face lifts transform our appearance; hormone-replacement therapy staves off menopause; surgery can (arguably) change our gender. The body has become malleable; it is no longer a given.

Some of these technologies of self-transformation provoke anxiety, but people find it very hard to articulate the grounds for their anxiety. Sometimes they appeal to bad side effects—breast implants might be carcinogenic—but that is an argument for better breast implants, not an objection to breast-enlargement technology as such. Sometimes people call breast implants "unnatural." This takes us closer to the heart of the matter, but it is hard to say why this should be an objection, or even what exactly it means. If I want to be muscular, I could go to the gym every day, or else I could have some pectoral implants inserted. The latter is much more convenient and probably less costly in the long run. Is it really more unnatural and more objectionable than visiting a gym? Is losing weight by dieting more natural than losing weight by taking a drug that speeds up your metabolism?

Anyone who has absorbed the scientific picture of the world will conclude that there is no answer to such questions. We must drop this talk of "natural" and "unnatural" where the human body is concerned. The body is a machine that is there to serve our purposes. Once we know how this machine works, we can treat it just as we would our car or our house. There is a rough-and-ready distinction between merely repairing the body, removing some defect in it and changing our body, transforming it in accordance with our wishes. After all, we make such a distinction in the case of cars and houses, why not for bodies also? But this distinction has no ethical significance: it is no worse to improve your house than it is to repair it. Why should it be any different with your body?

The image of the human body as an organic machine is meant to be liberating. By disenchanting the human body, science ensures that the body makes no demands on us, that it does not require to be treated in a certain way. Like the rainforests, the parts of the body have no purposes that we must respect, no modes of working and living that we must not interfere with. Of course we may encounter technical difficulties in dealing with our bodies—the body may fail to do what we want because of disease or physical limitation—but, in principle, all such technical obstacles can be overcome given the necessary knowledge and resources. There is nothing about the human body that must be taken as a given.

David Hume drew the logical conclusion: the very existence of the human body need not be treated as a given either. From the point of view of the universe, a human life is no more (and no less) valuable than an oyster.[4] The world puts no value on the life of a human being; only human beings do that. Once we cease to value a human life, once its continuance is no longer desired either by the person whose life it is or by other people, that life loses its value. Nature sees nothing wrong in "turning a few ounces of blood from their natural channels."[5] If that is what we want, nature will not stop us.

Hume's essay "Of Suicide" remained unpublished in the eighteenth century because it attacked a firmly entrenched prohibition. Since then attitudes have gradually changed until the view that there need be nothing wrong with suicide became almost the conventional wisdom. But doubts remain. Lawmakers who are happy to decriminalize suicide hesitate to authorize euthanasia because, they say, one can't be sure that the choice is truly voluntary, that people are not persuading their elderly relatives to move on before their time, and so on. Yet such worries do not prevent us sending "volunteers" to their deaths in war. I suspect there is a deeper concern here that our lawmakers are less ready to articulate.

Though many claim that there need be nothing wrong with suicide, far fewer endorse Hume's reason for thinking this. People still maintain that a human life is more valuable than the life of a cat or, indeed, an oyster. This can't mean that the continuance of a human life is wanted more than that of a cat or an oyster. Many cats want to say alive quite as much as any human being, and we humans may feel more concern about the fate of a beautiful oyster than we do about certain fellow humans. Nevertheless, we admit, human life is more important. And we treat what human beings want as more important than what cats want precisely because we think human beings are more important than cats. But if the value of a human life is not a function of how much anybody wants it to continue, how can the simple fact that nobody wants a particular human life to continue make it right to end it?

The continued prevalence of notions of natural value and purpose helps explain other aspects of our attitude to the human body. A few years ago, I saw a television program about a man who fervently wished to be rid of his healthy left leg: this leg was a part of his body he simply did not want to have. His left leg felt like an imposition, an encumbrance, even a deformity. The man's misery was clearly genuine, and we watched him search desperately for a surgeon willing to amputate. Unsurprisingly, all the doctors he approached turned him down. In the meantime, the man rendered the leg useless by strapping it in a brace, a measure that seemed to relieve his distress a little.

The makers of the television program did everything they could to present things from this man's point of view. Nevertheless, despite all their efforts, I had no doubt that the doctors were right to refuse him: it was psychiatric help he needed, not surgery. But why shouldn't the man be allowed to have the body he wishes, a body that fits his self-image, especially if this need to be rid of his leg simply won't go away? Why should he be condemned to misery when the solution is so near at hand? Toward the end of the program, our man was visited by another sufferer who had destroyed his leg with a shotgun in order to force doctors to amputate it. This man's life had been transformed: he was much more comfortable with the prosthetic leg that had replaced the amputated limb. He had no regrets. Why should we?

The fact is a healthy human body has two legs. A desire to be rid of a perfectly healthy leg is a perverse desire, one that has little claim to be satisfied however strongly felt. This desire should be eliminated, by pill or other therapy. The doctors refused this man because, they thought, a doctor's job is to make people healthy, not to give them whatever they want. It was not biochemistry, physiology, or anatomy that taught them this. These sciences explain only how human bodies actually work and how they came to exist. Evolutionary biology no more prevents doctors from cutting off a man's leg to make him happy than it forbids me to cut down the ancient oak in my garden because it makes me happy. What we ought and ought not do with the human body is beyond science's scope.

Yet we seem to have opinions about such matters, we seem to differentiate making a body healthy again, restoring its natural functioning, from simply bending it to our will. Is such thinking mere superstition, a harmful vestige of a prescientific age we should have outgrown long ago?

Disenchanting the Human Mind

> We can construct a railway across the Sahara, we can build the Eiffel Tower and talk directly with New York, but we surely cannot improve man. No, we can! To produce a new 'improved version' of man—that is

> the future task of Communism. And for that we have first to find out everything about man, his anatomy, his physiology and that part of his physiology which is called his psychology. Man must look at himself and see himself as a raw material, or at best as a semi-manufactured product, and say: "At last, my dear *homo sapiens,* I will work on you."[6]

Science drains the natural world of purpose; it disenchants our world. But science does leave some remnant of meaning and purpose behind: it acknowledges that human beings have purposes, that they have objectives that explain their behavior. Human beings don't just want to understand the world, they want to change it, and scientists respond to this by giving us a technology, not just a theory. There would be little point in doing so if human life were devoid of purpose. But how should scientists describe what happens when a human being acts for a purpose? How can they find a place in their disenchanted world for the meaningful activities of human beings?

I'm getting out of my chair and walking toward the cupboard. Why? Because I want a drink and believe the drinks are in the cupboard. Here my action is purposive, and it is purposive because it is motivated in a certain way. I have a *desire* for a drink, and I have a *belief* about how to get that desire satisfied. That belief is based on further things I believe about the world: I think the drinks are in the cupboard, I think I can get to the cupboard by getting out of my chair, and so forth. In general, purposive action is motivated by a combination of two different kinds of mental state: *desires* for various things and *beliefs* about how to get those desires satisfied. To have a purpose is to have a certain combination of beliefs and desires.

This picture of human action requires elaboration, but it will do for now. Certainly, there is nothing in it to which the scientist need take exception. In the scientist's view, beliefs and desires are both states of human organisms, states that causally explain the behavior of those organisms. When we say that a person has a purpose, all we are saying is that they are in a state that will dispose them to behave in certain ways. There's nothing superstitious or mysterious about that.

Normally, we act in an effort to satisfy our desires. But once we understand how behavior is caused, once we understand the physical basis of desire, for instance, we can exercise control over our behavior at an earlier stage, by manipulating its causes in the brain. Science tells us that we human beings are bags of chemicals. By discovering the chemistry of the brain, we will understand how desires and beliefs are produced and then we shall know the physical basis of behavior. And once we understand human behavior, we can predict and manipulate human behavior, our own included. A science of the mind yields a technology of the mind.

In fact, this is something we can do on a small scale without employing any science of the mind. If you feel a great desire for a mid-afternoon nap, you could take to your bed. But suppose you have to work and can't afford to sleep; then go to your kitchen and make yourself a coffee. That will not satisfy your desire to sleep, but it will remove it. By drinking the coffee you have engaged in a simple bit of self-manipulation. You have altered your psychology to ensure that you behave in the way you want to.

As our knowledge of the brain deepens, our technology of self-transformation becomes more powerful. For example, one of the chemicals in our brain is serotonin. Psychiatrists have discovered that by manipulating the levels of serotonin in our brain, they can change our desires. This discovery lay behind the development of the drug Prozac. Prozac affects all sorts of emotions, reactions, and attitudes. For example, those who find themselves more inclined than they would wish to help deadbeat friends or remain with abusive partners (perhaps because of their low self-esteem) can change their behavior by taking Prozac. They can deal with this oppressive desire to help deadbeats, and so on, not by satisfying it but by destroying it. Having rubbed it out, they are free of any compulsion to help others. Such desires need no longer be taken as a given: we can simply decide not to have them.[7]

What a beautiful illustration of the liberating potential of science. Prozac's popularity is huge: between its introduction in 1987 and the year 2000, some thirty-five million people made use of it. Yet Prozac has been causing concern. Why? Isn't it wonderful that Prozac is helping so many of us deal with the stresses of life? The public debate takes a familiar course. The opponents of Prozac, rather than making any direct objection to its use, point to regrettable side effects. But one of the main advantages of Prozac over previous generations of antidepressants is precisely its lack of obviously harmful side effects. It has been claimed that Prozac causes violent or self-destructive behavior, but the evidence here is inconclusive. The opponents of this new technology of the self find themselves unable to articulate the real grounds for their concern.

To advance the debate, let's focus on the idea that drugs like Prozac are liberating. It is not hard to see why fans of Prozac think so. Before Prozac, we were at the mercy of powerful psychic forces over which we had no control. Now Prozac gives us a way of controlling (at least some of) these forces, or else of extinguishing them altogether. Surely, Prozac can liberate us from the misery of mental illness just as the discovery of penicillin freed us from the tyranny of tuberculosis. Without strong evidence of bad side effects, isn't anyone who objects to widespread use of Prozac merely erecting superstitious obstacles to human happiness? In refusing to acknowledge that human beings are bags of chemicals whose mixture can sometimes be improved by psychiatric drugs, we may be cutting off our nose to spite our face.

What lies behind this gospel of liberation is a certain picture of what human freedom consists in.[8] In this view, human beings are free when they can get what they want. I am in control when my desires determine what happens. I freely get the drinks out of the cupboard because that is what I want to be doing in order to quench my thirst. Now, a psychiatric drug helps us get what we want in a rather special way: by enabling us to change what we want. So we now have a whole new level of freedom: not only can we perform the actions that we want, we can also have the desires that we want. Isn't this new freedom to be welcomed?

Vertigo is more likely. Science invites us to exercise control over our lives by finding out what we want, working out how to get it, and then acting accordingly. But now we are being told that we shouldn't take our desires as given, that we can act to change them as well. But if we can change what we want, what basis is left for choice or decision? If, when I want a holiday, I can either act to satisfy this desire or else, just as easily, act to remove it, how can that desire give me any reason to go on holiday rather than stay at home? Once the science of the mind is completed and we can alter our desires in any way we please, how shall we decide what to do? Far from expanding our powers of self-control, these drugs threaten to deprive us of any grounds for making a choice.

Is this all a fuss about nothing? Don't we decide every day how many cups of coffee we shall have and thus how sleepy we want to feel without experiencing metaphysical vertigo? Don't many of us drink alcohol on an evening when we want to feel relaxed and sociable, and abstain when we don't, without fear of depriving ourselves of the ability to choose? Isn't such self-transformation a common and unproblematic feature of everyday life?

Yes, it is, but, as things currently stand, our powers of self-transformation are very limited. We must take many of our desires for granted. For example, I can easily remove the desire to sleep by ingesting some caffeine, but there is no easy way to remove the desire to work. Most people feel a need for financial security and know they have to work regularly to get it: they have no way of making themselves want to live for the day, just like that. This fixed desire constrains their choices: their need to work gives them a strong motive for drinking a coffee. In the last paragraph, I was discussing the idea that such needs, needs we can't be rid of, are a limitation on our freedom, so that a drug that enabled us to decide whether we wanted to work or preferred to live for the day would be an important extension of our self-control. But this seems the opposite of the truth. Such drugs, by liberating us from desire, would tend to remove any grounds for choice. Only someone who takes at least some of his or her desires as given has any basis for action at all.

The Pharmacy of the Future

Your relationship is in trouble. The two of you get along well and seem compatible in most things, but nagging doubts about your partner's fidelity spoil your happiness. Sometimes you tell yourself these doubts are irrational, and you try to put them out of your mind. And perhaps they are irrational: it's so hard to judge from the inside. That lingering glance at the party, a late return from work: are these genuine grounds for suspicion, or events that any normal person would hardly notice? Whether reasonable or not, your doubts just won't go away, so what to do? Those who hire private investigators are beneath contempt, and raising the matter with your partner would inflame their anger without quieting your suspicions.

Clearly, your troubled psyche is badly in need of repair, and so you visit The Pharmacy of the Future. You walk through the door intending to purchase the new anti-doubt pill Credon. Credon will lull your suspicions, will make you credit your partner's stories and stop your scrutinizing their every movement at parties. Credon isn't an all-round gullibility pill: it won't make you believe whatever a random second-hand car salesman tells you. It works only in the context of intimate relationships. True, the manufacturers warn that, in trials, Credon has generated a level of trust between lovers that some might consider excessive. But who can say when it is reasonable to stop trusting your loved ones? That is for you to decide.

Having made up your mind about this, you ask for Credon, but your conscientious pharmacist suspects that you have yet to consider all the options. Aren't you taking it for granted that you should *want* your partner to be faithful to you? Why take that for granted, the pharmacist asks? Why not resolve your psychic tensions by taking the anti-possessiveness pill Libermine instead? Those on Libermine don't care whether their partners have the occasional tryst, just so long as these flings don't come to anything. On Libermine you can speculate with tender curiosity about your partner's fidelity.

Seeing you hesitate between an anti-doubt and an anti-possessiveness pill, the pharmacist can't resist making a further suggestion. If you think the choice must be between Credon and Libermine, you obviously haven't reflected on the relationship itself. This relationship might be as fulfilling as any you could reasonably hope for. But why must you be part of a couple at all? True, in the past you always felt miserable living alone and couldn't be happy without the knowledge that you were someone's top priority. Solox, the emotional independence pill, can change all that. Those taking Solox have a wide and satisfying circle of friends, can travel the world unconstrained by a partner's schedule, may leave their accommodation in just the state they like it. And they escape the costs of romantic intimacy, jealously included.

The choice among Credon, Libermine and Solox is bewildering. All resolve the psychic tension that oppresses you, but in quite different ways. Nor will the pharmacist hand over one of these drugs until it is clear to him that you have made a properly informed decision on the matter. But how are you to decide? Suppose Credon is the same price as a Mars bar, while Libermine and Solox both cost the equivalent of a good bottle of wine. Does that tilt the balance in favor of Credon? No self-respecting person would take Credon simply because it was cheaper. You are not short of money, and the price of a good bottle of wine is not going to make the difference between choosing to live in a trusting and monogamous relationship and opting for a quite different lifestyle. So what is?

You might try telling the pharmacist that it is natural to want to be in a relationship and abnormal not to care about whether or not your partner is sleeping around. Isn't that a good reason to choose Credon? But, at this, the pharmacist grows stern. Such judgmental attitudes have no scientific basis and should not influence your decisions, let alone your view of others. Many people, he reminds you, are born with Solox in their brains: they have no interest in romance as traditionally conceived. What exactly is "unnatural" about their psychology? Such people are just as much a product of nature as you or me. Why should the rest of us regard these free spirits as inadequates simply because they differ from us? Chastened by the pharmacist's outburst, you retreat to safer ground and appeal to the desires you find yourself with, carefully avoiding any evaluation of them and simply reporting their relative strength. Perhaps Solox would make it easier to travel, or leave your place in a tip, you say, but in fact you have no desire to travel and put great weight on a tidy house. Of course, the pharmacist will be unimpressed by this. You are still failing to appreciate the huge power of modern psychopharmacology. You are forgetting about Wanderlust (even cheaper than Credon), which will have you fleeing the country whenever you can. On Wanderlust, everyone can benefit fully from the effects of Solox. And though, of course, one shouldn't be judgmental about the house-proud, some might regard strict tidiness as a symptom of what used to be called obsessive-compulsive disorder, a condition that is still treated (in those who experience it as a problem) with the penicillin of psychopharmacology, Prozac.

In desperation, you change tack. "Perhaps I could live happily in an open relationship on Libermine but then it wouldn't really be *me* anymore; I would have destroyed myself by taking Libermine; I would have turned myself into someone else. And taking Solox would be even worse. I don't look down on those who are happy without a monogamous relationship, but *I* could never be such a person, and I want a life that expresses who *I* am." The pharmacist is unmoved. He reminds you that you were perfectly willing to take Credon: you didn't think that destroying your suspicious nature, and replacing it with a trusting soul, would make you a different person. Why should it be more of a change to alter the strength of your desire for a monogamous relationship?

How do we draw a line here? Science won't help us. In the 1960s, many people in the Western world who had sought monogamy abandoned that romantic ideal and opted for open relationships. Were they adopting new selves, or finding their true selves at last? Who can say? The "true self" looks like a piece of superstition.[9]

Bewilderment has now turned to frustration. You thought you had made a decision and that science would enable you to implement that decision. Instead, science seems to be putting obstacles in the way of your making any decision at all. The pharmacist is giving you too much choice, more choice than you can think of any grounds for making. By insisting that you take nothing as given, that you regard every aspect of your character as mutable, as subject to your will, the pharmacist puts you in an irresolvable quandary. You can't handle such total control.[10]

Why not cut this knot by making an *arbitrary* choice? Tell the pharmacist that you just want Credon and that's the end of it. After all, it is cheaper. In the absence of any other reason for choosing among the bewildering variety of equally coherent characters, personalities, needs, and interests on offer, you may as well choose the cheapest. At any rate, you know that, once Credon has taken effect, you won't regret the choice, being willing to believe virtually anything your partner tells you. But then, you reflect, you'd be equally happy with having taken Libermine. To decide between Credon and Libermine, you need to discover something that strikes you as a good reason for preferring one to the other *before* you make the choice. In a grocery store, you can happily choose between two brands of biscuits on the basis of a slight difference in price because this choice does not really matter to you. In the pharmacy, the choices you make are fundamental. If anything at all really matters to you, these choices must seem to matter. And if nothing seems to matter, there is no point in having the capacity to choose in the first place.

Conclusion

For Trotsky, the better we understand how human beings work, the freer we shall be. But The Pharmacy of the Future suggests that the more we learn about ourselves, the less free we shall be. A scientific understanding of man is a threat to our freedom because it undermines our capacity to govern our own lives by making decisions. If man is a just bag of chemicals, once we know what these chemicals are, we can re-mix them at will. And by re-mixing them at will, we can give ourselves whatever character we like. But if we can choose a character at random, our current needs and interests lose their authority as grounds for making any decision. And what other grounds for making decisions are there?

It is often said that science threatens human freedom when it insists that a person's actions are determined by factors outside that person's control: his character and environment. Several people wish to marry me and, it seems, I can choose one of them, or else choose not to marry at all. But science tells me that things over which I have no control (i.e., "character" and "circumstance") already determine which decision I shall make and what I shall do. People like me, people with my genes and upbringing, people with my education, in my economic position, at my age, choose to marry people like that. So, really, I have no option: choice is an illusion. I am no more in control than an autumn leaf, imagined by Wittgenstein, which floats to the ground while thinking "Now I'll go this way . . . Now I'll go that."

My worry is rather different. My worry is not that a successful science of the human mind will deprive us of the ability to make decisions by subjecting us to the immutable facts of our nature and situation, but rather that it threatens to remove the fixed points that are needed to make decision making possible at all. I feel not constrained but vertiginous. In a purely scientific picture of man, there is no obstacle to indefinite transformation of both self and environment. When learning the science of what we actually are, we also learn the science of what we might become. To be sure, man finds himself with certain needs in a certain situation. But science tells us that there is nothing normative about man's actual needs or his actual situation.

In Western Europe, religious belief used to be the principle source of those fixed points that make decision making possible. In the rest of the world, it still is. These beliefs may all be delusions but, as technology advances, the need for such fixed points becomes more, not less, pressing. Should science be the whole truth about human beings, that truth will not set us free.

I am grateful for the comments of Leif Wenar, Louise Antony, Sam Ishii-Gonzales, and Tim Crane on earlier drafts.

FIFTEEN

Religion and Respect

Simon Blackburn

Friday Dinner

Some years ago, without realizing what it might mean, I accepted a dinner invitation from a Jewish colleague for dinner on Friday night. I should say that my colleague had never appeared particularly orthodox, and he would have known that I am an atheist. However, during the course of the meal, some kind of observance was put in train, and it turned out I was expected to play along—put on a hat, or some such. I demurred, saying that I felt uncomfortable doing something that might be the expression of some belief that I do not hold, or of joining a "fellowship" with which I felt no special community and with which I would not have any particular fellow-feeling beyond whatever I feel for human beings in general. I was assured that what it would signify, if I went through with the observance, was not that I shared the world views or beliefs of my host, or wished myself to identify uniquely with some particular small subset of humanity, but only that I respected his beliefs, or perhaps his stance. I replied that in that case, equally, I could not in conscience do what was required.

The evening was strained after that. But, I argued to myself, why should I "respect" belief systems that I do not share? I would not be expected to respect the beliefs of flat-Earthers or those of the people who believed that the Hale–Bopp comet was a recycling facility for dead Californians and killed themselves in order to join it. Had my host stood up and asked me to toast the Hale–Bopp hopefuls, or to break bread or some such in token of fellowship with them, I would have been just as embarrassed and indeed angry. I lament and regret the holding of such beliefs, and I deplore the features of humanity that make them so common. I wish people were different. And as far as toasting some particular subset of humanity goes, I also wish people were not keen on separating themselves from others, keen on difference and symbols of tribalism. I don't warm to badges of allegiance, flags, ostentatious signs of apartness, because I do not think they are good for the world. I am glad that the word "race" has lost most of its reputation recently, and I would rather like the word "culture," as it occurs in phrases like "cultural diversity" to follow it. More moderately, we might keep it, but also keep a beady eye on it. When people do things differently, sometimes it is fine, but sometimes it is not. This is especially so with overt signs of religious affiliation. By all means be apart, if you wish, but don't expect me to jump up and down with joy.

"Respect," of course is a tricky term. I may respect your gardening by just letting you get on with it. Or, I may respect it by admiring it and regarding it as a superior way to garden. The word seems to span a spectrum from simply not interfering, passing by on the other side, through admiration, right up to reverence and deference. This makes it uniquely well placed for ideological purposes. People may start out by insisting on respect in the minimal sense, and in a generally liberal world they may not find it too difficult to obtain it. But then what we might call "respect creep" sets in, where the request for minimal toleration turns into a demand for more substantial respect, such as fellow-feeling, or esteem, and finally deference and reverence. In the limit, unless you let me take over your mind and your life, you are not showing proper respect for my religious or ideological convictions.

We can respect, in the minimal sense of tolerating, those who hold false beliefs. We can pass by on the other side. We need not be concerned to change them, and in a liberal society we do not seek to suppress them or silence them. But once we are convinced that a belief is false, or even just that it is irrational, we cannot respect in any thicker sense those who hold it—not on account of their holding it. We may respect them for all sorts of other qualities, but not that one. We would prefer them to change their minds. Or, if it is to our advantage that they have false beliefs, as in a game of poker, and we am poised to profit from them, we may be wickedly pleased that they are taken in. But that is not a symptom of special substantial respect, but quite the reverse. It is one-up to us, and one-down to them.

I shall not in this essay dwell on the infirmity of "anything goes" postmodernism. In the present context, that would be the view that belief is a purely personal matter, and furthermore one that is free from normative control. That is, any state of mind on such subjects is as good as any other, and it is some kind of infringement of a person's right to suppose otherwise. The bull's-eye is drawn wherever the arrow of belief lands, and everyone, always, scores the same. I think this is inconsistent with any proper conception of belief, which essentially requires a contrast between getting something right and failing to do so. An archery where you are allowed to draw the bull's-eye wherever the arrow lands is not a sport in which you always score highly. It is an activity in which there is no score at all. But here I can rest on the simple reminder that in everyday life nobody for a moment believes in this promiscuous equality of belief. If high tide is at midday, the tide table that says it is at midday is better than the one that says it is at six o'clock, and thereby puts you on the rocks.[1]

Religion may try to occupy a position where such inequalities of opinion do not apply. Perhaps there is no such thing as getting the nature of the gods right. I think the only honest way to follow this path would be to query the cognitive trappings of religion, or in other words, to admit that we are in the domain of emotion or attitude or stance rather than the domain of belief. I return to this below, but meanwhile I want to stick with the more traditional idea that there is such a thing as religious belief and that those who express themselves by claiming that they believe things are sometimes right about themselves. They do have beliefs.

People sometimes say they respect the "sincerity" of those who display passionate conviction, even when what they are convinced about is visibly false. Tony Blair is regularly given credit for his sincerity, at least by the right-wing media, as he remains the only person in the world to believe in Iraqi weapons of mass destruction. But surely we ought to find passion and conviction in such a case dangerous and lamentable. The tendency of mind that they indicate is the vice of weakness, not the virtue of strength. Far from being a sign of sincerity, passionate conviction in these shadowy regions is a sign of weakness, of a secretly known infirmity of representational confidence. If we sympathize with the doughty Victorian W. K. Clifford, we will see it as a sign of something worse: a dereliction of cognitive duty, or a crime against the ethics of belief, and hence, eventually, a crime against humanity.[2]

Sincerity is different from passion and conviction, since it is possible, and often appropriate, to be sincerely undecided. Here I like a remark of David Hume, who was perplexed by the frequent juxtaposition, in classical times, of bawdy or irreverent attitudes to the gods with apparently contradictory tendencies to show real respect for the gods, and especially real horror at impiety:

> Men dare not avow, even to their own hearts, the doubts which they entertain on such subjects: They make a merit of implicit faith; and disguise to themselves their real infidelity, by the strongest asseverations and most positive bigotry. But nature is too hard for all their endeavours, and suffers not the obscure, glimmering light, afforded in those shadowy regions, to equal the strong impressions, made by common sense and by experience. The usual course of men's conduct belies their words, and shows, that their assent in these matters is some unaccountable operation of the mind between disbelief and conviction, but approaching much nearer to the former than to the latter.[3]

This unaccountable state of mind is better accounted for, I shall later argue, from an emotional rather than a cognitive perspective. But it could be interpreted, rather literally, in terms of "being in two minds" about the Gods, in which case it oversimplifies to say that the subject believes, or that he does not believe. Rather he half believes, and whether his state approximates more to disbelief may vary with the context. The context of relaxed conversation with friends is very different from the context of an opportunity to beat up an avowed heretic.

Phrases like "equal concern and respect" trip off the tongue. But in any more than the most minimal sense of "deserving equal protection of the law" or equal toleration, there are, quite properly, gradations of respect. We respect skill, ability, judgment, and experience. The opinion of someone who has demonstrated these qualities is more important to us than the opinion of a newcomer, or someone who is foolish and wild in his reasonings. We defer to some people more than we defer to others, and this deference is a measure of respect.

Equally, we respect some believers with whom we disagree more than others. The quality of mind that got someone to believe something with which, all the same, we do not agree, may itself be more or less admirable. Sometimes, we can easily see how someone careful and honest and cautious fell into error. The illusion to which they have succumbed may have been very tempting; perhaps we can see how we ourselves would have been taken in had something fortunate not happened. In this case, we suppose, the defect of their judgment is minimal. They may maintain a reputation for general trustworthiness. At the other end of the scale, we can barely see how somebody could be so deluded at all, and we begin to think that they must be of infirm or unsound mind.

I think that intuitively we understand that beliefs are contagious. So if someone goes along with the herd and follows one of the major surrounding religions of their culture, this need not demonstrate much of a defect. But if someone gets taken in by a minority cult, there is less excuse. It might seem more or less wilful, or the result of an unfortunate stage of life at which they were especially at sea. Other things being equal, someone who believes that Jesus walked on water is not, in our culture, so many bricks short of a load as someone who believed that the Hale–Bopp comet was his vehicle to heaven. Holding the first belief is excusable, given that so many people have been repeating it to you since childhood, whereas you have to go out of your way to pick up the second. You have to acquiesce in your own deception, or want to be deluded. It is said that religions are just cults with armies, but they are also cults with a greater number of practitioners and louder voices, and those greater numbers exert more pressure on children and even adults to join in. So joining in is less of a measure of cognitive vice. Quite sensible people get taken in. But it remains true that we cannot both hold that they believe a lot of things that it is perfectly irrational to believe, and respect them on that account.

Whence, then, the demand for respect, the demand that even if you are not with us, you must admire us, or salute us, or smilingly stand aside for us? And why do many people go along with it? For to my surprise, I found that people split fairly evenly over the dinner party. I think it was tactless, or perhaps provocative, to lead me into a kind of trap; it was demanding "respect creep" to expect me to join in. Others think I was an insensitive and ungrateful guest to make any kind of issue of it. Indeed, I am not sure I would behave in the same way now (I might have to raise analytic questions broached above about just where on the spectrum of respect I would be being supposed to stand. But would such questions be well received?). So why not just be a good chap and play along? After all, it would not have been sacrilegious to do so, not in my eyes.

Religion and Onto-Religion

Perhaps we learn part of the answer if we turn to the non-cognitive side of religious practice. In postmodernist writings on religion, it is the done thing to distinguish between theology and "onto-theology," or religion and "onto-religion." Onto-theology makes existence claims. It takes religious language in the same spirit in which people calling themselves scientific realists take science. It makes claims about what exists, and these claims are more or less reasonable and convincing, and when they are true they point to explanation of the way things are in one respect or another. Onto-theology believes that there is, literally, a three-decker universe, somehow governed by a unified intelligence akin to a person who has various plans and preferences, and rewards and punishments at his disposal. The objects of religious belief—god or the gods—make things happen. They are part of the causal order. Religious beliefs are among the kinds of thing they make happen. Onto-theologians see no real difference between the way a chair explains my perception of a chair and subsequent belief that there is a chair there in front of me, and the way in which God explains the production of fire in a bush and the appearance of a couple of stones with commandments written on them.

Onto-religion is probably that which the ordinary person in the pew supposes himself to be holding and voicing by his observances. This is clearest when the observances include beliefs about this order of space–time and the causally connected events that may be expected within it. A friend of mine at Cambridge once had a room cleaner who was a Jehovah's Witness. Her life seemed to be passed mainly in happy expectation of shortly being among the few saved who would be privileged to ascend Castle Hill (a kind of hillock barely higher than the tallest buildings) and "watch the slaughter." She lived with a very definite expectation, just on a par with the expectation of night and day (or perhaps she did not quite, if Hume is to be believed). Much of what passes for religion in the so-called religious right seems about the same. When the shining day of Rapture comes, the air will be full of flying Christians, toting ghostly guns and riding ghostly SUVs, exulting over the slaughter of everyone else below. It is but a short step to supposing that there may be definite strategies for hurrying this desirable event along, such as blowing people up, or voting for President Bush.

Onto-theologians are the cheerleaders for this kind of religion. They puzzle, for instance, over questions such as whether or not heaven will make room for domestic animals, or what kinds of bodies, if any, we will find ourselves inhabiting after resurrection, or exactly what will happen to unbelievers. They may not be quite as unsophisticated as the Jehovah's Witness or the millions stocking up food and gas for the Rapture, but they are in the same line of business.

In more sophisticated circles, onto-theology is old hat. Instead we should see religion in the light of poetry, symbol, myth, practice, emotion, and attitude, or, in general, a *stance* toward the ordinary world, the everyday world around us. Religion is not to be taken to describe *other* worlds, or even past and future events in *this* world, but only to orientate us toward this world. Religious language is not representational, giving an account of disconnected parts of the cosmos, regions of space–time, or even of something like space and something like time, but in which all kinds of different things are going on. It is symbolic or expressive, orientating us toward each other, or toward our place in this world.

Let us call this interpretation of religious practice the expressive interpretation. Like other antirealist or anti-representational theories, it could be offered in a number of different ways. It might be offered as a description of the "somewhat unaccountable" state of mind of the ordinary practitioner in the pew. But this is unlikely, for as we have already seen, there may be a good deal of actual expectation and causal belief in the repertoire of the man in the pew. It may be offered normatively: the people in the pew may think of themselves as representing mysterious regions of space and time, but they ought to see themselves as expressing stances. Following David Lewis, we might call expressive theology the "minimal unconfused revision" of the confused state of mind of the person in the pew.[4]

However we take it, expressive theology makes it harder to be an atheist. In the days of onto-theology, we knew what went on when someone claimed that "God exists," and we knew how to argue that there is not the slightest reason to believe it. But once all that is dismissed as old hat, the plot thickens. If someone thinks the events depicted in the Harry Potter films really happened, or are the kinds of event that really happen, we can hope to mobilize observation and science and human testimony to disabuse them. But if someone claims that the movies express emotions and dreams that it is good that people have, it is harder to mount resistance. Nobody wants to disallow uplifting fiction.

If "God exists" becomes the expression of a stance toward the world, then rejection must be rejection of that stance. But we don't know how to reject a stance until we know what it is, and unfortunately, just here, matters become somewhat indeterminate. Perhaps "God exists" is to be seen as an expression of love or delight—and who wants to be put down as against love and delight?

But equally perhaps "God exists" functions largely as a license to demand "respect creep." It turns up an amplifier, and what it amplifies is often the meanest and most miserable side of human nature. I want your land, and it enables me to throw bigger and better tantrums, ones that you just have to listen to, if I find myself saying that God wants me to want your land. A tribe wants to enforce the chastity of its women, and the words of the supernatural work to terrify them into compliance. We don't like our neighbors, and it works if we say that they are infidels or heretics. This is religion used to ventilate and to amplify emotions of fear, self-righteousness, vengefulness, bitterness, hatred, and self-hatred. If this is how the religious language functions, we on the sidelines should not want people to be using it, and we should not use it ourselves.

I do not think the expressive account of religion could possibly be the whole story. This is because I doubt whether religion could perform this amplifying function if expressive theology were accurate to the sociology or the sentiments of the ordinary believer. In other words, I believe that the amplification works only because in the "somewhat unaccountable" state of mind there is a fair mix of onto-religion. The thought that God wants us to take the land or punish the women could not get its extra punch if everyone knew, and knew that everyone knew, that it was no more than a symbolic or metaphorical expression of the desire for the land or the repression of women that we have decided upon by ourselves. The idea of authority coming down, being delivered from outside, is crucial to the working. I believe it may be crucial even if we cannot find anyone who puts their hand on their heart and admits to believing the ontological bit. It might still affect them as an imagining that they cannot shake—and just as imaginings that we know to be such can all the same be possible sources of emotions such as terror, so they can form a possible source of self-righteousness, and its associated "respect creep."

All this is very depressing, as is the apparently unstoppable human need for it. Still, religions are human productions, and although human beings are bad, they are not all bad. Some of their productions and expressions of emotion are rather good. So if we are clear that onto-theology is no longer on the table, I fear that I become only an impure atheist. After all, I enjoy English parish churches, with their comfortable spaces and simple pieties, their quiet graveyards remembering past generations, the shadows of rooted lives in peaceful rural settings, the overwhelming sadness of lives cut short by events over which they had no control: outsiders' wars, pestilences, accidents. Inside these buildings, I do not feel the ghosts of people who wanted to watch the slaughter of others. Nor would I like to see such places disappear; I slip furtive coins or small notes into the preservation fund.

It is hard to confess, but I can enjoy religious music, and even religious poetry. I think the *Book of Common Prayer* and the King James Bible are great glories of the English language, and I am grateful for an education that did something to immerse me in their vocabulary and rhythms. I suppose I regard the Church of England as an old family pet: a bit moth-eaten, prone to scratch at its own fleas (gay marriages, female bishops) but familiar and somehow comforting, best when it is not making too much noise.

I do not think of these small and sporadic pieties of mine as themselves religious. I see them as second-order pieties, piety for those pieties of others with which I feel some empathy. The pieties of the people are human pieties, representing desire, hope, disappointment, remembrance, attempts to give public meaning to the great events of birth, marriage, and death. Even Christians are human. So these are pieties about which I am myself pious. I might even have to admit that I respect them in a fairly thick sense. I admire people who try to give voice to the great events and emotions of human life, and perhaps approach reverence if they do it as well as John Donne or Milton or Bach.

I would not be surprised if I took a visitor to such a place, and they felt no weight of English history—probably largely mythical, as history always is—and I would not be particularly surprised or disappointed if I had expected a shared response that then was not forthcoming. But in some corner, I myself "demand" that other people respect my little spasm of second-order piety. How would I feel if someone were not only left cold but, in turn, found me sentimental, or embarrassing, or just laughable for feeling moved? I fear I would be upset, as I know I am if I visit a foreign country and others of the party avert their eyes from the new scenes around them and wilfully, as it seems, just chatter on about their own concerns.

De gustibus non est disputandum, but there are very few such matters of taste. Kant thought that the judgment that something is beautiful instanced a paradox. Itself, it is subject to no rule, no deduction or proof of the one right way in which it is to be conducted. So it seems to be nothing but the expression of wayward pleasure. The paradox is that this pleasure "can be demanded" of others. Almost magically, it turns itself from a subjective expression of a personal reaction into a public requirement. "Demand" probably first seems too strong to us, twenty-first-century relativists, not very concerned about the diverse ways in which judgments of beauty bubble up in others. But when we know ourselves better, it may start to seem right. If we go to the Grand Canyon, and my experience of awe and terror and elevation are met only by your indifference and wish for an ice cream, the rift between us is serious. Of course, you may excuse yourself—you were tired, out of sorts, preoccupied, angry at something, had seen it often before—but unless you at least feel the need to excuse yourself, we are on the road to alienation and potential hostility. If you see the Grand Canyon only as an opportunity for starting franchises and tourist camps, then I would be disappointed in you. We might have to split up.

And it is a degree worse if you see the productions of human beings only in that light. The nave of Durham, the Taj Mahal, Stonehenge, Lindisfarne make moral demands because they testify to a human spirit that deserves some admiration, and even awe. It is not that we have to respect the beliefs that lay behind them (in the case of Stonehenge, nobody has any idea what these were, and in the case of the Taj Mahal few visitors do). It is the beauty and the energy, the sheer single-mindedness, and the pageant of the past that strike us as sublime and awe-inspiring and command our respect. If you cannot respond to that demand, we have to split up even more definitively than in the case of the Grand Canyon.

Emotions and Respect

Expressive theology is rightly an object of suspicion. People who go in for it sound like atheists in dog collars. It sounds as though they have discovered a nice cheat. You need only defend religious sayings as a kind of fiction, which is not too hard, for who can object to fictions? But then you can go ahead and use the sayings with all the force of conviction and belief. You have relieved yourself of epistemic obligations but kept the old fire and fury. And, as I have said, I think that a cheat is embodied in the whole procedure: the function of the language (the legitimation of attitudes and attitudes to attitudes) actually depends on ontological imaginings that the position officially disavows. Otherwise "God has told me this is my land," and "get off!" would function no differently, and if one were prey to uncertainty in issuing the injunction, it would be no help to couch it the first way.

On the other hand, expressivist theologians have a point. In the eighteenth century, people gradually realized that the classical arguments for the existence of God did not get you as far as you wanted. Even if the cosmological argument, or the argument from design, convinced you as proofs of existence, you then had to go on to think of some attributes for the god or gods you had arrived at. And that was bound to be a process of projection. If your culture applauds vengeance, you find a vengeful god; if your culture applauds jealousy, you find a jealous god, and so on. But in that case, why bother with the theological journey in the first place? The cash value of religious sayings and doings becomes the emotional license they give you. The apparent representations of transcendental fact simply serve to reinforce the stances of the culture.

The expressivist theologian says that this is exactly the core that is to be retained. The appearance that we are describing a transcendental part of reality is to be downplayed. It is but window dressing, clothing the emotional realities in ways that make them salient, or enable them to be communicated and practiced. It is like the myth of a journey up the mountain, to find words about how to live. But by keeping the people in the pews, it keeps them on side. The myth, and the dignities of the setting, the familiar repetitions, or the ritual or the priest then impress whatever stance is celebrated upon the minds of the congregation. To the outsider, however, it is more sinister than that. It is not just that the dignities of the setting and the rest express what was there before. The trouble lies in the amplification, the joyous rejection of reason, doubt, negotiation, and compromise.

I have said that holding a false belief does not give anyone a title to respect. Insofar as I cannot share your belief, I have no reason to respect you for holding it—quite the reverse, in fact. But the same is not true of emotions. If I happen upon the funeral of a stranger, I cannot feel the same grief as the close relatives and mourners. But I don't think they are making any kind of mistake, or displaying any kind of fault or flaw or vice. On the contrary, we admire them for giving public expression to their grief, and if they did not show this kind of feeling, they would be alien to us, and objects of suspicion. It is fair to say that we ought to respect their grief, and in practice we do. We may withdraw from the scene. Or we may inconvenience ourselves to let them go ahead (we turn down our radio). Or, we may waive demands that would otherwise be made (we give them time off work). Similarly, a birth or wedding is a happy occasion, and it is bad form to intrude on them with trouble and grief (let alone prophesies of such, as in many fairy stories).

So, expressivist theology can profit from distinguishing cognitive disagreement, which very likely does not coincide with substantial respect, from emotional difference, which often does coincide with respect. Peoples' emotions are important, and whether or not we can empathize with them, we do accord them time and space and a kind of shelter.

Putting emotion at the center also helps with Hume's "somewhat unaccountable" states of mind. Emotions can easily display exactly the ambiguity or ambivalence he notices, and without our thinking that the subject is in two minds about anything. A mother may berate her errant son, call down all the imprecations of heaven upon his bad behavior, find his music or his amours just a joke, yet simultaneously fight for him like a tigress if others try the same. It is not so much that she is in two minds about her son, as that she is in a position to claim privileges she denies to others less close to him. Classical authors making licentious jokes about the gods but then prepared to attack infidelity present exactly the same case.

Unfortunately, it is a gross simplification to bring the essence of religion down to *emotion*. The stances involved are far more often ones of *attitude*. And it is a fraud to take the space and shelter we rightly offer to emotional difference, and use it to demand respect for any old divergence of attitude. The relevant attitudes are often ones where difference implies disagreement, and then, like belief, we cannot combine any kind of disagreement with substantial respect. Attitudes are public.[5]

Suppose, for example, the journey up the mountain brought back the words that a woman is worth only a fraction of a man, as is held in Islam. This is not directly an expression of an emotion. It is the expression of a practical stance or attitude that may come out in all sorts of ways. It is not an attitude that commends itself in the egalitarian West. So should we "respect" it? Not at all. The case is the same as that of the Hale–Bopp comet. I think it is a dreadful attitude and it is a blot on the face of humanity that there are people who hold it and laws and customs that express it.

I have said that the "surplus meaning," or the ontological parts that the expressivist theologian would like to jettison, is in fact essential to the working of the attitude that he wants to retain. What does this mean? It is easy to imagine a stance toward women that more or less coincides with that of Islam but where the people who hold it are subject to no religious beliefs or imaginings or somewhat unaccountable fusions of the two. I think that the ontological imaginings do their work at a slightly different place. They work to close off questions and doubts and, in effect, to fend off reason. They cement a particular way of associating "ought" and "is" and insulate it from criticism. So it would be almost impossible to defend the view that women are worth a fraction of men on purely secular grounds (which is not to deny its purely secular origin—its origin in indefensible attitudes and practices). It would be much harder to say that the facts as we find them in the world make the evaluation not only reasonable but also secure, beyond doubt, such that it is a grave sign of villainy to query it. It is this bit that the ontological imaginings bring with them. It is not just that the right way to kill a goat is by cutting its throat, but that denial of this sets you so far beyond the pale as to jeopardize your membership in the group, or even your life. By closing its eyes to this bit, expressivist theology in fact repudiates everything that makes religious language the power that it is.

One of the more depressing findings of social anthropology is that societies professing a religion are more stable and last longer than those that do not. It is estimated that breakaway groups like communes or New Age communities last some four times longer if they profess a common religion than if they do not. We can now see why this should be so. A religious community can be defined in terms of the grip of imaginings that sprinkle fairy dust on the transition between "is" and "ought," ensuring communal support for whatever transition has become salient, enforcing uniformity, and making dissent difficult or impossible.

Meaning in the World

In this final section, I want to challenge the idea that religion itself occupies the entire territory of spirituality, or the search for meaning in life.

There are two directions in which people look for the meaning of life. One is beyond life itself; this is the transcendent and ontological option. We are to fix our gaze and our hopes on another world, another way of being, that is free of the mess and sorrow, the meaningless motions and events of present life. We are to transcend the small, squalid, contingent, finite, animal nature of earthly existence. Our insignificance in this cosmos is compensated only by assurance of significance in a wider scheme of things. There is hope in another world. And if this is hard to believe, spiritual disciplines of contemplation and prayer are there to help us. Others who have made the journey, wise men and mystics, inspire us with their reports, telling us of glimpses of the world beyond.

In this picture, the source of meaning transcends the ordinary mundane world of our bounded lives and bounded visions. The literature, art, music, and practices of religion are then thought to give voice to this attitude to meaning. This is, of course, onto-religion, since the attitudes are possible only if we believe in a world beyond.

But there is another option for meaning, and for our interpretation of religious art, which is to look only within life itself. This is the immanent option. It is content with the everyday. There is sufficient meaning for human beings in the human world—the world of familiar, and even humdrum, doings and experiences. In the immanent option, the smile of the baby, the grace of the dancer, the sound of voices, the movement of a lover, give meaning to life. For some, it is activity and achievement: gaining the summit of the mountain, crossing the finish line first, finding the cure, or writing the poem. These things last only their short time, but that does not deny them meaning. A smile does not need to go on forever in order to mean what it does. There is nothing beyond or apart from the processes of life. Furthermore, there is no one goal to which all these processes tend, but we can find something precious, value and meaning, in the processes themselves. There is no such thing as *the* meaning of life, but there can be many meanings within a life.

A fine expression of the immanent option comes in the scene that culminates in the death of Bergotte, the writer, in Proust:

> At last he came to the Vermeer which he remembered as more striking, more different from anything else he knew, but in which, thanks to the critic's article, he noticed for the first time some small figures in blue, that the sand was pink, and, finally, the precious substance of the tiny patch of yellow wall. His dizziness increased; he fixed his gaze, like a child upon a yellow butterfly that it wants to catch, on the precious patch of wall. "That's how I ought to have written," he said. "My last books are too dry, I ought to have gone over them with a few layers of colour, made my language precious in itself, like this little patch of yellow wall."

Just as Renoir or Hals enable us to see pleasure in the everyday, so Vermeer enables us to discover something precious in it, a dignity and tranquillity that require no purpose beyond the objects of everyday life themselves. In this vision there is only the simple harmony of everyday being, beautifully captured by André Gide when he described how in his still-life paintings Jean-Baptiste-Siméon Chardin depicted "la vie silencieuse des objets"—the silent life of objects.

Some find themselves pointing in a transcendental direction and some in the immanent direction. I suspect this is not a matter of deliberate choice but more a matter of temperament and experience, aided and abetted by the surrounding culture and accidents of education. Some are more comfortable in the everyday world than are others, and some are more comfortable with transcendent hopes than are others. Many lives have few or no moments of either dignity or tranquillity, and for those living them, the consolations of belief in something higher may prove irresistible. In moments of despair and desolation, the belief that this is all that there is may be hard to bear.

But equally, many hopes are vain and reports of the transcendent realm strike many of us as nothing but wish fulfilment, fiction, and delusion. And there is surely something self-defeating about imagining a world modeled on this, yet whose existence would give meaning to this, as if we could grasp a mode of being that would not, at the bottom, be just more of the same. And things do not gain meaning just by going on for a very long time, or even forever. Indeed, they lose it. A piece of music, a conversation, even a glance of adoration or a moment of unity have their allotted time. Too much and they become boring. An infinity and they would be intolerable.

Centuries of propaganda have left many people vaguely guilty about taking the immanent option. It is stigmatized as "materialistic" or "unspiritual": the transcendental option uses every device it can to demand "respect creep." But one must not allow the transcendental option to monopolize everything good or deep about the notion of spirituality. A piece of music or a great painting may allow us a respite from everyday concerns, or give us the occasion for uses of the imagination that expand our range of sympathy and understanding. They can take us out of ourselves. But they do not do so by taking us anywhere else. The imagination they unlock, or the sentiments and feelings they inspire, still belong to this world. In the best cases, it is this world, only now seen less egocentrically, seen without we ourselves as at the center of it, seen as Vermeer saw the patch of wall, or as Bergotte (or Proust) saw the representation by Vermeer. Such experiences can be called spiritual if we wish, although the word may have suffered so much from its religious captivity that it cannot be said without embarrassment. Fortunately, the phenomenon it describes does not die with it.

This is why an atheist should not feel guilt about responding to great religious works of art. If they are great, it is not because they excite the ontological imaginings, the bit that serves, if I am right, to inflame and cement peoples' moral convictions. Their greatness lies in the domain of emotion rather than that of ontology, and when there is a distinction, more in the domain of emotion than that of attitude. And emotions are reactions to this life, to the here and now. As I said above, even Christians are human, and their common humanity is expressed in the greatest Christian art. And the same applies to other religions.

The same strictures apply to ontological religious appropriation of the idea of something sacred, which blurs the distinction between emotion and attitude. The attitude part is that which really matters however. To regard something as sacred is to see it as marking a boundary to what may be done. Something is regarded as sacred when it is not to be sacrificed to other things, not to be weighed in a cost–benefit analysis, not to be touched. The memory of a loved one is sacred when it is not to be questioned or assessed. The scientist says that truth is sacred, when he regards deception, or even just inaccuracy, as shocking, and regards the idea that we might go in for a bit of it, say, for financial gain, undiscussable. We regard the night sky as sacred if, no matter how many people want it, or how much money they would pay, the idea of putting a large advertising satellite up in it, permanently reflecting Coca-Cola or McDonald advertisements, is not even discussable. We do not have to be conventionally religious to give these things their absolute importance. If someone tramples on them, it would be quite in order to talk of desecration.

If too many things are regarded as sacred, we have a life surrounded and hedged by fetishes. If too few things are so regarded, we slide into a world where everything is to be bought and sold, a matter of profit and loss. There is a balance to be struck, and it may well be a regrettable feature of modernity that we have not found it, and a severe condemnation of the capitalist world that it may make it impossible to give it political expression. What Big Business wants, Big Business gets, and just as that now includes the human genome and interesting prime numbers, so may it well come to include compromise with truth, and the invasion of the night sky.

If I think the night sky is to be treated as untouchable, and feel profoundly shocked and despondent at the idea of commercial exploitation of it, then I cannot respect those who feel otherwise. That is, I cannot respect them for that different feeling (even while I may grudgingly admire their ingenuity or the scale of their ambition). We have an issue. Nor can we agree to differ, for in practice that amounts to letting them have their way, if they can raise the money or interest the sponsors. I have to hold that they are wrong. Having the wrong attitudes is as bad or worse than having the wrong beliefs. The fault or flaw is more obvious here, when it is not buried inside a cognitive architecture, than in other cases where we think something must have gone wrong with a belief system but find it difficult to say just what it is. As epistemologists all know, it is not easy to locate the various vices of belief formation or to defend the view that they are vices.

But in this kind of case it is easier. Here it is insensitivity and willingness to impose, the equivalent at least of playing loud and often unwanted music everywhere, all the time. It is denying people a solace they want, or a set of feelings that can no longer be easily expressed, and that is a crime against humanity. We may call it a crime against the night sky, but I see that as shorthand for what is really going wrong. The cosmos is big enough to take the odd McDonald's advertisement, but we are not.

So in the end, should I have behaved differently that Friday night? I fear the matter is indeterminate. Was I being asked to express substantial respect for an ontological self-deception whose primary purpose includes protecting arbitrary attitudes and customs from the scrutiny of reason? Or was I being asked to show minimal respect, not much more than toleration, for remembrances and pieties that it is human to have and that desperately need protection against the encroaching world of cost-benefit analysis and the surrendering of unbridled power to economic interest? I fear there is no one answer. I fear that the somewhat unaccountable state of mind of my host may be interpreted in either way, and no doubt in yet other ways again.

The section entitled "Meaning in the World" rehearses material I originally presented at a Nexus conference in Tijburg in 2003, responding to an address by Roger Scruton. It has hitherto appeared in Dutch, and I am grateful to the Nexus trustees for permission to use it here.

SIXTEEN

Reasonable Religious Disagreements

Richard Feldman

A few years ago I co-taught a course called "Rationality, Relativism, and Religion" to undergraduates majoring in either philosophy or religion. Many of the students, especially the religion majors, displayed a pleasantly tolerant attitude. Although a wide variety of different religious views were represented in the class, and the students disagreed with one another about many religious issues, almost all the students had a great deal of respect for the views of the others. They "agreed to disagree" and concluded that "reasonable people can disagree" about the issues under discussion. In large part, the point of this essay is to explore exactly what this respectful and tolerant attitude can sensibly amount to. The issue to be discussed is a general one, applying to disagreements in many areas other than religion. However, I will focus here on religious disagreement.

Clearly, not everyone responds to apparent disagreements with the tolerance and in the respectful way my students did. Sometimes people respond by being intolerant and dismissive of those with whom they disagree. Some people advocate a kind of "relativism," according to which everyone is in some sense right. I will discuss these two responses in Section I. The rest of the essay will be about "reasonable disagreements" of the sort my students had.

My own religious beliefs will not figure prominently in this essay. However, it probably is best to acknowledge the point of view I had when I began thinking carefully about the issues I will address. I have long been what might plausibly be described as a "complacent atheist." I grew up in a minimally observant Jewish family. I went to Hebrew school and Sunday school for several years, had my bar mitzvah, and soon afterward acknowledged that I did not believe in the existence of God and did not feel much attachment to the religion. In fact, I felt some disapproval of the businesslike aspect of our temple, which, as I recall, refused to allow the younger brother of one of my friends to celebrate his bar mitzvah because my friend had reneged on an alleged commitment to continue attending, and paying for, classes beyond his own bar mitzvah. In college and graduate school, I found the arguments about the existence of God philosophically interesting, but studying them did nothing to change my beliefs. I remain a relatively complacent atheist, though the issue discussed in this essay challenges that complacency.

Intolerance and Relativism

Intolerance

Intolerance can be found on all sides of all issues. I react strongly, perhaps intolerantly, to intolerance, perhaps because it conflicts so sharply with what I have learned in the areas of philosophy that I have studied most extensively, epistemology and critical thinking. Epistemology is the abstract study of knowledge and rationality. Critical thinking, as I understand it, is a kind of applied epistemology, the underlying idea being that thinking clearly and carefully about any issue requires understanding and applying some fundamental epistemological concepts. These include the ideas of truth and rationality, the difference between good reasons and mere persuasiveness or rhetorical effectiveness, and the fundamental concepts of logic. In my view, to think critically and effectively about hard issues requires reconstructing in clear and precise terms the important arguments on the issue with the aim of discovering whether or not those arguments succeed in establishing or lending rational support to their conclusions. So conceived, arguments are tools for helping us figure out what it is most reasonable to believe. They are decidedly not tools with which we can clobber our "opponents."[1]

In fact, the idea that people with different views are opponents gets us off on the wrong foot. It is better to see others, as far as possible, as engaged in a collective search for the truth, with arguments being precise ways of spelling out reasons supporting a particular conclusion. Intolerant and dismissive responses fail to engage these arguments and therefore fail to conform to the most fundamental requirements of effective thinking. To respond to someone's argument in a dismissive way has the effect, perhaps intended, of cutting off discussion. It is as if one said, "I refuse to think carefully about what you said. I will simply stick to my own beliefs about the topic." This is inconsistent with the rigorous, careful, and open-minded examination of real issues, which is the essence of critical thinking.

Although religious matters often are discussed rigorously, carefully, and open-mindedly, some discussions appealing to religious ideas constitute blatant refusals to engage in intellectually serious argument analysis. An example of the kind of thinking I have in mind can be found in a column by Cal Thomas, a widely syndicated columnist whose foolish and simplistic words regularly disgrace my local newspaper. In a column about gay marriage, Thomas writes:

> Let's put it this way. If you tell me you do not believe in G-d and then say to me that I should brake for animals, or pay women equally, or help the poor, on what basis are you making such an appeal? If no standard for objective truth, law, wisdom, justice, charity, kindness, compassion and fidelity exists in the universe, then what you are asking me to accept is an idea that has taken hold in your head but that has all of the moral compulsion of a bowl of cereal. You are a sentimentalist, trying to persuade me to a point of view based on your feelings about the subject and not rooted in the fear of G-d or some other unchanging earthly standard.[2]

There is much that is troubling about this brief passage. For one thing, Thomas wrongly equates atheism with a denial of "objective" standards of truth, justice, and the rest. In addition, as anyone who has thought hard about arguments knows, there are difficult questions about when it is sensible to appeal to authority to resolve an issue. There are surely times when a sensible person does defer to authority. Many people who have looked under the hood of a malfunctioning car will understand why. To attempt to resolve a contemporary social issue by appeal to the authority of the difficult-to-interpret words in an ancient text is quite another matter. Furthermore, even if Thomas made his case more politely, it is hard to see the point of arguing about such an issue in a mass circulation public newspaper when you know that your premises are widely disputed among the readers. Good argument proceeds, whenever possible, by appeal to shared premises. Dismissing without argument the views of those with whom you disagree is of no intellectual value. Given all the time and energy I've put into teaching critical thinking, I react strongly to things that represent such small-minded departures from it.

It is difficult to say how, or if, we can get knowledge or justified beliefs about moral issues. Some sophisticated thinkers believe that all moral thoughts really are just "sentiments." Most disagree. But the idea that your moral thoughts are based entirely in sentiments if you do not believe in God, but have some more legitimizing force if you do believe in God is not at the forefront of enlightened thought. Let's put it this way. Cal Thomas is no insightful philosopher, and his thoughts about moral epistemology are scarcely worth more than a moment's reflection. The remarks quoted are from a column asserting that same-sex marriage should not be permitted. That is a complex issue. Judgments about what social arrangements are best for our society are difficult to establish. Well-intentioned people come to different conclusions. Religious bigotry makes no useful contribution to the discussion.

What is most irritating about Thomas's column is its bigotry. Imagine replacing the word "atheist" with names for other groups of people in the sentence, "If you are an atheist, then your moral views are not worth a bowl of cereal."

Imagine what an editor would do with the column if it said this about Jews or Muslims. Or if it dismissed in the same way the views of people of some ethnic or racial group in the country. But attacking atheists in this way passes the mainstream acceptability test. Cal Thomas may be dismissed as a lightweight, fringe thinker. But the view he expresses is a more extreme version of the altogether too common idea that atheists are somehow less than decent people. This attitude is revealed in the undeclared axiom of contemporary American politics that any remotely serious candidate for president, and for many other offices as well, must proclaim religious faith. Acknowledged atheists need not apply. A few months before I wrote this essay (in 2004), a candidate in the Democratic presidential primaries (Howard Dean) got into considerable trouble because he was forced to profess his devoutness in order to remain a viable candidate. I have no idea what his actual religious beliefs were, but it was difficult to dismiss the thought that he was not a religious man and knew that he couldn't acknowledge this fact without giving up all chances of winning the nomination. The reason he could not admit this truth—if it is in fact a truth—is the idea that somehow he could not be a decent person or a good leader were he not religious. I have no idea how widespread this nonsense is, but it is at least prevalent enough to insert itself into the popular press from time to time. The asymmetry of this situation is notable. While it is acceptable for atheists to be treated with disrespect by the likes of Cal Thomas, it seems (at least to me) that it is widely accepted that atheists are supposed to treat theists with respect and to approach theistic views with attitudes of tolerance.

The Cal Thomases of the world illustrate one intellectually bankrupt response to disagreement: intolerance and dismissiveness. I turn next to what may seem to be a diametrically opposed response.

Relativism

Relativists shy away from acknowledging that there really are disagreements. Relativists wonder why there must be just one right answer to a question and they often say that while one proposition is "true for" one person or one group of people, different and incompatible propositions are "true for" others. I think of this view as "mindless relativism." This sort of relativism is not at all unusual, and it may well be that some of my students had a response along these lines. These relativists think that somehow it can be that when you say that there is a God, you are right, and when I say that there is not, I am right as well.

Appealing as it may be to some, this kind of relativism cannot be right.[3] It is true that people on different sides of a debate do have their respective beliefs. But in many cases they really do disagree. They simply cannot both be right, even if we are not in a position to know who is right. To say that the different propositions are "true for" people on the different sides of the issue is just another way to say that they believe different things. It does not make the disagreement go away.

While mindless relativists are in some ways more tolerant and respectful than those who respond in the first way described here, it is notable that they also fail to engage with the arguments of others. Since their own view is "true for them," relativists do not see their own positions as challenged by the views of others. Therefore, they need not examine with care the arguments for those dissenting views. It is as if they responded to arguments on the other side of an issue by saying, "Well, that argument may be a good one for you, but I have my own view and I will stick to it since it is true for me." In a way, this response is almost as dismissive as the intolerance displayed by Cal Thomas, but it is coupled with a difficult-to-interpret assertion that the other view is right also. Of course, relativists need not respond in this way. It is consistent with their relativism to take competing arguments seriously. However, it is difficult to make sense of their overall position and hard to see just what they think the arguments are supposed to accomplish.

Neither intolerance nor relativism is an acceptable response to disagreement. Advocates of both tend to fail to take seriously the arguments for views opposed to their own. I will set them aside and turn to the more subtle and sophisticated view that I think most of my students had in mind.

Disagreements

Unlike relativists, most of my students saw that there were real disagreements about religious issues. Unlike Cal Thomas, they took other views seriously. They thought that reasonable people could disagree about the issues, and that this was exactly what was going on in their case. But what, exactly, can this respectful and tolerant attitude really amount to? A brief discussion of disagreements generally will help set the stage for a more-detailed investigation of this question in the remainder of this essay.

Genuine Disagreements

The students in my class disagreed with one another about significant religious matters. Some—the atheists like me—believed that there is no God. The majority believed that God does exist. Among the theists there were notable differences about the nature of God and about God's relation to the world. The details of those differences will not matter for the discussion that follows, and I will not attempt to spell them out here. It just matters that there were some such differences. As my central example, I'll use the disagreement between the atheists and the theists. But most of what I will say could just as well be applied to disagreements among the theists, or to disagreements about other topics.

In saying that there were disagreements among the students I am saying only that there were propositions that some of them affirmed and some of them denied. When there is a disagreement, it is not possible for both sides to be right. Most obviously, if there is a God, then the atheists are mistaken no matter how sincere, well meaning, and thoughtful they were. If there is no God, then theists are mistaken. The same goes for the other propositions about which they disagreed: What some of them believed was not simply different from what the others believed. Their beliefs were incompatible. If one side had it right, then the other had it wrong.

Some disagreements are merely apparent and not genuine. That is, there are situations in which people seem to disagree about some proposition but actually do not. For example, people arguing about such things as pornography may not have any real disagreement. Those "against" it may think that it has harmful social consequences. Those "for" it may think that it should not be made illegal. There may be no disagreement about any specific proposition. Of course, there may be real disagreements about one of these more specific propositions concerning pornography. But the example illustrates one way in which an apparent disagreement can be merely apparent.

Disagreements can also be merely apparent when people use words in different ways without realizing it. If you and I are arguing about whether John went to the bank, but you are thinking of a financial institution and I am thinking about a riverside, then we may have no genuine disagreement. Our disagreement is merely apparent, resulting from our different interpretations of the word. The unnoticed ambiguity of the word masks our agreement about the underlying facts.

There are several differences among people of different faiths that do not amount to genuine disagreements. For example, one difference between people of different religious faiths is that they commit to following differing practices. The holidays they observe and the character of their places of worship will differ. And a variety of other customs and practices will differ. These differences are not, in their own right, disagreements about the truth of any specific propositions.

Another difference that need not involve a genuine disagreement involves the presence or absence of a "spiritual" attitude. There is a sense of wonder or awe that some people experience, and this may play a role in religious belief. Of course, atheists sometimes express feelings of awe at the size, complexity, and natural beauty of the world and may express this as a feeling of spirituality. I do not know exactly what spirituality is, but a difference that amounts to the presence or absence of this feeling is not a disagreement over the truth of religious propositions.

One could try to reinterpret professions and denials of religious faith not as statements of beliefs about how things are but as expressions of commitment to different ways of life or as mere expressions of spiritual attitudes. But any such effort is an evasion. It is obvious that theists and atheists do not merely differ in how they live their lives. They really do disagree about the truth of the proposition that God exists. Any attempt to turn religious disagreements into mere differences in lifestyles fails to do justice to the plain facts of the case and is, perhaps, part of an effort to paper over troublesome questions. In the remainder of this essay, I will assume that religious differences are not merely differences involving commitments to ways of living or differences concerning the presence or absence of feelings of spirituality. They include genuine disagreements.

It is important to emphasize the existence of genuine disagreement does not rule out significant areas of agreement. There are obviously many things about which theists and atheists can agree. And there are many things about which theists of different types can agree. It may be that the points of agreement among the theists are in some ways more important than the points of disagreement. It is no part of my goal to overstate the extent of disagreement. Rather, I begin with the fact that there is disagreement and raise questions about reasonable attitudes toward it.

Clarifying the Questions

My students seemed to feel uncomfortable if they were forced to acknowledge that they actually thought that those with whom they disagreed were wrong about the proposition about which they disagreed. But that, of course, is what they must think if they are to maintain their own beliefs. If you think that God exists, then, on pain of inconsistency, you must think that anyone who denies that God exists is mistaken. You must think that this person has a false belief. You must think that, with respect to the points about which you disagree with someone, you have it right and the other person has it wrong.

Thinking someone else has a false belief is consistent with having any of a number of other favorable attitudes toward that person and that belief. You can think that the person is *reasonable,* even if mistaken. And this seems to be what my students thought: while they had their own beliefs, the others had reasonable beliefs as well. I think that the attitude that my students displayed is widespread. It is not unusual for a public discussion of a controversial issue to end with the parties to the dispute agreeing that this is a topic about which reasonable people can disagree. (Think of *The NewsHour* on PBS.)

Some prominent contemporary philosophers have expressed similar views. For example, Gideon Rosen has written:

> It should be obvious that reasonable people can disagree, even when confronted with a single body of evidence. When a jury or a court is divided in a difficult case, the mere fact of disagreement does not mean that someone is being unreasonable. Paleontologists disagree about what killed the dinosaurs. And while it is possible that most of the parties to this dispute are irrational, this need not be the case. To the contrary, it would appear to be a

> fact of epistemic life that a careful review of the evidence does not guarantee consensus, even among thoughtful and otherwise rational investigators.[4]

But how exactly can there be reasonable disagreements? And how can there be reasonable disagreements when the parties to the disagreement have been confronted with a single body of evidence? And can they sensibly acknowledge, as I have suggested they do, that the other side is reasonable as well?

To sharpen these questions, I will introduce some terminology. Let's say that two people have a *disagreement* when one believes a proposition and the other denies (i.e., disbelieves) that proposition. Let's say that two people have a *reasonable disagreement* when they have a disagreement and each is reasonable (or justified) in his or her belief. Let's say that people are *epistemic peers* when they are roughly equal with respect to intelligence, reasoning powers, background information, and so on.[5] When people have had a full discussion of a topic and have not withheld relevant information, we will say that they have *shared their evidence* about that topic.[6] There is some question about whether people can ever share *all* their evidence. This issue will arise later.

With all this in mind, I can now pose in a somewhat more precise way the questions the attitudes of my students provoked.

> Q1 Can epistemic peers who have shared their evidence have reasonable disagreements?
>
> Q2 Can epistemic peers who have shared their evidence reasonably maintain their own belief yet also think that the other party to the disagreement is also reasonable?

The point about the people being peers and sharing their evidence is crucial. No doubt people with different bodies of evidence can reasonably disagree. Suppose Early and Late both watch the six o'clock news and hear the weather forecast for rain the next day. Early goes to sleep early, but Late watches the late news and hears a revised forecast, calling for no rain. When they get up in the morning, they have different beliefs about what the weather will be that day. We may assume that each is reasonable. Their differing evidence makes this easy to understand. But if they were to share the evidence, in this case by Late's telling Early about the revised forecast, it would be harder to see how a reasonable disagreement would still be possible. So the puzzling case is the one in which each person knows about the other's reasons.

People who are not peers because of vastly different experiences and life histories can justifiably believe very different things. For example, the ancients may have justifiably believed that the Earth is flat and thus "disagreed" with our view that it is approximately round. There is nothing particularly mysterious about this. But this does not help explain how there could be a reasonable disagreement in my classroom. No matter how isolated my students had been earlier in their lives, they were not isolated anymore. They knew that there were all these smart kids in the room who believed very different things. And they had a good idea of why these other students believed as they did. Q1 asks whether they could reasonably disagree under those conditions. In effect, Q2 asks if a party to one of these disagreements can reasonably think that his or her disagreement is in fact a reasonable one. This is a way of asking if a party to a disagreement can reasonably come away from that disagreement thinking "reasonable people can disagree about this." Can they think something like, "Well, my answer is correct, but your answer is a reasonable one as well"?

Affirmative answers to Q1 and Q2 will support the tolerant and supportive attitudes my students wanted to maintain. In most of what follows, I will emphasize Q2, but Q1 will enter the discussion as well. Unfortunately, I cannot see a good way to defend affirmative answers, at least when the questions are interpreted in what I take to be their most straightforward senses. As will become apparent, open and honest discussion seems to have the puzzling effect of making reasonable disagreement impossible.

Avoiding Misinterpretations

It will be useful to distinguish the questions I am focusing on from some others that might be expressed in similar language. The need for this clarification of the questions arises from the fact that the word "reasonable" is used in many different ways. To be clear about our questions, it is necessary to separate out the intended usage from some others.

One might describe a person who generally thinks and behaves in a reasonable way as a "reasonable person." Just as an honest person might tell an infrequent lie, a reasonable person might have an occasional unreasonable belief. When he had such a belief, the reasonable person would disagree with another reasonable person who has similar evidence but is not suffering from this lapse of rationality. The issue that puzzles me is not whether or not generally reasonable people can disagree in a specific case, even when they have the same evidence. Surely they can. The issue is whether they are both reasonable in the contested case.

People sometimes use the word "reasonable" in a watered-down way, so that anyone who is not being flagrantly unreasonable counts as being reasonable. If a person holding a belief is trying to be sensible and is not making self-evident blunders, then the belief counts as "reasonable" in this watered-down sense. This strikes me as far too lenient a standard. It counts as reasonable a variety of beliefs that rest on confusions, misunderstandings, incorrect evaluations of evidence, and the like. If this is all that is required to be reasonable, then it is easy to see that there can be reasonable disagreements among people who have shared their evidence. But this minimal concept of reasonableness is not what I have in mind, and it is surely not what my students had in mind. They did not want to say of their fellow students merely that they were not making obvious blunders. They wanted to say something more favorable than that. According to this stronger notion of being reasonable, a belief is reasonable only when it has adequate evidential support.

Sometimes a belief has enormous practical significance for a person. Consider, for example, a hostage and a neutral reporter on the scene. They may have the same evidence about the prospects for the hostage's release. However, the hostage may have a better chance of surviving his ordeal if he has the optimistic belief that he will be set free, while the reporter may have no special interest in the case. The hostage, therefore, has a motive for believing he will be released that the reporter lacks. Even if he has only a very limited amount of supporting evidence, we might say that the hostage is reasonable in so believing, given the practical value the belief has for him. The reporter would not be reasonable in that same belief. This, however, is not an evaluation of the evidential merit of the belief, but rather of its prudential or practical value. One somewhat odd way to put the point is to say that it is (prudentially or practically) reasonable for the hostage to have an (epistemically) unreasonable belief in this situation. My interest is in the epistemic, or evidential, evaluations.

This point is particularly significant in the present setting. The issue I am raising about religious beliefs, and disagreements involving them, is not about whether religious belief is beneficial. It may in fact be beneficial to some people and not others. It may be that some or all of the theists in my class led better lives partly as a result of their theism, and it may be that the atheists are better off being atheists. Nothing I will say here has any direct bearing on that question. My topic has to do with questions about what to make of disagreements about whether or not religious beliefs are true.

Finally, my questions have to do with belief, not with associated behavior. There are cases in which people with similar evidence reasonably behave differently. Suppose that we are on the way to an important meeting and we come to a fork in the road. The map shows no fork, and we have no way to get more information about which way to go. We have to choose. You choose the left path and I choose the right path. Each of us may be entirely reasonable in choosing as we do. Of course, we would have been reasonable in choosing otherwise. But, as you go left and I go right, neither of us is reasonable in believing that we've chosen the correct path. Believing differs from acting, in a case like this. The reasonable attitude to take toward the proposition that, say, the left path is the correct path is suspension of judgment. Neither belief nor disbelief is supported. Each of us should suspend judgment about which path is best, while picking one since, as we envision the case, not taking either path would be the worst choice of all. As this case illustrates, acting and believing are different. Sometimes it is reasonable to act a certain way while it is not reasonable to believe that that way of acting will be successful.

It is possible that the choice about being religious or not, or the choice among the various religions, is in some ways like the fork-in-the-road example. This is an extremely important choice we must make, and our information about the matter is limited. No one is to be criticized for making a choice. If this is right, it may show that our religious choices have a kind of practical rationality. However, it does not show that our religious beliefs are epistemically rational.

All the cases described in this section are cases in which one might plausibly say that epistemic peers who have shared their evidence about a proposition can reasonably disagree. But they are not the sorts of cases I want to examine. I take it that the students in my class wanted to say that other students with other beliefs were epistemically reasonable with respect to their specific beliefs, and not just generally reasonable folks. They were not saying merely that others were not patently unreasonable. And they weren't saying that the beliefs of the others were merely of practical value. Nor were they saying that some related behavior was reasonable. They were saying that these were genuinely reasonable disagreements with shared, or at least nearly shared, evidence. These are the core cases of apparent reasonable disagreement.

Defenses of Reasonable Disagreements

In this section, I will consider four lines of thought supporting the view that my students could have been having a reasonable disagreement.

Drawing Different Conclusions from the Same Evidence

One might think that it is clear that people can reasonably draw different conclusions from the same evidence. A simple example seems to support that claim. I will argue, however, that reflection on the example shows that it supports the opposite conclusion.

There are situations in which one might say that a good case can be made for each of two incompatible propositions. For example, suppose a detective has strong evidence incriminating Lefty and also has strong evidence incriminating Righty of the same crime. Assume that the detective knows that only one suspect could be guilty. One might think that since a case could be made for either suspect, the detective could reasonably believe that Lefty is guilty and Righty is not, but could also reasonably believe that Righty is guilty and Lefty is not. She gets to choose. If anything like this is right, then there can be reasonable disagreements in the intended sense. If there were two detectives with this same evidence, they could reasonably disagree, one believing that Lefty is guilty and the other believing that Righty is guilty. Each could also agree that the other is reasonable in drawing the contrary conclusion.

I think, however, that this analysis of the case is seriously mistaken. It is clear that the detectives should suspend judgment in this sort of case (given only two possible candidates for guilt). The evidence for Lefty is evidence against Righty. Believing a particular suspect to be guilty on the basis of this combined evidence is simply not reasonable. Furthermore, it is hard to make clear sense of the thought that the other belief is reasonable. Suppose one of the detectives believes that Lefty is guilty. She can then infer that Righty is not guilty. But if she can draw this inference, she cannot also reasonably think that it is reasonable to conclude that Righty is guilty. This combination of beliefs simply does not make sense.

Thinking about the case of Lefty and Righty suggests that one cannot reasonably choose belief or disbelief in a case like this. The only reasonable option is to suspend judgment. These considerations lend support to an idea that I will call "The Uniqueness Thesis." This is the idea that a body of evidence justifies at most one proposition out of a competing set of propositions (e.g., one theory out of a bunch of exclusive alternatives) and that it justifies at most one attitude toward any particular proposition. As I think of things, our options with respect to any proposition are believing, disbelieving, and suspending judgment. The Uniqueness Thesis says that, given a body of evidence, one of these attitudes is the rationally justified one.

If The Uniqueness Thesis is correct, then there cannot be any reasonable disagreements in cases in which two people have exactly the same evidence. That evidence uniquely determines one correct attitude, whether it be belief, disbelief, or suspension of judgment. And reflection on the case of Lefty and Righty lends strong support to The Uniqueness Thesis.

It is worth adding that the order in which one gets one's evidence on the topic makes no difference in cases like this. Suppose the detective first learns the evidence about Lefty, and reasonably concludes that Lefty is guilty. She then acquires the comparable evidence about Righty. The fact that she already believes that Lefty is guilty makes no difference. She still should suspend judgment. The principles of rational belief do not include a law of inertia.

Different Starting Points

One might think that, in addition to the evidence one brings to bear on an issue, there are some fundamental principles or starting points that affect one's conclusions. Whether these starting points amount to fundamental claims about the world or epistemological principles about how to deal with evidence, the idea is that these differences enable people with the same evidence to reasonably arrive at different conclusions.

The idea behind this thought can be developed as an objection to my analysis of the case of Lefty and Righty. It is possible that two detectives looking at the same evidence may come to different conclusions because they weigh the evidential factors differently.[7] Suppose part of the case against Lefty includes the fact Lefty has embezzled money from the firm, while part of the case against Righty includes the fact he is suspected of having had an affair. One detective might think that one factor is more significant, or a better indicator of guilt, while the other weighs the other factor more heavily. Hence, they have the same evidence, yet they weigh the elements of that evidence differently and thus come to different conclusions. To make a case for reasonable disagreements out of this, it must be added that either way of weighing these factors counts as reasonable.

I think, however, that this response just pushes the question back a step. We can now ask which factor should be weighed more heavily. It could be that the detectives have reasons for weighing the factors as they do. If so, then they can discuss those reasons and come to a conclusion about which really is most significant. If not, then they should acknowledge that they do not really have good reasons for weighing them as they do and thus for coming to their preferred conclusions. To think otherwise requires thinking that, in effect, they get their preferred ways to weigh the factors for "free"—they do not need reasons for these preferences. But I see no reason at all to grant them this license.

A related idea is that people may have different fundamental principles or worldviews. Perhaps there are some basic ways of looking at things that people typically just take for granted. Maybe acceptance of a scientific worldview is one such fundamental principle. Maybe a religious outlook is another. Or, maybe there are some more-fundamental principles from which these differences emerge. A difficult project, which I will not undertake here, is to identify just what these starting points or fundamental principles might be and to explain how they might affect the sorts of disagreements under discussion. But whatever they are, I do not think that they will help solve the problem. Once people have engaged in a full discussion of issues, their different starting points will be apparent. And then those claims will themselves be open for discussion and evaluation. These different starting points help support the existence of reasonable disagreements only if each side can reasonably maintain its starting point after they have been brought out into the open. And this idea can support the tolerant attitude my students wanted to maintain only if people can think that their own starting point is reasonable and that different and incompatible starting points are reasonable as well.[8] I cannot understand how that could be true. Once you see that there are these alternative starting points, you need a reason to prefer one over the other. There may be practical benefit to picking one. But it does not yield rational belief. The starting points are simply analogues of the two forks in the road, in the example considered earlier.

The Evidence Is Not Fully Shared

In any realistic case, the totality of one's evidence concerning a proposition will be a long and complex story, much of which may be difficult to put into words. This makes it possible that each party to a disagreement has an extra bit of evidence,

evidence that has not been shared. You might think that each person's unshared evidence can justify that person's beliefs. For example, there is something about the atheist's total evidence that can justify his belief, and there is something different about the theist's total evidence that can justify her belief. Of course, not all cases of disagreement need to turn out this way. But perhaps some do, and perhaps this is what the students in my class thought was going on in our class. And, more generally, perhaps this is what people generally think is going on when they conclude that reasonable people can disagree.

On this view, the apparent cases of reasonable disagreement are cases in which people have shared only a portion of their evidence. Perhaps if *all* the evidence were shared, there could not be a reasonable disagreement. This is the consequence of The Uniqueness Thesis. But, according to the present idea, there are no cases of fully shared evidence, or at least no realistic cases. If we take (Q1) and (Q2) to be about cases in which all the evidence is shared, then the answer to both questions is "no." But if we take the questions to be about cases in which the evidence is shared as fully as is realistically possible, then the answers are "yes." We might say that the reasonable disagreements are possible in those cases in which each side has private evidence supporting its view.

It is possible that the private evidence includes the private religious (or non-religious) experiences one has. Another possible way to think about private evidence is to identify it with the clear sense one has that the body of shared evidence—the arguments—really do support one's own view. The theist's evidence is whatever is present in the arguments, plus her strong sense or intuition or "insight" that the arguments, on balance, support her view.[9] Likewise for the atheist. A similar idea emerges in Gideon Rosen's discussion of disagreement in ethics. He talks of the sense of "obviousness" of the proposition under discussion. He writes:

> If the obviousness of the contested claim survives the encounter with . . . [another person] . . . then one still has some reason to hold it: the reason provided by the seeming. If, after reflecting on the rational tenability of an ethos that prizes cruelty, cruelty continues to strike me as self-evidently reprehensible, then my conviction that it is reprehensible has a powerful and cogent ground, despite my recognition that others who lack this ground may be fully justified in thinking otherwise.[10]

The idea, then, is that the seeming obviousness, or the intuitive correctness, of one's position counts as evidence. The theist and the atheist each have such private evidence for their respective beliefs. Hence, according to this line of thought, each is justified. That's how both parties to the disagreement can reasonably draw different conclusions.

This response will not do. To see why, compare a more straightforward case of regular sight, rather than insight. Suppose you and I are standing by the window looking out on the quad. We think we have comparable vision and we know each other to be honest. I seem to see what looks to me like the dean standing out in the middle of the quad. (Assume that this is not something odd. He's out there a fair amount.) I believe that the dean is standing on the quad. Meanwhile, you seem to see nothing of the kind there. You think that no one, and thus not the dean, is standing in the middle of the quad. We disagree. Prior to our saying anything, each of us believes reasonably. Then I say something about the dean's being on the quad, and we find out about our situation. In my view, once that happens, each of us should suspend judgment. We each know that something weird is going on, but we have no idea which of us has the problem. Either I am "seeing things," or you are missing something. I would not be reasonable in thinking that the problem is in your head, nor would you be reasonable in thinking that the problem is in mine.

Similarly, I think, even if it is true that the theists and the atheists have private evidence, this does not get us out of the problem. Each may have his or her own special insight or sense of obviousness. But each knows about the other's insight. Each knows that this insight has evidential force. And now I see no basis for either of them justifying his own belief simply because the one insight happens to occur inside of him. A point about evidence that plays a role here is this: evidence of evidence is evidence. More carefully, evidence that there is evidence for *P* is evidence for *P*. Knowing that the other has an insight provides each of them with evidence.

Consider again the example involving the two suspects in a criminal case, Lefty and Righty. Suppose now that there are two detectives investigating the case, one who has the evidence about Lefty and one who has the evidence incriminating Righty. They each justifiably believe in their man's guilt. And then each finds out that the other detective has evidence incriminating the other suspect. If things are on a par, then suspension of judgment is called for. If one detective has no reason at all to think that the other's evidence is inferior to hers, yet she continues to believe that Lefty is guilty, she would be unjustified. She is giving special status to her own evidence with no reason to do so, and this is an epistemic error, a failure to treat like cases alike. She knows that there are two bodies of equally good evidence for incompatible propositions, and she is favoring the one that happens to have been hers originally.

In each case, one has one's own evidence supporting a proposition, knows that another person has comparable evidence supporting a competing proposition, and has no reason to think that one's own reason is the non-defective one. In the example about seeing the dean, I cannot reasonably say, "Well, it's really seeming to me like the dean is there. So, even though you are justified in your belief, your appearance is deceptive." I need some reason to think you, rather than me, are the one with the problem. The detective needs a reason to think it is the other's evidence, and not her own, that is flawed. The theist and the atheist need reasons to think that their own, rather than the other's, insights or seemings are accurate. To think otherwise, it seems to me, is to think something like this: "You have an insight according to which *P* is not true. I have one according to which *P* is true. It's reasonable for me to believe *P* in light of all this because, gosh darn it, *my* insight supports *P*." If one's conviction survives the "confrontation with the other," to use Rosen's phrase, this seems more a sign of tenacity and stubbornness than anything else.

Thus, even though the parties to a disagreement might not be able to share all their evidence, this does not show that they can reasonably disagree in the cases in which their evidence is shared as well as possible. Their bodies of evidence are very similar, and each has evidence about what the other's private evidence supports. It is especially clear that neither person can justifiably believe both sides are reasonable. If I think that you do have good evidence for your view, then I admit that there is this good evidence for your view, and thus my own beliefs must take this into account. I need a reason to think that you, not me, are making a mistake. The unshared evidence does not help.

Having a Reasonable Disagreement without Realizing It

I have considered and found unsatisfactory three ways in which one might attempt to defend the view that the participants in a purported case of reasonable disagreement can reasonably maintain their own beliefs yet grant that those on the other side are reasonable as well. These were unsuccessful attempts to support affirmative answers to (Q1) and (Q2). In this section, I will consider a view according to which people can reasonably disagree, but the participants to the disagreement cannot reasonably see it that way. On this view, they will think (mistakenly) that the other side is unreasonable. This view, then, gives an affirmative answer to (Q1) but a negative answer to (Q2).

The fundamental assumption behind the view under discussion in this section is that one can reasonably weigh more heavily one's own experiences or perspective than those of another person. When confronted with a case of disagreement on the basis of shared evidence, according to this view, one can reasonably conclude that the other person is not adept at assessing the evidence or that the person is simply making a mistake in this particular case as a result of some sort of cognitive failing. One way or another, then, the conclusion drawn is that the other person does not have a reasonable or justified belief. And the idea is that *both* parties to the disagreement can reasonably draw this conclusion. Thus, both parties have a reasonable belief, yet they reasonably think that the other side is not reasonable.

Applied to our specific case of disagreement about the existence of God, this situation might work out as follows. The theists reasonably think that the atheists are assessing the evidence incorrectly or that they have a kind of cognitive defect. Thus, for example, the theists can think that in spite of their general intelligence, the atheists have a kind of cognitive blindness in this case. They are unable to see the truth in religion and they are unable to appreciate the significance of the theists' reports on their own experience. The theists, then, are justified in maintaining their own beliefs and rejecting those of the atheists as false and unjustified. The atheists, on the other hand, are justified in thinking that the theists are making some kind of mistake, perhaps because psychological needs or prior conditioning blind them to the truth. Thus, the atheists are justified in maintaining their own beliefs and rejecting those of the theists as false and unjustified.[11] A neutral observer, aware of all the facts of their respective situations, could correctly report that both sides have justified beliefs. As a result, the answer to (Q1) is "yes," since there can be a reasonable disagreement. Yet the answer to (Q2) is "no," since the participants cannot see it that way.

Since my main goal in this essay is to examine the tolerant and supportive view that implies an affirmative answer to (Q2), I will not pursue this response at length. I will say, however, that I think that this defense of reasonable disagreements rests on an implausible assumption. Beliefs about whether expertise or cognitive illusions are occurring in oneself or in a person with whom one disagrees depend for their justification on evidence, just like beliefs about other topics. If the atheists or the theists in our central example have any reasons for thinking that they themselves, rather than those on the other side, are the cognitive superiors in this case, then they can identify and discuss those reasons. And the result will be that the evidence shows that all should agree about who the experts are, or the evidence will show that there is no good basis for determining who the experts are. If the evidence really does identify experts, then agreeing with those experts will be the reasonable response for all. If it does not, then there will no basis for anyone to prefer one view to the other, and suspension of judgment will be the reasonable attitude for all. There is no way this setup can lead to reasonable disagreement.

The Remaining Options

In the previous section, I considered and rejected some lines of thought according to which there can be reasonable disagreements. I argued that none of them succeeded. Suppose, then, that there cannot be reasonable disagreements. What can we say about people, such as my students, in the situations that are the best candidates for reasonable disagreements? What is the status of their beliefs? In this section, I will examine the possibilities. There are really only two.

The Hard Line

You might think that the evidence must really support one side of the dispute or the other. This might lead you to think that those who take that side have reasonable beliefs, and those who believe differently do not have reasonable beliefs.

The answer to both (Q1) and (Q2) is "no." We can apply this idea to the dispute between the theists and the atheists in my class. Assume that they have shared their evidence to the fullest extent possible. Their disagreement is not about which belief is more beneficial or morally useful or any of the other matters set aside earlier. In that case, according to the present alternative, one of them has a reasonable belief and the other does not. Of course, one of them has a *true* belief and the other does not. But that is not the current issue. The current issue is about rationality, and the hard line says that the evidence they share really must support one view or the other, and the one whose belief fits the evidence is the rational one. Either the evidence supports the existence of God, or it doesn't. Either the theists or the atheists are rational, but not both. There can be no reasonable disagreements. This is the hard-line response.

The hard-line response seems clearly right with respect to some disagreements. Examples may be contentious, but here is one: Suppose two people look carefully at the available relevant evidence and one of them comes away from it thinking that astrological explanations of personality traits are correct, and the other denies this. The defender of astrology is simply making a mistake. That belief is not reasonable. As Peter van Inwagen says, belief in astrology is "simply indefensible."[12] Similarly, the hard-line view may be correct in Rosen's example about a person who favors an ethos prizing cruelty. That person is just missing something. It is likely that a detailed discussion of the rest of the person's beliefs will reveal enough oddities to render the whole system suspect. Such a person's moral view is simply indefensible.

However, the hard line is much harder to defend in other cases. These other cases are the ones in which any fair-minded person would have to admit that intelligent, informed, and thoughtful people do disagree. In these moral, political, scientific, and religious disputes, it is implausible to think that one side is simply unreasonable in the way in which (I say) the defenders of astrology are.

The hard-line response is particularly difficult to accept in cases in which people have been fully reflective and openly discussed their differing responses. In our example, once people discuss the topic and their evidence, they are forced to consider two propositions:

1. God exists.
2. Our shared evidence supports (1).

The theist says that both (1) and (2) are true. The atheist denies both (1) and (2). Notice that after their discussion their evidence includes not only the original arguments themselves and their own reactions to them, but also the fact that the other person—an epistemic peer—assesses the evidence differently. So consider the theist in the dispute. To stick to his guns, he has to think as follows: "The atheist and I have shared our evidence. After looking at this evidence, it seems to me that (1) and (2) are both true. It seems to her that both are false. I am right and she is wrong." The atheist will, of course, have comparable beliefs on the other side of the issue. It is difficult to see why one of them is better justified with respect to (2) than is the other. But it also is clear that for each of them, (1) and (2) sink or swim together. That is, it is hard to imagine it being the case that, say, the theist is justified in believing (1) but should suspend judgment about (2). Analogous remarks apply to the atheist. It looks like both should suspend judgment. It is difficult to maintain the hard-line position once the parties to the dispute are reflective about their situations and their evidence includes information about the contrary views of their peers.

Admittedly, it is difficult to say with complete clarity just what differentiates the cases to which the hard-line view is appropriate (astrology, Rosen's ethos of cruelty) from the cases to which it is not (the serious disputes). One difference, perhaps, is that an honest look at what the evidence supports in the latter cases reveals that our evidence is decidedly modest to begin with. Even if our individual reflections on these hard questions provides some justification for the beliefs that may seem correct to us, that evidence is counterbalanced when we learn that our peers disagree. This leads us to our final view about disagreements.

A Modest Skeptical Alternative

One reaction of a party to an apparent reasonable disagreement might go something like this:

> After examining this evidence, I find in myself an inclination, perhaps a strong inclination, to think that this evidence supports *P*. It may even be that I can't help but believe *P*. But I see that another person, every bit as sensible and serious as I, has an opposing reaction. Perhaps this person has some bit of evidence that cannot be shared, or perhaps he takes the evidence differently than I do. It's difficult to know everything about his mental life and thus difficult to tell exactly why he believes as he does. One of us must be making some kind of mistake or failing to see some truth. But I have no basis for thinking that the one making the mistake is him rather than me. And the same is true of him. And in that case, the right thing for both of us to do is to suspend judgment on *P*.

This, it seems to me, is the truth of the matter. At least for some range of hard cases. There can be apparent reasonable disagreements, as was the case in my classroom. And when you are tempted to think that you are in one, then you should suspend judgment about the matter under dispute. If my students thought that the various students with varying beliefs were equally reasonable, then they should have concluded that suspending judgment was the right thing to do.[13]

This is a modest view, in the sense that it argues for a kind of compromise with those with whom one disagrees. It implies that one should give up one's beliefs in the light of the sort of disagreement under discussion. This is a kind of modesty in response to disagreement from one's peers. This is also a skeptical view, in the limited sense that it denies the existence of reasonable beliefs in a significant range of cases.

This may see to be a distressing conclusion. It implies that many of your deeply held convictions are not justified. Worse, it implies that many of my deeply held, well-considered beliefs are not justified. Still, I think that this is the truth of the matter. And perhaps the conclusion is not so distressing. It calls for a kind of humility in response to the hard questions about which people so often find themselves in disagreement. It requires us to admit that we really do not know what the truth is in these cases. When compared to the intolerant views with which we began, this is a refreshing outcome.

Conclusion

My conclusion, then, is that there cannot be reasonable disagreements of the sort I was investigating. That is, it cannot be that epistemic peers who have shared their evidence can reasonably come to different conclusions. Furthermore, they cannot reasonably conclude that both they and those with whom they disagree are reasonable in their beliefs. Thus, I cannot make good sense of the supportive and tolerant attitude my students displayed. It is possible, of course, that the favorable attitude toward others that they expressed really only conceded to the others one of the lesser kinds of reasonableness that I set aside in section II, part C. If this is correct, then either the hard-line response applies, and this is an example in which one side is reasonable and the other simply is not, or it is a case to which the more skeptical response applies. If that's the case, then suspension of judgment is the epistemically appropriate attitude. And this is a challenge to the complacent atheism with which I began.

I have not here argued for a conclusion about which category the disagreements between theists and atheists, or the various disagreements among theists, fall into. For all I've said, some of these cases may be ones in which one side simply is making a mistake and those on the other side are justified in both sticking to their guns and ascribing irrationality to the other side. Others may be cases that call for suspension of judgment. To defend my atheism, I would have to be justified in accepting some hypothesis explaining away religious belief—for example, the hypothesis that it arises from some fundamental psychological need. And, while I am inclined to believe some such hypothesis, the more I reflect on it, the more I realize that I am in no position to make any such judgment with any confidence at all. Such psychological conjectures are, I must admit, highly speculative, at least when made by me.

This skeptical conclusion does not imply that people should stop defending the views that seem right to them. It may be that the search for the truth is most successful if people argue for the things that seem true to them. But one can do that without being epistemically justified in believing that one's view is correct.

I am grateful to Louise Antony, John Bennett, Allen Orr, and Ed Wierenga for helpful comments on earlier drafts of this paper. The paper is a revised version of talks given at Ohio State University, Washington University, the University of Miami, the University of Michigan, the Inland Northwest Philosophy Conference, and the Sociedad Filosofica Ibero-American. I am grateful to the audiences on all those occasions for helpful discussion.

SEVENTEEN

If God Is Dead, Is Everything Permitted?

Elizabeth Anderson

At the Institute for Creation Research Museum in Santee, California, visitors begin their tour by viewing a plaque displaying the "tree of evolutionism," which, it is said (following Matt. 7:18), "bears only corrupt fruits." The "evil tree" of evolution is a stock metaphor among proponents of the literal truth of the biblical story of creation. In different versions, it represents evolutionary theory as leading to abortion, suicide, homosexuality, the drug culture, hard rock, alcohol, "dirty books," sex education, alcoholism, crime, government regulation, inflation, racism, Nazism, communism, terrorism, socialism, moral relativism, secularism, feminism, and humanism, among other phenomena regarded as evil. The roots of the evil tree grow in the soil of "unbelief," which nourishes the tree with "sin." The base of its trunk represents "no God"—that is, atheism.

The evil tree vividly displays two important ideas. First, the fundamental religious objection to the theory of evolution is not scientific but moral. Evolutionary theory must be opposed because it leads to rampant immorality, on both the personal and political scales. Second, the basic cause of this immorality is atheism. Evolutionary theory bears corrupt fruit because it is rooted in denial of the existence of God.

Most forms of theism today are reconciled to the truth of evolutionary theory. But the idea of the evil tree still accurately depicts a core objection to atheism. Few people of religious faith object to atheism because they think the evidence for the existence of God is compelling to any rational inquirer. Most of the faithful haven't considered the evidence for the existence of God in a spirit of rational inquiry—that is, with openness to the possibility that the evidence goes against their faith. Rather, I believe that people object to atheism because they think that without God, morality is impossible. In the famous words (mis)attributed to Dostoyevsky, "If God is dead, then everything is permitted." Or, in the less-famous words of Senator Joe Lieberman, we must not suppose "that morality can be maintained without religion."

Why think that religion is necessary for morality? It might be thought that people wouldn't *know* the difference between right and wrong if God did not reveal it to them. But that can't be right. Every society, whether or not it was founded on theism, has acknowledged the basic principles of morality, excluding religious observance, which are laid down in the Ten Commandments. Every stable society punishes murder, theft, and bearing false witness; teaches children to honor their parents; and condemns envy of one's neighbor's possessions, at least when such envy leads one to treat one's neighbors badly.[1] People figured out these rules long before they were exposed to any of the major monotheistic religions. This fact suggests that moral knowledge springs not from revelation but from people's experiences in living together, in which they have learned that they must adjust their own conduct in light of others' claims.

Perhaps, then, the idea that religion is necessary for morality means that people wouldn't *care* about the difference between right and wrong if God did not promise salvation for good behavior and threaten damnation for bad behavior. On this view, people must be goaded into behaving morally through divine sanction. But this can't be right, either. People have many motives, such as love, a sense of honor, and respect for others, that motivate moral behavior. Pagan societies have not been noticeably more immoral than theistic ones. In any event, most theistic doctrines repudiate the divine sanction theory of the motive to be moral. Judaism places little emphasis on hell. Christianity today is dominated by two rival doctrines of salvation. One says that the belief that Jesus is one's savior is the one thing necessary for salvation. The other says that salvation is a free gift from God that cannot be earned by anything a person may do or believe. Both doctrines are inconsistent with the use of heaven and hell as incentives to morality.

A better interpretation of the claim that religion is necessary for morality is that *there wouldn't be a difference between right and wrong* if God did not make it so. Nothing would really be morally required or prohibited, so everything would be permitted. William Lane Craig, one of the leading popular defenders of Christianity, advances this view.[2] Think of it in terms of the authority of moral rules. Suppose a person or group proposes a moral rule—say, against murder. What would give this rule authority over those who disagree with it? Craig argues that, in the absence of God, nothing would. Without God, moral disputes reduce to mere disputes over subjective preferences. There would be no right or wrong answer. Since no individual has any inherent authority over another, each would be free to act on his or her own taste. To get authoritative moral rules, we need an authoritative commander. Only God fills that role. So, the moral rules get their authority, their capacity to obligate us, from the fact that God commands them.

Sophisticates will tell you that this moralistic reasoning against atheism is illogical. They say that whether God exists depends wholly on the factual evidence, not on the moral implications of God's existence. Do not believe them. We know the basic moral rules—that it is wrong to engage in murder, plunder, rape, and torture, to brutally punish people for the wrongs of others or for blameless error, to enslave others, to engage in ethnic cleansing and genocide—with greater confidence than we know any conclusions drawn from elaborate factual or logical reasoning. If you find a train of reasoning that leads to the conclusion that everything, or even just these things, is permitted, this *is* a good reason for you to reject it. Call this "the moralistic argument." So, if it is true that atheism entails that everything is permitted, this is a strong reason to reject atheism.

While I accept the general form of the moralistic argument, I think it applies more forcefully to theism than to atheism. This objection is as old as philosophy. Plato, the first systematic philosopher, raised it against divine command theories of morality in the fifth century BCE.[3] He asked divine-command moralists: are actions right because God commands them, or does God command them because they are right? If the latter is true, then actions are right independent of whether God commands them, and God is not needed to underwrite the authority of morality. But if the former is true, then God could make any action right simply by willing it or by ordering others to do it. This establishes that, if the authority of morality depends on God's will, then, *in principle,* anything is permitted.

This argument is not decisive against theism, considered as a purely philosophical idea. Theists reply that because God is necessarily good, He would never do anything morally reprehensible Himself, nor command us to perform heinous acts. The argument is better applied to the purported *evidence* for theism. I shall argue that if we take the evidence for theism with *utmost seriousness,* we will find ourselves committed to the proposition that the most heinous acts are permitted. Since we know that these acts are not morally permitted, we must therefore doubt the evidence for theism.

Now "theism" is a pretty big idea, and the lines of evidence taken to support one or another form of it are various. So I need to say more about theism and the evidence for it. By "theism" I mean belief in the God of Scripture. This is the God of the Old and New Testaments and the Koran—the God of Judaism, Christianity, and Islam. It is also the God of any other religion that accepts one or more of these texts as containing divine revelation, such as the Mormon Church, the Unification Church, and Jehovah's Witnesses. God, as represented in Scripture, has plans for human beings and intervenes in history to realize those plans. God has a moral relationship to human beings and tells humans how to live. By focusing on theism in the Scriptural sense, I narrow my focus in two ways. First, my argument doesn't immediately address polytheism or paganism, as is found, for example, in the religions of Zeus and Baal, Hinduism, Wicca. (I'll argue later that, since the evidence for polytheism is on a par with the evidence for theism, any argument that undermines the latter undermines the former.) Second, my argument doesn't immediately address deism, the philosophical idea of God as a first cause of the universe, who lays down the laws of nature and then lets them run like clockwork, indifferent to the fate of the people subject to them.

What, then, is the evidence for theism? It is Scripture, plus any historical or contemporary evidence of the same kind as presented in Scripture: testimonies of miracles, revelations in dreams, or what people take to be direct encounters with God: experiences of divine presence, and prophecies that have been subject to test. Call these things "extraordinary evidence," for short. Other arguments for the existence of God offer cold comfort to theists. Purely theoretical arguments, such as for the necessity of a first cause of the universe, can at most support deism. They do nothing to show that the deity in question cares about human beings or has any moral significance. I would say the same about attempts to trace some intelligent design in the evolution of life. Let us suppose, contrary to the scientific evidence, that life is the product of design. Then the prevalence of predation, parasitism, disease, and imperfect human organs strongly supports the view that the designer is indifferent to us.

The core evidence for theism, then, is Scripture. What if we accept Scripture as offering evidence of a God who has a moral character and plans for human beings, who intervenes in history and tells us how to live? What conclusions should we draw from Scripture about God's moral character and about how we ought to behave? Let us begin with the position of the fundamentalist, of one who takes Scripture with utmost seriousness, as the inerrant source of knowledge about God and morality. If we accept biblical inerrancy, I'll argue, we must conclude that much of what we take to be morally evil is in fact morally permissible and even required.

Consider first God's moral character, as revealed in the Bible.[4] He routinely punishes people for the sins of others. He punishes all mothers by condemning them to painful childbirth, for Eve's sin. He punishes all human beings by condemning them to labor, for Adam's sin (Gen. 3:16–18). He regrets His creation, and in a fit of pique, commits genocide and ecocide by flooding the earth (Gen. 6:7). He hardens Pharaoh's heart against freeing the Israelites (Ex. 7:3), so as to provide the occasion for visiting plagues upon the Egyptians, who, as helpless subjects of a tyrant, had no part in Pharaoh's decision. (So much for respecting free will, the standard justification for the existence of evil in the world.) He kills all the firstborn sons, even of slave girls who had no part in oppressing the Israelites (Ex. 11:5). He punishes the children, grandchildren, great-grandchildren, and great great-grandchildren of those who worship any other god (Ex. 20:3–5). He sets a plague upon the Israelites, killing twenty-four thousand, because some of them had sex with the Baal-worshiping Midianites (Num. 25:1–9). He lays a three-year famine on David's people for *Saul*'s slaughter of the Gibeonites (2 Sam. 21:1). He orders David to take a census of his men, and then sends a plague on Israel, killing seventy thousand, for David's sin in taking the census (2 Sam. 24:1, 10, 15). He sends two bears out of the woods to tear forty-two children to pieces, because they called the prophet Elisha a bald head (2 Kings 2:23–24). He condemns the Samarians, telling them that their *children* will be "dashed to the ground, their pregnant women ripped open" (Hosea 13:16).[5] This is but a sample of the evils celebrated in the Bible.

Can all this cruelty and injustice be excused on the ground that God may do what humans may not? Look, then, at what God commands humans to do. He commands us to put to death adulterers (Lev. 20:10), homosexuals (Lev. 20:13), and people who work on the Sabbath (Ex. 35:2). He commands us to cast into exile people who eat blood (Lev. 7:27), who have skin diseases (Lev. 13:46), and who have sex with their wives while they are menstruating (Lev. 20:18). Blasphemers must be stoned (Lev. 24:16), and prostitutes whose fathers are priests must be burned to death (Lev. 21:9). That's just the tip of the iceberg. God repeatedly directs the Israelites to commit ethnic cleansing (Ex. 34:11–14, Lev. 26:7-9) and genocide against numerous cities and tribes: the city of Hormah (Num. 21:2–3), the land of Bashan (Num. 21:33–35), the land of Heshbon (Deut. 2:26–35), the Canaanites, Hittites, Hivites, Perizzites, Girgashites, Amorites, and Jebusites (Josh. 1–12). He commands them to show their victims "no mercy" (Deut. 7:2), to "not leave alive anything that breathes" (Deut. 20:16). In order to ensure their complete extermination, he thwarts the free will of the victims by hardening their hearts (Deut. 2:30, Josh. 11:20) so that they do not sue for peace. These genocides are, of course, instrumental to the wholesale theft of their land (Josh. 1:1–6) and the rest of their property (Deut. 20:14, Josh. 11:14). He tells eleven tribes of Israel to nearly exterminate the twelfth tribe, the Benjamites, because a few of them raped and killed a Levite's concubine. The resulting bloodbath takes the lives of 40,000 Israelites and 25,100 Benjamites (Judg. 20:21, 25, 35). He helps Abijiah kill half a million Israelites (2 Chron. 13:15–20) and helps Asa kill a million Cushites, so his men can plunder all their property (2 Chron. 14:8–13).

Consider also what the Bible *permits.* Slavery is allowed (Lev. 25:44–46, Eph. 6:5, Col. 3:22). Fathers may sell their daughters into slavery (Ex. 21:7). Slaves may be beaten, as long as they survive for two days after (Ex. 21:20–21, Luke 12:45–48). Female captives from a foreign war may be raped or seized as wives (Deut. 21:10–14). Disobedient children should be beaten with rods (Prov. 13:24, 23:13). In the Old Testament, men may take as many wives and concubines as they like because adultery for men consists only in having sex with a woman who is married (Lev. 18:20) or engaged to someone else (Deut. 22:23). Prisoners of war may be tossed off a cliff (2 Chron. 24:12). Children may be sacrificed to God in return for His aid in battle (2 Kings 3:26–27, Judg. 11), or to persuade Him to end a famine (2 Sam. 21).

Christian apologists would observe that most of these transgressions occur in the Old Testament. Isn't the Old Testament God a stern and angry God, while Jesus of the New Testament is all-loving? We should examine, then, the quality of the love that Jesus promises to bring to humans. It is not only Jehovah who is jealous. Jesus tells us his mission is to make family members hate one another, so that they shall love him more than their kin (Matt. 10:35–37). He promises salvation to those who abandon their wives and children for him (Matt. 19:29, Mark 10:29–30, Luke 18:29–30). Disciples must hate their parents, siblings, wives, and children (Luke 14:26). The rod is not enough for children who curse their parents; they must be killed (Matt. 15:4–7, Mark 7:9–10, following Lev. 20:9). These are Jesus' "family values." Peter and Paul add to these family values the despotic rule of husbands over their silenced wives, who must obey their husbands as gods (1 Cor. 11:3, 14:34–5; Eph. 5:22–24; Col. 3:18; 1 Tim. 2:11–12; 1 Pet. 3:1).

To be sure, genocide, God-sent plagues, and torture do not occur in the times chronicled by the New Testament. But they are prophesied there, as they are repeatedly in the Old Testament (for instance, in Isaiah, Jeremiah, Ezekiel, Micah, and Zepheniah). At the second coming, any city that does not accept Jesus will be destroyed, and the people will suffer even more than they did when God destroyed Sodom and Gomorrah (Matt. 10:14–15, Luke 10:12). God will flood the Earth as in Noah's time (Matt. 24: 37). Or perhaps He will set the Earth on fire instead, to destroy the unbelievers (2 Pet. 3:7, 10). But not before God sends Death and Hell to kill one quarter of the Earth "by sword, famine and plague, and by the wild beasts" (Rev. 6:8). Apparently, it is not enough to kill people once; they have to be killed more than once to satisfy the genocidal mathematics of the New Testament. For we are also told that an angel will burn up one third of the Earth (8:7), another will poison a third of its water (8:10–11), four angels will kill another third of humanity by plagues of fire, smoke, and sulfur (9:13, 17–18), two of God's witnesses will visit plagues on the Earth as much as they like (11:6), and there will be assorted deaths by earthquakes (11:13, 16:18–19) and hailstones (16:21). Death is not bad enough for unbelievers, however; they must be tortured first. Locusts will sting them like scorpions until they want to die, but they will be denied the relief of death (9:3–6). Seven angels will pour seven bowls of God's wrath, delivering plagues of painful sores, seas and rivers of blood, burns from solar flares, darkness and tongue-biting (16:2–10).

That's just what's in store for people while they inhabit the Earth. Eternal damnation awaits most people upon their deaths (Matt. 7:13–14). They will be cast into a fiery furnace (Matt. 13:42, 25:41), an unquenchable fire (Luke 3:17). For what reason? The New Testament is not consistent on this point. Paul preaches the doctrine of predestination, according to which salvation is granted as an arbitrary gift from God, wholly unaffected by any choice humans may make (Eph. 1: 4–9). This implies that the rest are cast into the eternal torments of hell on God's whim. Sometimes salvation is promised to those who abandon their families to follow Christ (Matt. 19:27–30, Mark 10:28–30, Luke 9:59–62). This conditions salvation on a shocking indifference to family members. More often, the Synoptic Gospels promise salvation on the basis of good works, especially righteousness and helping the poor (for example, Matt. 16:27, 19:16–17; Mark 10:17–25; Luke 18:18–22, 19:8–9). This at least has the form of justice, since it is based on considerations of desert. But it metes out rewards and punishments grossly disproportional to the deeds people commit in their lifetimes. Finite sins cannot justify eternal punishment. Since the Reformation, Christian thought has tended to favor either predestination or justification by faith. In the latter view, the saved are all and only those who believe that Jesus is their savior. Everyone else is damned. This is the view of the Gospel of John (John 3:15–16, 18, 36; 6:47; 11:25–26). It follows that infants and anyone who never had the opportunity to hear about Christ are damned, through no fault of their own. Moreover, it is not clear that even those who hear about Christ have a fair chance to assess the merits of the tales about him. God not only thwarts our free will so as to visit harsher punishments upon us than we would have received had we been free to choose, He also messes with our heads. He sends people "powerful delusions" so they will not believe what is needed for salvation, to make sure that they are condemned (2 Thess. 2:11–12). Faith itself may be a gift of God rather than a product of rational assessment under our control and for which we could be held responsible. If so, then justification by faith reduces to God's arbitrary whim, as Paul held (Eph. 2:8–9). This at least has the merit of acknowledging that the evidence offered in favor of Christianity is far from sufficient to rationally justify belief in it. Granting this fact, those who do not believe are blameless and cannot be justly punished, even if Jesus really did die for our sins.

And what are we to make of the thought that Jesus died for our sins (Rom. 5:8–9, 15–18; 1 John 2:2; Rev. 1:5)? This core religious teaching of Christianity takes Jesus to be a scapegoat for humanity. The practice of scapegoating contradicts the whole moral principle of personal responsibility. It also contradicts any moral idea of God. If God is merciful and loving, why doesn't He forgive humanity for its sins straightaway, rather than demanding His 150 pounds of flesh, in the form of His own son? How could any loving father do that to his son?

I find it hard to resist the conclusion that the God of the Bible is cruel and unjust and commands and permits us to be cruel and unjust to others. Here are religious doctrines that on their face claim that it is all right to mercilessly punish people for the wrongs of others and for blameless error, that license or even command murder, plunder, rape, torture, slavery, ethnic cleansing, and genocide. We know such actions are wrong. So we should reject the doctrines that represent them as right.

Of course, thoughtful Christians and Jews have struggled with this difficulty for centuries. Nothing I have said would come as a surprise to any reflective person of faith. Nor are theists without options for dealing with these moral embarrassments. Let us consider them.

One option is to bite the bullet. This is the only option open to hard-core fundamentalists, who accept the inerrancy of the Bible. In this view, the fact that God performed, commanded, or permitted these actions demonstrates that they are morally right. This view concedes my objection to theism, that it promotes terrible acts of genocide, slavery, and so forth. But it denies the moral force of this objection. We know where this option has led: to holy war, the systematic extirpation of heretics, the Crusades, the Inquisition, the Thirty Years War, the English Civil War, witch-hunts, the cultural genocide of Mayan civilization, the brutal conquest of the Aztecs and the Inca, religious support for ethnic cleansing of Native Americans, slavery of Africans in the Americas, colonialist tyranny across the globe, confinement of the Jews to ghettos, and periodic pogroms against them, ultimately preparing the way for the Holocaust.[6] In other words, it has led to centuries steeped in bloodshed, cruelty, and hatred without limit across continents.

Since this is clearly reprehensible, one might try a stopgap measure. One could deny that the dangerous principles in the Bible have any application after biblical times. For example, one might hold that, while it is in principle perfectly all right to slaughter whoever God tells us to, in fact, God has stopped speaking to us. This argument runs into the difficulty that many people even today claim that God has spoken to them. It is hard to identify any reason to be comprehensively skeptical about current claims to have heard divine revelation that does not apply equally to the past. But to apply such skepticism to the past is to toss out revelation and hence the core evidence for God.

Another option is to try to soften the moral implications of embarrassing biblical episodes by filling in unmentioned details that make them seem less bad. There is a tradition of thinking about "hard sayings" that tries to do this.[7] It imagines some elaborate context in which, for instance, it would be all right for God to command Abraham to sacrifice his son, or for God to inflict unspeakable suffering on His blameless servant Job, and then insists that that was the context in which God actually acted. I have found such excuses for God's depravity to be invariably lame. To take a typical example, it is said of David's seemingly innocent census of his army that he sinned by counting what was not his, but God's. Even if we were to grant this, it still does not excuse God for slaughtering seventy thousand of David's men, rather than focusing His wrath on David alone. I also find such casuistic exercises to be morally dangerous. To devote one's moral reflections to constructing elaborate rationales for past genocides, human sacrifices, and the like is to invite applications of similar reasoning to future actions.

I conclude that there is no way to cabin off or soft-pedal the reprehensible moral implications of these biblical passages. They must be categorically rejected as false and depraved moral teachings. Morally decent theists have always done so in practice. Nevertheless, they insist that there is much worthy moral teaching that can be salvaged from the Bible. They would complain that the sample of biblical moral lessons I cited above is biased. I hasten to agree. There are many admirable moral teachings in the Bible, even beyond the obvious moral rules—against murder, stealing, lying, and the like—that are acknowledged by all societies. "Love your neighbor as yourself" (Lev. 19:18, Matt. 22:39, Mark 12:31, Luke 10:27, James 2:8) concisely encapsulates the moral point of view. The Bible courageously extends this teaching to the downtrodden, demanding not just decency and charity to the poor and disabled (Ex. 23:6, 23:11; Lev. 19:10, 23:22; Deut. 15:7–8, 24:14–15; Prov. 22:22; Eph. 4:28; James 2:15–16), but provisions in the structure of property rights to liberate people from landlessness and oppressive debts (Deut. 15, Lev. 25:10–28). Although the details of these provisions make little economic sense (for instance, canceling debts every seven years prevents people from taking out loans for a longer term), their general idea, that property rights should be structured so as to enable everyone to avoid oppression, is sound. Such teachings were not only morally advanced for their day but would dramatically improve the world if practiced today.

So, the Bible contains both good and evil teachings. This fact bears upon the standing of Scripture, both as a source of evidence for moral claims, and as a source of evidence for theism. Consider first the use of Scripture as a source of evidence for moral claims. We have seen that the Bible is morally inconsistent. If we try to draw moral lessons from a contradictory source, we must pick and choose which ones to accept. This requires that we use our own independent moral judgment, founded on some source other than revelation or the supposed authority of God, to decide which biblical passages to accept. In fact, once we recognize the moral inconsistencies in the Bible, it's clear that the hard-core fundamentalists who today preach hatred toward gay people and the subordination of women, and who at other times and places have, with biblical support, claimed God's authority for slavery, apartheid, and ethnic cleansing, have been picking and choosing all along. What distinguishes them from other believers is precisely their attraction to the cruel and despotic passages in the Bible. Far from being a truly independent guide to moral conduct, the Bible is more like a Rorschach test: which passages people choose to emphasize reflects as much as it shapes their moral character and interests.

Moral considerations, then, should draw theists inexorably away from fundamentalism and toward liberal theology—that is, toward forms of theism that deny the literal truth of the Bible and that attribute much of its content to ancient confusion, credulity, and cruelty. Only by moving toward liberal theology can theists avoid refutation at the hands of the moralistic argument that is thought to undermine atheism. Only in this way can theists affirm that the heinous acts supposedly committed or commanded by God and reported in the Bible are just plain morally wrong.

The great Enlightenment philosopher Immanuel Kant took this line of reasoning to its logical conclusion for morality. He considered the case of an inquisitor who claims divine authority for executing unbelievers. That the Bible commends such acts is undeniable (see Ex. 22:20, 2 Chron. 15:13, Luke 19:27,

Acts 3:23). But how do we know that the Bible accurately records God's revealed word? Kant said:

> That it is wrong to deprive a man of his life because of his religious faith is certain, unless . . . a Divine Will, made known in extraordinary fashion, has ordered it otherwise. But that God has ever ordered this terrible injunction can be asserted only on the basis of historical documents and is never apodictically certain. After all, the revelation has reached the inquisitor only through men and has been interpreted by men, and even did it appear to have come from God Himself (like the command delivered to Abraham to slaughter his own son like a sheep) it is at least possible that in this instance a mistake has prevailed. But if this is so, the inquisitor would risk the danger of doing what would be wrong in the highest degree; and in this very act he is behaving unconscientiously.[8]

Kant advances a moral criterion for judging the authenticity of any supposed revelation. If you hear a voice or some testimony purportedly revealing God's word and it tells you to do something you know is wrong, don't believe that it's really *God* telling you to do these things.

I believe that Kant correctly identified the maximum permissible moral limits of belief in extraordinary evidence concerning God. These limits require that we reject the literal truth of the Bible. My colleague Jamie Tappenden argues in this volume that such a liberal approach to faith is theologically incoherent. Perhaps it is. Still, given a choice between grave moral error and theological muddle, I recommend theological muddle every time.

But these are not our only alternatives. We must further ask whether we should accept *any* part of the Bible as offering evidence about the existence and nature of God. Once we have mustered enough doubt in the Bible to reject its inerrancy, is there any stable position short of rejecting altogether its claims to extraordinary evidence about God? And once we reject its claims, would this not undermine all the extra-biblical extraordinary evidence for God that is of the same kind alleged by believers in the Bible? Here we have a body of purported evidence for theism, consisting in what seem to be experiences of divine presence, revelation, and miracles, testimonies of the same, and prophecies. We have seen that such experiences, testimonies, and prophecies are at least as likely to assert grave moral errors as they are to assert moral truths. This shows that these sources of extraordinary evidence are deeply unreliable. *They can't be trusted.* So not only should we think that they offer no independent support for *moral* claims, but we should not think they offer independent support for *theological* claims.

Against this, defenders of liberal theology need to argue that the claims derived from these extraordinary sources fall into two radically distinct groups. In one group, there are the purported revelations that assert moral error, which should not be accepted as having come from God and offer no independent support for any claim about God. In the other group, there are the genuine revelations that assert moral truths or some morally neutral proposition (for example, claims about historical events and prophecies of the future), as well as testimonies of miracles and experiences of divine presence, which should be accepted as having come from God and do provide evidence for the existence and nature of God.

I think this fallback position should be rejected for two reasons. First, it does not explain why these extraordinary types of evidence should be thought to fall into two radically distinct groups. Why should they *ever* have generated grave moral errors? Second, it does not explain why all religions, whether monotheistic, polytheistic, or non-theistic, appear to have access to the same sources of evidence. Believers in any one religion can offer no independent criteria for accepting their own revelations, miracles, and religious experiences while rejecting the revelations, miracles, and religious experiences that appear to support contradictory religious claims. I believe that the best explanation for both of these phenomena–that the extraordinary sources of evidence generate grave moral error as well as moral truth and that they offer equal support for contradictory religious claims–undermines the credibility of these extraordinary sources of evidence altogether.

So first, why were the ancient biblical peoples as ready to ascribe evil as good deeds to God? Why did they think God was so angry that He chronically unleashed tides of brutal destruction on humanity? The answer is that they took it for granted that *all* events bearing on human well-being are willed by some agent for the purpose of affecting humans for good or ill. If no human was observed to have caused the event, or if the event was of a kind (e.g., a plague, drought, or good weather) that no human would have the power to cause, then they assumed that some unseen, more-powerful agent had to have willed it, precisely for its good or bad effects on humans. So, if the event was good for people, they assumed that God willed it out of love for them; if it was bad, they assumed that God willed it out of anger at them. This mode of explanation is universally observed among people who lack scientific understanding of natural events. It appears to be a deeply rooted cognitive bias of humans to reject the thought of meaningless suffering. If we are suffering, someone *must* be responsible for it!

Why did these representations of God as cruel and unjust not make God repugnant to the authors of Scripture and their followers? They were too busy trembling in their sandals to question what they took to be God's will. The seventeenth-century philosopher Thomas Hobbes observed that people honor raw power irrespective of its moral justification:

> Nor does it alter the case of honour, whether an action (so it be great and difficult, and consequently a sign of much power) be just or unjust: for honour consisteth only in the opinion of power. Therefore the ancient heathen did not think they dishonoured, but greatly honoured the Gods, when they introduced them in their poems, committing rapes, thefts, and other great, but unjust, or unclean acts: insomuch as nothing is so much celebrated in Jupiter, as his adulteries; nor in Mercury, as his frauds, and

> thefts: of whose praises, in a hymn of Homer, the greatest is this, that being born in the morning, he had invented music at noon, and before night, stolen away the cattle of Apollo, from his herdsmen.[9]

Hobbes's psychological explanation applies even more emphatically to the authors of Scripture, the ancient Hebrews and the early Christians, whose God commits deeds several orders of magnitude more terrible than anything the Greek gods did.

Ancient social conditions also made God's injustice less obvious to the early Jews and Christians. Norms of honor and revenge deeply structure the social order of tribal societies. These norms treat whole clans and tribes, rather than individuals, as the basic units of responsibility. A wrong committed by a member of a tribe could therefore be avenged by an injury inflicted on any other member of that tribe, including descendents of the wrongdoer. Given that people in these societies habitually visited the iniquities of the fathers on the sons, it did not strike the early Hebrews and Christians as strange that God would do so as well, although on a far grander scale.[10]

So the tendency, in the absence of scientific knowledge, to ascribe events having good *and bad* consequences for human beings to corresponding benevolent *and malevolent* intentions of unseen spirits, whether these be gods, angels, ancestors, demons, or human beings who deploy magical powers borrowed from some spirit world, explains the belief in a divine spirit as well as its (im)moral character. This explanatory tendency is pan-cultural. The spiritual world everywhere reflects the hopes and fears, loves and hatreds, aspirations and depravities of those who believe in it. This is just as we would expect if beliefs in the supernatural are, like Rorschach tests, projections of the mental states of believers, rather than based on independent evidence. The same cognitive bias that leads pagans to believe in witches and multiple gods leads theists to believe in God. Indeed, once the explanatory principle–to ascribe worldly events that bear on human well-being to the intentions and powers of unseen spirits, when no actual person is observed to have caused them–is admitted, it is hard to deny that the evidence for polytheism and spiritualism of all heretical varieties is *exactly on a par* with the evidence for theism.

Every year in my town, Ann Arbor, Michigan, there is a summer art fair. Not just artists, but political and religious groups, set up booths to promote their wares, be these artworks or ideas. Along one street one finds booths of Catholics, Baptists, Calvinists, Christian Orthodox, other denominational and nondenominational Christians of all sorts, Muslims, Hindus, Buddhists, Baha'i, Mormons, Christian Scientists, Jehovah's Witnesses, Jews for Jesus, Wiccans, Scientologists, New Age believers–representatives of nearly every religion that has a significant presence in the United States. The believers in each booth offer evidence of exactly the same kind to advance their religion. Every faith points to its own holy texts and oral traditions, its spiritual experiences, miracles and prophets, its testimonies of wayward lives turned around by conversion, rebirth of faith, or return to the church.

Each religion takes these experiences and reports them as conclusive evidence for *its* peculiar set of beliefs. Here we have purported sources of evidence for higher, unseen spirits or divinity, which systematically point to *contradictory* beliefs. Is there one God, or many? Was Jesus God, the son of God, God's prophet, or just a man? Was the last prophet Jesus, Muhammad, Joseph Smith, or the Rev. Sun Myung Moon?

Consider how this scene looks to someone like me, who was raised outside of any faith. My father is nominally Lutheran, in practice religiously indifferent. My mother is culturally Jewish but not practicing. Having been rejected by both the local Lutheran minister and the local rabbi (in both cases, for being in a mixed marriage), but thinking that some kind of religious education would be good for their children, my parents helped found the local Unitarian church in the town where I grew up. Unitarianism is a church without a creed; there are no doctrinal requirements of membership. (Although Bertrand Russell once quipped that Unitarianism stands for the proposition that there is *at most* one God, these days pagans are as welcome as all others.) It was a pretty good fit for us, until New Age spiritualists started to take over the church. That was too loopy for my father's rationalistic outlook, so we left. Thus, religious doctrines never had a chance to insinuate themselves into my head as a child. So I have none by default or habit.

Surveying the religious booths every year at the Ann Arbor art fair, I am always struck by the fact that they are staffed by people who are convinced of their own revelations and miracles, while most so readily disparage the revelations and miracles of other faiths. To a mainstream Christian, Jew, or Muslim, nothing is more obvious than that founders and prophets of other religions, such as Joseph Smith, the Rev. Moon, Mary Baker Eddy, and L. Ron Hubbard, are either frauds or delusional, their purported miracles or cures tricks played upon a credulous audience (or worse, exercises of black magic), their prophecies false, their metaphysics absurd. To me, nothing is more obvious than that the evidence cited on behalf of Christianity, Judaism, and Islam is of exactly the same type and quality as that cited on behalf of such despised religions. Indeed, it is on a par with the evidence for Zeus, Baal, Thor, and other long-abandoned gods, who are now considered ridiculous by nearly everyone.

The perfect symmetry of evidence for all faiths persuades me that the *types* of extraordinary evidence to which they appeal are not credible. The sources of evidence for theism—revelations, miracles, religious experiences, and prophecies, nearly all known only by testimony transmitted through uncertain chains of long-lost original sources—systematically generate contradictory beliefs, many of which are known to be morally abhorrent or otherwise false. Of course, ordinary sources of evidence, such as eyewitness testimony of ordinary events, also often lead to conflicting beliefs. But in the latter case, we have independent ways to test the credibility of the evidence—for instance, by looking for corroborating physical evidence. In the former cases, the tests advanced by believers tend to be circular:

don't believe that other religion's testimonies of miracles or revelations, since they come from those who teach a false religion (Deut. 13:1–5). It is equally useless to appeal to the certainty in one's heart of some experience of divine presence. For exactly the same certainty has been felt by those who think they've seen ghosts, been kidnapped by aliens, or been possessed by Dionysus or Apollo. Furthermore, where independent tests exist, they either disconfirm or fail to confirm the extraordinary evidence. There is no geological evidence of a worldwide flood, no archaeological evidence that Pharaoh's army drowned in the Red Sea after Moses parted it to enable the Israelites to escape. Jesus' central prophecy, that oppressive regimes would be destroyed in an apocalypse, and the Kingdom of God established *on Earth, within the lifetime of those witnessing his preaching* (Mark 8:38–9:1, 13:24–27, 30), did not come to pass.[11] If any instance of these extraordinary sources of evidence is what it purports to be, it is like the proverbial needle in the haystack—except that there is no way to tell the difference between it and the hay. I conclude that none of the evidence for theism–that is, for the God of Scripture—is credible. Since exactly the same types of evidence are the basis for belief in pagan Gods, I reject pagan religions too.

It follows that we cannot appeal to God to underwrite the authority of morality. How, then, can I answer the moralistic challenge to atheism, that without God moral rules lack any authority? I say: the authority of moral rules lies not with God, but with each of us. We each have moral authority with respect to one another. This authority is, of course, not absolute. No one has the authority to order anyone else to blind obedience. Rather, each of us has the authority to make claims on others, to call upon people to heed our interests and concerns.[12] Whenever we lodge a complaint, or otherwise lay a claim on others' attention and conduct, we *presuppose* our own authority to give others reasons for action that are not dependent on appealing to the desires and preferences they already have. But whatever grounds we have for assuming our own authority to make claims is equally well possessed by anyone who we expect to heed our own claims. For, in addressing others as people to whom our claims are justified, we acknowledge *them* as judges of claims, and hence as moral authorities. Moral rules spring from our practices of reciprocal claim making, in which we work out together the kinds of considerations that count as reasons that all of us must heed, and thereby devise rules for living together peacefully and cooperatively, on a basis of mutual accountability.

What of someone who refuses to accept such accountability? Doesn't this possibility vindicate Craig's worry, that without some kind of higher authority external to humans, moral claims amount to nothing more than assertions of personal preference, backed up by power? No. We deal with people who refuse accountability by restraining and deterring their objectionable behavior. Such people have no proper complaint against this treatment. For, in the very act of lodging a complaint, they address others as judges of their claims, and thereby step into the very system of moral adjudication that demands their accountability.

I am arguing that morality, understood as a system of reciprocal claim making, in which everyone is accountable to everyone else, does not need its authority underwritten by some higher, external authority. It is underwritten by the authority we all have to make claims on one another. Far from bolstering the authority of morality, appeals to divine authority can undermine it. For divine command theories of morality may make believers feel entitled to look only to their idea of God to determine what they are justified in doing. It is all too easy under such a system to ignore the complaints of those injured by one's actions, since they are not acknowledged as moral authorities in their own right. But to ignore the complaints of others is to deprive oneself of the main source of information one needs to improve one's conduct. Appealing to God rather than those affected by one's actions amounts to an attempt to escape accountability to one's fellow human beings.

This is not an indictment of the conduct of theists in general. Theistic moralities, like secular ones, have historically inspired both highly moral and highly immoral action. For every bloodthirsty holy warrior we can find an equally violent communist or fascist, enthusiastically butchering and enslaving others in the name of some dogmatically held ideal. Such observations are irrelevant to my argument. For my argument has not been about the *causal consequences* of belief for action. It has been about the *logical implications* of accepting or rejecting the core evidence for theism.

I have argued that if we take with utmost seriousness the core evidence for theism, which is the testimonies of revelations, miracles, religious experiences, and prophecies found in Scripture, then we are committed to the view that the most heinous acts are morally right, because Scripture tells us that God performs or commands them. Since we know that such acts are morally wrong, we cannot take at face value the extraordinary evidence for theism recorded in Scripture. We must at least reject that part of the evidence that supports morally repugnant actions. Once we have stepped this far toward liberal theological approaches to the evidence for God, however, we open ourselves up to two further challenges to this evidence. First, the best explanation of extraordinary evidence—the only explanation that accounts for its tendency to commend heinous acts as well as good acts—shows it to reflect either our own hopes and feelings, whether these be loving or hateful, just or merciless, or else the stubborn and systematically erroneous cognitive bias of representing all events of consequence to our welfare as *intended* by some agent who cares about us, for good or for ill. Extraordinary evidence, in other words, is a projection of our own wishes, fears, and fantasies onto an imaginary deity. Second, all religions claim the same sorts of extraordinary evidence on their behalf. The perfect symmetry of this type of evidence for completely contradictory theological systems, and the absence of any independent ordinary evidence that corroborates one system more than another, strongly supports the view that such types of evidence are not credible at all. And once we reject such evidence altogether, there is nothing left that supports theism (or polytheism either). The moralistic argument, far from threatening atheism, is a critical wedge that should open morally sensitive theists to the evidence *against* the existence of God.

I thank Ed Curley, Chris Dodsworth, David Jacobi, and Jamie Tappenden for helpful advice concerning this paper.

EIGHTEEN

Divine Evil

David Lewis

A Neglected Argument

Standard versions of the argument from evil concern the evils God fails to prevent: the pain and suffering of human beings and non-human animals, and the sins people commit. The most ambitious versions of the argument claim that the existence of evil is logically incompatible with the existence of an omnipotent, omniscient, and completely benevolent deity. More-cautious approaches maintain that the existence of pain and sin ought to make us skeptical about any such deity. Or that the extent of the suffering in the millions of years of sentient life on Earth gives us strong reason to think no such deity exists. Or that particular cases of extreme anguish and human cruelty make belief in this sort of deity irrational. And so on.

In my view, even the most ambitious version succeeds conclusively. There is no evasion, unless the standards of success are set unreasonably high. Those who try to escape the conclusion have to insist that no use can be made of disputable premises, however antecedently credible those premises may be.[1] But philosophers can and do dispute anything. Some, for example, are prepared to argue about the law of non-contradiction. The faithful who claim that the strong argument from evil leaves open a bare possibility—the sort of possibility only a philosopher could cherish—gain a victory in name only.

What interests me here, however, is a simpler argument, one that has been strangely neglected. The standard versions, I said, focus on evil that God fails to prevent. But we might start instead from the evils God himself perpetrates. There are plenty of these, and, in duration and intensity, they dwarf the kinds of suffering and sin to which the standard versions allude.

For God, if we are to believe an orthodox story, has prescribed eternal torment as a punishment for insubordination. There are, of course, disagreements about what it takes to be insubordinate. Some say that the mere fact of not believing in him is enough to mark you out. Others think that you must violate one of the divine commandments. However the test is set up, it is clear that there is some complex of psychological attitudes and actions that suffices for damnation.

The orthodox story is explicit about the temporal scale of the punishment: it is to go on forever. Many of those who tell the orthodox story are also concerned to emphasize the quality of the punishment. The agonies to be endured by the damned intensify, in unimaginable ways, the sufferings we undergo in our earthly lives. So, along both dimensions, time and intensity, the torment is infinitely worse than all the suffering and sin that will have occurred during the history of life in the universe. What God does is thus infinitely worse than what the worst of tyrants did. However clever they were at prolonging the agonies of their victims, their tortures killed fairly quickly. God is supposed to torture the damned forever, and to do so by vastly surpassing all the modes of torment about which we know.

Although those who elaborate the orthodox account are sometimes concerned with the fit between crime and punishment, there is no possibility of a genuine balance.[2] For the punishment of the damned is infinitely disproportionate to their crimes. Even the worst of this-worldly offenders is only capable of inflicting a finite amount of suffering. However many times that offender endures the exact agony he caused, there will still be an infinite number of repetitions to come. Moreover, in each of these repetitions, the torment will be intensified and extended across all possible modes.

This is to assume, of course, that the damned have committed some crime. If the orthodox story supposes only that they fail to believe in God, then the injustice is even more palpable. Alice the agnostic may live a life full of charity and good works, notable for its honesty, fairness, and loving care of those around her. If lack of faith suffices for damnation, then the divine reward will be an eternity of the most exquisite agony.

Varieties of Theism

So I think the usual philosophical discussions of the problem of evil are a sideshow. We seem to strain at the gnat and swallow the camel. Why is this?

Many will say that what I have called the "orthodox story" is a cartoon theism. Real, grownup theists believe something much more sophisticated. The standard versions of the argument from evil prove attractive to philosophical unbelievers because they are taken to deploy only uncontroversial premises, the sorts of premises grownup theists can be expected to have to grant.

I reply that this overlooks two important points. First, the neglected argument does apply against mainstream versions of theism preached all around us. There is a strong case for claiming that the overwhelming majority of Christians and Muslims, both in North America and the rest of the world, are committed to the "orthodox story." There are many passages in the New Testament (and in the Koran) that tell, or presuppose, that story, if they are read at face value.[3]

Second, the reply fails to appreciate how difficult it is to avoid the "orthodox story" while simultaneously retaining the distinctive doctrines of Christianity. To evade the neglected argument, you must contend that prominent passages of scripture should not be read literally. Perhaps there are alternative ways of reading the idea of God's punishment or understanding torment. But we need to hear not just that there *are* such ways but *what* they are.

I concede that the neglected argument doesn't apply against deism. If you simply hold that there is an omniscient, omnipotent, completely benevolent deity but have no views about his plans for rewarding and punishing people in any hereafter, then you can save your energies to defend against the more familiar problems of evil. But, I shall suggest, you will have to acknowledge that your doctrine isn't Christianity.

There are several ways in which you might try to elaborate a more substantial theism. Perhaps you think that talk of *judgment* and of *punishment* isn't to be taken literally. Maybe what happens in this life is that people make choices. Some choose salvation, and others damnation. Those who are damned receive what they have chosen. But if damnation is torment, or if it is a state for which eternal torment is an apt metaphor, then trouble recurs. For if we suppose that the alleged choice is ill informed and irrevocable, then God does evil. He places people in a situation in which they must make a judgment that binds them for eternity, and he knows that some will be so inadequately informed that they will opt for an eternity of torment (or for a state for which torment is an apt metaphor). It is hard to distinguish between God and the parent who equips the nursery with sharp objects galore and plenty of matches, fuses, and dynamite. Moreover, it is very difficult to see how our actual choices could be anything except ill informed. For the world in which we live is one in which we have scanty evidence about any hereafter of potential torment, and one in which those who tell tales about God's judgments and punishments offer incompatible suggestions about what should be done to avoid torment. On many versions of Christianity, of course, our lack of evidence is an integral part of the divine plan, for it is supposed that the greatness of faith consists in the ability to trust in the absence of—or even in the teeth of—the evidence.[4]

Things would be different if those who are damned are stubborn, persisting in their choice even when fully informed. What would these people be like? They must prefer a state of torment (literal or metaphorical) to the alternative of salvation. Why do they see subordinating themselves to God as worse? Perhaps because they set supreme value on their own independence. But, if God is genuinely worthy of our worship, then to be fully informed is to recognize all the attributes that make this so. It is hard to recognize how resistance could survive an eternity of demonstrations of the divine magnificence.

Even if we suspend doubts about the possibility of stubbornness in the face of full information, we can still ask why God fails to prevent damnation. This returns us to the familiar versions of the argument from evil. A standard explanation is on offer: incompatibilist freedom is of supreme value. It is alleged that even an omnipotent, omniscient, and completely benevolent deity who wished to create a world in which incompatibilist freedom was found might have to allow for the existence of stubborn beings who chose eternally to remain in torment.

I reply in two parts. First, I question the supreme value of incompatibilist freedom. Imagine two worlds. In one of these, actions are produced by psychological states, themselves caused by prior psychological conditions and by the pressures of the environment, those conditions and environments in turn being caused by earlier circumstances, all in accordance with the conditions philosophers introduce to allow for compatibilist freedom. In the second world, just the same actions are performed, but in accordance with your favorite incompatibilist account. Why should we think of the second world as a great advance on the first? In what, precisely, does its superiority reside?

If you are inclined to think, as I do, that there is no superiority to be found, you will not be satisfied with the thought that God may have to allow some people who eternally choose damnation. You will think that God could have settled for a world with compatibilist freedom and that he could have set things up so as to keep his creatures out of trouble. So, to escape the problem, theists will have to explain why the value of incompatibilist freedom is so great that it outweighs the extraordinary torment endured by those who continue forever to resist.

Yet even if we allow that incompatibilist freedom is a great value, it's still worth asking why God has arranged things in the way we find them. He could leave incompatibilist freedom intact while doing far more luring and urging than he does. Assuming we have to make a choice, why must it be made through a glass darkly? Once again, God seems negligent, at best.

Instead of substituting our free choice for God's judgment and punishment, theists may contend that we should reinterpret the notion of torment. Lurid anecdotes about unquenchable fire, sulfur, and brimstone are not to be taken literally. Damnation simply consists in the state of being insubordinate to God.[5] This proposal depends on supposing that torment is an apt metaphor for insubordination.

I deny that it is. Contented atheist that I am, my state of alienation from the deity is *not* one for which torment is an apt metaphor. Christians may respond that this judgment is shallow: From my mundane perspective, I may judge myself happy enough in my denial of God. Once I am fully informed, however, I will appreciate the grossness of my swinish satisfaction, and torment will be an apt description of my insubordinate condition.

Now familiar troubles arise. Suppose, first, that my state of insubordination is unmodifiable: insubordinate on Earth, insubordinate eternally. Then indeed, I can envisage my eternal separation from God as being one of great anguish, as I come to appreciate the glorious bliss that is forever beyond my reach. But, as before,

I have been placed in a dangerous situation, one in which my eternal prospects were determined by a choice I was forced to make in ignorance. Once again, I have been treated unjustly.

A second possibility is that I can make amends in the hereafter. When acquainted with the divine greatness and the divine plan, I accede and subordinate myself to God. Now, it seems, the metaphor dissolves. My state of insubordination is remedied, and I am no longer in torment. Perhaps the response will be that my torment endures because of the memory of my past insubordination. But why should the memory cause me more than a pang, if I rightly see myself as insubordinate because of ignorance and as remedying my insubordination in light of the facts? I might come to applaud those who made the correct choice from the earthly perspective, but it would be hard to justify chiding myself so severely that it would amount to anything like torment. Furthermore, if the memory *does* serve as a source of torment, then, once again, God has failed to prevent evil by permitting me to hazard my eternal felicity in a state of radically incomplete knowledge.

The charge was that the neglected argument depended on a cartoon version of the hereafter. I reply that the strategy of reading the scriptures non-literally either fails to take torment as an apt metaphor for the state of damnation or else reinstates the problem. If the texts (and the doctrines drawn from them) are not radically misleading, then God remains as a source of divine evil.

But the strategy has exposed another possibility: what if everyone repents and is saved?

Universal Salvation

It is plainly possible for God to avoid perpetrating evil. He might not punish anyone. Or, perhaps, he might just administer ordinary finite punishments, designed, in some way, to change the psychological condition of those who had resisted him.

I find the option of limited punishment mysterious. Presumably there is some great end that God has designed his creation to achieve, an end that is furthered by the repentance of those who had failed the earthly test. An obvious rejoinder, from those of us who find no great value in incompatibilist freedom, is that God could have saved himself the trouble of limited punishment by setting up the causal conditions so that the resisters didn't go astray to begin with. Even if we acquiesce in the supreme value of incompatibilist freedom, however, inflicting torment seems quite unnecessary. An omnipotent God could be expected to convert resisters by other means—displays of magnificence, for example. If it is suggested that these are not guaranteed to do the trick, that the resistance may persist, then it should also be noted that, under the conditions of incompatibilist freedom, punishment also comes without any guarantee of repentance. Why should sticks work better than carrots?

The idea of limited punishment supposes that God is disposed to punish his creatures so long as they remain insubordinate. If one of us resists eternally, then that person will suffer eternal torment. But perhaps this never happens. All of us may eventually knuckle under. We come to love Big Brother. We find the ministry of love irresistible. Yet this only diminishes the force of the neglected argument. God retains the disposition to punish those who resist, and to punish them eternally if they resist forever. In other words, even if he never inflicts the infinite torment, he is prepared to do so. He is ready to perpetrate evil far in excess of the sum total of pain, suffering, and cruelty manifested in the created universe. Divine evil continues to exist in the cast of the divine will.

Some Christians are universalists. They maintain that God saves all of us. This happens not because everyone eventually falls into line, but because God isn't disposed to punish any of his creatures. Now God is genuinely exempt from divine evil. He neither causes the infinite torment nor has any disposition to do so.

Is universalism really a *Christian* option? Can Christians afford to deny divine evil? Christianity, properly so-called, requires a redemption. At its heart is the claim that Jesus was born to save us from something. The condition from which we have been redeemed must be truly horrible. What can be horrible enough except for eternal torment?

Finite torment, perhaps. But for the sacrifice of Christ, God would have had to purify each of us individually, and that would have involved significant torment in the hereafter. God envisaged two possible scenarios. In the first, sinful humanity is unredeemed and all of us must be punished before achieving union with the deity. In the second, the crucifixion serves to cleanse us from our state of sin, and no punishment after death is needed. Because God has no wish to punish any of us, he chose the second.

But this apology fails. If each of us can be saved without punishment under the second scenario, then there is no differentiation between those who acknowledge the sacrifice of Christ and those who scoff, between the most devout saints and the greatest sinners. All of us can instantly be forgiven and brought into the bliss of salvation. If that were so, then there would be no need for punishment in the first scenario. The choice is between universal acceptance without the sacrifice of Christ and universal acceptance with that sacrifice. There is no redemption, no distinguishing the faithful from the insubordinate. Alternatively, if salvation is made possible for all by the death of Christ, but some who fail to appreciate this act of redemption need further cleansing in order to be saved, then we return to the idea of limited punishment. Universalism cannot be sustained.

Orthodox Christians think that the sufferings of Jesus give all of us a second chance but that some of us don't avail ourselves of the opportunity. The redemption works for all of us by freeing us from the stain of sin (part of our human condition), but it doesn't provide instant salvation for all. That's why Christian theologians, and Christian preachers everywhere, emphasize the importance of faith, of following the precepts of Christ, and so on.[6] If everyone wins without regard to performance, not only do all these doctrines drop away, but so too does the rationale of the earthly life. If even the most-wicked of people can be immediately forgiven without punishment, then there is no point to our life of trial in the vale of tears.

So if there's a redemption, there'll have to be a distinction between those who take advantage of it and those who don't. What happens to those who don't? According to universalism, they are not to be punished. God will place them in some condition without perpetrating divine evil.

One possible condition would be nonexistence. Those who take advantage of the sacrifice of Christ, the faithful, are called to salvation. The rest of us simply die.[7] You might worry, perhaps, that this is something of a waste. Couldn't God have done better by increasing the fraction of those who would rise to the opportunity? Once again, the theist is likely to sing the praises of incompatibilist freedom. A world with fewer who are saved and more who depart into eternal sleep is better than one in which the ratio of sleepers to saved is decreased (even to zero), if the decrease is purchased by exchanging incompatibilist freedom for its compatibilist counterpart. Even granting that, it seems appropriate to worry about the justice for individuals. Imagine a happy atheist, one for whom the earthly life goes well. From the standpoint of eternity, we might (and God presumably does) observe a life truncated. Our atheist didn't turn to Christ, and so bodily death came as the end. Overall, however, we can see the life in positive terms because of the success of its mundane phase (its only phase as it turns out). The trouble is that other atheists (as well as agnostics and heathen worshippers) have earthly lives that are not so wonderful; some of them indeed endure sufferings that are, by our mundane standards, excruciating (although, of course, their pains are nothing in comparison with those inflicted in the orthodox story with which we started). From the eternal perspective, this life looks like an utter mistake, for its only phase is utterly dreadful. By bringing this person into being, God has brought about divine evil.

The universalist Christian might reply that my assessment is wrong. God creates someone who turns out to suffer horribly. Bodily death comes as the end because, despite having the opportunity for faith, the atheist failed to turn to Christ; the resistance was free (in the incompatibilist sense). Arguments we have met before apply here too. Why is this type of freedom of such great value? Why does that freedom compensate *this individual* for the horrible suffering? Why not make the inducements to faith a bit stronger?

I think universalists have a better reply. The afterlife is a more heterogeneous affair than people have thought. The point of our earthly lives isn't to divide us into two groups, one to live forever in unimaginable bliss, the other to suffer unimaginable torment. Instead of being tried, we simply discover who we are. Some, perhaps the most fortunate, find out that they are people for whom the adoration of the deity is the highest form of rapture; they appreciate Christ's sacrifice and are summoned to the presence of God. Others resist the Christian message and develop different ideals for their lives. They are assigned to places in the afterlife that realize those ideals for them. Atheist philosophers, perhaps, discover themselves in an eternal seminar of astonishing brilliance. Each of us finds an appropriate niche.[8]

This fantasy allows the sufferings of our mundane lives to be redeemed. Not all of us are destined for Christian salvation, for God's eternal Sabbath, but everyone will receive a well-adapted reward.[9] God does not treat all of us alike. But there is no divine evil.

Redemption is taken to consist in making available to some, those who freely turn to Christ, the highest form of bliss. We are freed from sin, not so that we avoid the terrors of eternal damnation but so that we have the chance of gaining the most wonderful reward. We are as much freed *for* as freed *from.* But as I read the scriptures, the fantasy involves ignoring (or denying) crucial texts. It underplays the importance of sin.[10] And, of course, it passes very lightly over the references to the torments of the damned.

Most Christians follow a version of the religion that is committed to divine evil, evil perpetrated by God. Most, therefore, fall afoul of the neglected argument. Perhaps some do not. Perhaps some are inclined to accept the universalist fantasy I have just outlined. Can that count as a genuine style of Christianity? I shall leave that for the theologians to decide.

Can We Admire the Believers?

Many Christians appear to be good people, people worthy of the admiration of those of us who are non-Christians. From now on let us suppose, for simplicity's sake, that these Christians accept a God who perpetrates divine evil, one who inflicts infinite torment on those who do not accept him. Appearances notwithstanding, are those who worship the perpetrator of divine evil themselves evil?

Consider Fritz. Fritz is a neo-Nazi. He admires Hitler. Fritz's admiration of an evil man suffices, we might think, to make Fritz evil.

But perhaps this is too quick. Fritz's evil character, we might say, arises not from his admiration for Hitler but from his willingness to behave in the same way. Simply admiring Hitler isn't enough. One must also be disposed to emulate Hitler's deeds; and if this disposition is present, one is evil, whether or not the admiration remains.

Modest Fritz is not so disposed. He thinks himself unworthy. "Great deeds are reserved for great men," he says. (Compare: "Vengeance is mine," saith the Lord.[11]) Fritz wouldn't even beat up a defenseless weakling—not even with a dozen of his mates at his side. He might even go so far as to restrain them. "This is the Führer's work, not ours," he argues. Fritz knows very clearly what Hitler would want done. Even though he admires Hitler, he does not do it.

Fritz is evil, it seems, simply because it is evil to admire someone who is evil. Or more exactly, it is evil to admire someone evil in full recognition of the characteristics and actions that express their evil. Evil is contagious, transmitted by clear-eyed admiration.

Some worshippers of the perpetrator are obviously evil. They relish contemplating the torment of the damned. Some of them even think that delight in the eternal sufferings of worldly sinners will be a component of the bliss of the saved.[12] Like Fritz, they may think that inflicting such suffering, or even any suffering at all, is beyond their humble station. They are glad that the perpetrator has instituted a division of labor. Their part is to forgive those who insult them, to turn the other cheek. They are happy in the thought that, by doing so, they will heap coals of fire on the heads of their enemies.[13]

Many other Christians are not like this at all. They are sincerely compassionate; they genuinely forgive their enemies. Yet they knowingly worship the perpetrator. Perhaps they do not like to think about it, but they firmly believe that, in the hereafter, their God will consign people they know, some of whom they love, to an eternity of unimaginable agony. Moved by this thought, they do whatever they can to urge others to join them in faith. Their deep sympathy with the unbelievers is expressed in efforts to persuade others to play by the rules the perpetrator has set. In worshipping the perpetrator, however, they acquiesce in those rules. They are well aware that many will not fall in line with the rules. They think that, if that happens, the perpetrator will be right to start the eternal torture. They endorse the divine evil. And that's bad enough.

Among those of us who do not worship the perpetrator, there are many who admire worshippers of the perpetrator. We admire some of our neighbors, recognizing their honesty, fairness, kindness, courage, and so forth. We admire religious people famed for their selflessness, their courage, or their scholarship—Mother Teresa, Father Murphy, Jean Buridan.[14] Yet we know that they worship the perpetrator. Moreover, since they worship the perpetrator, endorsing his judgments about the propriety of eternal torment for some (including us), the perpetrator's evil extends to them. They admire evil and are tainted by it. In admiring them, we too admire evil. Does the evil spread by contagion to us?

What of those who admire those who admire those who worship the perpetrator? Are they too infected? If admiration transmits evil, then so do chains of admirers of arbitrary length. Eventually, almost every living person will be infected. It is almost impossible to avoid being hooked up to a chain that will terminate, possibly at a very long distance, in admiration of the perpetrator. Ecumenicism only makes matters worse. The more we are prepared to be tolerant in religious matters, the more we'll be prepared to overlook the details of others' theological views; the more we'll focus on their exemplary behavior toward those around them; as more admire the perpetrator's admirers, there will be more people for others to admire, and the contagion will spread.

This will occur even if, someday, there are no more worshippers of the perpetrator, even if nobody remembers the perpetrator, even if nobody remembers anyone who worshipped the perpetrator, even if nobody remembers anyone who remembered worshippers of the perpetrator. The only ones to escape will be the committed misanthropes. Leaving aside those who find nothing admirable in humanity, everyone will be tainted with divine evil.

The conclusion is absurd. It is also depressing. How can it be morally permissible to be tolerant of others and to appreciate their worth? What saves us from chains of contagion?

Perhaps what saves us is that sometimes those who admire are not well enough informed. If Fritz did not know about Hitler's evil deeds, thinking of the Führer only as a strong and patriotic leader who was restoring morale, then the misguided admiration would not mark Fritz as evil. Similarly, if I admire a worshipper of the perpetrator, recognizing that the worshipper appreciates the divine commitment to eternal torment, and if you admire me, not knowing of my admiration of the worshipper but recognizing my (occasional) good deeds, then the taint of divine evil does not spread from me to you. You are in the dark about the source of the evil in me. Like Fritz, you are an innocent. And, perhaps, your ignorance is far less culpable than his.

Admiration, we might suppose, is a bit more selective than the examples suggest. We don't just give it or withhold it. We admire people for particular qualities; sometimes we admire them despite perceived defects. I may admire the worshipper because he does so much for the poor and the sick. If I admire the worshipper despite his endorsement of the perpetrator, I place great weight on qualities that are genuinely good. You may admire me because you take me to be responding to that good. You do not know of my knowledge of the worshipper's acquiescence in the perpetrator's rules, and my decision to give that relatively little weight in my overall assessment. If you did know that, you might have second thoughts about me; you might not admire me after all. So the chain of contagion would be broken.

It is possible, then, to limit the spread of divine evil. Chains of contagion can be broken because admirers are often not fully informed about the attitudes of those they admire, because admiration can be a selective matter, a response to particular qualities. This is probably how things work in actuality. We are not all tainted with evil.

A residual difficulty remains. What of the worshippers themselves? And what attitude should we non-believers have toward our Christian friends? Can they avoid contagion? Can we admire them and not be infected?

If our friends believe the universalist fantasy, there's no problem. They don't worship a perpetrator, and we can freely admire them. But I suspect that the vast majority are more orthodox. They genuinely think that their God will commit those who do not accept him to eternal torment. They may prefer not to dwell on the point, but when they consider it, they accept his judgment. Of course, they do not see this as divine evil. Instead they talk of divine justice and the fitting damnation of sinners. If Fritz is clear about Hitler's actual deeds, he will tend to use similar locutions. He won't talk about evil and genocide but will praise the proper purification of the highest form of culture and the justified wiping out of a disease.

Modest Fritz isn't disposed to persecute the Jews in his neighborhood. Nor are our Christian friends inclined to rain suffering and humiliation upon us. Yet if Hitler, or one of his appropriate representatives were there, beside Fritz and his mates and the potential Jewish victim, Fritz would approve of the persecution's being carried out by the proper authorities. So, too, with the worshippers. If the day of judgment were to arrive now, and they were to stand by and observe God's decision to punish us—their unbelieving friends—they would endorse it. Perhaps they would grieve for the fact that the punishment was prescribed for *us;* they would be full of regrets that we had not listened to their warnings and urgings; perhaps they would blame themselves for not having done more. But, in the end, they would worship the perpetrator; they would label divine evil as divine justice.

Can we absolve them of evil for their collaboration? We might try to recall the many good things they do, the sufferings they alleviate, the comforts they bring. There is plenty to throw into the balance in their favor. We can admire their compassion, their perseverance, their selflessness. But can we admire them, despite their preparedness to worship the perpetrator?

The balance seems to tilt in the negative direction. For, as the original neglected argument makes clear, the evil that God causes is infinitely greater than the entire sum of mundane suffering and sin. It is infinitely intense, and it lasts forever. However much pain our friends forestall or relieve, it is infinitesimal in comparison with the torment inflicted on a single individual who receives God's damnation. Yet they are willing to testify to the perpetrator's rightness in passing so severe a sentence. They are prepared to go on worshipping.

Overall, it seems, our evaluation must be negative. They are like the tyrant whose many small contributions to his subjects' welfare pale in contrast to the monstrous repression he will countenance. If we think of them as clear-headed, as fully aware of the character of their commitments in worshipping the perpetrator, we cannot excuse them.

But most of us do, at least most of the time. Are we too conniving at the divine evil? Probably not, precisely because the neglected argument is neglected. The magnitude of the torment isn't taken seriously. We dodge the consequence by keeping it all in soft focus, consoling ourselves with the thought that hellfire and brimstone are mere conceits, that grownup theists have gotten beyond the cartoon scenarios. That is probably the stance most favored by those who worship the perpetrator; starting from their trust in God, they suppose that there must be some nice version of the story, one that will not literally end with billions of damned souls writhing in eternal agony. Can they articulate a nice version that retains the distinctive ideas of Christianity?

Non-believers have been able to excuse their religious friends on the grounds that they are probably not clear-headed about the commitments of their worship. We can think of them as good people who have not seen the perpetrator's dark side. In bringing the problem of divine evil to their attention, I am presenting them with a choice they have previously avoided. Ironically, I may be making it impossible for myself to admire many whom I have previously liked and respected.

Editorial Note (Philip Kitcher). In March 2001, David Lewis finished a short outline of a paper he planned on "Divine Evil." He sent me a copy of the outline, and we had two conversations about it. Around this time, he also wrote a letter to Michael Tooley about the project.

After David's untimely death, Stephanie Lewis and I discussed some of his unfinished work. Further exchanges between us, and with Louise Antony, led to a decision that I would try to turn David's outline into a full essay, drawing on the letter about it and my memory of our conversations. (In particular, I have kept a promise I made to David to supply him with some references.) I am grateful to John Collins, Patricia Kitcher, and Michael Tooley for their advice and encouragement. Comments from Louise, and, especially Steffi, have been extremely helpful in composing the final version.

David's marvelous philosophical voice is inimitable. I have tried to preserve it by using as many phrases from the outline as I could. But this is surely, neither in substance nor in style, the paper he would have written. I trust readers to attribute its insights to David, and its deficiencies to me.

NINETEEN

Meta-atheism: Religious Avowal as Self-Deception

Georges Rey

When I was very young, I attended a Methodist church for several years, and, purchasing the little books offered for the purpose, prayed morning and night, confessing my peccadilloes and asking for happier times. I found particularly compelling the singing of the chorales by the congregation: the combination of the simple tunes with complex inner harmonies being sung by ordinary folk struck me as simultaneously sublime and democratic and aroused in me a sense of good will toward people and much of the world that still plays a significant role in my life (among other things, making me particularly vulnerable to the religious music of Bach and the moral writings of Kant).

Around the age of eight or nine, however, I recall learning some of the rudiments of science, and, after a little reflection, it seemed to me pretty obvious that most of the claims about God, although still attractive, were wishful thinking. Ironically enough, the very humility that I had been taught to be a virtue made me think that we ought to respect the independence of the world from our wishes, and it came to seem to me that atheism was therefore the only genuinely religious attitude (I was actually barred from the Boy Scouts for describing my religion as atheism!).

One might think that with greater maturity I would have come to more moderate views. But I'm afraid the reverse has happened. What with teaching the standard theistic arguments in my introductory philosophy courses, attending and discussing religious services with various observant friends, and just reading the daily paper, I frequently find myself having to confront religious views. But the more I do so, the more I actually fasten upon and think about upon the claims being made, the more bizarre and incredible do I find them. I really mean no offense to religious people, but, increasingly, the claims seem to me not merely wishful thinking, but, quite frankly, *mad.* At any rate, beliefs that there are incorporeal psychological agents, with infinitely great powers, with whom one is some special "super-natural" communication, who love, scold, disapprove, command, forgive—whatever else one may think about the legitimacy of religion, surely one has to acknowledge that these are the *sorts of claims* that, in any other, non-religious context, are associated with patently psychotic delusions!

Now, of course, I don't think for a moment that most religious people are psychotic. Nor do I share the view suggested by (at least the title of) the recent "brights" movement of Richard Dawkins (2003a, 2003b) and D. C. Dennett (2003) that religious people are lacking in intelligence, taken in by bad science or some common logical fallacies (I will, though, discuss some of these errors below). To the contrary, I'm often impressed by the intelligence of many religious people and by fact that they stand by the claims in a way that is manifestly insensitive to exposure of the fallacies. It is the maintenance of the claims despite an understanding of the errors that leads me to speculate there must be something else going on, and this has led me to wonder whether they really do believe them.

Well, clearly lots of people claim to, and seem to live and sometimes die for their religious views. It's certainly risky for me to second-guess them on that score just because I think their arguments are bad—after all, don't people know what they themselves believe, and believe what they sincerely avow, whether or not their arguments are any good? Maybe not. People seem to be susceptible to all manner of ignorance, confusion, and often deeply motivated distortions of their own psychological lives. Indeed, my interest in the present topic stems in part from my interest in the quite general discrepancies that seem to me and others to arise between the things people sincerely say, or avow, and what, according to objective evidence of their states and behavior, they actually believe. For starters, note the formidable difficulties of expressing oneself clearly in language, of saying, and even consciously thinking, exactly "what one means." Related to that, there is the familiar phenomenon of adjusting what one says–and thinks–in the light of the demands and expectations of one's audience: here there are not only the intricate issues regarding how we efficiently use language in conversation (e.g., limiting the "context," taking for granted background knowledge), but also simpler facts regarding verbal impulsiveness, pig-headedness, unnoticed empathy with one's audience, and adjustments to what they do or don't want to hear.

But, in addition to these difficulties, there's also the phenomenon of *self-deception:* people often claim to believe things that they merely *want* or are in some way *committed* to believing, even though "at some level" they know the belief is false (see my and other essays in McLaughlin & Rorty 1988, as well as Bach 1981 and Moran 2001 for discussion). Simple examples are the standard one of people ignoring the symptoms they have of some dread disease, or the obvious evidence of the infidelities of a spouse; or doting parents exaggerating, even to themselves, the talents of their child. But some cases are more systematic and "ideological." For example, people frequently espouse claims about universal freedom, rights, or justice that they often blatantly ignore in their own (or their party's) activities, as in the case of many well-intentioned communists disregarding the horrors of Stalin, or defenders of American foreign policy tolerating the death squads in Latin America. Some of this is, of course, simply lies and hypocrisy; but I bet some of it is perfectly sincere self-deception. In all these cases, it is because we have reason to suppose that the people involved are otherwise quite intelligent enough to draw the conclusions that they consciously resist that we suppose there must be something else at work.

My hunch about what passes as "religious belief" is that it frequently involves self-deception, particularly along the latter ideological lines. And so I find myself taking seriously the following hypothesis, which (for lack of a better name) I call *meta-atheism:*

> Despite appearances, many Western adults who've been exposed to standard science and sincerely claim to believe in God are self-deceived; at some level they believe the claim is false.

Note that I am restricting the scope of the claim to members of my culture exposed to standard science. Although I fully expect it could be extended beyond them, I don't want to speculate here on the psychology of people not so exposed. My view is, of course, a kind of extension of the usual claims about wishful thinking and rehearsal of childhood and other social dramas that one finds in, for example, Marx and Freud. But I would also want to include other influences, such as loyalty to one's family or other social groups, powerful commitments and identifications, or simple resistance to changing significant public stances (see also Boyer 2001, 2004, and Atran 2002, for interesting speculations about innate cognitive influences).

Note that I'm not at all concerned to criticize religious *practices*—meditating, keeping a sabbath, attending church, or engaging in rituals surrounding birth, marriage, and death. I am certainly not unsympathetic to religious resistance to the crass "materialism" and commerciality of much contemporary culture, nor even opposed to some sense of what people call the "spiritual," understood as a certain respectful feeling toward the world and other people, and a valuing of their less superficial properties. I am concerned only with the *content* of the *supernatural claims* that are made on behalf of these practices and attitudes. It is only these that I suspect are understood by most people in my culture to be obviously false.

One reason my view may seem initially absurd is that religious claims are so intensely familiar that we tend not to hear how truly bizarre and unbelievable they are. They can cast a kind of spell on us–they certainly did on me when I was young—and we can easily mouth the words, even meaningfully, without really attending to what they literally mean. For this reason, in trying to make my case for meta-atheism, I will want to distance myself a little from the claims, and, in order to bring out what I find bizarre in them, will sometimes use harsh language (e.g, "psychotic delusion") that may already have offended religious readers. I ask them to bear with it. It's really not intended to be insulting. May it simply provide the occasion for the religious to say precisely why such language is unwarranted and where I've gone wrong.

I should emphasize that I don't mean to be particularly smug or self-righteous about my hypothesis, or pretend to be very much less self-deceived than the next person. Self-deception and other discrepancies between our real and avowed attitudes seem to me quite widespread, may be unavoidable, and are often entirely salutary and benign (nothing like a little self-deception to keep an otherwise querulous family together!). Paradoxical though it may sound, I can think of a number of areas in my own life where I regularly practice self-deception (though, for it to be effective, I mustn't dwell on the fact for too long). I might well turn out to be self-deceived even about my own atheism—explaining why I still like all that Bach—and perhaps about this meta-atheism as well! My point would remain that there's still a level at which I, like everyone else, nevertheless know better. Of course, some cases may be more benign than others, an issue I'll address at the end.

I don't presume for a moment to be able to *establish* the claim of meta-atheism. I certainly recognize that there's a lot to be said that would appear to argue against it. Much depends upon far more detailed empirical research than I'm in a position to do, and, in any case, on having a much clearer understanding of such really quite complex states and processes of "belief," "avowal," and "self-deception"—and, indeed, a clearer conception of the mind generally—than I think anyone yet has (see my 1997 and 2001b work for discussion). I expect that the right story in the area will allow for a wide variety of different sorts of "belief." All that I really hope to do here is to put my hypothesis in the running, calling attention to a number of striking peculiarities of religious thinking that I think it may help explain. I'll set out these peculiarities shortly. Indeed, it's really they, more than the conclusion itself, that interest me.

God as a Mental Being

I should say roughly what I shall mean by "God." I'm most familiar with Christian conceptions, and in the short space here will focus upon them, although I presume much of what I say could be applied to others. What seems to me essential to most conceptions, and is at issue with atheists, is that *God is a supernatural, psychological being,* that is, a being not subject to ordinary physical limitations but capable of some or other mental state, such as knowing, caring, loving, disapproving—and indeed, at least in Christianity, is eternal, omniscient, omnipotent, and necessarily benevolent (for brevity, I'll refer to these latter properties as "omni" properties, a being possessing them as an "omni"-being). What the theist usually asserts that the atheist denies is that there is some such being who knows about our lives, cares about the good, either created the physical world or can intervene in it, and is in charge of a person's whereabouts in an "afterlife" (my talk of "God" will sometimes be short for some cluster of these standard claims). If you think of God as something other than a psychological being of this sort or think that talk of God is simply a metaphorical or "symbolic" way of talking about love, the possibility of goodness, or the Big Bang, then much of what I say may not apply (although such weakened construals are, of course, further evidence that people don't really believe the literal theistic assertions).

Now, it doesn't seem to me even a remotely serious possibility that such a God exists. His nonexistence is, in the words of the American jury system, far "beyond a reasonable doubt." I am, of course, well aware that plenty of arguments and appeals to experience have been produced to the contrary, but they seem to me obviously fallacious and would be readily seen to be so were it not for the social protections religious claims regularly enjoy. For those who might be waylaid by some of the latest versions of the standard defenses, I will offer a few observations here, focusing on the arguments of two recent influential Christian philosophers, William Alston (1991) and Alvin Plantinga (2000). However, I shall presuppose some acquaintance with standard criticisms of the standard defenses, as they are presented in almost every introductory philosophy text (e.g., Sober 2004, pt. 2).

Philosophy vs. Common Sense

It is crucial to my case for religion being self-deception that the reasons for atheism are *obvious,* not depending upon some subtle metaphysics or sophisticated theories of knowledge. I submit that, once one abstracts away from the issues the powerful motivations of religious commitment, the errors in the standard versions of arguments for the existence of God are ones that can be easily appreciated by anyone with an average high school education. (Of course, sophisticated versions of the arguments take sophistication to work through. But, naturally, the more sophisticated they are, the less likely they play a role in ordinary religious thought. In any case, I challenge the reader to produce versions of the arguments that are not in the end just as susceptible to the commonsense objections I raise.)

Not all metaphysical issues are obvious in this way. Our knowledge of the external world, the mind/body problem, the nature of meaning: these are notoriously difficult issues to sort out, often involving quite abstract, subtle, and sophisticated reflection. But some disputes don't involve anything of the sort. Arguments about the existence of ghosts, gremlins, or evil spirits are simply not worth any serious philosophical consideration. The straightforward reason not to believe in these things is simply that there is no serious evidence for them. If someone thinks there is, then they need to produce the evidence. Merely citing the spooky feeling you get in your attic, or the baleful stare of the village madman isn't enough.

I submit that claims about God are of this latter sort. There's simply no reason to take them more seriously than one does claims about witches or ghosts. The idea that one needs powerful *philosophical theories* to settle such issues I like to call the "philosophy fallacy." We will see that people are particularly prey to it in religious discussions, both theist and atheist alike; indeed, atheists often get trapped into doing far more, far riskier philosophy than they need.

Atheism and the Absence of Evidence

The simplest argument for atheism is that one should disbelieve a hypothesis whose expected consequences don't mesh with any evidence. More bluntly: *absence of evidence is evidence of absence*—at least after you've looked. If you poke around enough in the places where it would reasonable to expect evidence of *X* and you don't find any, that's a pretty good reason to believe there is no *X*. This is surely why sensible people don't believe in elves, fairies, or the bogeyman under the bed. You look under the bed at random times, check the locks on windows and doors, make discreet inquiries about other beds in the neighborhood, and so forth. Of course, a sufficiently frightened child could remind you that no finite number of inquiries or peeks under the bed could *logically* establish there wasn't a *very clever* and maybe *incorporeal* bogeyman; but you then might point out that common sense and science wouldn't get very far if they took *every* such mere "logical" possibility equally seriously. At a certain point, we simply have to rely on "inference to the best explanation" of all the evidence we can get, and accept, at least provisionally, conclusions that have been shown in this way to be true "beyond a reasonable doubt." These are not processes that anyone yet seriously understands, but they are ones on which jury trials and the rest of our lives manifestly depend.

The well-known "problem of evil" in the case of God is just a special case of this strategy: one would reasonably expect an omni-being to have created a moral world; the patent lack of such a world (in the plethora of cases that have nothing to do with "free will") provides reason to doubt there's any such being, as does the overall poor record of answered prayers (where one remembers to count not only positive anecdotes, but all of the *failures* people tend not to remember). And note that this argument doesn't justify mere agnosticism: people are presumably not agnostic about bogeymen; rather, it justifies full *disbelief*. What's bad enough for bogeymen is bad enough for God.

There are two sorts of replies theists have made to this argument: theoretical appeals, and appeals to special, religious experience. A few remarks about each.

The Standard Theoretical Arguments

The standard theoretical arguments for the existence of God are the "ontological argument," which tries to include "existence" in the very "definition" of a "perfect" being, and Aquinas's "five ways," which turn on abstract issues about infinity and ultimate explanations. Although these arguments raise many interesting issues, I very much doubt that anyone really bases their religious beliefs upon them. Existence may or may not be a "predicate," the universe may or may not be infinite, and there may or may not be unmoved movers, uncaused causers, necessary substances, and undesigned purposeful systems, but most of these arguments don't even begin to establish the existence of anything like the traditional Christian God with His astounding omni-properties. Apart from the standard errors and fallacies (e.g., about the nature of motion, the intelligibility of infinite series; see Sober 2004), the simplest thing to notice about them is that they don't establish the existence of a *psychological* being of any sort: after all, why should a necessary, even "perfect" being, or an unmoved mover, uncaused causer, or unexplained explainer, have *a mind* any more than it might have a liver or a gall bladder, much less have (or be) a *unique* one with the hyperbolic properties in question?

It's true that we ordinarily take for granted the operations of a mind and so often rest content with an explanation of something that ends with some appeal to what someone wanted or intended. Thus, God's wanting to create the world can seem like an ultimately satisfying explanation of why it exists. This is "the argument from design" and, until Darwin, seemed like the "best explanation" of why, in particular, species displayed so many adaptive traits. But such "watchmaker" analogies, as well as more recent arguments from the "improbability" of the universe having the constants it has, are quite generally inapt, since, conspicuously unlike the case of a watchmaker, *no one has the slightest evidence of God's intentions (and/or the real probabilities of our universe existing) apart from the universe itself,* and so it risks patent circularity to claim that His intentions explain the way the universe is. Even a serious theist could wonder what on Earth God had in mind in creating the world when and as He did (had He had a bad night?), and so why that particular mental being would suffice as an unexplained explainer.

Religious Experience

Many religious people, however, base their claims not on theoretical arguments, but on special experiences and intuitions (I won't distinguish). Standard Christian reports of religious experiences speak about sensing the "presence" of God or Christ as disembodied spirits, accompanied by overwhelming feelings of "goodness" and "love" (see Alston 1991, 12ff, for quotation of many such reports). On the face of it, however, no matter how distinctive such experiences may be, it's perfectly obvious that they themselves can't establish much of anything beyond themselves, any more than dreams of ghosts do: what would need to be shown is that God—or ghosts—would be the best explanation of those experiences; but this no one has even seriously begun to do. Indeed, ask yourself how local, personal experiences could possibly provide serious evidence for the existence of a *necessary, eternal, omni*-being responsible for *the creation of the world.* How does the presence of such a being feel differently from that of a merely contingent, finitely old and powerful one? How does one know one is in the presence of the genuine creator of *everything*? (Imagine someone claiming the universe was fifteen billion years old *only* on the basis of a gut feeling.) In addition to maybe securing some corroborative evidence for such lavish claims, it would, of course, also be a good idea to run some controlled experiments on such experiences to rule out the effects of, for example, lively and hyperbolic imaginations, wishful thinking, and, of course, the massive religious indoctrination imposed on everyone in our culture since earliest childhood. These are tall orders, patently not satisfied by isolated experiences alone. This is, of course, where the traditional theoretical arguments would have to take over, fallacies and all.

Note that attention to such reasoning is not a demand that needs to be satisfied in the actual *formation* of beliefs. It's a demand for *reflection.* Plantinga (2000, 105, 175, 370) reasonably claims that many of our ordinary beliefs based on memory and perception are not arrived at by (conscious) *reasoning,* for example, to a best explanation of one's experience, but are automatically "triggered" or "occasioned" by experience, involving little or no reasoning at all. For example, someone doesn't *infer* from certain sensations that she remembers seeing a cat last week; she just *remembers* seeing one. Whether or not she arrived at this belief by a "justified" route, she is "warranted" in believing she saw a cat insofar as her eyes and memory are reliable.

Plantinga then proceeds to claim that human beings are endowed with a special faculty, a "*sensus divinitatus,*" which similarly doesn't provide so much a *rational* basis for religious belief as a means by which such belief "is triggered or occasioned by a wide variety of circumstances, including . . . the marvelous, impressive beauty of the night sky; the timeless crash and roar of the surf that resonates deep within us; the majestic grandeur of the mountains," not to mention "awareness of guilt" (2000, 174–75). He then points out that whether or not this belief is warranted in this way depends, as in the case of a memory of a cat, upon whether the faculty is reliable, which depends, then, on whether on not God exists: "a successful atheological objection will have to be to the *truth* of theism, not to its rationality, justification . . . or whatever" (2000, 191).

But this latter is a false dilemma. The question that the "atheologian" is raising is not whether theistic beliefs are *formed* by some process of justification, but whether, *on reflection,* there is any independent reason to think that extravagant beliefs occasioned by mountain peaks and free-floating guilt are in fact caused by (the reliable operation of a *sensus divinitatus*–detecting) God. Of course there isn't, any more than there's any reason to think that beliefs about ghosts "occasioned" by misty graveyards and decrepit old houses are caused by real ghosts (much less through the operation of a "*sensus spiritatus*"). . . . And that's partly because there's no reason to think that ghosts or God exists.

Skeptical Worries and the Philosophy Fallacy

At this point, many theists are fond of claiming that this sort of demand for independent evidence for a religious faculty of knowledge is illegitimate, mounting a *tu quoque,* along the lines of traditional skepticism, to the effect that there is no independent evidence for memory and sensory perception either (see e.g., Alston 1991, ch. 3, and Plantinga 2000, 119). After all, any test would seem to presuppose at least some reliability of those very faculties. They conclude that we have to rely on "basic beliefs," which, for some people, may perfectly well include a belief in God.

Such a move seems to me a parade case of the "philosophy fallacy" I mentioned earlier. The question of how we manage to know anything (about *anything:* logic, mathematics, or the external world) is a terrifically hard one, and mounting a reply to the traditional skeptic is perhaps even harder. But it's a serious mistake to suppose that discussions about theism really wait on these difficult issues, any more than does a reasonable verdict in court, or a dismissal of claims about ghosts. As the philosopher G. E. Moore observed, it's a requirement of any credible theory of knowledge that it not deny that normal people know such ordinary things as that they have two hands. A corollary of that observation is that it should also not tolerate the delusions of psychotics. Quite apart from answering the skeptic, any theory of knowledge that would successfully include knowledge of a god would need to present a theory that meets both of these demands, and it is difficult to see how it could do so. In particular, Plantinga's defense of the "warrant" of theism by appeal to a *sensus devinitatas* would have to be shown to be in some rationally relevant way different from analogous defenses by (a community of) psychotics or believers in ghosts or gremlins. The question is not whether there are or aren't "basic" or foundational beliefs, but why anyone should think that belief in the existence of anything with the extravagant implications of God should figure among them; or, even if it does, why the failure of any of these implications to be independently confirmed wouldn't be an overwhelming reason to scotch the belief, basic or otherwise. Beliefs acquired by unassisted vision, be they ever so basic, are soon undermined by noticing you're not seeing things smack in front of you—or are "seeing" things for which there's no independent evidence. You don't need an answer to the philosophical skeptic to know that!

At least as things are presently understood in epistemology, the ordinary practice of justification consists in strengthening evidential relations among the vast network of interlocking beliefs we have about the world (see Quine, 1960): beliefs based on memory are confirmed by the evidence of sight, sound, touch and the testimony of others, which in turn receive confirmation from that of still others, and so forth. I believe I have two hands because it looks to me as though I do, my eyes seem perfectly good in other cases, no one has told me that I or others like me are deluded in this regard, and all this accords with massive amounts of information I have about people, the world, the past, and so forth. Perhaps *the whole network* (or, anyway, a great deal of it) could be an elaborate hoax of an evil demon. But circles get less vicious as they get bigger, and include things you haven't the slightest reason to abandon. Even if there is no noncircular justification for *all* of our beliefs (whatever that would be like), at least the circle does involve pretty much that *totality,* many parts of which, as Moore also emphasized, we have far more reason to trust than we do any of the arguments of the philosophical skeptic (always remember: the skeptic needs to base his argument on some premises, so, if he invites you to question *all* your beliefs, you have every right to question *his* premises as well—which many philosophers have often successfully done). Moreover, it's crucial to note that, in the debate about God, these beliefs are shared by theist and atheist alike. By comparison, the circle of religious beliefs is viciously small and involves hosts of claims that the atheist has raised substantial reasons to doubt. The theistic claims just dangle, at best *compatible* with the rest of our network, but not in the least *confirmed* by it.

The thesis I want to defend in the rest of this paper is that *almost everyone knows all of this:* the contemporary theist's disregard of such obvious standards is simply the result of a variously motivated self-deception, to which I now turn.

Reasons for Meta-Atheism

There seem to me to be roughly the following eleven reasons to suppose that anyone subjected to a standard Anglo-European high school education knows at some level that standard theistic claims are false (some of the reasons overlap):

Obviousness of the Considerations Raised Above

The kinds of considerations I raised in the previous section are ones to which, it seems to me, any moderately educated adult is readily sensitive. Perhaps non-philosophers wouldn't bother to put it the ways I have, and doubtless most people have not really even thought very much about the standard theological arguments or about how their ordinary beliefs form a vast interlocking network. But in discussing these things I have been at pains to raise only *commonsensical* considerations, of the sort that are regularly raised in, for example, popular science, courtroom arguments, and mystery novels, where people regularly second-guess detectives, juries, and attorneys about relevant evidence and argument. Imagine a jury hearing testimony by a defendant appealing to a *sensus spiritatus* on behalf of a claim that there was someone else at the scene of the crime: is it really in the cards that they would take it seriously "beyond a reasonable doubt"?

Patent Weakness of Religious Arguments

As regards the standard theological arguments, I submit that *were any of the reasonings presented in any other context, their advocates would readily recognize them as unsound.* Unless one came to the arguments with a preconceived theism, few would conclude that Creationism is really a serious alternative to evolutionary biology, or, for those who accept evolution, that God was needed as a further factor, any more than they would think that angels would be needed to push the planets in addition to gravitation. Nor (along the lines of the "ontological argument") would they think that "perfect" islands or demons must exist, lest their nonexistence be an imperfection; nor conclude from the fact that everything had a cause that there was a *single* cause for everything—much less that that cause must have involved a mind.

Tolerance of Otherwise Delusional Claims

I don't think you need to be an atheist to have the reaction I've mentioned to the content of religious claims. Were the claims about a supernatural entity who loves, commands, scolds, forgives, and so on, to be encountered in a fashion removed from the rich, "respectable" aesthetic and cultural traditions in which they are standardly presented, they would be widely regarded as delusional, if not psychotic. As a child, a friend of mine thought the lives of saints were the models by which one was supposed to live, and so one day proceeded to eat ashes with her breakfast, in emulation of St. Thérèse of Liseux. Her otherwise quite devout mother was horrified, and admonished her never to do anything so foolish again. (Consider how much more horrified she would have been were she to be presented at communion with an actual piece of a human body and a glass of real blood!) Or, think of how most normal, even religious people react to hippies who—sometimes in emulation of Jesus—forsake their worldly goods to wander and proselytize among the poor; or to people who murder their children because "God told them to" (just as He told Abraham!); or to the claims of the Koresh cult in Texas, or those claims about the Hale-Bopp comet made by the recent Heaven's Gate cult—and then remember that many religions were themselves once just such "cults" (see in this regard the work of the noted biblical scholar, Elaine Pagels 1979).

It's a useful exercise in general to note people's reactions when idiosyncratic religious claims are presented to them in a way that disguises their usual religious context. I regularly begin a class casually recounting to my students a story I claim to have read about a local judge who, confronted with a confessed murderer whom he knew and loved, decided to release him, and went home and shot his son to atone for the crime instead (or, alternatively, sacrificed his son as a way of *thereby* sacrificing *himself*). If I tell the story casually enough, the look of horror and incredulity is striking on the faces of many students who don't immediately see the analogy with the familiar sacrifice of Christ. In a similar vein, even the noted theistic philosopher Robert Adams (1999) writes: "What would you think if you asked your neighbor why he was building a large stone table in his backyard, and he said, 'I'm building an altar, because God has commanded me to sacrifice my son as a whole burnt offering. Won't you come to the ceremony tomorrow morning?' All agree that the neighbor should be committed to a mental hospital" (p. 284).

Reliance on Texts and Authorities

Many of the otherwise outlandish religious claims derive an air of legitimacy, of course, from their reliance on a specific set of usually archaic texts or other ultimate religious authorities, whose claims are presented "dogmatically" (indeed, the primary meaning of "dogma" has precisely to do with religious proclamations). The texts or authorities standardly serve as the *sole* basis for various claims (e.g., that God exists, that Jesus is the son of God) that are regarded as essentially incontestable—certainly not often contested on the basis of any *non*-textual evidence.

Faith in texts and ultimate authorities, of course, raises countless theoretical and practical problems, familiar from the history of religious strife. Most obviously: how do you know which (translation or interpretation of a) text or authority to trust? Why believe one of them does and the other does not express "the word of God"? It is common knowledge that the familiar Bible we possess is at least in part the result of the efforts of a great many ordinary mortals, as susceptible to "sin" and error as anyone, working in very different languages, times, and conditions and embroiled in now this, now that religious and political controversy (see Pagels, 1979, 2003). One would think it would behoove someone worried about which version genuinely reflected God's word to be constantly trying to sift through the intricate historical details, anxiously ascertaining which writers really did have a main line to God, before placing their faith imprudently in the wrong ones. However, so far as I have heard, serious biblical scholarship has little effect on most people's actual religious practices. (How many Christians, for example, will worry about the admonitions against prayer and charity seriously attributed to Jesus in the recently discovered Thomas Gospel [see Pagels, 2003, 229, #14])?

This all contrasts dramatically with science and common sense, where there are patently no such sacred creeds, texts, or ultimate authorities. Of course, there are *textbooks* and *provisional* authorities, but these are quite frequently challenged, the texts revised and updated as the result of further research (Newton's classic *Principia* is seldom read outside of historical research; Einstein's specific proposals for a unified-field theory are viewed as forlorn). In general, we know very well that truths about the world are not revealed per se by the contents of some text or the revelation of some individual. Indeed, as the history of quantum physics has shown in often startling ways, there is no claim so sacrosanct that some good scientist—or scientifically minded philosopher—might not reasonably challenge it (some have proposed revising even basic logic in view of the results!). Of course, the challenge is based on other beliefs—it makes no sense to challenge *all* of one's beliefs at once—but those beliefs in turn can be challenged in terms of still others, and so forth, with no particular belief having to be based upon faith or revelation. The noted philosopher W. V. Quine (1960), developing a metaphor of Otto Neurath, often compared our position in science and common sense to that of mariners on the open sea who have to repair their boat while remaining afloat in it, standing now on one plank to repair a second, and on a second to repair a third, only to stand on the third to repair the first.

Detail Resistance

This continual revision and adjustment of ordinary beliefs is related to the multifarious ways I mentioned earlier in which they are interconnected, any one of them having logical or evidential relations to indefinite numbers of the others. For example, beliefs about whether or not O. J. Simpson murdered Nicole Simpson are connected to beliefs about cars, freeways, airports, police, and DNA—which in turn connect them to beliefs about cities, governments, history, and even cosmology. And one expects there to be in this way *indefinite numbers of details* that could be filled out in regard to these connections. If doubts are raised about the details, they can rebound to any one of the connected beliefs: thus, evidence against a particular theory of DNA would have given jurors less reason to believe that O. J. was at the scene of the crime. And if someone were to suggest that some third party murdered Nicole Simpson, then one would expect there to be further details—for example, further fingerprints, DNA—that would serve as crucial evidence. If there were *no* such details, one would be (as many were) reasonably skeptical: again, as everyone knows, absence of evidence is evidence of absence.

By contrast, literally understood, religious claims are oddly *detail-resistant.* Perhaps the most dramatic cases are the claims about creation. Whereas scientists regularly ask about the details of the "Big Bang"—there is an entire book, for example, about what happened in the first three minutes (see Weinberg, 1977)—it seems perfectly silly to inquire into similar details of just how God did it. Just how did His saying, "Let there be light," actually bring about light? How did He "say" anything at all? Or, if He merely "designed" the world or the species in it, how did He do this? Does anyone really think there is some set of truths answering these questions? Perhaps; but it is striking how there is nothing like the systematic research on them, in anything like the way that there is massive, ongoing systematic research into the indefinitely subtle details of biology, physics, and cosmology. As the philosopher Philip Kitcher (1982, ch. 5) points out, even "Creation Science" is concerned only with resisting evolutionary biology, not with seriously investigating any of the massive details that would be required for the Creation story actually to be confirmed. And even for those who regard evolution as simply the manner of God's creation, there is (so far as I know) not the slightest interest in investigating, say, radioisotopes, sedimentary layers, and the fossil record to establish precisely how, when, and where God had any role whatsoever in the creation of atoms, compounds, amino acids, DNA, and so forth that are manifestly required for the development of life, consciousness, and intelligent capacities. Despite what they claim, theists in fact treat Him as an idle wheel that does no serious explanatory work.

Of course, theologians do discuss details. I'm not a scholar of theology; however, I'm willing to wager that few of the details they discuss are of the *evidential* sort that we ordinarily expect of ordinary claims about the world, that is, claims that link the theological to *crucial data that would be better explained by the theological than by any competing hypothesis* (as I noted earlier, rendering theistic claims *compatible* with the rest of one's beliefs is not the same as rendering them *confirmed*). Mere elaborations of the theological stories without this property—mere stories about "angels on the head of a pin"—don't constitute such details. If there really are serious attempts to narrow down the details of God's activities by, for example, reference to the fossil record, or systematic studies of the effects of prayer, then I stand corrected. But I'd also wager that most "believers" would find such efforts silly, perhaps even "sacrilegious."

Some of this resistance to detail could, of course, be attributed to intellectual sloth. But not all of it. After all, if the religious stories really were true, an incredible lot would depend upon getting the details right (for many religious people, if you believe the wrong story, you could risk winding up in hell forever!). However, when I ask "believers" these kinds of questions of detail, I am invariably met with incredulity that I even think they're relevant. Usually the questions themselves are regarded as sacrilegious.

Similarity to Fiction

This resistance to detail is strikingly similar to the same resistance one encounters in dealing with fiction. It seems as silly to ask the kind of detailed questions about God as to ask for details about fictional characters; for example, What did Hamlet have for breakfast? Just how did the tornado get Dorothy and Toto to Oz? These questions are obviously silly and have no real answers—the text pretty much exhausts what can be said about the issues. In keeping with the reliance on texts and appeals to non-literality that we've already noted, religious claims seem to be understood to be fiction from the start.

Another indication that religious stories are understood as more akin to fiction than to factual claims is the aforementioned toleration of what would otherwise be patently delusional and bizarre claims. In fictions, we standardly enjoy all manner of deviation from "naturalism" not only in matters of fact, but even in how we react. My own favorite examples in this regard are Wagner operas, which (I confess) move me terribly. But it matters a lot that it's fiction. In the first act of *Lohengrin,* for example, Elsa is accused of having murdered her brother. Instead of demanding some evidence for such an awful charge, she falls to her knees and prays that a knight in shining armor should come and vanquish her accuser; and when he shows up—on a swan!—he agrees to do so and marry her on the spot—but only on condition she never asks who he is! Were I to witness an event like this in real life, and the people were serious, I would regard them as completely out of their minds. But in the opera I am deeply moved—just as I am by the Passion story of the sacrifice of Christ, as a *story,* even though I would be thoroughly appalled and disgusted were it the history of an *actual, intentional sacrifice.*

Merely Symbolic Status of the Stories

Indeed, notice that much of the power of religious claims doesn't really consist in their literal *truth.* Imagine, again, a judge in a real court, considering an appropriate punishment for the sins of man, and let's accept the idea of an innocent person being sacrificed to expiate *someone else's* sins. But, now ask if, in the specific case of Jesus, He actually did suffer *enough*? I don't mean to say that His betrayal and crucifixion weren't pretty awful; but can one afternoon on a cross (with the prospect of Sunday in heaven) really "balance" *all* of the "sins" of Genghis Khan, Hitler, Stalin, or what death squads routinely do to their victims in Latin America? These are crucifixions multiplied *many a million-fold.* But, of course, all this is less relevant if we are to take the Passion story as merely symbolic fiction, that is, not as an actual rectifying of wrongs. Mere symbols, after all, needn't share the magnitudes of what they symbolize.

Peculiarly Selective Perspectives

Related to detail resistance is a peculiar skewing of perspective on the world that keeps obviously disturbing details conveniently out of sight. As mentioned earlier, Alvin Plantinga (2000, 174) notes that religious feelings are often triggered by various bits of natural scenery, for example, mountains, the sea, the night sky. Such effects are quite familiar and easy to appreciate, even by a godless sinner like myself. But, of course, these bits are not really very representative of the world as a whole. Tastes may vary here, but it's not clear that on balance the majority of the devout are seriously prepared to regard most portions of the universe as suggestive of an omni-God. They know very well that the universe consists, overwhelmingly, of vast tracts of empty space, dotted with horrendous explosions and careening rubble, amid most of which any living thing would be annihilated in an instant. Even sticking to the minuscule Earth, they know that a biological war of all against all likely leaves most animals starving, diseased, and scared; and that most of human life ends in humiliating misery, perfectly nice people wasting away from awful diseases and mental deteriorations, often unable to recognize family and friends, much less retain any wisdom they may have earlier acquired (Can anyone seriously think that Alzheimer's helps in the building of a better immortal soul?). Of course, it's perfectly fine to be selective about what one focuses upon and enjoys; it's self-deception only if it leads one to avow hypotheses that one knows to be belied by the majority of the evidence.

Or consider the striking cultural bias of especially (but not only) Christian views. Until the colonization of the rest of the world by Europe beginning in the sixteenth century, most of the world hadn't heard a thing about the Judeo-Christian omni-God—and presumably prior to around 2000 BC virtually no one had (perhaps there'd been a few seers). These non-Europeans and earlier peoples worshipped a multitude of very different sorts of divinities, if any at all, and, of course, a great many of them still do. This should be a most peculiar and extraordinary fact with regard to an omni-being who created the world and remains significantly in charge of it, particularly one keen that people "don't worship any gods before Him." It would be a little like learning that the vast majority of Romans hadn't the faintest idea about their proud and powerful emperor, and took themselves to ruled by other figures entirely—and that the emperor hadn't a clue about them either! Why does the "word of God" not even *mention* all these other people? Leave aside the issue of their moral status, and what fate awaits them in the Hereafter: the simpler question is just what Christians are to make of these people's complete ignorance of Christianity and (up until their worldly discovery) Christianity's utter disregard of them.

One standard story (at least about all these people's ignorance) seems to be that all humans are tainted with "original sin" that makes them "blind" to God and His commands. For example, Alston (who, to his credit, is quite worried by this problem) writes:

> It may be that God makes basic truths about Himself readily available to all persons, regardless of race, creed or color, but many of us are too preoccupied with other matters to take sufficient notice. This angle on the matter has been stressed in the Christian tradition under the rubric of "original sin," and it provides another alternative to supposing that persistent disagreement can best be explained by a total lack of genuine cognition. (Alston 1991, 268)

The emperor is deciding the eternal and possibly horrific fate of billions of people, and they are all "too preoccupied" to notice?! Well, according to Plantinga (2000), "sin carries with it a sort of blindness, a sort of imperceptiveness, dullness and stupidity.... I [the sinner] am inclined to seek my own personal glorification and aggrandizement, bending all my efforts toward making myself look good" (pp. 207–8).

Indeed, "Were it not for sin and its effects, God's presence and glory would be as obvious and uncontroversial to us all as the presence of other minds, physical objects and the past" (p. 214). Now *perhaps* Alston, Plantinga, and other Christians may believe this sort of thing about many of their secular *compatriots* (although, *really!*). But they and other Christians know very well they're in no position to insist upon it with regard to the *many hundreds and hundreds of millions* of, for example, Chinese, Indians, Polynesians, Africans, and Native Americans who hadn't or haven't had the good fortune to be visited by missionaries or evangelicals (or *conquistadores*). At any rate, I *hope* Christians don't seriously think that *all* of these peoples were and are so "dull, stupid and self-aggrandizing" as to be "blind" to the presence of something "as obvious as physical objects"!

There may be other, slightly more plausible stories that other Christians tell here—I've heard that George Bush once claimed "we all believe in the same God"—but, whatever the story, it's hard to see how anyone could take themselves to be in a position to seriously believe it. And so it's hard to see how anyone could take him or herself to be in a position to seriously believe that the Bible is the word of God.

Appeals to Mystery

Confronted with many of the above problems, many theists claim God is a "mystery"—indeed, I once heard a famous convert, Malcolm Muggeridge, claim "mystery" as his main reason for believing! But ignorance (read: mystery) is standardly a reason to *not* believe something. Imagine the police arresting you merely because it's a "mystery" how you could have murdered Smith! Just so: if it's really a complete mystery how God designed or created the world and permits so much pointless suffering, then obviously that's a reason to suspect it's simply not true that He did—and my point is that this is sufficiently obvious that everyone knows it and people simply pretend that religion affords some very odd exception.

Many theists are often willing to tolerate the mysteries surrounding God because they have an additional belief, which is that they also can't know about God's ways. Now, first of all, this is contradicted by all the claims they make about His omni-properties, as well as, crucially, about what He likes and dislikes. Moreover, many people claim that He's responsible for when people live and die, and think He's the sort of being that will be responsive to petitionary prayer. But these then are precisely the points at which the God hypothesis is vulnerable to obvious disconfirmation: too much happens that's hard to believe is the result of an omni-being, too little that is plausibly an answer to prayer.

Of course, people do tolerate plenty of mysteries about how the world works. Most people have only the dimmest idea about how things live and grow, or how intentions actually bring about action. But in these cases the evidence for the postulated processes is overwhelming and uncontroversial: Ordinary people haven't the slightest reason to doubt that things grow, or that thought causes action, despite the mystery about how it occurs. By contrast, anyone aware of the basic ideas of contemporary science and the lack of evidence of God has plenty of reason to doubt His existence. In such a case, mystery can be no refuge.

What's particularly odd about the belief about our supposed inability to know God's ways is that the inability is so arbitrarily and inexplicably strong: why should there be no normal evidence of His existence? Why shouldn't it be possible to establish it in the same way as the existence of bacteria or the Big Bang? In any case, it's not as though the religious try to do what they might do in these other cases, namely, think of clever, indirect ways of finding out. No, the "mystery" is supposed to be "deeper" and far more impenetrable than that. I can't imagine what sustains such conviction—mind you, not merely about *God*, but about the *knowability* of God's ways—except perhaps an unconscious realization that there, of course, couldn't ever be serious evidence for something that doesn't actually exist.

Appeals to "Faith"

Of course, many religious people readily recognize the failure of evidence but then go on to claim that religious beliefs are matters of "faith," not evidence (in an extreme case, like that of Tertullian or Kierkegaard, claiming to believe precisely "because it is absurd"). But try thinking something of the form:

p, however I don't have adequate evidence or reasons for believing it.

or

p, but it is totally absurd to believe it.

where you substitute for *p*, some non-religious claim, for example, "2 + 2 = 37," "the number of stars is even," or "Columbus sailed in 1962." Imagine how baffling it would be if someone claimed merely to "have faith" about these things. As Jonathan Adler (2002) points out, there seems to be something "impossible," even "conceptually incoherent" about it, a little like the incoherence of thinking you know something, but being nevertheless convinced it isn't true.

On the other hand, issues of faith do arise precisely in those cases in which a person is asked to manifest loyalty to a person or cause despite the evidence that might otherwise undermine it: thus, a father has faith in his son's honesty despite what the police say, or someone remains "true" to a political cause in the face of evidence of bribes. Indeed, I suspect one reason for the odd removal of many religious beliefs from empirical (dis-)confirmation may be due to the useful role of "unfalsifiable" claims in keeping a group together. Groups aligned around political or social causes, for example, are forever destabilized by people's discovering evidence that undermines some specific claim on which the cause may have been based (people don't benefit from "trickle down" effects; Stalin really did do horrific things), although, they, too, notoriously struggle to keep people to a "party line," which often comes to look "religious" in its rigidity. But, of course, cases of loyalty are precisely ones that lay the ground for the kind of self-deception that I have been arguing is characteristic of religious claims.

Betrayal by Reactions and Behavior

Most people's reactions and behavior—for example, grief or mourning at a friend's death—do not seem seriously affected by the claimed prospects of a Hereafter (one wonders about the claimed exceptions). Contrast the reactions in two situations of a young, loving, "believing" couple who are each seriously ill: In the first, the wife has to be sent off to a luxurious convalescent hospital for care for two years before the husband can come and join her for an indefinite time thereafter. In the second, the wife is about to die, and the husband has been told he will follow in two years. If, in the second case, there really were the genuine belief in a heavenly Hereafter that (let us suppose) they both avow, why shouldn't the husband feel as glad as in the first case—indeed, even gladder, given the prospect of eternal bliss! However, I bet he'd grieve and mourn "the loss" like anyone else. Indeed, note how most religious music for the dead is deeply lugubrious, and imagine the absurdity of performing the Mozart requiem for someone you won't see for a few years because she has gone to a luxurious resort!

Or consider petitionary prayer (in contrast to a merely meditative sort): in the first place, the idea of an omni-god that would permit, for example, children to die slowly of leukemia is already pretty puzzling; but to permit this to happen unless someone *prays* to Him to prevent it—this verges on a certain sort of sadism and moral incoherence (imagine a doctor who acted in this way!), and one wonders what people have in mind in worshipping Him. One can well understand the desperation of someone praying in such circumstances, or in a foxhole, or in the throes of unrequited love; but such desperations are just that, and do not per se manifest serious belief (as Neils Bohr is reputed to have said in being asked why he kept a horseshoe over his door, "I've been told they work even if you don't believe they do").

Indeed, if petitionary prayer were a matter of serious belief, then why aren't those who engage in it disposed to have the National Institutes of Health do a (non-intrusive) demographic study, say, of the different sorts of prayers, as they would were they interested in the claim that soy beans prevent cancer? And why do none of them expect prayer to cure wooden legs? Or bring Lazarus back after two thousand years? I suggest that there are obvious limits to people's self-deception, and they know full well that God couldn't really intervene in such obviously impossible ways.

Are the Self-Deceptions of Religion Benign?

There seem to me a great many motivations for the self-deceptions of religion. As I've mentioned (and others have detailed), many of them seem purely sociological: loyalty to one's family, culture, or tribe, and maintaining public stances. Others may be more psychological: taking refuge in the consoling stories of one's childhood, or giving expression to sensitivities that can be difficult to articulate regarding what's important about people and the world. Some of the self-deception may simply be due to uncontrolled responses to overwhelming personal experiences, or to desperate situations, as when recovering alcoholics rely on a "Higher Power" or turn to religion in their lonely and miserable old age. But a few of them are philosophical, and deserve to be addressed here.

One thing many people find satisfying is being a part of some emotionally fulfilling *community* or *project* they endorse that goes beyond their own individual lives: one's family, community, tribe, or nation, or projects of art, knowledge, and so on. At any rate, people pretty regularly find depressing the thought that their labors, especially their sufferings, are "meaningless," in that they don't contribute to some larger good. And it can be gratifying (but by no means required) that these projects are effectively nested: one slaves away, say, as the cook on an expedition to discover a fossil, which contributes to geology, which contributes to knowledge, which (perhaps) contributes to human welfare. Insofar as someone might look for still further nestings of one's projects, wondering, perhaps, what's so important about human welfare, it apparently can be gratifying to be told there is some still-larger project, perhaps a largest conceivable project, of which humanity is an integral part ("For the glory of God and that my neighbor may benefit thereby," Bach inscribed on his manuscripts). This last, hyperbolic move seems to be one of the appeals of religion, and, I presume, explains why many people think of a life without God as "meaningless."

It seems to me that there are two responses one can have to this familiar fact. The first is to notice that the appeal to some "largest possible" project is really only a temporary palliative. At any rate, if one really doesn't find some very large project, such as art, knowledge, or human welfare, somehow gratifying in itself, it is difficult to see how just increasing the project's community to include superhuman gods should be of any help. Why shouldn't one wonder and be depressed about the meaninglessness of these projects as well—indeed, if it were the largest possible project, then it would be metaphysically impossible for it to have any meaning beyond itself! (And would it help to be *eternal*? If something isn't meaningful over a finite time, it's hard to see how it would gain meaning by being extended *forever:* eternal pointlessness might well be worse than death!)

"Just so," the depressives among us might observe. But while the above consideration may well condemn our lives to necessary meaninglessness, there's nothing logically mandated by depression itself. Being depressed is not the conclusion of any argument; failing to be depressed even by the worst news in the world isn't *irrational.* At any rate, it is perfectly open to someone persuaded of the ultimate meaninglessness of life to find this a fact of profound indifference. It seems to me another instance of the "philosophy fallacy" to think that one needs grand metaphysical, religious stories in order to genuinely or legitimately enjoy the good things that life does sometimes afford.

Of course, most human beings are so constituted that they do in fact get depressed by certain sorts of things, notably the pointlessness of their projects, and especially by the suffering and death of themselves and their friends. With regard to these latter, I'm afraid I have nothing more helpful to say than anyone else—including the theist. Philosophers have, I think, rightly pointed out that death may not be as bad as people suppose, but it's hard to think of *any* story—least of all the glory of God!—that would justify the sufferings of, for example, children slowly dying from a plague, cancer, or AIDS, or people wasting away with Alzheimer's or completely debilitating strokes.

With regard to our projects, however, there does seem to be a good deal of plasticity. At least the economically fortunate can usually focus their attention on one group or project rather than another. Most of life, after all, is a pretty local affair, seldom requiring attention to all one's concerns, least of all to the "big" questions. Frustration with family can be replaced by (again, at least for the lucky) satisfaction with work, or maybe with just hanging out and schmoozing with friends.

Perhaps, though, this is where a little self-deception may be in order. Thinking your efforts are worthwhile for some larger project you approve is probably necessary to get your heart into those efforts. But—and here I tread with caution for fear of disrupting my own heart—serious reflection might well lead you to find such a thought pathetic. Someone recently quoted to me a statistic to the effect that the average philosophy article gets read maybe once. I'm not going to research this statistic more carefully. It helps that the facts here are unclear—continually muddied by local professional encouragements—so that I can pretty successfully sustain the thought that what I'm doing matters, which sufficiently motivates me to engage in the efforts, and—who knows?—maybe something will come of it (fortunately it's not the *only* reason I write the stuff). This is a benign self-deception that I'm happy to keep intact. Similar reasonings, of course, might apply to "turning a blind eye" to the faults of your friends and family, or to ignoring the signs of an in fact hopeless illness.

But there are limits. If my doing philosophy really required me to think of myself as the best philosopher since Kant, well, it'd be time to consider a new career. Some self-deceptions would be obviously demented. What I've tried to suggest above is that religious ones—at least abstracted from their social protections—seem to be of this sort, involving, I daresay, claims far more grandiose than my being the best since Kant. Pace William James's (1897/1992) famous discussion of "the will to believe," these sorts of claims are well beyond any evidential ambiguity and so seem far beyond the pale of benign self-deception or other "pragmatic" reasoning.

My chief qualms about most religion, even as self-deception, are not, however, with regard to the rational absurdity of the claims, but to the use of those claims to buttress claims in other domains, specifically, ethics and psychology. Claims, for example, about which people God has "chosen," what He has promised them, whose side He favors in a war, and which sexual arrangements He approves, are somehow supposed to provide some special grounding to moral views, and have, of course, been enlisted to this effect on behalf of conquest, racism, slavery, and persecution of sexual minorities. If you think some particular war is right, or some sexual practice wrong, fine; then provide the reasons you think so. But don't try to intimidate yourself and others with unsupportable, peculiarly medieval claims about how the "Lord of the Universe" approves or disapproves and will punish people accordingly. What, after all, does His disapproval have to do with morality in the first place? It's by no means obvious that even creators of a world get to say what's supposed to go on in it.

But an equally serious qualm is the way religion often encourages too simple an understanding of ourselves. Some aspects of religious psychology are, of course immensely admirable: the Christian concern with a certain serious kind of respect and love (or agape) for all human beings that so moved me as a child, is, I think, on to something interesting and important in our emotional repertoire. And there's certainly something to be said for "faith, hope, and charity," if they simply involve the virtue of putting a good face on things, and hanging in there, for yourself and others, despite it all. But too much of traditional religion seems to be based on dangerously simplistic conceptions of human life and its troubles, leading people to see conflicts not in terms of the complex conflicting interests and situations of the different parties, but rather as a war between "good" and "evil," "virtue" and "sin," good guys and bad guys. For example, Plantinga (2000, 207–8) goes so far as to claim that "the doctrine of original sin . . . has been *verified* in the wars, cruelty and general hatefulness that have characterized human history from its very inception to the present" (p. 207, italics mine). (See also Alston, 1991, 268). But does Plantinga really think this is a serious historical hypothesis about the causes of all the world's wars and the like? For one thing, these wars are often fought by people willing to sacrifice themselves for a "greater cause"; for another, weren't people like Hitler and Stalin paranoid? (Or is that also "original sin"?) For still another, aren't many people often trapped in "prisoner's dilemmas," being rationally obliged to do what they know is neither in their own or nor anyone else's ultimate best interest (as in a standard "arms race")? To be sure, the world has some nasty people in it; but it also has some pretty intricate social and psychological problems that are challenges for theist and atheist alike. It's the temptation to disregard the complexities in these and other domains that strikes me as one of the most frightening risks of standard religious thinking.

In any case, judging from, for example, the Crusades, the Inquisition, the wars of the Reformation, and present-day conflicts in Northern Ireland and the Middle East, it would appear that religious affiliation and these sorts of simplistic categories play as much a role in the horrors of the world as do any of the standard "sins" (pride, avarice, adultery). Reason enough, I should think, to be wary about religion as self-deception, not to mention as genuine belief.

This is a revised and shortened version of Rey (2001a) that appeared with a similar title in Martin and Kolak (2001), a much more expanded version of which will appear in the sixth edition of that same anthology, Martin and Kolak (2004), which readers should consult for more details than could be included here. The central idea for all these papers arose from the various stray remarks some years ago of Rogers Albritton, Ted Kompanetz, and Hilary Putnam, although I doubt they would recognize, much less endorse, what I have made of them. I'm also grateful to Jonathan Adler, Louise Antony, Sally Bogacz, Chris Bernard, Boran Berčić, Lisa Leigh, Joe Levine, Ray Martin, Chris Morris, Ryan McKay, and Michael Slote for useful discussions and comments; and to Antony, Martin, and Kolak for the encouragement to write up my views and their permission to reproduce the result in these several forms.

TWENTY

Faith and Fanaticism

Jonathan E. Adler

How do you explain the intellectual dimension of fanaticism, particularly as it leads to terrorism? The fanatics I focus on strive to justify their single-minded pursuit, as I illustrate initially from the guilty plea of Eric Rudolph, the convicted bomber.[1] Fanatics put forth arguments with which they try to persuade others to share their commitments.[2] An intellectual thread joins the traits we associate with fanaticism: self-righteousness, intolerance, excessive certainty, zealotry. So convinced are the fanatics that their cause is just that they are willing to pursue actions—including terrorism—that shatter the most fundamental of ethical boundaries.

The explanation that I develop is intellectual. I do not address the conditions that breed fanaticism—a history of political humiliation, economic deprivation, authoritarian education. These conditions are not sufficient—they do not provide an understanding of fanatical reasoning.

Fanatical reasoning, I argue, resides in a lack of commonplace *self-restraints* (or controls), not just from how the fanatic acts but from how he reasons and how he maintains his beliefs. Yet the need for self-restraint is a lesson we all learn. When, as a young student, you are angry that a teacher gave you an unfair grade, you conclude that you should get even by calling in a fire scare during a holiday event. You do not lose your head, however: either you distract yourself from the conclusion by going to the movies, or you realize that something was wrong with your reasoning, even if you do not know what.

Since, as I further argue, supernatural religious faith promotes denial of these self-restraints, the explanation that I develop also provides understanding of why faith is fertile ground for fanaticism. Regardless of the efforts of various faiths to teach in opposition to fanaticism and terrorism, essential tenets of supernatural religion are integral to fanatical reasoning. In fundamentalist faiths these tenets are incorporated in practices hospitable to fanaticism.

Rudimentary ways in which each of us undermines self-restraints on our reasoning are familiar. Prominent among these means are defensive maneuvers to protect one's favored beliefs, when threatened, that each of us has had occasion to indulge, including using self-deception or attending mainly to sympathetic sources. The contribution of faith to fanaticism depends on these defensive maneuvers systematically, extensively, and intellectually. Rather than invoking them haphazardly, as we all sometimes do, and with some tinge of shame and embarrassment, particularly when discovered, the day-to-day practices of supernaturalist faiths regularly both involve these maneuvers and invoke them to support religious claims.

Understanding your Response to the Fanatic's Conclusion

Because I focus on the reasoned basis that the fanatic claims for his acts, I center discussion on what I presume to be a fanatical argument—specifically, one to justify murder to stop abortions.[3] Recently, Eric Rudolph admitted to the 1996 bombing at the Summer Olympics in Atlanta and at other sites that resulted in 3 deaths and more than 115 injuries. In his eleven-page guilty plea, he argues:

> Abortion is murder. And when the regime in Washington legalized, sanctioned and legitimized this practice, they forfeited their legitimacy and moral authority to govern. At various time in history men and women of good conscience have had to decide when the lawfully constituted authorities have overstepped their moral bounds and forfeited their right to rule. This took place in July 1776 when our Forefathers decided that the British Crown had violated the essential rights of Englishmen, and therefore lost its authority to govern. And when in January of 1973 the government in Washington decided to descend into barbarism by sanctioning the ancient practice of infanticide by that act consigned 50 million unborn children to their graves. There is no more legitimate reason to my knowledge, for renouncing allegiance to and if necessary using force to drag this monstrosity of a government down to the dust where it belongs. I am not an anarchist. I have nothing against government or law enforcement in general. It is solely for the reason that this govt [sic] has legalized the murder of children that I have no allegiance to nor do I recognize the legitimacy of this particular government in Washington. Because I believe that abortion is murder, I also believe that force is justified and [sic] in an attempt to stop it. Because this government is committed to the policy of maintaining the policy of abortion and protecting it, the agents of this government are the agents of mass murder, whether knowingly or unknowingly. And whether

> these agents of the government are armed or otherwise they are legitimate targets in the war to end this holocaust, especially those agents who carry arms in defense of this regime and the enforcement of its laws. This is the reason and the only reason for the targeting of so-called law enforcement personnel.
>
> ...There is no more fundamental duty for a moral citizen than to protect the innocent from assault.... You have the right, the responsibility and the duty to come to the defense of the innocent when the innocent are under assault. Would you protect your children from the clutches of a murderer? Would you protect your neighbors' children when they were under assault? If you answered yes to both of these, then you must support the use of force as justified in attempting to prevent the murder that is abortion.... However if you do recognize abortion is murder and that unborn children should be protected and you still insist that force is unjustified to stop abortion, then you can be none other than cowards standing idly by in the face of the worst massacre in human history.
>
> There are those who would say to me that the system in Washington works. They say that pro-life forces are making progress, that eventually Roe v. Wade will be overturned, that the culture of life will ultimately win over the majority of Americans and that the horror of abortion will be outlawed. Yet, in the meantime thousands die everyday [sic]. They say that the mechanism through which this will be achieved is the Republican party, and under the benevolent leadership of men like George W. Bush the wholesale slaughter of children will be a thing of the past. But with every day that passes another pile of corpses is added to the pyre. George W. will appoint the necessary justices to the Supreme Court and Roe will be finished, they say. All of this will be achieved through the lawful, legitimate democratic process. And every year a million and a half more die. I ask these peaceful Christian law-abiding Pro-Life citizens, is there any point at which all of the legal remedies will not suffice and you would fight to end the massacre of children?[4]

I expect that you find this excerpt impassioned and filled with rage but nevertheless informed, controlled, and well reasoned. The core position that abortion is murder is prevalent in the United States, and its grounds or principles are recognized as credible, even by those who reject it. Rudolph's argument treats the retaliation as a last resort, not really murder but the attempt to save the innocent.[5]

What is it about the argument that arrests your attention and clues you that the underlying reasoning is fanatical, even if you bracket your knowledge of the horrid activities that it seeks to explain? Although there are glaring problems in the details, especially the highly strained analogies to the American Revolution and genuine cases of self-defense, I'm sure that you recoil and reject the argument when you realize where it is going. Rudolph's argument claims the right to murder as a tactic. Even though his elaborate written explanation is undoubtedly toned down, polished, and censored compared to the real thoughts and motives that drove him, you think that, along these lines, almost any action, however horrendous, could be justified.

In this excerpt and elsewhere in the document, Rudolph claims specifically the right to murder any officer of the government and, in order to realize that aim, he grants himself permission to use methods whose likely effects will be the death and maiming of many innocent bystanders. He thus goes beyond the fanatics who narrow their focus to the intentional murder of abortion-physicians and the destruction of abortion clinics. For the sake of discussion, let us explicitly state only the latter, more restricted, fanatical conclusion:

> We should commit ourselves to killing abortion-physicians, as opportunity permits.

I will refer to this conclusion as "Should Kill."

When you grasp Should Kill, you reject it such that you are puzzled as to how anyone sane could actually endorse it, even if the initial reasoning strikes you as credible, as with Rudolph's plea. Once you appreciate the conclusion—Should Kill—you are convinced that the reasoning is distorted, without your knowing, or even needing to know, where it goes wrong. The conclusion evokes a response in you that amounts to a restraint on your own reasoning. What is the basis for your response? The fanatic's conclusion strikes you as (a) starkly offensive to common sense and decency, (b) in sharp violation of the most rudimentary ethical prohibitions, (c) unacceptable to almost everyone of highly varied views and backgrounds, even those who endorse the core, strong "pro-life," position, and (d) bluntly disrespectful of democratic institutions and the rule of law.

Your initial response to the fanatic's argument also includes (e) emotional repugnance at his conclusions. In the "Conscience of Huckleberry Finn," Jonathan Bennett (1974) discusses the perspective of the Nazi commander Heinrich Himmler, a fanatic of ideology, not faith.[6] Himmler commanded his soldiers that though they are sickened, they should not hide from themselves their victims' anguish. Grappling with their own hesitancy and ambivalence will help steel their conscience—keep them "decent" and make them "hard." Himmler views feelings of revulsion and emotional distress as sentimental obstacles to be confronted, without concession.

Your view is the opposite: the depth of repugnance should cast doubt on the commands. The doubts are not, of course, conclusive. But before you will take them seriously, you require testimony on their behalf, independent of your own or the fanatic's reasoning.

The beliefs and values (a–e) that back your revolt at the fanatic's conclusion (Should Kill) rest on a huge bedrock of learning, critical evaluation, and mutual support. No argument to a conclusion that would nullify these beliefs and values could be endorsed, except under the most far-out circumstances. Even if you went along with the initial part of the fanatic's argument, you would not allow your own reasoning to overrule this wealth of knowledge. Your modesty extends to not demanding that you first understand exactly where the fanatic's argument goes wrong, as a condition on its rejection. Your deference to this wealth of knowledge is not even choice: The conclusion simply *cannot* be believed. Effectively, your well-founded beliefs and values are not merely reasons to object to the fanatic's argument, but controls or restraints on your own reasoning.

Attempting to Overrule Well-Founded Beliefs and Values

Religious commands can readily justify overruling the restraints of your background beliefs and values, since the authority of those commands ultimately derives from an all-knowing supernatural being. Religious commands demand obedience even when they violate basic ethical prohibitions and when their rationale reaches beyond the grasp of the faithful. (The demand for obedience is often backed by a promise of an eternally blessed life for the faithful, and its opposite for others.) Extreme devotional practices and an authoritarian educational upbringing reinforce this demand for obedience, and it is one path to the single-mindedness—the constricted focus—of fanaticism.

Although the appeal to divine authority within extreme devotional practices will be part of an explanation of the faith–fanaticism connection, it is insufficient. The primary weakness is the most obvious: Scant few of the faithful are fanatics. The appeal refers only to fanaticism that develops out of a severely directed and intolerant religious community, not the lone or isolated fanatic, as Rudolph seems to be.[7] A final weakness is that the appeal, instead of exposing the glaring defects in the fanatic's reasoning, defends it as according with divine commands.

The latter is illustrated at its most vivid and troubling in God's order to Abraham to sacrifice his son Isaac. Although the tale (the *akedah*—the *binding* of Isaac) is subject to interpretational disputes, it is read like the *Book of Job* as a triumph of faith. Unlike the *Book of Job*, however, the faith demonstrated is in Abraham's willingness to perform an act normally construed as a brutal, unthinkable murder. Because, within a supernatural setting, there is a strong tendency to tune out a range of commonsense questions and responses, think of the version of the *binding* that Robert Adams offers to his students:

> What would you think if you asked your neighbor why he was building a large stone table in his backyard, and he said, "I'm building an altar because God has commanded me to sacrifice my son as a whole burnt offering. Won't you come to the ceremony tomorrow morning?" All agree that the neighbor should be committed to a mental hospital.[8]

Nevertheless, the Abraham–Isaac tale is a parable of faith as well as an instance of Divine Command Theory:

> God commands me to do A, e.g., to sacrifice my son.
> If God commands me to do A (to sacrifice my son), it is right [my duty] to do so.
> So it is right [my duty] to do A (to sacrifice my son).

From the perspective of Divine Command Theory, for Abraham (or the neighbor) to rebel is the sin and conceit of placing human beliefs and values above divine authority.

By stark contrast, your rejection of the fanatic's argument applied to Abraham or to the neighbor would be to take the command as evidence that it cannot really be God speaking. You exercise self-restraint on your judgment, one expression of which is offered by Kant: "Abraham should have replied to this supposedly divine voice: 'That I ought not to kill my good son is quite certain. But that you, this apparition, are God—of that I am not certain, and never can be, not even if this voice rings down to me from (visible) heaven.'"[9]

Exceptions and Isolation: Lifting Restraints for Self-Protection

Despite their appeal to supreme authority, religious fanatics do not justify their acts on divine command alone. Perhaps even they are troubled by the lack of clear textual support for what they are doing. (How could any ancient text really speak to contemporary issues of the viability of a fetus in relation to the U.S. Constitution?[10]) Usually, the fanatic's argument is supplemented. Religious terrorists are likely to claim that their proposed killings are *exceptions* or special cases: "Because the true faith is purportedly in jeopardy, emergency conditions prevail, and the killing of innocents becomes, in their [religious terrorists'] view, religiously and morally permissible."[11] Rudolph's argument for the bombings as self-defense implies urgency. He rejects any (further) democratic delays:

> No politician in Washington will ever seriously threaten abortion on demand. And the fools who listen to them, in their hearts, know this but do not care. You so-called "Pro-Life," "good Christian people" who point your plastic fingers at me saying that I am a "murderer," that "two wrongs don't make a right" that even though "abortion is murder, those who would use force to stop the murder are morally the same," I say to you that your lies are transparent.

Despite his recognition that the particular weapons he had on hand "could potentially lead to a disaster wherein many civilians could be killed or wounded,"

Rudolph acknowledges no reason to delay his plan until less-dangerous, more-controllable weapons can be secured.

These claims of alleged emergencies are not genuine judgments of an exception but more of a strategy that I'll call "exceptionalism." Allowing seeing-eye dogs on buses, despite the law that no animals are permitted on public transportation, is a valid exception because it makes sense, given the rule or law itself. With little additional burden on users, seeing-eye dogs aid the public transportation system to realize its goal of availability to all.

Even if you do think of abortion as murder, it is unlikely you really believe that the current situation in the United States constitutes an emergency—large-scale infanticide. Were it otherwise, it would involve an unprecedented breakdown of law, decency, and ethics, generating widespread panic and rebellion. However strongly pro-life, you would respond very differently than you do to legal abortions, and that indicates a lack of real belief that the current situation amounts to, in Rudolph's term, "infanticide." (A thought experiment borrowed from Peter Unger brings the point home. Imagine that conception was visibly and biologically very much as Rudolph alleges. At conception, a tiny but fully developed infant forms. Gestation amounts to the infant's merely growing larger. Would the responses to abortion in these circumstances be at all like the muted responses currently, not only for those who are pro-life, but even for those who are pro-choice?)

Exceptionalism is the norm of religious faith. Religious stories are exempted from minimal demands for empirical credibility, as with miracles, and religious commands are exempted from ethical restrictions, as with the *binding* of Isaac. The attempt to immunize religious claims from everyday requests for validation is pervasive. When it is held that ritual can turn wine into blood, the obvious question is whether we can corroborate this claim chemically. Or, when eternal life is promised to the faithful, one asks for real details: How is this is known, especially when so much else, like why God allows evil, is "mysterious"? How could a disembodied soul be me? When bumper stickers, and religious leaders, proclaim that "prayer works," common sense, if it is not turned off, asks for evidence of the most unobtrusive sort: How often does prayer help the ill recover compared to crossing one's fingers or wishful thinking?[12]

The response that many liberal theists would give to these ordinary requests for corroboration for the Eucharist or Communion or other "miracles" is that they are too literal-minded and so miss the point. These are just *symbolic* representations. (Orthodox readings do take the miracle claims literally. They simply deny that the ordinary requests for corroboration are really capable of testing the veracity of these claims.) As merely symbolic, the rituals amount to a kind of communal pretense that we are accustomed to in reading or watching science fiction—you "suspend disbelief."[13] Still, even if these tales are only symbolic or mythical, thcy are nevertheless reported in the language of belief, and it is belief that is supposed to be the realization of faith.

Are these dull questions about the veracity of alleged miracles or ethical commands gratuitous, obtuse, or mean-spirited, like spilling the beans about Santa Claus to a young child? No—not in a discussion about fanatical beliefs and actions, which are way out and yet taken as righteous. To understand fanaticism requires a flat-footed inquiry into how it is possible to believe the unbelievable. We are trying to understand those very few, like Rudolph or the neighbor, who confuse parables with reality, though they suffer no serious mental disturbance.

In fact, religious assaults on evidence, belief, and truth arise outside the protective, ritualistic domains of religious institutions. In a *New York Times* op-ed article published July 7, 2005, Christoph Schonborn, the Roman Catholic cardinal archbishop of Vienna and the former "lead editor of the official 1992 Catechism of the Catholic Church," concludes his "Finding design in nature": "Scientific theories that try to explain away the appearance of design as the result of 'chance and necessity' are not scientific at all, but, as John Paul put it, an abdication of human intelligence" (p. A23).[14] Although Schonborn's article does not involve an overt affirmation of the supernatural, its offense to reason is far more brazen. A high-ranking Church official declares that evolution, the pillar of modern biology, is false, despite the overwhelming evidence in its favor. Schonborn, like all of us, depends on modern biology for treating illness, in appreciating environmental dependencies, in explaining the development of bacterial resistance to various drugs, in understanding genetic inheritance, and in countless other ways. How can he make sense of the consequence of his position—that biologists can be right in all these cases and yet so uniformly wrong when it comes to the fundamental theory of evolution? In his view, it must be that the biologists suffer a mammoth blind spot about the origins of life, the development of species, and the nature of genetic informational transfer.

If you deny the force of empirical evidence, exempting your own biological and cosmological claims from its reach, how are you going to stand up to all sorts of mysticism, superstition, and pseudo-scientific hucksterism? When the Catholic Church purported to offer a thorough critique of various "new age" beliefs and practices (e.g., psychic healing, astrology, communication with the dead, channeling, crystal-ball prophecies, feng shui, reincarnation), their criticisms all centered on the "new age" texts' arising from condemned sources that promote a self-centered spirituality.[15]

The Church is conspicuously silent on the primary failings, that is, that there are no replicable or controlled studies demonstrating the purported new-age phenomena. New-age predictions fail, when not hopelessly vague and untestable, and their claims are incompatible with well-confirmed natural laws. The Church's attempt to insulate itself from the reach of evidential assessment backfires. It misses the target not out of oversight, misjudgment, or even ineptitude but for unavoidable self-protection. The fear is that if it did strike at the real empirical vulnerability, the same weapon could be turned on the Church. In not cutting new-age claims at their manifest Achilles' heel, the Catholic Church appears more bent on maintaining authority and followers than searching for truth.

A strategy closely related to exceptionalism is *isolationism.* The isolationist strategy is to limit sources of corroboration or critical control to those who share one's views. The faithful cannot take seriously as challenges whether or not randomly selected physicists or biologists will allow that a person can literally walk on water, a woman can have a virgin birth, the dead can be alive. Respected historians are not to be relied on to determine the origins of religious texts and their stories. Authority on these matters does not rest with experts on the subjects, but with priests and ministers with prior commitments to the veracity of these texts and stories.

Isolationism by a group shrinks the set of acceptable ideas or beliefs, homogenizing the range of thought. As a group becomes more insular, dissent, beyond very restricted bounds, is treated as disloyalty, to be eliminated. Yet, social scientists teach us that in the absence of dissent groups tend to *polarize,* a crucial step toward extremism.[16]

Indulgence of this isolationist strategy has already been cited: the nullification or overriding of our background beliefs and values (a–e). A striking illustration of a narrower form of isolationism occurred when an author interviewed a religious terrorist in prison for murdering two CIA workers and injuring three others. The terrorist claims justification based on his reading of sacred texts. The interviewer–author asks him, "What if a respected Islamic scholar told you it would be wrong to shoot CIA employees?" The terrorist responds, "If a respected Islamic scholar would have told me not to do it then I would have asked him questions, and if he would have satisfied me completely then I would have not done it."[17] The interviewer's suggesting consultation with a scholar is not offered only as a way for the terrorist to gain greater knowledge, but as a check on the terrorist's judgments. The terrorist is taking back with one hand what he has granted—the authority of the scholar—with the other. The terrorist accords himself the final word, akin to a business's agreeing to have an auditor check its books on the condition that the auditor's report is subject to the company's own inspection.[18]

Denying the Gap between Belief and Action

In my opening example, a student concludes that he should call in a false alarm, but he dodges action by distracting himself. I have, though, not yet provided room for this crucial self-restraint, since the fanatic's conclusion is only, recall, Should Kill:

> We should commit ourselves to killing abortion-physicians, as opportunity permits.

However, the fanatic endorses a further conclusion, which I'll call "Intend to Kill":

> We commit ourselves to killing abortion-physicians as opportunity permits.

You find it hard to reason with someone who endorses Should Kill. But if that person resists acting on that endorsement, not proceeding to Intend to Kill, you would take him to be a fanatic of a much less extreme sort.

Yet, this judgment leaves you with another puzzle: Why isn't the move from Should Kill to Intend to Kill no real step at all, as the fanatic will insist? After all, to intend to kill (or to pull the trigger) is just to act consistently with the recommendation that you endorse. Rudolph's presentation does not draw this distinction, which I'm sure he would mock as pedantic hair-splitting.

If, though, you reflect on the example of the student, the puzzle dissolves. The student does not recognize that he is reasoning along a bad path until he is shaken awake by vivid confrontation with the action that his conclusion demands—it is one thing to be persuaded to call in the alarm; it is another to do so, which is far more consequential. In the case of the fanatic's argument, the powerful background beliefs and values that lead you to jump ship immediately at Should Kill kick in for this extreme pro-lifer only at the next step to Intend to Kill, when action is really demanded. That is why, even though the extreme pro-lifer goes along with much of the fanatic's argument, he is closer to you in moral character than is the fanatic.

The rationale for a break between Should Kill and Intend to Kill is an obvious delay principle: As the costs or risks of acting increase, we are more reluctant to follow out a belief's guidance, as long as circumstances permit. Merely believing a strong proposition rarely has any serious risks, in enormous contrast to acting upon it.

We learn lessons of the delay principle from many angles. Besides the opening example, think of some action you have come to regret. You are incensed that a friend stands you up. You confront him only to learn that he had to rush his wife to the hospital for emergency surgery, as he intended to tell you, with apology, had you just given him the chance. Or, imagine that your child convinces you that a neighbor's son bullied him. You resolve to speak to the neighbor. Still, you hesitate. Before you call the neighbor, and risk causing offense, straining relations, and placing your child in an embarrassing situation, you inquire of others what really happened.

Predominantly, the beliefs that we acquire issue in no action at all (e.g., the belief I pick up through passive observation that my neighbor is wearing a blue tie). Even for those beliefs that do direct action (e.g., I should call my aunt for her birthday), there is a lapse between "should" and "does"—the *belief–action gap.* When you reach fury at a perceived offense, your friends suggest you cool down ("count to ten") to think through an irrevocable retaliation. Frequently, we hope the pressure to act will just go away. A student who could not complete his homework because of a printer malfunction believes that if the teacher confronts him, he should tell the teacher what happened. But what he hopes is that the teacher will forget about today's homework and collect it tomorrow.

Hamlet may be neurotic in his search for certainty as a condition for his performing a momentous act. But if it is neurotic, it is still only an exaggeration of a wise pattern of self-critical caution. Unless you are perfect, you will be very familiar with not fully living up to your ideals. You can be a devoted environmentalist and still occasionally take that long, decadent hot shower.

With little effort, the belief–act gap allows us to respect our fallibility. Delaying action, we increase opportunities to discover if the guiding belief is mistaken. The delay principle presupposes fallibility, since from the point of view only of what we believe, there is nothing to discover.

The fanatic's closing of the belief–action gap illuminates characteristic charges against him of impatience and of not taking his fallibility seriously. From the fanatic's perspective, the delay principle makes no sense: If you really believe that you should act a certain way, then, when opportunity arises, you should so act, without hesitation. Not to do so is a kind of inconsistency, or worse. This is why fanatics will accuse those who profess a shared belief, but who do not act with them, of hypocrisy or cowardice, as Rudolph does in his plea. But from the perspective of our everyday lives, the principle is undeniably prudent.

In various ways, religious faith shrinks the gap between belief and action. How can you be commanded to act by biblical authority and just respond, "Well, maybe tomorrow"? The argument to take a divine command as a duty to act is extremely simple, lending the fanatic his needed certainty, the flip side of not taking his fallibility seriously. Lives of extreme religious devotion direct a great deal of time and energy toward a singular focus, at the expense of the rich variety of human pursuits. Religious practices dominate one's life because of their pervasive and righteous directives, thereby moralizing many human activities. Religious texts are filled with action-implying or -prescribing beliefs and stories, leaving little room, if taken seriously, for the normal gap between belief and action–prudence, laziness, distraction, wishful thinking, diverse personal interests, limited time. Narrowing that gap feeds into a sense of urgency, impatience to act, and intolerance for those with ordinary lives of more-relaxed ethics.

What if the Fanatic is Sincere?

In our discussing the connection between faith and fanaticism, a pointed question arises: What if the fanatic is *sincere*—really believes his claims (e.g., that the scholar's reading of the text has to be filtered through the terrorist's own understanding; that the Bible authorizes the killings of abortion-physicians; that the regular, legal performance of abortion is, to use Rudolph's terms, "mass murder," a "holocaust")? This question can actually serve as the basis to generate three different objections to our analysis of fanatical reasoning and to our corresponding explanation of why religious faith is fertile ground for fanaticism. I'll respond to each objection in turn.

First, if the fanatic is sincere, is he really different from the moral hero? The implied objection is that the moral hero also must overrule various restraints in defending an extreme conclusion and in acting on it. He opposes popular opinion, and he is bound to treat some well-regarded sources of information as biased. The objector will admit that the fanatic goes further than the moral hero, but he will reply that this is just a difference of degree.

Well, yes, but only as a fistfight is a difference of degree from a bloodbath. Moral heroes do not engage in the murder of the innocent, the more the better, as a tactic to terrorize. (Rudolph's original plan was to "use five low-tech timed explosives" at the Olympics. Why?: "The purpose of the attack on July 27th was to confound, anger and embarrass the Washington government in the eyes of the world." The likely infliction of harm on a large number of innocents was just a strategy to garner the government's attention, clearly not, by any stretch, self-defense.[19])

Even if we put aside this stark disanalogy between the fanatic and the moral hero, what still remains incredible is that the various potential sources of self-restraint should be as uniformly tainted as the fanatic requires. The moral hero needs to be open-minded, since his goal is to move opinion toward his point of view by reasoned argument, not by fear. The arguments of Gandhi or early civil rights workers drew heavily on the democratic and ethical principles of their respective governments and its citizens. Open-mindedness is advantageous because if one is wrong, one wants to discover it before one acts. If one is right, one expects corroboration, even if the occasional source is mistaken.

Second, the question—"What if the fanatic is sincere?"—raises the objection that the fanatic is less blameworthy than I allege. If the fanatic genuinely believes his conclusions, for example, that killing abortion-physicians is self-defense, then he is guilty only of serious error in judgment and reasoning, no deeper evil.

This objection misfires in a number of ways. Most simply, it mistakes my purposes. Blame is of only peripheral interest here. The focus is on the moral character of fanatics and its expression in their arguments.

In any case, sincerity, and acting with good intentions, is compatible with blame. When a police officer kills someone because he really had good reason to believe that the child's play pistol was a gun, not merely because he believed it, that is excusable. The leading Nazi doctors are not excused because they sincerely believe that the Jews spread a racial defect that could be stopped only by extermination, regardless, unsurprisingly, of whether or not they took themselves to be acting with good intentions. Their belief had to be reasonably well founded, insofar as the relevant evidence was available to them. So, at most, the blame is mitigated to the extent that their insulated and threatening social environments made it very difficult for them, even as doctors, to appreciate the evidence against their poisoned ideology.[20]

The third and most far-reaching way to construe the question as an objection is to say that if the fanatic is sincere, then he does not adopt any of these strategies purposefully. The fanatic does not intend the isolation. He genuinely believes that the other sources are prejudiced or unreliable.

This way of construing the question, rather than generating an objection to my presentation, actually advances it, although not till later does my reply become complete. The ways the fanatic protects his beliefs by making exceptions, isolating them from normal controls, and ignoring the belief–action gap do amount to strategies, even if that is not his intent. In fact, the fanatic's sincerity measures the great depth of his distortions, thereby pressing the puzzle of how his facade of reasoned argument is to be explained.

Self-Deception: Believing the Unbelievable

In order to engage these strategies while maintaining sincerity, the fanatic must hide from himself what he is doing. He requires extensive self-deception, forms of which are essential for the realization of faith as belief.

Faith reflects a personal choice to believe, in the absence of proof or evidence. God's "divine hiddenness" is sometimes construed as "grace," since it allows for faith. This view of faith accords with standard readings of well-known biblical passages, and it is found in much stronger form in influential presentations (that of Kierkegaard's "leap of faith," specifically).[21] William James in a famous paper explicitly defends the right to believe as a matter of choice.[22] He limited his thesis, however, to those beliefs whose content could not be established by reason or evidence, where his primary examples are religious and ethical beliefs.[23]

However, belief cannot be based on faith or choice, and that is because the fundamental claim of belief is that what is believed is true. To believe that the #2 train stops at Eastern Parkway is to hold it to be true. So only reasons that imply the truth of what is believed can serve as backing. Of these indicators of truth, evidence is only the most prominent. I can believe that my son did not throw spitballs in class because a trustworthy classmate told me so. But I cannot believe it merely because I want to. The classmate's testimony is a reliable indicator that what it reports is true, but my wanting to believe my son innocent is no indicator at all that he did not throw the spitballs.

These claims enjoy parallels with the common speech-act of assertion: When you ask a stranger if the #2 stops at Eastern Parkway and he answers yes, you would normally come to believe it because you take him to believe it. If you challenge the stranger as to how he knows it, he might answer your challenge by noting that he is a lifelong New Yorker. If, however, he responds that he believes it because he chooses to or because he thought that's what you wanted to hear, you would not accept what he said. This demand—that reasons to believe must be reasons only of truth—derives from the concept of belief itself, indifferent to what is believed. The same concept of belief is involved in believing that Jim is in Texas or murder is wrong or $2 + 2 = 4$ or angels fly. It is not restricted to some subject, empirical rather than, say, ethical, as James and other theologians proclaim.

The attempt of faith to exempt religious beliefs from the demands that reasons for those beliefs must be reasons only of truth is self-defeating. For those demands follow from the truth claim of belief. Because what we believe is what we take to be true, belief is central to our lives. We care deeply about being correct, since our beliefs guide our actions. Because you correctly believe that the #2 train stops at Eastern Parkway, you board it and efficiently get to your destination.

The failure of belief based on faith is shown by the impossibility of overtly believing that there is a God or an afterlife or a heaven on the basis of faith. It is as contradictory to assert

> There is an afterlife because I have faith that there is.
> as
> The #2 stops at Eastern Parkway because I have faith that it does.

In either case, you, as hearer, would not proceed, in the standard way, of coming to believe what is (literally) asserted. The speaker's faith that there is an afterlife is no indicator of it. In either case, the speaker could not believe himself. The impossibility of belief matches Adams's students' reaction to the neighbor in the contemporary version of the *binding* of Isaac and your initial response to Rudolph or other fanatical defenses of terrorism. You think: "How *can* anyone believe that?" Though far less emotionally engaged, it is the same reaction you would have to someone who claimed to believe various miracles in a literal, everyday setting: "How *can* anyone believe that the chemistry of wine is instantly transformable into that of blood?"[24]

In a well-known passage, Pascal argues that it is a wise strategy to believe in God, regardless of whether or not God exists. (Briefly, Pascal's argument for belief is that you lose little if there is no God; but you will be infinitely blessed if there is, and infinitely damned otherwise.) An agnostic is persuaded, but he responds: " 'I confess, I admit it. But still, is there no means of seeing the faces of the cards?'—'Yes, Scripture and the rest, etc.—'Yes, but I have my hands tied and my mouth closed; I am forced to wager, and am not free. I am not released, and am so made that I *cannot* believe. What, then, would you have me do?' " (my emphasis).

Pascal replies:

> True. But at least learn your inability to believe, since reason brings you to this, and yet you cannot believe. *Endeavour then to convince yourself,* not by increase of proofs of God, but by the abatement of your passions. You

would like to attain faith, and do not know the way; you would like to cure yourself of unbelief, and ask the remedy for it. Learn of those who have been bound like you, and who now stake all their possessions. . . . Follow the way by which they began; by acting as if they believed, taking the holy water, hearing masses said, etc. Even this will naturally make you believe, and *deaden your acuteness.*[25] (my emphasis)

Pascal acknowledges the agnostic's plea but provides no reason to actually believe there is a God. Rather, Pascal recommends an indirect way for the agnostic to induce the belief he wants. He is to convince himself by a procedure of imitation, whereby the desired belief arises in him without notice. Pascal's recommendation is for a long-term project of self-deception to evade the impossibility of straightforward belief that there is a God.

Admittedly, self-deception is often innocent, an analogue of white lies. In the case of fanaticism, though, the consequences are profound. Since the perversion of belief is extensive, the self-deception required is not occasional self-trickery but more of a mental fog or massive self-delusion. But this much self-deception is normally impossible, since belief is so fundamental to the guidance of our lives. No one can deceive himself that he is Superman or Napoleon and proceed with his routine life, without mental breakdown.

The limited possibility of way-out beliefs, which is the flip side of our pretend treatment of religious tales, is one reason that scant few of faith are fanatics, to revert to an opening perplexity. The miracle stories, the exotic ethical prohibitions and taboos, and the efficacy alleged for petitionary prayers are unbelievable taken at face value, rather than within the insulated setting of supernatural religion.

Reality as Restraint

Self-deception is vulnerable to reality. To persuade yourself that you are very popular, you need to adopt the isolationist strategy of maintaining close association only with those who like you, while avoiding or denigrating (as "losers") those groups and individuals who do not think well of you. The fanatic's dependence on a variety of strategies to keep reality at a distance requires his rigid lack of openness. A psychoanalyst makes the following observation in regard to paranoia, a cousin of fanaticism:

Flexibility—not rigidity—reflects an active self-direction. Furthermore, flexibility—not rigidity—reflects a genuinely objective attitude toward the world.[26]

The paranoid person's thought and judgment become so narrowly restricted by the requirements of guardedness . . . as to forbid increasingly any point of view except that of defensive bias. His detachment and

> critical judgment are lost. There is no genuine thinking-about, considering objective reality...
>
> The very rigidity of suspicious thinking, its prejudice and imperviousness to influence, may endow it, just as it does dogmatism, with a semblance of critical detachment that it does not actually possess.[27]

The flexibility is necessary for complex judgments because, in trying to align one's beliefs with the way the world really is, there will have to be adjustments before we align rightly. C. S. Peirce understood this relation of flexibility and objectivity when he praised the self-corrective power of scientific method: "To satisfy our doubts, therefore, it is necessary that a method should be found by which our beliefs may be determined by nothing human, but by some external permanency."[28]

The fundamental outlook of belief involves restraint because it is the world that determines what I am to believe. Think of perception. You believe that Joe is in his office, but then you see him at the local diner. Immediately, you stop believing he is in his office and come to believe he is at the diner. Your prior belief does not override your current, clear perception, but just the reverse. Our background beliefs and values have the dominant and foundational status they have because they are most clearly reflective of the world. Allowing them to restrain present reasoning is not to lack either confidence or commitment. Reliance on these restraints serves then the same ends as reliance on evidence—to get things right. The very idea that belief is a matter of choice or faith, whether in forming beliefs or in validating their grounds ("religious experiences"), looks in the wrong direction. It is to look inward to oneself, whereas belief demands one look outward to the conditions of the truth of what is believed.

Self-deception, which is a way to evade the restraint of reality, plays a distinctive role for the fanatic. It is normally highly risky for a person who believes something out of self-deception to highlight that belief, as that invites critical attention. The fanatic, though, brags of the righteousness of his cause. This distinguishes him not only from the ordinary crook but from the genuinely righteous, who do not commit vividly despicable acts. Nor are contemporary fanatics mentally disturbed, though their conclusions are far out. Rudolph's elaborate, though highly refined plea is an illustration both of his drive to give public voice to his rationale and of self-deception. On this latter count, one passage is particularly telling. Rudolph justifies his plan by saying, "This is the reason and the only reason for the targeting of so-called law enforcement personnel." In decisions that intricately involve a variety of our personal interests and values, most of us are hesitant to take our motives as stemming solely from the merits of the case. To claim otherwise is to presume a superhuman goodness, as well as superior self-knowledge. But a facet of Rudolph's fanaticism is his self-ascribed purity of motives. He represents himself as acting only as reason and morality dictate. He does not act for personal gain or even to express personal animosity (against those who perform abortions).

How is it that the fanatic's self-deception and other distortions of belief do not lead him to shy away from exposure? The answer is implicit in the argument so far, specifically, in the depth of the fanatic's conviction, in his abnormal surety of the righteousness of his cause. But let's first widen this question.

Familiar self-restraints or self-controls work upon action, not the desires that motivate those actions. A diet operates to curb acting on one's craving for food, not on the craving itself, which is why diets so often fail. But self-restraints on belief are easier. The restraints of your background beliefs and values are already active. Unlike a diet, they require neither an effort to impose nor any sacrifice to maintain. When you automatically filter your reasoning through your beliefs and values, wild conclusions give way immediately, as in the opening example of the student. If the student does not just distract himself from his conclusion to set off a false alarm, he simply realizes that his reasoning went astray. That is your quick way, too, in rejecting the religious fanatic's conclusion (Should Kill) or (Intend to Kill). How come it is not his?

Compare divine commands with military commands. The officer orders you to drive a jeep to the edge of the base and then walk back. The order makes no sense, but still you must obey. There are limits, however. You would not obey if the officer told you to place a foul chemical in the soup for lunch. The command is filtered through your knowledge of right and wrong and the fact that officers are subject to constant review.

But now a crucial disanalogy between religious and military commands surfaces, in addition to the obvious one that only the former claims divine authority. Unlike military commands, which you can regard as dopey or arbitrary or even irrational, you are called on to follow the commands of divine authority *and* to believe them correct.

Since you are obliged to believe these commands, even if you do not understand them, and to treat them as overriding, you are granted an impeccable ground to deny any need for restraints. Recall, for example, how Himmler wants his soldiers to respond to their revulsion at carrying out their orders. Since they have convincing arguments that the Jews should be exterminated, the logical force of those feelings or emotional responses are nullified. Or, think of the role that the apparent immorality and lawlessness of the fanatic's conclusion Should Kill or Intend to Kill plays for you, in contrast to its role for the fanatic. The fanatic views these appeals to immorality and lawlessness only as objections to his proposal to kill abortion-physicians or to do worse, as in Rudolph's case. The fanatic replies from the point of view within his argument alone that the killings are permissible exceptions due to emergency conditions. He refuses to take these objections and concerns as a reason to step back to take a detached view of the reasoner who endorses that argument.

When you treat these grounds of your resistance to the fanatic's argument as restraints, however, their role is not exhausted by their success or not as objections to his argument. They are reasons to reject the fanatic's reasoning, even if you found his reasoning otherwise persuasive. Just as you can reject the fanatic's argument without knowing where it went wrong, the opening example of the student shows that you can reject your own argument without knowing where it went wrong.

This intellectual modesty and honesty is essential to common sense. We all recognize that our experience and learning, which helps constitute common sense, is severely limited. Common sense thinks, for example, that events must have determinate causes and that any intricate, fine-tuned mechanism like the eye must have resulted from an intentional design. But recognizing its own limits, common sense defers here to physicists and biologists, respectively. Common sense also recognizes our own vulnerability to self-deception in forming judgments that reflect on ourselves. You want to know whether you are teaching well, but realize that your own observations are bound to be biased. So you seek the observations of colleagues and students, under conditions favorable to objectivity.

The example of the religious terrorist illustrates how the fanatic rejects such evident checks on his own potential biases. Because all such checks are viewed by him just in the single role as objections, he can take himself to be acting reasonably, since as objections they are nullified by his argument. He refuses to recognize these objections in a different, though related, role. They amount to reasons not to trust himself as the arguer, which requires not a rejection of his argument, but independent support for it, a kind of check of which we all sometimes avail ourselves. You crave a hot new sports car, but since you care about safety, cost, and dependability, too, you consult the ratings in *Consumer Reports*.

The fanatic's refusal to accept any independent controls on his judgment provides an explanation for both the frustrating puzzle of how the fanatic, though suffering a distortion of reason, can proudly attempt to justify his acts with a bold veneer of reason, and the role of religious faith in supplying its intellectual foundation.

Trust and Restraint

The denial of restraints enters early on: Appeals to divine mysteries are not invitations to investigate but a signal not to ask. How are any of us supposed to treat as just what is clearly unjust? Here there are numerous choices available, but let's list one that is very well known as the second of the Ten Commandments:

> You shall not bow down to them or worship them [carved images]; for I, the Lord your God, am a jealous god. I punish the children for the sins of the fathers to the third and fourth generations of those who hate me. (Ex. 20]

Like Abraham, we are asked to allow faith and trust to overrule our clear ethical judgments. Relying on faith and trust as a response to supernatural or unethical claims is sometimes compared to our receiving *testimony* from strangers—we trust them even though we do not know that they will speak truly. But let us look more closely at the comparison. As with our earlier, everyday example in which you ask a stranger for directions on a visit to New York City, and the stranger responds, "Take the #1 downtown to the last stop." You accept his word without further investigation, though you do not know him, and you are not gullible. You know that his answer can be wrong out of error or malice. You filter his answer, however, through the restraint of plausibility. You would not accept his response if he told you to go to JFK airport to catch a commuter jet.

Aside from this *internal* restraint, there are also powerful *external* restraints in the conversational setting, knowledge of which strengthens your confidence in the stranger's word. An earlier example provides a good illustration of the role of knowledge of external restraints as supporting one's judgment and reasoning. You trust the military command because, in part, you know that the officer who issues the command is subject to careful review by his military superiors.

The external restraints of the testimonial practice explain its overwhelming success in transmitting true information, despite our seeming vulnerability to dishonest or incompetent informants. The stranger, who supplies you with the train directions, benefits enormously from conversational practices that require truthfulness, and when that norm is violated its effects pose threats beyond this interaction. Since the information you seek is easy for a native to provide, your main worry is that the stranger might lie. But he has no motive to lie. He has nothing to gain from it. This powerful restraint—external from your point of view—is simply to act rationally.

I stress the restraint of acting on rational motives to clarify why belief depends on both internal restraints and external ones. Typically, internal restraints just reflect knowledge of the external ones. It is this lawfulness, and our knowledge of it, even if rudimentary, that allows for our understanding of the world. These internal and external restraints do not, of course, guarantee that the stranger will speak correctly. But they set tight limits, as you know from a huge number of your encounters with informants who give you correct, useful answers to your inquiries. You trust the stranger, but far from blindly.

Imagine how untrustworthy testimony would be if these internal and external restraints were removed. That is the worry over supernatural, biblically based teachings and commands, and it lies behind my selection of examples, however few. The internal restraints of your own ethical values and sense of what is empirically possible must be surrendered; the external restraints of natural laws are also abandoned.

But the comparison of religious faith with beliefs in the supernatural actually understates the lack of restraints implied by faith. Assume that, contrary to the evidence, there is a supernatural realm, one not governed by natural laws (like gravitation or rational motives for actions). We would not have any inkling of the grounds rules for the supernatural realm, so we would not know if claims about psychic healing were any more credible than crystal balls or pyramids or astrology. Still, were there a supernatural realm, it would be law governed.

But God's omnipotence means that He is not subject to any laws; He is beyond the supernatural realm. God can do anything possible, there being a complete absence of restraint.

The goodness attributed to God adds no restraint upon which we can rely. If biblical texts are treated as authoritative, God commands what is unjust (e.g., the second commandment's condemning children for their father's sins) and permits terrible evils. He actively orders and commits atrocities. The binding of Isaac is actually less consequential ethically than those incidents in the Bible in which God orders the slaughter of all members of an enemy or sinning community. Such tales, as ones of righteous retribution, illuminate the religious terrorist's intellectual path.

Fortunately, religious belief is unnecessary for commitment to an ethical life and community, as the banal example of testimony already shows. We know that for simple informational requests, people predominantly speak to you truthfully, even though the speaker generally derives no benefit. Our reasons for honesty call upon no deity. Truthfulness is explicable on rational grounds: We appreciate the value of honesty, particularly evident in the difference we all experience between communities that have a high level of trust and those that do not. We are competent in many ordinary matters, including knowing when we do not know. We usually lack motivation to deceive, but if we do lie, our reputation is threatened. Finally, our upbringing and fellow feeling runs contrary to dishonesty.

These grounds to explain the basic, prevalent honesty and reliability of ordinary testimony expose the falsity in the saying "If God is dead everything is permitted." But the account of why testimony works so well as a result of natural internal and external restraints actually argues for a conclusion much stronger and just the reverse: if God is alive, everything is permitted.

My thanks to Jeff Blustein, Chris Gowans, Charles Blustein Ortman, Georges Rey, Michael Stocker, Lisa Warenski, and, especially, Louise Antony for many useful comments and suggestions.

NOTES

1. FAITH AND REASON, THE PERPETUAL WAR: RUMINATIONS OF A FOOL

1. Editor's note: One's "noetic framework" is one's set of background assumptions about knowledge: how one can come to know things, what counts as good reason to believe, which authorities are reliable, etc.
2. Editor's note: Foundationalism is the view that knowledge is arranged hierarchically, with the most-certain beliefs serving as evidence for all the rest. The American philosopher Willard V. O. Quine rejected this view, arguing that all our beliefs are mutually supporting, so that none is immune from challenge by emerging evidence or argument.

2. FROM YESHIVA BOCHUR TO SECULAR HUMANIST

1. I prefer this term to the more common "Orthodox Jewish." Its significance will become apparent soon.
2. The word "yeshiva" comes from the Hebrew word for sitting; the idea is that you are constantly "sitting and learning" when in yeshiva. A "bochur" is a young man or boy, so to be a "yeshiva bochur" is just to be a male student in a yeshiva.
3. And I mean "literally." I remember once having it explained to me that God made the Earth round so that at every moment someone would be awake and studying Torah, for otherwise it couldn't continue to exist.
4. Another commentary points out that when God tells Moses to "leave me" to destroy the people, it's odd since there's no indication that Moses was in any way standing in His way. The implication is (this is how Midrashic hermeneutics works) that God was suggesting to Moses that he should in fact get in His way.
5. Elijah, according to biblical legend, never died but ascended to Heaven alive. There are many stories in the Talmud of his appearing to various scholars.

6. Did I ever really take it seriously? Georges Rey (this volume) will tell you I didn't. Maybe he's right. I certainly thought I did (which is consistent with his thesis, of course). But whatever the case about the past, I really can't take it seriously now.
7. What I'm describing is a central tendency of current Jewish communal life, and its relation to traditional Torah doctrine. It's important to note, however, that there are many, many individual Jews, both in Israel and around the world, who have shown great moral courage by speaking out, and even risking their lives, to oppose the Israeli oppression of Palestinians. There are now a number of Jewish organizations, again both in Israel and around the world, that are working hard for the cause of peace and justice in Israel/Palestine.
8. Whether this idea is actually Nietzsche's or I read it into his work, I don't know, and for our purposes it doesn't matter.

3. RELIGIO PHILOSOPHI

1. Quotations from Pascal are taken from Blaise Pascal, *Pensées,* trans. A. J. Krailsheimer (Harmondsworth, UK: Penguin, 1966), and will be indicated in the text according to the Lafuma numbering, which Krailsheimer uses.

4. FOR THE LOVE OF REASON

1. As the *Catholic Encyclopedia* certifies: "Limbus Infantium" is "the permanent place or state of those unbaptized children and others who, dying without grievous personal sin, are excluded from the beatific vision on account of original sin alone." See *New Advent* (www.newadvent.org/cathen/09256a.htm). Apparently, the Church has recently revised its teachings, and eliminated Limbo.
2. Not Eve—*her* sin didn't count—but leave *that* alone for now.
3. Jean-Baptiste Lamarck (1744–1829) was a naturalist, a predecessor of Darwin's. Like Darwin, he believed that species evolved, but unlike Darwin, he held that characteristics *acquired* by the organism during its lifetime could be passed on to future generations.
4. You can view it at www./time/covers/0,16641,1101660408,00.html.
5. The American Civil Liberties Union.
6. *Raleigh News and Observer,* July 7, 1994.
7. Valentine Davies, Screenplay, *Miracle on 34th Street* (transcribed).
8. Davies, *Miracle on 34th Street.*
9. Rey argues, in this volume, that this is typically the case.
10. "Tubular Bells"—released, as irony will have it, on Virgin Records. Amazon.com will let you listen: www.amazon.com/gp/product/B00000WG4/104-4076158-4010317?v=glance&n=5174.

6. OVERCOMING CHRISTIANITY

1. Editor's Note: The book is William Lane Craig and Walter Sinnott-Armstrong, *God? A Debate between a Christian and an Atheist* (New York: Oxford University Press, 2004).

7. ON BECOMING A HERETIC

1. How much acceptance of those doctrines was really required is a matter I'm not at all clear about now. Certainly it's now possible to rise to high office in the Church without accepting much of its official theology, as the career of Bishop Spong illustrates. See John Shelby Spong, *Why Christianity Must Change or Die* (San Francisco: Harper, 1998).
2. See particularly chapters 8 and 9.
3. Some Christian philosophers will say that God's omniscience requires only that he know everything that is knowable, and that propositions about the future (or more modestly, propositions about future human free actions, and all others that depend on them) lack a truth value; not being knowable, they are not in fact known, even by an omniscient being. This may be a way of reconciling God's omniscience with human freedom, but it does so only by creating problems for the doctrine of divine providence.
4. See Thomas Aquinas, *Summa theologiae* I, xxiii.
5. I suppose there must have been some Jews in our town, but I don't recall being aware of their presence.
6. The most explicit passage endorsing strong salvific exclusivism—the doctrine that belief in Jesus as one's savior is both necessary and sufficient for salvation—is John 3:16–18, though other passages may also be cited: John 14:6; Mark 16:15–16; and Acts 4:12. The traditional doctrine of the Roman Catholic Church, enunciated at the Council of Florence in the fifteenth century, was that there was no salvation outside the Church. In the 1960s, the Second Vatican Council seemed to endorse a less strict view of the requirements for salvation. More recently, however, in *Dominus Iesus*, a declaration promulgated in 2000, the Church cautioned against too pluralistic a reading of the Second Vatican Council: "If it is true that the followers of other religions *can* receive divine grace, it is also certain that *objectively speaking* they are in a gravely deficient situation in comparison with those who, in the Church, have the fullness of the means of salvation" (para. 22, my emphasis). This document is available on the Vatican Web site: www.vatican.va/roman_curia/congregations/cfaith/documents.
7. See, for example, W. K. Jordan, *The Development of Religious Toleration in England, from the Convention of the Long Parliament to the Restoration, 1640–1660* (Cambridge, MA: Harvard University Press, 1938).
8. Perhaps the most influential modern statement of this defense, dubbed the free-will defense because it emphasizes the value of human freedom as the greater good that justifies the permission of evil, is in Alvin Plantinga's *God, Freedom and Evil* (Grand Rapids, MI: Eerdmans, 1974), pt. 1.
9. I realize, of course, that—in the United States, at least—a great many Christians do not accept the theory of evolution. This seems to me a sad comment on our culture. It lies outside the area of my expertise to respond to the deceptive means by which some Christian apologists have tried to sow doubt about this fundamental advance in our understanding of life on this planet. I will simply recommend that anyone taken in by the likes of Philip Johnson or Michael Behe read, first, Philip Kitcher's *Abusing Science, the Case against Creationism* (Cambridge, MA: MIT Press, 1982) and, then, his more recent "Born Again Creationism," in *In Mendel's Mirror* (New York: Oxford University Press, 2003).
10. I first became aware of the importance of this point through reading Michael Tooley's "The Argument from Evil," *Philosophical Perspectives 5, Philosophy of Religion,* ed. James E. Tomberlin (Atascadero, CA: Ridgeview, 1991). But acceptance of it has also motivated the recent work on this issue of Marilyn McCord Adams, e.g., in her *Horrendous Evils and the Goodness of God* (Ithaca, NY: Cornell University Press, 1999).

11. See, for example, the essays on divine command ethics collected in his *The Virtue of Faith and Other Essays in Philosophical Theology* (New York: Oxford University Press, 1987) and the chapter on Abraham's dilemma in his *Finite and Infinite Goods, a Framework for Ethics* (New York: Oxford University Press, 1999).
12. Deuteronomy 7:1–2 (New Revised Standard Version, translation). This and numerous other such passages are helpfully discussed in Gerd Lüdemann's *The Unholy in Holy Scripture: The Dark Side of the Bible* (Louisville, KY: Westminster John Knox Press, 1997). Lüdemann is a German theologian whose numerous works, intended to get Christians to deal honestly with the difficulties their scriptures present for modern believers, might easily prompt some believers to reject the faith altogether.

8. MERE STRANGER

1. I John 4:18 (New International Version). The passage continues: "We love because he first loved us. If anyone says, 'I love God,' yet hates his brother, he is a liar. For anyone who does not love his brother, whom he has seen, cannot love God, whom he has not seen" (Verses 19–20).
2. C. S. Lewis, *Mere Christianity* (New York: Macmillan, 1943), 65.
3. Lewis, *Mere Christianity,* 65.
4. John Wesley felt the same way (although I was not aware of this when I was young). Randy Maddox writes that Wesley was convinced of the "unfailing justice and universal love of God" that made "it impossible for him to believe that people who lacked knowledge of Christ through no fault of their own . . . would be automatically excluded from heaven.. . . He argued that Scripture gave no authority for anyone to make definitive claims about them." See Maddox, "Wesley and the Question of Truth or Salvation through other Religions," *Wesley Center Online* (July 2004), wesley.nnu.edu/wesleyan_theology/theojrnl/26-30/27.1.htm.
5. Lewis, *Mere Christianity,* 56.
6. According to Maddox, Wesley held that "it was more reasonable to be an atheist than to affirm a God who was capable of unconditional reprobation." See Randy Maddox, *Responsible Grace: John Wesley's Practical Theology* (Nashville: Abingdon Press, 1994), 56.
7. Philippians 2:6 (New International Version). See Joseph Campbell's discussion of this passage in *The Hero's Journey* (San Francisco: Collins, 1991), 226.
8. Dietrich Bonhoeffer (July 21, 1944), *Letters and Papers from Prison* (London: Collins Fontana Books, 1953), 122–23.
9. Lewis, *Mere Christianity,* 65–66.
10. Campbell, *Hero's Journey,* 106.
11. For good descriptions of these and other forms of meditation, see Jack Kornfield, *A Path with Heart* (New York: Bantam, 1993), and Henepola Gunaratana, *Mindfulness in Plain English* (Boston: Wisdom Publications, 2002).
12. See Lama Thubten Yeshe, *Introduction to Tantra* (Boston: Wisdom Publications, 1987), 104–6; *The Bliss of Inner Fire* (Boston: Wisdom Publications, 1998), 62–63; Dalai Lama, *The Union of Bliss and Emptiness* (Ithaca, NY: Snow Lion, 1988), 18–19; and Glenn Mullin, *Tsongkhapa's Six Yogas of Perfection* (Ithaca, NY: Snow Lion, 1996), 227–31.
13. See, for example, Stephen Batchelor, *Buddhism without Beliefs* (New York: Riverhead Books, 1997).

10. THANK GOODNESS!

1. Elsewhere, Dennett provides the following characterization of the " movement: "A bright is a person with a naturalist as opposed to a supernaturalist worldview. We brights don't believe in ghosts or elves or the Easter Bunny—or God. We disagree about many things, and hold a variety of views about morality, politics and the meaning of life, but we share a disbelief in black magic—and life after death." See Daniel Dennett, "The Bright Stuff," *New York Times,* July 12, 2003.

11. TRANSCENDENCE WITHOUT GOD: ON ATHEISM AND INVISIBILITY

1. Charles Mills, "Non-Cartesian *Sums:* Philosophy and the African American Experience," reprinted in his *Blackness Visible* (Ithaca, NY: Cornell University Press, 1998), 6.

12. AN ARISTOTELIAN LIFE

1. When Aristotle asks this question, it is not clear if he is referring to the traditional Greek conception of the gods or if he is referring to his own conception of divinity. Neither conception matches the God of the Judeo-Christian tradition. According to the traditional Greek conception (as found, for example, in Homer), there are many gods, not one. Unlike the one God of the Judeo-Christian tradition, these Greek gods did not create the world and are not separate from it. They do not love human beings or act to bring about what is good for the world. They do not impose codes of belief or morality on humans. Rather, individual gods have their special concerns and interests, and they struggle with each other and with humans to promote their own interests. Traditional Greek gods have many of the same character traits, and hence many of the same character failings, as humans. In Aristotle's view of divinity, a god cannot have human personalities or traits of character, for a god is a wholly rational being that is unchanging and permanent. As such, a god does not love or even care about human beings or about the state of the world, and so a god is not a proper object of worship, prayer, or sacrifice.
2. Aristotle, *Nicomachean Ethics*, 2nd ed., trans. Terence Irwin (Indianapolis: Hackett, 1999).
3. For insightful discussion of Aristotle's views on friendship and political activity, see John M. Cooper, "Aristotle on Friendship," in *Essays on Aristotle's Ethics,* ed. Amelie Rorty (Berkeley: University of California Press, 1980), 301–40.
4. For more information on the work that Occidental students do with the community-oriented advocacy organization described in the text, see www.uepi.oxy.edu.
5. I should note, however, that the low-wage workers on campus are represented by a union and that some of the Occidental students are working with "United Students Against Sweatshops" to press for a living wage for these workers. For information on this national student group, see their Web site at www.unionvoice.org/studentsagainstsweat/home.html.
6. In fact, his main recommendations are not so very different from the more liberal political proposals one finds in contemporary political philosophy. See, for example, John Rawls, *A Theory of Justice,* rev. ed. (Cambridge, MA: Harvard University Press, 1999). Rawls describes his version of a just society as "realistically utopian."

14. DISENCHANTMENT

1. Max Weber, "Religious Rejections of the World and Their Directions" in *From Max Weber: Essays in Sociology* (New York: Oxford University Press, 1946), 350–51.
2. The Scientific World View would not have been offered as a justification for such activities when the need for a justification was first felt. Before the scientific revolution, man's dominion over nature was often thought of as an authority delegated by God. What may be distinctive about the Scientific World View is that it has returned many of us to a state in which we feel no need for any such justification.
3. David Hume, "Of Suicide," in *Selected Essays,* Oxford World Classics (New York: Oxford University Press, 1993), 321.
4. Hume, "Of Suicide," 319.
5. Hume, "Of Suicide," 320.
6. Leon Trotsky, *Sochineniia* XXI; 110–12 (Moscow 1925–27). I take the reference and translation from O. Figes, *A People's Tragedy* (New York: Penguin, 1996), 734.
7. For a thoughtful (and mildly enthusiastic) account of the history and impact of Prozac, see Peter Kramer, *Listening to Prozac* (London: Fourth Estate, 1994).
8. For an early sketch of the picture, see Thomas Hobbes, *Leviathan* (Indianapolis: Hackett, 1994), ch. 21, paras. 1–4.
9. In *Being and Nothingness* (London: Routledge, 1969), Sartre approaches the same conclusion from a different direction. Much of that book bears on the present topic.
10. For a recent, crisp statement of the problem, see Harry Frankfurt, *The Importance of What We Care About* (Cambridge: Cambridge University Press, 1988), 177–78. Could we solve the problem by appealing to Frankfurt's "higher-order desires," i.e., desires to have certain desires? Suppose I simply want to want monogamy: that is the desire I want to have. Wouldn't that get me to take Credon? Yet the same sort question recurs. If there is a pill that will rid me of this higher-order desire, why shouldn't I take it? This question can be repeated until we get to a point where the person is indifferent between satisfying the desire and taking the desire-destroying pill.

15. RELIGION AND RESPECT

1. This paragraph summarizes a longer treatment in my *Truth: A Guide for the Confused,* forthcoming from Penguin and Oxford University Press, New York.
2. W. K. Clifford, "The Ethics of Belief," in *The Ethics of Belief Debate,* ed. Gerald D. McCarthy (Atlanta: Scholars Press, 1986).
3. David Hume, *The Natural History of Religion*, XII.
4. David Lewis, "Quasi Realism Is Fictionalism," in *Fictionalism,* ed. Mark Kalderon, forthcoming.
5. See, for instance, Allan Gibbard, *Thinking How to Live* (Cambridge, MA: Harvard University Press, 2003).

16. REASONABLE RELIGIOUS DISAGREEMENTS

1. I develop this method of argument analysis in *Reason and Argument,* 2nd ed. (Englewood Cliffs, NJ: Prentice Hall, 1999).
2. Rochester *Democrat and Chronicle,* March 3, 2004.

3. This assumes that we use the word "God" in the same way. See the discussion of ambiguity in the section titled "Agreements."
4. "Nominalism, Naturalism, Philosophical Relativism," *Philosophical Perspectives* 15 (2001): 69–91. The quotation is from pp. 71–72.
5. I borrow this term from Tom Kelly.
6. People who aren't peers can share their evidence. But the interesting case involves peers who share their evidence.
7. I thank Allen Orr for pressing me on this point.
8. It is also possible that each side is justified in maintaining its own "starting point" and rejecting the starting point of the others. This would make the present idea just like the ideas discussed in the subsection titled "Having a Reasonable Disagreement without Realizing It."
9. Peter van Inwagen suggests this in "Is It Wrong Everywhere, Always, and for Anyone to Believe Anything on Insufficient Evidence?" in *Faith, Freedom, and Rationality,* eds. Jordan and Howard-Snyder (Lanham, MD: Rowman & Littlefield, 1996). He does not refer to the insight as evidence.
10. "Nominalism, Naturalism, Philosophical Relativism," 88.
11. Both sides can still regard the others as peers because of their general capacities. The difference over this case does not disqualify them as peers.
12. "Is It Wrong Everywhere, Always, and for Anyone to Believe Anything on Insufficient Evidence?" 137–54.
13. There are technical puzzles here. There are many varieties of theism. If the view proposed implies that you should think that they are equally probable, then you can't also think that each of those versions of theism is as probable as atheism and also think that theism is as probable as atheism. I will not attempt to deal with this here.

17. IF GOD IS DEAD, IS EVERYTHING PERMITTED?

1. This agreement exists at the level of generality with which the moral rules are expressed in the Ten Commandments. It does not exist for more fine-grained descriptions of moral rules, where exceptions, justifications, and excuses for violations are articulated. All moral systems, including those found in Scripture, acknowledge exceptions to the basic moral rules. But societies vary dramatically in the exceptions they allow. For example, some permit killing in retaliation for insults; others permit killing for the greater glory of God; others permit suicide in the face of terminal illness. Societies also often vary dramatically in their views of who is included within the scope of protection of the moral rules. Are only fellow tribe members included, or fellow nationals, or all people, without exception? Finally, the rules of sexual morality are even more variable than the rules against killing, theft, and lying. While most societies have condemned adultery, this is by no means universal, and adultery has often been defined much more permissively for men than for women. My point is simply that all societies agree that certain types of conduct are morally objectionable on their face and so require some kind of special justification if exceptions are to be allowed. This recognition is not based on any kind of revelation or divine inspiration. Nor is recognition of the right exceptions based on divine sources. For as we shall see, societies founded on biblical morality are hardly superior to others in discerning the allowable exceptions.
2. William Lane Craig, "The Indispensability of Theological Meta-Ethical Foundations for Morality," *Foundations* 5 (1997): 9–12, www.leaderu.com/offices/billcraig/docs/meta-eth.html.

3. Plato, "Euthyphro," in *Collected Dialogues of Plato,* eds. Edith Hamilton and Huntington Cairnes (Princeton, NJ: Princeton University Press, 1961).
4. I here omit any parallel critique of the Koran, on the assumption that most readers of this essay are not Muslim. But the Koran does not differ fundamentally from the Old and New Testaments in characterizing God as committing, commanding, and permitting great evil. See Ibn Warraq, *Why I Am Not a Muslim* (New York: Prometheus Books, 1995).
5. All quotations are drawn from the *Holy Bible: New International Version* (NIV) (Grand Rapids, MI: Zondervan, 1978). This modern translation softens some of the harsh verses found in the King James Version (KJV) of the Bible, which tends to be favored by fundamentalists. For example, in the KJV, David tortures his enemies with God's support, cutting them with saws, harrows, and axes (1 Chron. 20:3). The same verse in the NIV represents David merely "consigning them to labor" with these tools.
6. This is not to say that the Holocaust was a specifically Christian enterprise. My point is rather that without centuries of Church-sponsored anti-Semitism in Eastern Europe, Hitler could not have recruited in these countries the legions of executioners, whose religiously inspired enthusiasm was needed to enable the Holocaust to proceed as far as it did. Christian anti-Semitism does, of course, have a textual grounding in the Gospels. For instance, John calls the Jews the children of the devil (8:44) and stresses their role in the death of Christ (18:35, 19:12–13). Matthew 27:25 has the Jews accepting responsibility for murdering Christ ("Let his blood be upon us and on our children!").
7. See, for example, Walter Kaiser et al., *Hard Sayings of the Bible* (Downers Grove, IL: InterVarsity Press, 1996).
8. Immanuel Kant, *Religion within the Limits of Reason Alone,* trans. and ed. Theodore Greene and Hoyt Hudson, (1793; repr., New York: Harper & Row, 1960), 175.
9. Thomas Hobbes, *Leviathan,* ed. Edwin Curley, (1651; repr., Indianapolis: Hackett, 1994), ch. 10, para. 48, p. 54.
10. Yet we should also not suppose that the ancient Hebrews lacked the moral concepts necessary to recognize God's injustice. When God smites seventy thousand men for David's sinful census, David tells him, "I am the one who has sinned and done wrong. These are but sheep. What have they done? Let your hand fall upon me and my family" (2 Sam. 24:17).
11. That this was Jesus' central teaching is the dominant view among biblical scholars writing today. See Bart Ehrman, *Jesus: Apocalyptic Prophet of the New Millennium* (Oxford: Oxford University Press, 1999) for a compelling and accessible account of the evidence for this interpretation.
12. Stephen Darwall has developed this conception of morality as equal accountability in his book *The Second-Person Standpoint: Morality, Respect, and Accountability* (Harvard University Press, 2006).

18. DIVINE EVIL

1. See, for example, Alvin Plantinga, *God, Freedom, and Evil* (Grand Rapids, MI: Eerdmans, 1977).
2. Dante's *Inferno* tries to match punishments to crimes and sins. The torment is immeasurably worse than the evil produced by the sinner. Yet the entire arrangement is set up—as the sign at the entrance announces—in the service of what claims to be divine justice, and even love.
3. For a sample, see Matthew 11:20–24, 13:47–50, 18:1–10, 25:31–46; Mark 9:42–49; Luke 10:13–15, 16:19–31, 17:20–37; Romans 12:14–21; 2 Thessalonians 1:5–10; He-

brews 6:7–8, 10:26–31, 12:18–29; James 5:1–3; 2 Peter 2:4–22; Jude 13, 23; *Revelation passim*. *Qur'an* Suras 82–85, 87–89.

4. Søren Kierkegaard, *Fear and Trembling*.
5. Although Christians are sometimes inclined to offer this identification, unbelievers can find it difficult to grasp. Is the idea that actively opposing God's will is a form of damnation? Or that having the disposition to oppose constitutes damnation? In either case, I'll argue, it's very hard to see why this state should prove painful, or why, if it were painful, the person damned wouldn't change his attitude.
6. See Paul's letters, Romans in particular.
7. Perhaps there could be a version of Christianity emphasizing the Gospel of John and the uncontroversially Pauline letters that adopted this view. In these Christian texts, salvation and eternal life are usually contrasted with a vaguely characterized state of death. I shall leave it to Christian theologians to decide whether the sorts of passages cited in note 3 can simply be jettisoned.
8. This is the mirror image of the vision of the afterlife offered in a favorite story of the late Sidney Morgenbesser. According to that vision, we find ourselves after death studying Talmud; for some that's heaven, for others hell.
9. Augustine, *City of God* XXII, 30.
10. See Romans, chs. 7–12.
11. Romans 12:19.
12. Most obviously, Tertullian. "You are fond of spectacles; expect the greatest of all spectacles, the last and eternal judgment of the universe. How shall I admire, how laugh, how rejoice, how exult, when I behold so many proud monarchs and fancied gods groaning in the lowest abyss of darkness; so many magistrates, who persecuted the name of the Lord, liquefying in fiercer fires than they ever kindled against the Christians; so many sage philosophers blushing in red-hot flames, with their deluded scholars." Interestingly, this passage is quoted both by Gibbon (*Decline and Fall of the Roman Empire,* ch. XV) and by Nietzsche (*Genealogy of Morals,* essay 3).
13. Romans 12:20.
14. Father John Murphy was a courageous leader in the Wexford battles of the Uprising of 1798. He is much celebrated in popular song.

20. FAITH AND FANATICISM

1. I draw on Jessica Stern, *Terror in the Name of God: Why Religious Militants Kill* (New York: Harper & Collins, 2003).
2. See Stern, *Terror in the Name of God.* Of special relevance: pp. xix, 18–20, 28, 52, 84, 90, 106, 142.
3. Stern cites the abortion-physician's argument as most reasonable.
4. The whole statement is found on www.npr.org for April 14, 2005. Since, in trying to generalize about fanaticism, which can be directed to very different issues or opinions, the search is for deviant causes commensurate with intentionally deviant acts, it is not surprising that details of individual cases will vary a great deal and fit the generalizations only roughly. In Rudolph's case, specifically, the following paragraph occurs in the Wikipedia article on him:

   > It has been alleged that Rudolph is an adherent of the extremist group Christian Identity, a sect that holds that white Christians are God's chosen people, and that others will be condemned to Hell. However, in a statement released after he entered a guilty plea, Rudolph denied being a supporter of that movement, claiming

that his involvement amounted to a brief association with the daughter of a Christian Identity adherent. In one of the more than two hundred undated letters provided to *USA Today* by Rudolph's mother, Rudolph states, "I really prefer Nietzsche to the Bible."

5. The conclusion could be argued as well on grounds of leading to the best consequences.
6. Jonathan Bennett, "Conscience of Huckleberry Finn," *Philosophy* 69 (1974): 123–34.
7. If, because scant few of faith are fanatics, it is thought that there is no real perplexity, recall that very few teenagers are involved in serious car accidents, yet the correlations are significant and call for explanation.
8. Robert M. Adams, *Finite and Infinite Goods: A Framework for Ethics* (Oxford: Oxford University Press, 1999), 284.
9. Immanuel Kant, *The Conflict of the Faculties,* trans. M. J. Gregor and R. Anchor, in *Kant, Religion and Rational Theology,* eds. Alan W. Wood and G. Di Giovanni (Cambridge: Cambridge University Press, 1996), 283. Here is Woody Allen's version from *Without Feathers* (New York: Random House, 1983):

> And Abraham awoke in the middle of the night and said to his son Isaac, "I have had a dream where the voice of the Lord sayeth that I must sacrifice thou, so put your pants on."
>
> And Isaac trembled and said, "So what did you say? I mean when He brought this whole thing up?" "What am I going to say?" Abraham said. "I'm standing there at two a.m. in my underwear with the Creator of the Universe. Should I argue?" And Sarah, who heard Abraham's plan, grew vexed and said, "How doth thou know it was the Lord and not, say, thy friend who loves practical jokes?" And Abraham answered, "because it was a deep, resonant voice, well-modulated, and nobody in the desert can get a rumble in it like that." And so he took Isaac to a certain place and prepared to sacrifice him, but at the last minute the Lord stayed Abraham's hand and said, "How could thou do such a thing?" And Abraham said, "But thou said,"
>
> "Never mind what I said," the Lord spake. "Doth thou listen to every crazy idea that comes thy way?" And Abraham grew ashamed. "I jokingly suggest thou sacrifice Isaac and thou immediately runs out to do it." And Abraham fell to his knees. "See, I never know when you're kidding." And the Lord thundered, "No sense of humor! I can't believe it!" "But doth this not prove I love thee, that I was willing to donate mine only son on thy whim?" And the Lord said, "It proves that some men will follow any order, no matter how asinine, as long as it comes from a resonant, well-modulated voice."

10. Neither in the religious quotations offered by Rudolph and in the numerous ones sprinkled throughout the right-wing extremist Web site "armyofgod" does one actually find a biblical injunction that commands the proposed terrorists acts, on anything close to a literal reading. The opening quotation of the Web site, whose main target is abortion, is this: "Ye, who have not resisted unto blood, striving against sin" (Heb. 12:4). If you think "blood" must be to death, keep in mind that lying and theft are also sins. (Also, the injunction seems to be directed to those who resist, to shed their own blood, not that of the sinners.)

    It is not as if there is never any condemnations not calling for highly speculative interpretational leaps. In the part of the armyofgod site attacking homosexuality, by contrast, a literal reading does accord with their view: "If a man also lie with mankind, as he lieth with a woman, both of them have committed an abomination: they shall surely be put to death; their blood shall be upon them" (Lev. 20:13). Elsewhere in this passage, however, a death sentence is placed on adulterers, as well.

11. Stern, *Terror in the Name of God,* xix.
12. As to why so many people appear to believe that prayer works, one proposal is offered in Richard Nisbett and Lee Ross, *Human Inference: Strategies and Shortcomings of Social Judgment* (Englewood Cliffs, NJ: Prentice Hall, 1980), 92.
13. On the fictional stance, see Georges Rey's "Meta-atheism" (this volume).
14. For a follow up, see *New York Times*, July 9, 2005, 1.
15. My text here is *"New Age": A Christian Reflection* by the Working Group on New Religious Movements. The authors are listed as: Members of the Holy See: The Pontifical Councils for Culture and for Interreligious Dialogue, the Congregation for the Evangelization of Peoples; and the Pontifical Council for Promoting Christian Unity. Kenya: Paulines Publications, 2003. I was referred to it by Sophie Arie's January 31, 2003, article in the *Guardian*, which is headlined "Beware New Age, Vatican Tells Flock."
16. For discussion and references, see Cass R. Sunstein, *Why Societies Need Dissent* (Cambridge, MA: Harvard University Press, 2003).
17. Stern, *Terror in the Name of God,* 181.
18. I assume that the terrorist's proposal to test the scholar is on matters of interpretation, where the terrorist lacks any independently certifiable set of answers.
19. In his statement, he details logistical problems that interfered with his original plan to provide warnings so as not to harm "innocent civilians," though he knew that "the weapons used (highly uncontrollable timed explosives) and the choice of tactics . . . could potentially lead to a disaster wherein many civilians could be killed or wounded."
20. The ease of worldwide communications today renders isolation extremely difficult. But the very varied quality of the Internet renders its power two-edged. All good evidence is available over the Internet, but also loads of misinformation.
21. See, for example, John 11:14–15; 20:24–29, *The New English Bible* (New York: Cambridge University Press, 1971).
22. William James, "The Will to Believe," in *Essays on Pragmatism,* ed. A. Castelli (New York: Harner, 1951), 88–109.
23. One of the ironies of religious faith is that in order to defend themselves against commonsense questions of validation, they voice skepticism about establishing ethical principles and rules. Skepticism about ethical knowledge follows from Divine Command Theory itself: Only if ethical judgments are backed by divine command do they have legitimacy, so that ethics lacks integrity or autonomy. Human reason and the benefits of social community are not enough to explain our allegiance to ethical principle, even as its basis. At the end, I briefly oppose this skepticism.
24. For development of the arguments in this section, see Jonathan E. Adler, *Belief's Own Ethics* (Cambridge, MA: MIT Press, 2002), chs. 1, 4, and 11.
25. Blaise Pascal, *Pensées.* Intro. by T. S. Eliot (New York: E.P. Dutton, 1958), frag. 233.
26. David Shapiro, *Autonomy and Rigid Character* (New York: Basic Books, 1981), 74–75.
27. Shapiro, *Autonomy and Rigid Character,* 170–71.
28. Charles S. Peirce, "The Fixation of Belief," in *Essays in the Philosophy of Science,* ed. V. Thomas (New York: Bobbs-Merrill, 1957), 24.

REFERENCES

1. FAITH AND REASON, THE PERPETUAL WAR: RUMINATIONS OF A FOOL

Barth, Karl. 1956. *Church Dogmas*. Trans. G. T. Thompson and Harold Knight. Edinburgh, UK: T. & T. Clark.

Plantinga, Alvin. 1983. "Reason and Belief in God." In *Reason and Rationality: Reason and Belief in God*, eds. Alvin Plantinga and Nicholas Wolterstorff, 16–93. Notre Dame, IN: University of Notre Dame Press.

Pojman, Louis P. 1998. "Can Religious Belief Be Rational?" In *Philosophy of Religion,* 3rd ed., 483–92. Belmont, CA: Wadsworth.

Russell, Bertrand. 1930. *Has Religion Made Useful Contributions to Civilization*? Little Blue Book.

Girard, K. S. "Emmanuel Haldeman-Julius." Reprinted in B. Russell, *Why I Am Not a Christian and Other Essays on Religion and Related Subjects,* 24–47. New York: Touchstone Books, Simon & Schuster, 1967.

19. META-ATHEISM: RELIGIOUS AVOWAL AS SELF-DECEPTION

James, William (1897/1992). "The Will to Believe and Other Essays in Popular Philosophy." In *William James: Writings 1878–1899*. New York: Living Library, pp. 445–704.

Rey, Georges (2000a/2006). "Does Anyone Really Believe in God?" In *Experience of Philosophy,* sixth edition, ed. by Raymond Martin and Daniel Kolak. New York: Oxford University Press, pp. 335–54.

Rey, Georges. 2001b. "Physicalism and Psychology: A Plea for Substantive Philosophy of Mind." In *Physicalism and Its Discontents,* ed. by Carl Gillet and Barry Loewer. Cambridge: Cambridge University Press, pp. 99–128.

20. FAITH AND FANATICISM

Adams, Robert (1999). *Finite and Infinite Goods: A Framework for Ethics.* Oxford: Oxford University Press.

Adler, Jonathan. 2002. *Belief's Own Ethics.* Cambridge: MIT Press.

Alston, William. 1991. *Perceiving God: The Epistemology of Religious Experience.* New York: Cornell University Press.

Atran, Scott. 2002. *In Gods We Trust: The Evolutionary Landscape of Religion.* Oxford: Oxford University Press.

Bach, Kent. 1981. "An Analysis of Self-deception." *Philosophy and Phenomenological Research* 41 (March): 351–70.

Boyer, Pascal. 2001. *Religion Explained: Evolutionary Origins of Religious Thought.* New York: Basic Books.

Boyer, Pascal. 2004. Why Is Religion Natural? *Skeptical Inquirer* 28 (2) (March–April): 25–31.

Dawkins, Richard. 2003a. Now Here's a Bright Idea. *Free Inquiry* (October/November).

Dawkins, Richard. 2003b. "Religion Be Damned." *Wired* 11 (10) (October).

Dennett, Daniel C. 2003. The Bright Stuff. *New York Times,* op-ed page. July 12, 2003.

James, William. 1897/1992. The Will to Believe and Other Essays in Popular Philosophy. In *William James: Writings 1878–1899.* New York: Living Library.

Kitcher, Philip. 1982. *Abusing science: The case against creationism.* Cambridge: MIT Press.

Martin, Raymond, and Daniel Kolak, eds. 2001. *The Experience of Philosophy,* 5th ed. Oxford: Oxford University Press.

McLaughlin, Brian, and Amelie Rorty. 1988. *Perspectives on Self-deception.* Berkeley: University of California.

Moran, Richard. 2001. *Authority and Estrangement: An Essay on Self-knowledge.* Princeton: Princeton University Press.

Pagels, Elaine. 1979. *The Gnostic Gospels.* New York: Vintage.

Pagels, Elaine. 2003. *Beyond Belief: The Secret Gospel of Thomas.* New York: Random House.

Plantinga, Alvin. 2000. *Warranted Christian Belief.* New York: Oxford University Press.

Quine, Willard. 1960. *Word and Object.* Cambridge, MA: MIT Press.

Rey, Georges. 1988. "Towards a Computational Account of Akrasia and Self-deception." In *Perspectives on Self-deception,* eds. Brian McLaughlin and Amelie Rorty, 264–96.

Rey, Georges. 1997. *Contemporary Philosophy of Mind: A Contentiously Classical Approach.* Oxford, UK: Blackwell.

Rey, Georges. 2001a. Meta-atheism: Reasons for Thinking Few People Actually Believe in God. In *Experience of Philosophy,* eds. Raymond Martin and Daniel Kolak.

Rey, Georges. 2001b. Physicalism and Psychology: A Plea for Substantive Philosophy of Mind. In *Physicalism and Its Discontents,* eds. Carl Gillet and Barry Loewer. Cambridge: Cambridge University Press.

Sober, Elliot. 2004. *Core Questions in Philosophy,* 4th ed. New York: Macmillan.

Weinberg, Scott. 1977. *The First Three Minutes: A Modern View of the Origin of the Universe.* New York: Basic Books.

NOTES ON CONTRIBUTORS

Jonathan E. Adler is Professor of Philosophy at Brooklyn College and the City University of New York Graduate Center. His research interests lie mainly in epistemology, especially issues about rationality, testimony, and the ethics of belief. In addition to authoring many essays, he wrote *Belief's Own Ethics* (2002).

Elizabeth Second Anderson is John Rawls Collegiate Professor of Philosophy and Professor of Women's Studies at the University of Michigan, Ann Arbor. She is the author of *Value in Ethics and Economics* (1993) and numerous articles on equality, democratic theory, value theory, the philosophy of the social sciences, and feminist theory.

Louise M. Antony is Professor of Philosophy at the University of Massachusetts, Amherst. Her research interests are in the philosophy of mind, epistemology, and feminist theory. Two of her most recent essays are "Everybody Has Got It: A Defense of Non-Reductive Materialism in the Philosophy of Mind," forthcoming in *Contemporary Debates in the Philosophy of Mind*, ed. Brian McLaughlin and Jonathan Cohen; and "The Socialization of Epistemology," in *Oxford Handbook of Contextual Political* Studies, ed. Robert Goodin and Charles Tilley (2006). She is co-editor, with Charlotte Witt, of *A Mind of One's Own: Feminist Essays on Reason and Objectivity,* 2nd ed. (2002), and with Norbert Hornstein of *Chomsky and His Critics* (2003).

Marvin Belzer is Associate Professor of Philosophy at Bowling Green State University. He has published many essays on deontic logic and practical reasoning, including: "Dyadic Deontic Detachment" (with Barry Loewer) in *Synthese* (1983), and "Normative Kinematics I" and "Normative Kinematics II" in *Law and*

Philosophy (1984). Recently, he has become interested in metaphysics, especially the topic of personal identity, and in Buddhist philosophy. He is a consultant and teacher of meditation.

Simon Blackburn is Professor of Philosophy at the University of Cambridge, a Fellow of Trinity College, Cambridge, and a Fellow of the British Academy. He has authored scores of essays on the philosophy of language, philosophy of mind, and ethics. His books are: *Reason and Prediction* (1973), *Spreading the Word* (1984), *Essays in Quasi-Realism* (1993), *The Oxford Dictionary of Philosophy* (1994), *Ruling Passions* (1998), *Think* (1999), *Being Good* (2001), *Lust* (2004), and *Truth: A Guide* (2005).

Edwin Curley is the James B. and Grace J. Nelson Professor of Philosophy at the University of Michigan, and a member of the American Academy of Arts and Sciences. His research interests are mainly in the history of early modern philosophy, especially the work of Spinoza. In addition to having written many essays, he is the author of *Spinoza's Metaphysics* (1969), *Descartes against the Skeptics* (1978), and *Behind the Geometrical Method* (1988), and has produced an edition of Hobbes's *Leviathan* (1994).

Daniel C. Dennett is the Austin B. Fletcher Professor of Philosophy and co-director of the Center for Cognitive Studies at Tufts University. He is the author of nearly a dozen books and hundreds of articles on the philosophy of mind and cognitive science. Recently, he has been supplementing his scholarly work with books and essays aimed at a general audience, focusing on science and religion and their respective rôles in contemporary society. Some of his books are *Content and Consciousness* (1969), *Consciousness Explained* (1991), *Darwin's Dangerous Idea* (1995), *Kinds of Minds* (1996), *Sweet Dreams: Philosophical Obstacles to a Science of Consciousness* (2005), and *Breaking the Spell: Religion as a Natural Phenomenon* (2006).

Daniel M. Farrell is Professor of Philosophy at The Ohio State University. He works primarily in the areas of political philosophy and the philosophy of law and has published extensively on the issues of threats, deterrence, and punishment. His most recent contribution to these issues, "Capital Punishment and Societal Self-defense," appeared in *Philosophy and Its Public Role,* ed. William Aiken and John Haldane, St. Andrews Studies in Philosophy and Public Affairs (2004).

Richard Feldman is Professor of Philosophy at the University of Rochester. He specializes in epistemology and metaphysics. His publications include scores of essays, and the books *Evidentialism: Essays in Epistemology* (with Earl Conee) (2004), and *Epistemology* (Foundations of Philosophy Series) (2003).

Daniel Garber is Professor of Philosophy, and Associate Member of the Program in the History of Science at Princeton University. His research is on the history of philosophy, and he is especially interested in issues arising from the interactions among philosophy, science, and society in the period of the Scientific Revolution. In addition to many translations and edited volumes, his books include *Descartes' Metaphysical Physics* (1992), *Descartes Embodied: Reading Cartesian Philosophy through Cartesian Science* (2001).

Marcia Homiak is Professor of Philosophy at Occidental College, where she teaches courses in philosophy, ancient history, and women's studies. She writes in the areas of ancient ethics and moral psychology. She is the author of "Feminism and Aristotle's Rational Ideal" in *A Mind of One's Own*, ed. L. Antony and C. Witt (2002), and "On the Malleability of Character" in *On Feminist Ethics and Politics*, ed. C. Card (1999).

Anthony Simon Laden is Associate Professor of Philosophy at the University of Illinois at Chicago. He works in moral and political philosophy, where his interests include democratic theory, feminism, identity politics, and practical reason. He is the author of *Reasonably Radical: Deliberative Liberalism and the Politics of Identity* (2001), and "Evaluating Social Reasons: Hobbes vs. Hegel," *Journal of Philosophy* 102:7 (July 2005).

Joseph Levine is Professor of Philosophy at the University of Massachusetts, Amherst. His research interests include the philosophy of mind (especially the topic of conscious experience), the philosophy of language, and metaphysics. He is the author of many articles, and also of *Purple Haze: The Puzzle of Consciousness* (2001).

David Lewis was the Class of 1943 Professor of Philosophy at Princeton University at the time of his death in 2001. One of the most eminent philosophers of the twentieth century, he was the author of four highly influential books, *Convention: A Philosophical Study* (1969), *Counterfactuals* (1973), *On the Plurality of Worlds* (1986), and *Parts of Classes* (1991), and numerous essays on a wide range of philosophical topics, including metaphysics, philosophy of language, philosophical logic, epistemology, ethics, and social philosophy. Five volumes of his collected papers have been published, two by Oxford University Press, and three by Cambridge University Press.

David Owens teaches at the University of Sheffield, United Kingdom. His recent work is on ethics, moral psychology, and early modern philosophy. He is the author of *Causes and Coincidences* (1992), and *Reason without Freedom* (2000).

Georges Rey works primarily on the foundations of cognitive science and has published on issues of consciousness and qualia, concepts and intentionality, and the philosophy of linguistics. He is the author of *Contemporary Philosophy of Mind* (1997), and edited (with Barry Loewer) *Meaning in Mind: Fodor and His Critics* (1991). He is currently Professor of philosophy at the University of Maryland at College Park.

Stewart Shapiro is the O'Donnell Professor of Philosophy at The Ohio State University and serves as Professorial Fellow at the Arché Research Centre at the University of St. Andrews. His major research interests lie in the philosophy of mathematics, logic, and language, notably vagueness. He teaches a wide range of courses, including Jewish Philosophy. Among his many publications are *Thinking about Mathematics* (2000), *Foundations without Foundationalism: A Case for Second-order Logic, Philosophy of Mathematics: Structure and Ontology,* and *Vagueness in Context* (2006), all published by Oxford University Press. He recently edited the *Oxford Handbook for the Philosophy of Mathematics and Logic* (2005).

Walter Sinnott-Armstrong is Professor of Philosophy and Hardy Professor of Legal Studies at Dartmouth College. His main areas of research include applied ethics, moral theory, philosophy of law, theory of knowledge, and informal logic. His most recent books are *Pyrrhonian Skepticism* (2004), *God? A Debate between a Christian and an Atheist* (with William Lane Craig) (2003), and *Moral Skepticisms* (2006), and he is the editor, with Richard Howarth, of *Perspectives on Climate Change: Science, Economics, Politics, Ethics* (2005).

James Tappenden is Associate Professor of Philosophy at the University of Michigan. His many publications concern mainly the philosophy of mathematics and philosophical logic, and the history of these topics. His book *Philosophy and the Origins of Contemporary Mathematics: Frege and His Mathematical Context* is forthcoming from Oxford University Press.

Kenneth A. Taylor is Professor of Philosophy at Stanford University. His main areas of research are the philosophy of language and the philosophy of mind. In addition to many essays, he is the author of *Meaning and Truth: An Introduction to the Philosophy of Language* (1998), *Reference and the Rational Mind* (2003), and *Referring to the World: An Introduction to the Theory of Reference*. With his colleague, the philosopher John Perry, he developed and hosts a popular radio show, "Philosophy Talk."

INDEX